1005083165

# THE CALVERT SITE

## An Interpretive Framework for the Early Iroquoian Village

Peter A. Timmins

Mercury Series
Archaeological Survey of Canada
Paper 156

Published by
Canadian Museum of Civilization

© Canadian Museum of Civilization 1997

Canadian Cataloguing in Publication Data

Timmins, Peter Andrew, 1958 –

The Calvert site: an interpretive framework for the early Iroquoian village

(Mercury series, ISSN 0316-1854)
(Paper/Archaeological Survey of Canada,
ISSN 0317-2244 ; no. 156)
Includes an abstract in French.
Includes bibliographical references.
ISBN 0-660-15969-4

1. Calvert Site – Ontario – London Region.
2. Iroquoian Indians – Ontario – London Region – Antiquities
3. Excavations (Archaeology) – Ontario – London Region.
4. Archaeology – Methodology.
I. Candian Museum of Civilization
II. Archaeological Survey of Canada.
III. Title: An interpretative framework for the early Iroquoian village.
IV. Series
V. Series: Paper (Archaeological Survey of Canada) ; no. 156.

E99.169T55 1997   971.3'26   C97-980007-2

 PRINTED IN CANADA

Published by
Canadian Museum of Civilization
100 Laurier Street
P.O. Box 3100, Station B
Hull, Quebec
J8X 4H2

**Senior production officer:** Deborah Brownrigg
**Cover design:** Ashton Station Creative Group Inc.
**Technical Editor:** Richard Morlan

**Front cover:** Golspie Swamp
(Upper Thames River Conservation Authority)

**Back cover:** Dorchester Swamp
(Upper Thames River Conservation Authority)

**Effigy and vessel:** William Fox

## OBJECT OF THE MERCURY SERIES

The Mercury Series is designed to permit the rapid dissemination of information pertaining to the disciplines in which the Canadian Museum of Civilization is active. Considered an important reference by the scientific community, the Mercury Series comprises over three hundred specialized publications on Canada's history and prehistory.

Because of its specialized audience, the series consists largely of monographs published in the language of the author.

In the interest of making information available quickly, normal production procedures have been abbreviated. As a result, grammatical and typographical errors may occur. Your indulgence is requested.

Titles in the Mercury Series can be obtained by calling in your order to 1-800-555-5621, or by writing to:

Mail Order Services
Canadian Museum of Civilization
100 Laurier Street
P.O. Box 3100, Station B
Hull, Quebec
J8X 4H2

## BUT DE LA COLLECTION

La collection Mercure vise à diffuser rapidement le résultat de travaux dans les disciplines qui relèvent des sphères d'activités du Musée canadien des civilisations. Considérée comme un apport important dans la communauté scientifique, la collection Mercure présente plus de trois cents publications spécialisées portant sur l'héritage canadien préhistorique et historique.

Comme la collection s'adresse à un public spécialisé, celle-ci est constituée essentiellement de monographies publiées dans la langue des auteurs.

Pour assurer la prompte distribution des exemplaires imprimés, les étapes de l'édition ont été abrégées. En conséquence, certaines coquilles ou fautes de grammaire peuvent subsister : c'est pourquoi nous réclamons votre indulgence.

Vous pouvez vous procurer la liste des titres parus dans la collection Mercure en appelant au 1-800-555-5621, ou en écrivant au :

Service des commandes postales
Musée canadien des civilisations
100, rue Laurier
C.P. 3100, succursale B
Hull (Québec)
J8X 4H2

Canad**ä**

# Abstract

This study develops a general methodology for the interpretation of archaeological data and applies the method to the study of an Early Iroquoian community that occupied the Calvert site near London, Ontario, between approximately A.D. 1150 and 1250. Contrary to previous interpretations of Early Iroquoian communities, the results show that the Calvert village was neither unplanned nor disordered. Rather, the Calvert people developed their village in a systematic manner through four sequential periods of rebuilding and spatial reorganization that involved substantial economic and sociopolitical change. At least some Early Iroquoian villages, then, were planned family communities approaching a higher level of sociopolitical organization than was previously thought.

The study is concerned with strengthening archaeological interpretations through the development and application of interpretive theory, that is, a body of archaeological principles employing analogical reasoning to relate archaeological residues to the natural processes or cultural behaviours inferred to have produced them. Interpretive theory represents a broadening of the concept of middle range theory to incorporate all social, cultural, and natural processes that condition the archaeological record.

The "interpretive pyramid" is introduced as an adaptation of the traditionally recognized ladder of archaeological inference that models the increasing difficulty of inference as one proceeds from interpretations relating to space and time through interpretations of technology, economy, sociopolitical organization, religion, and ideology. The spatio-temporal inferences at the base of the pyramid have the greatest scope for generalization; this scope narrows, however, as one rises within the pyramid. The interpretive pyramid forms the basic structure for organizing the substantive portion of the study, beginning with a spatio-temporal analysis of the Calvert community, and proceeding through techno-economic, sociopolitical, and cultural analyses.

To situate the Calvert site ecologically, its environmental setting is reconstructed. This analysis leads to the definition of five distinct micro-environmental zones within a five-kilometre radius of the site; it is demonstrated that the Calvert site was optimally situated to provide ready access to diverse natural resources.

At the spatio-temporal level, a detailed analysis of stratigraphic evidence (feature and post superpositions), spatial data, ceramic cross-mends, post mould densities, and radiocarbon dates is performed to provide interpretations of the site's occupational history. This analysis yields four sets of settlement pattern, artifactual and ecofactual data corresponding to four occupational episodes, as well as an estimate of the dating of the site and the duration of each occupational phase.

The occupation of the Calvert site began with the construction of a single house (House 1), which was probably used as a seasonal hunting camp in the mid-twelfth century. The Early village phase that followed — three longhouses and one small shed surrounded by a single row palisade — was occupied for about twenty years in the early thirteenth century. The Early phase was terminated and the Middle phase initiated by a village reorganization that involved dismantling the houses and rebuilding them in an east-west pattern. The palisade was contracted, and a second line of palisade constructed. This phase of occupation was sequential and continuous with the Early phase and may have lasted for about twenty years in the early to mid-thirteenth century. The Late phase was marked by the removal of the Middle phase houses and the construction of three or four much smaller east-west oriented houses, possibly surrounded by a single palisade. There was no major temporal gap between the Middle and Late phases. The Late phase may have been occupied intermittently for about twenty years in the mid-thirteenth century.

The economic analysis incorporates the results of floral and faunal analyses and involves a comparison of data from the four occupational phases to determine whether changes in site function occurred. The faunal data are divided into sub-samples and compared on a phase-by-phase basis, which indicates a focus on mammal hunting in House 1, a shift to a broad-spectrum hunting and fishing pattern in the Early and Middle phases, and a return to a strategy based on mammal hunting in the Late phase. The floral remains reveal no notable changes in the diversity of floral species among the three main phases, although fewer species were identified from House 1. While it is evident that maize was the main plant food of the Calvert people, squash, bean, and sunflower were also cultivated, and several fleshy fruits were collected during all phases. Evidence of seasonality from both faunal and floral indices leaves little doubt that the Calvert site was used in all seasons during all phases. Warm weather indicators, however, are less common in the Late phase and House 1, whereas cold weather indices are more plentiful in these samples. This suggests that the House 1 and Late phase occupations occurred primarily during the cold season, with some use in the warm seasons as well.

The analyses conducted at the technological level include lithic, ceramic, and bone, antler, and shell technology, feature formation and function, refuse disposal, building technology, and structure function. The pottery of the Early, Middle, and Late phases is found to be very similar, suggesting that it was the product of a single community evolving through time. House 1, on the other hand, yielded a highly distinctive ceramic assemblage, dominated by suture stamped ceramics that form only a minority of the main village ceramic samples. This suggests that the occupants of House 1 were not related to the group that later lived in the main village.

The analysis of feature function at Calvert relates directly to the study of refuse disposal technology. Ceramic cross-mends are analyzed from a behavioural point of view to help identify refuse streams, which, in general, involve movement of debris from hearth activity areas to interior features and the subsequent removal of debris to exterior refuse pits. This pattern is observed for both the Early and Middle phases. The Late phase, however, reveals a very different arrangement: mainly in-house refuse disposal streams and a high proportion of house-to-house refuse transfer. This pattern is interpreted as evidence of abandonment behaviour, which reflects a lack of concern for moving refuse out of houses and a high degree of interaction between households. These observations

support the interpretation of the Late phase as a hunting camp occupied mainly in the cold season.

The analyses of building technology result in the definition of four different structure types including the standard Early Iroquoian longhouse occupied by an extended family, the residential/storage house characterized by a very high proportion of interior storage pits, the small non-residential work/storage hut or shed, and the small houses occupied by families or task groups while on hunting expeditions.

Population estimates suggest an increase from the Early phase to the Middle phase, followed by a decline in the Late phase. It is noted that a contraction of the palisade during the Middle phase, coupled with the proposed population increase, would have led to more crowded conditions. The Middle phase reorganization also involved defensive considerations, including the construction of a second row of palisade and the radial alignment of houses to inhibit movement between them. This evidence suggests that the Calvert village was reorganized under some form of stress, possibly of a sociopolitical nature.

At the regional level, settlement patterns and ceramics from Glen Meyer communities in the Dorchester, Byron, Caradoc, and Norfolk Sand Plain areas are compared to evaluate their sociopolitical relationships. Ceramic styles among these site clusters are very heterogeneous, with each local group developing distinctive elements of its own ceramic tradition. Intra-village settlement patterns are less variable, but there are substantial differences in village layouts and feature distributions. Overall, it appears that these communities were largely politically autonomous and economically self-sufficient.

Finally, a new model of Early to Middle Iroquoian political development in southwestern Ontario is proposed, seeking to account for several aspects of Early and Middle Iroquoian settlement patterns and material culture. It is proposed that each of the clusters of Glen Meyer sites represents two or three village communities, living in a circumscribed area and sharing a diverse resource base that was exploited through a combination of hunting, collecting, and horticulture. Economic and sociopolitical cooperation among these people would have preconditioned them for the eventual amalgamation of several of these small villages to form much larger, segmented villages at the beginning of the Middle Iroquoian period around A.D. 1300. These communities were more easily defended, and by the mid-fourteenth century were located on heavier soils that were much more productive for horticulture. Thus the changes of the Early to Middle Iroquoian periods addressed both economic and sociopolitical needs.

Local developments also led to changes at the interregional level. With former neighbours now living together in large regional villages, new ties would have been established for political alliances, defense, trade, and perhaps spouse exchange. This unprecedented level of interregional interaction may have led to the rapid spread of Middle Iroquoian ceramic motifs across southern Ontario.

At the cultural level, interpretive data were drawn from ethnohistorical and ethnographic sources concerning Iroquoian calendrical ceremonies, curing societies, and mortuary programmes. Curing societies have a strong shamanistic element, and evidence for shamanic belief systems was discovered at Calvert in the form of the association of a Carolina parakeet skin and a stone pipe bowl with ritualistic implications.

Early Iroquoian villages may be successfully analyzed once their occupational histories have been reconstructed through the careful study of site formation processes. In the case of the Calvert community, reconstruction has permitted us to trace the development of a single community over the course of three generations. The result is our first clear picture of the economic and sociopolitical realities of stability and change in Early Iroquoian society. Contrary to earlier beliefs, this study shows that Early Iroquoian groups had developed effective sociopolitical institutions to cope with village planning and defense. These institutions were important as they laid the foundations for the highly developed political institutions of the historic Ontario Iroquoians.

# Résumé

Dans cette étude, on s'est servi de données archéologiques pour élaborer une méthode générale d'interprétation qui a encadré l'analyse d'une communauté de la Phase Iroquoienne ancienne dont l'occupation du site Calvert situé dans le voisinage de London, Ontario, remonte à environ 1150 et 1250 ap.J.-C. On démontre que le village de Calvert, contrairement à la perception antérieure qu'on avait des communautés de la Phase Iroquoienne ancienne, ne manifeste aucun signe d'improvisation ni de désordre. En effet, le village témoigne de quatre périodes de reconstruction systématique et de réorganisation sociale qui ont correspondu à des changements économiques et sociopolitiques importants. Au moins quelques villages de la Phase Iroquoienne ancienne étaient constitués de communautés familiales dont l'organisation sociopolitique atteignait un niveau plus élevé qu'on ne le croyait antérieurement.

Cette étude vise à mettre en valeur l'interprétation archéologique grâce à l'élaboration et à la mise en application d'une théorie interprétative, c'est-à-dire d'un ensemble de principes archéologiques qui a recours à un raisonnement analogique pour relier les vestiges archéologiques aux procédés naturels ou aux comportements culturels qui en sont la source. La théorie interprétative représente un élargissement du concept de la théorie de la moyenne qui incorpore tous les procédés sociaux, culturels et naturels contribuant à la formation de l'enregistrement archéologique.

La "pyramide interprétative" se veut une adaptation des niveaux traditionnellement reconnus de l'inférence archéologique dont le degré de difficulté augmente à mesure qu'on déborde de l'interprétation reliée à l'espace et au temps et qu'on s'adresse à l'interprétation reliée aux techniques, à l'économie, à l'organisation sociopolitique, à la religion et à l'idéologie. Les inférences spatio-temporelles se situent à la base de la pyramide et revêtent un caractère très général; la perspective se rétrécit, cependant, en montant vers le sommet de la pyramide. La pyramide interprétative constitue le noyau autour duquel s'organise la partie substantielle de l'étude, en commençant par l'analyse spatio-temporelle de la communauté de Calvert et en continuant avec l'analyse techno-économique, sociopolitique et culturelle.

Pour discuter de l'aspect écologique du site Calvert, on a reconstitué son milieu environnemental. Cette analyse a conduit à reconnaître cinq micro zones environnementales distinctes à l'intérieur d'un rayon de cinq kilomètres du site; on démontre que le site Calvert était idéalement situé au centre de ressources naturelles diverses et faciles d'accès.

Au niveau spatio-temporel, on fait une analyse détaillée du témoignage stratigraphique (la superposition des structures et des traces de pieux), des données spatiales, du raccord des tessons de céramique, du nombre relatif des traces de pieux, et des dates au radiocarbone dans le but de reconstituer l'histoire de l'occupation du site. L'analyse des objets et des restes de nourriture a permis de dégager quatre modes d'établissements correspondant à quatre épisodes d'occupation et de déterminer les dates du site ainsi que la durée de chaque phase d'occupation.

L'occupation du site Calvert a débuté par la construction d'une seule maison (Maison 1) qui a probablement servi de camp de chasse saisonnier au milieu du douzième siècle. La Phase ancienne du village qui a suivi - trois maisons-longues et un petit hangar entourés d'une palissade d'une seule rangée de pieux - témoigne d'une occupation qui a duré vingt ans au début du treizième siècle. La Phase moyenne a commencé par la réorganisation du village qui a impliqué la démolition et la reconstruction des maisons en direction est-ouest. La palissade a été resserrée et une deuxième palissade construite. Cette Phase d'occupation a succédé à la première mais se situe dans le prolongement de la Phase ancienne et a pu avoir duré environ vingt ans du début au milieu du treizième siècle. La Phase récente se caractérise par le déplacement des maisons de la Phase moyenne et la construction de trois ou quatre maisons plus petites orientées en direction est-ouest, vraisemblablement entourées d'une palissade d'une seule rangée de pieux. Il n'y a eu aucun hiatus temporel important entre les Phases moyenne et récente. Au cours de la Phase récente, l'occupation a pu avoir été intermittente pendant environ vingt ans au milieu du treizième siècle.

L'analyse de l'économie incorpore le résultat des analyses florales et fauniques et implique une comparaison des données des quatre phases d'occupation pour déterminer si la fonction du site a changé. Les données fauniques se divisent en quatre sous-échantillons; leur comparaison Phase par Phase indique une concentration sur la chasse aux mammifères dans la Maison 1, contrairement au modèle généralisé de chasse et de pêche à la Phase récente. Les restes floraux ne révèlent aucun changement notable quant à la diversité des espèces florales au cours des trois phases principales, quoique moins d'espèces aient été identifiées dans la Maison 1. Même s'il est évident que le maïs a été la principale plante alimentaire pour les habitants de Calvert, la courge, le haricot et le tournesol ont aussi été cultivés, et plusieurs fruits charnus ont été collectés au cours de toutes les Phases. Le témoignage saisonnier des restes fauniques et floraux laissent peu de doute quant à l'utilisation du site Calvert à toutes les saisons au cours de toutes les Phases. Les indicateurs de température chaude sont cependant moins nombreux à la Phase récente et dans la Maison 1 dont les échantillons comprennent en abondance des indicateurs de température froide; ce qui nous permet de croire que l'occupation de la Maison 1 et l'occupation au cours de la Phase récente ont eu lieu principalement durant la saison froide mais auraient été occasionnelles au cours des saisons chaudes.

Les analyses effectuées au niveau technique comprennent les industries de la pierre, de la céramique, de l'os, de l'andouiller et du coquillage, la formation et la fonction des structures, le traitement des déchets, les techniques de construction et la fonction des habitats. On arrive à la conclusion que les poteries des Phases ancienne, moyenne et récente sont très semblables, ce qui laisse entendre qu'elles étaient produites par une seule communauté qui évoluait dans le temps. La Maison 1, par contre, a livré des poteries très

distinctes dont la poterie, modelée à partir de plusieurs morceaux et impressionnée, est dominante mais ne représente qu'une poterie minoritaire par rapport aux poteries du village principal. Ce qui nous permet de croire que les occupants de la Maison 1 n'étaient pas reliés au groupe qui a plus tard vécu dans le village principal.

L'analyse des fonctions des structures retracées au site Calvert est étroitement liée à l'étude du traitement des déchets. Le raccord des tessons de céramique est examiné à la lumière des comportements susceptibles de révéler les courants de déchets qui, en général, impliquent le transport des débris des aires d'activités avoisinant les foyers vers l'intérieur des structures et le déplacement subséquent des débris vers les fosses à déchets à l'extérieur. Ce modèle est observé aux deux Phases ancienne et moyenne. La Phase récente révèle cependant un arrangement très différent: l'organisation des déchets principalement à l'intérieur des maisons et une proportion élevée de déchets échangés d'une maison à l'autre. À notre avis, ce modèle témoigne d'un comportement d'abandon, c'est-à-dire d'une négligence à dégager les débris des maisons, et un haut degré d'interaction entre les maisonnées. Ces observations renforcent l'interprétation qu'il s'agisse d'un camp de chasse occupé principalement durant la saison froide lors de la Phase récente.

L'analyse des techniques de construction permettent de déterminer quatre types d'habitations comprenant la maison-longe normale de la Phase ancienne occupée par une famille étendue, la maison servant de résidence-entrepôt caractérisée par une très haute proportion de fosses d'entreposage à l'intérieur, la petite hutte de travail-entrepôt non résidentielle ou hangar, et les petites maisons occupées par des familles ou groupes de travail au cours des expéditions de chasse.

L'évaluation des populations conclut à une augmentation démographique de la Phase ancienne à la Phase moyenne, suivie par un déclin à la Phase récente. On est conscient qu'un resserrement de la palissade à la Phase moyenne, combinée à une augmentation présumée de la population, aurait provoqué un encombrement. La réorganisation à la Phase moyenne impliquait aussi des mesures défensives, comprenant l'érection d'une seconde rangée de pieux dans la palissade et l'alignement radial des maisons pour décourager les déplacements entre elles. Ces constatations permettent de croire que le village de Calvert a été réorganisé sous l'effet d'un genre de stress, vraisemblablement de nature sociopolitique.

Au niveau régional, on compare les modes d'établissements et la céramique des communautés de Glen Meyer situées dans les régions de Dorchester, de Byron, de Caradoc et de Norfolk Sand Plain dans le but d'en dégager les liens sociopolitiques. Les styles de poteries provenant de ce groupe de sites sont très hétérogènes, chaque groupe local développant des éléments distincts à l'intérieur de sa propre tradition céramique. Les modes d'établissements à l'intérieur des villages sont moins variables, mais il y a des différences importantes dans la disposition des villages et la distributions des structures. Dans l'ensemble, ces communautés semblent jouir d'une grande autonomie politique et d'une autosuffisance économique.

Finalement, on propose un nouveau modèle de développement politique qui cherche à rendre compte de plusieurs aspects des modes d'établissements et de la culture matérielle chez les Iroquoiens du sud-ouest de l'Ontario aux Phase ancienne et moyenne. On propose que chacun des sous-groupes de sites de Glen Meyer se compose de deux ou trois villages communautaires, situés dans une région délimitée et partageant des ressources de base variées exploités en complément de la chasse, de la collecte et de l'horticulture. La coopération économique et sociopolitique requise de ces habitants aurait constitué une condition préalable à l'amalgamation éventuelle de plusieurs de ces petits villages en villages plus grands et segmentés au début de la Période Iroquoienne moyenne vers 1300 ap.J.-C. Ces communautés étaient plus facilement défendables et, vers la moitié du quatorzième siècle, vivaient sur des terres plus fermes, beaucoup plus productives pour l'horticulture. Ces changements qui ont eu lieu durant les Périodes Iroquoiennes ancienne et moyenne correspondaient donc à des besoins à la fois économiques et sociopolitiques.

Les développements locaux ont aussi entraîné des changements aux niveau interrégional. Ces anciens voisins vivant dorénavant ensemble dans de grands villages à caractère régional auraient tissé de nouveaux liens, favorables à des alliances politiques, à la défense, au commerce et peut-être à l'échange d'épouses. Ce niveau sans précédent d'interaction interrégionale peut avoir favorisé la diffusion rapide des motifs de la céramique de la Période Iroquoienne moyenne dans le sud de l'Ontario.

Au niveau culturel, les données interprétatives sont extraites des sources ethnohistoriques et ethnographiques en ce qui a trait aux cérémonies régulières des Iroquoiens, aux sociétés de la santé et aux rites mortuaires. Les sociétés de la santé comportent une forte composante de chamanisme, et des témoignages quant aux systèmes de croyances reliés au chamanisme ont été découverts au site Calvert sous la forme de l'association d'une peau de perruche de Caroline et une cheminée de pipe en pierre dans un contexte à caractère rituel.

Les villages de la Phase Iroquoienne ancienne donnent prise à des analyses significatives une fois l'histoire de leur occupation reconstituée suite à une étude soignée des procédés de formation des sites. Dans le cas de la communauté de Calvert, la reconstitution nous a permis de retracer l'évolution d'une seule communauté au cours de trois générations. Il en résulte une première image claire de la stabilité et du changement des réalités économiques et sociopolitiques chez la société de la Phase Iroquoienne ancienne. Contrairement aux croyances antérieures, cette étude montre que les groupes de la Phase Iroquoienne ancienne s'étaient dotés d'institutions sociopolitiques efficaces face à la planification et à la défense des villages. Ces institutions étaient d'autant plus importantes qu'elles constituaient les fondations des institutions politiques très élaborées qui régissaient les Iroquoiens historiques de l'Ontario.

# Acknowledgements

The publication of this monograph would not have been possible without the assistance of a wide range of funding agencies, institutions, and individuals who have supported the Calvert site project over the past several years.

The doctoral research on which the monograph is based was supported by a Doctoral Fellowship from the Social Sciences and Humanities Research Council of Canada, a Max Bell Fellowship in Canadian Studies from McGill University, and two Dissertation Research Grants from the Ontario Heritage Foundation. The financial support of these agencies is gratefully acknowledged.

During my graduate studies I was privileged to have the guidance of Professor Bruce Trigger as my thesis supervisor. Dr. Trigger gave generously of his time to assist my research and I thank him for his keen interest, critical insight, and meticulous editorial skills. Professors Fumiko Ikawa-Smith and Michael Bisson also served as members of my thesis committee and their expertise and assistance was greatly appreciated.

I thank Mr. William Fox (now of the Canadian Parks Service) and the Ontario Ministry of Citizenship, Culture and Recreation for excavating the Calvert site and making the data available for my use. I am particularly grateful to Bill for his encouragement and ready advice on the Calvert material. I also thank the members of the London Chapter of the Ontario Archaeological Society who assisted in the Calvert site excavations and processed many of the artifacts.

The completion and publication of this work benefitted from the support of Mr. Dave Wake and Mr. Paul Lennox of the Ontario Ministry of Transportation. Dr. William Finlayson and the London Museum of Archaeology, provided assistance for this research between 1985 and 1989. Professors Michael Spence and Chris Ellis of the Department of Anthropology, the University of Western Ontario, have also been a source of advice and encouragement.

I thank those who undertook specialized analyses of the Calvert site material. Rosemary Prevec conducted the faunal analysis, Glenna Ounjian analyzed the floral remains, and Rudy Fecteau provided a report on the carbonized wood. I am also grateful to Professor Gary Crawford of the University of Toronto who provided initial assistance with the Calvert site floral analysis. Mike Leonard and Mark Snowsell of the Upper Thames River Conservation Authority graciously provided me with data on the environment of the Dorchester area. Catherine Comrie and Janie Ravenhurst drew the artifact illustrations.

Over the years, several friends, colleagues and fellow students have assisted this research through discussions with the writer. They include Tom Arnold, Mark Borland, Bob Calvert, Dr. Brian Deller, David Denton, Christine Dodd, Arnie Feast, Neal Ferris, Dr. Bill Fitzgerald, Wayne Hagerty, Tom Hamilton, Les Howard, Bruce Jamieson, Ian Kenyon, Jim Keron, Harri and Karen Mattila, Moira McCaffery, Bev Morrison, Carl Murphy, Rob Pihl, Dana Poulton, Dave Riddell, Dr. Robert Pearce, Rob Pihl, Dr. David Smith, Dr. Alex von Gernet, Dr. Gary Warrick, Dr. Ron Williamson and Phil Woodley.

This study would never have been completed without a wide network of family support. I thank Bill and Sheila Timmins, Gabriel and Jane Kney, and all members of my extended family for several varied forms of assistance.

I owe a huge debt of gratitude to Dr. Richard Morlan of the Canadian Museum of Civilization for his hard work in editing and formatting the final page layout. Richard's editorial suggestions, especially with respect to the biological component of the study, were a great help during the revision process. I also thank Dr. Jean Luc Pilon for his thoughtful comments on the manuscript and for initiating the publication process.

Finally, I dedicate this work to my family: to my young sons Matthew and Michael, who have lived with this project all their lives, and to my wife Katharine, who has always been there.

P.T., November 1996

# Table of Contents

# List of Figures

# List of Tables

# Chapter 1

# Introduction and Theoretical Orientation

## Introduction

This study presents an interpretive framework for the Early Iroquoian village based upon the analysis of the Calvert site, a thirteenth century Glen Meyer village located near London, Ontario. Early Iroquoian villages in southern Ontario usually consist of several overlapping, non-stratified community patterns resulting from periodic rebuilding of the same village site. The Calvert site typifies villages of this period in displaying evidence for at least three separate and sequential periods of village construction. In the past the archaeological remains of Early Iroquoian villages have been difficult to interpret due to the confusing mixture of structures, features, and artifacts from different occupational periods. This has restricted our understanding of Early Iroquoian community patterns and village organization. Past researchers have characterized Early Iroquoian villages as disorganized and unplanned, an assessment that was extended to interpretations of their socio-political systems (Warrick 1984a:59; Noble 1969:19; 1975a:43); yet Early Iroquoian villages have not been analyzed in terms of their occupational histories to determine if this assessment is correct.

This study confronts these problems by developing and implementing a method for reconstructing the occupational history of the Calvert site. This method is employed to separate the Calvert data into sub-samples relating to each phase of occupation. The data from each phase are then analyzed in detail, and comparative analyses are performed to assess community change through time. The result is a holistic portrayal of the Calvert community drawing together interpretations of the occupational history of the village, the changing economy, the social organization of the community, and other cultural aspects of Early Iroquoian life. In attempting such a detailed reconstruction, the rich contextual background of Iroquoian culture, ethnohistory, and archaeology is drawn upon as source data for generating interpretive propositions.

The theoretical basis of the study concerns the relationship between archaeological remains and archaeological interpretations, and is related to the need to understand the formation processes of the Calvert site in order to reconstruct its occupational history. The study of the relationship between archaeological statics and cultural dynamics has been a focus of theoretical debate in archaeology over the past two decades, usually under the heading of middle range theory. In developing a holistic interpretive framework for the Early Iroquoian village the scope of middle range theory, as it is currently used in archaeology, is found to be too narrow, and a broader construct called interpretive theory is introduced.

The remainder of this chapter is concerned with a critique of middle range theory with a view to isolating its strengths and modifying our concept of it as holistic **interpretive theory**. A logical model of archaeological inference is presented as an aid to conceptualizing the holistic archaeological inquiry. The various steps in this interpretive pyramid represent different types of archaeological inference (i.e. spatio-temporal, techno-economic, social-political, cultural). The interpretive method proposed here is then integrated with the various levels of the pyramid through the identification of a common reasoning process found at all levels of archaeological analysis.

## The Status of Middle Range Theory

During the 1970s and 1980s, many North American archaeologists became preoccupied with the development of a body of archaeological theory that was specifically formulated to place archaeological interpretation on firmer ground. Much of this research was influenced by Lewis Binford's assertion that archaeologists require "a science of the archaeological record" that is concerned with establishing the nature of relationships between human behaviour and archaeological residues (Binford 1983b:50,413). This body of interpretive knowledge became known as middle range theory, to distinguish it from higher level general theory that seeks to explain characteristics of cultural systems (ibid:412).

Some archaeologists have aggressively pursued middle range research using strategies that range from experimental archaeology to ethnoarchaeology (Binford 1977, 1978a, 1978b, 1980, 1981a, 1981b, 1983a, 1983b, 1984, 1989; Coles 1973; DeBoer and Lathrap 1979; Gould 1980, 1990; Kramer 1979; Schiffer 1972, 1976, 1978, 1983, 1985, 1987; Tringham 1978; Yellen 1977). These studies draw on actualistic data to determine how the archaeological record may have been formed and how the observed patterns in the record may be assigned meaning in the present. Their goal is to amass a body of knowledge concerning the physical, natural, and cultural processes that have conditioned the archaeological record, and to use this body of knowledge to lend rigour to archaeological interpretations. Yet, while some archaeologists proclaimed that middle range theory building constituted the "archaeological agenda for the 1980s" (Moore and Keene 1983:17), others questioned the practical utility of the middle range interpretative method for achieving the substantive aims of archaeology.

The major criticisms of middle range studies have come either from archaeologists working outside the processual paradigm, who attack such studies on epistemic and philosophical grounds (i.e. Hodder 1982b, 1986), or from observers who see few successful applications of middle range theory in archaeological data interpretation (i.e. Thomas et al. 1983; Courbin 1987). The latter criticism illuminates a fundamental disjunction between theory and data in current American archaeology. It is also unfortunate that many archaeologists involved in middle range research in academic settings have turned their backs on the study of prehistory, while they busy themselves with actualistic studies aimed at refining interpretive methods. The "new archaeology" of the 1960s and 1970s became the "new methodology" of the 1980s:

> New Archaeologists have exacerbated substantive failure by subtly redirecting the goals of the discipline away from the creation of any systematic accumulation of knowledge, and by making the tools, methods and theories the goals of the discipline. ...the new archaeology has also become boring for all but those intently engaged in method (Dunnell 1984:502).

Many "post-processual" archaeologists hold a radically different view of the aims, interpretive methods, and epistemic limits of contemporary archaeology than do their processual counterparts (Wylie 1989). Followers of the emerging symbolic/contextual school, for example, reject middle range research as they do the positivist approach of the "new archaeology" (Hodder 1982a, 1982b, 1985, 1986). They favour a particularistic approach that gives primacy to the historical and cultural context of specific situations, rather than the development of general interpretive principles.

From a critical viewpoint, it is apparent that the middle range research program is paradigm dependent, insofar as it presupposes an eco-systemic view of culture in which all aspects of culture are interrelated (Wylie 1989:103-105; Trigger 1989). Yet alternative post-processual programs are equally paradigm dependent, and their proponents have not demonstrated that they have specific advantages in terms of interpretive security (Wylie 1989). I am not prepared to wholly reject middle range research in favour of less structured and largely unverifiable methodologies. Archaeological inferences must come from somewhere, and in most cases they involve analogies based on ethnographic data, historical records, actualistic data, and our own background and experience. Most archaeologists use a form of middle range reasoning every day, although they may not think of it as such.

## Rethinking Middle Range Theory

The concept of "middle range" theory was initially borrowed from sociology and introduced to archaeology in the 1970s (Raab and Goodyear 1984). Within sociology the term was used to designate a form of theorizing relating low level empirical data to higher level general theories (ibid:287). In archaeology, however, middle range theory has been closely identified with the study of natural and cultural site formation processes (Binford 1977:7, 1983b: 415, 422; Schiffer 1987). This view of middle range theory has been advocated by Lewis Binford, who contends that archaeologists require a body of theory that relates specifically to the study of the archaeological record:

> What we are seeking through middle range research are accurate means of identification, and good instruments for measuring specified properties of past cultural systems. We are seeking reliable cognitive devices...that permit the accurate conversion from observation on statics to statement about dynamics. We are seeking to build a paradigmatic frame of reference for giving meaning to selected characteristics of the archaeological record through a theoretically grounded body of research... (Binford 1983b: 415-416).

The formal structure of any middle range proposition, as conceived by Binford, involves the establishment of a **correlation** linking an archaeologically observable static entity to dynamic behaviour usually documented in contemporary societies. Binford's search for such correlations began as early as 1962, when he discussed the need for ethnographically based correlations between human behaviour and material culture as the basis for law-like generalizations concerning human behaviour in his seminal essay, "Archaeology as Anthropology" (1962; 1972:24-25). Much of Binford's subsequent work, including his actualistic studies, has been concerned with

attempts to identify and justify such behavioural generalizations in the interests of developing a "science of the archaeological record" (Binford 1983b:50).

Binford's middle range research program has won widespread support among academic archaeologists over the past two decades. The increasing number of ethnoarchaeological and experimental studies in the current literature demonstrates our acceptance of the need for such work. Yet recent critical literature on the subject has raised a number of issues that betray a confusion within the archaeological community over how middle range research should be defined, carried out, and put to practical use. In reviewing the recent literature, the following issues have been isolated:

1. It has been argued that middle range research has distracted archaeologists from the study of other substantive problems in archaeology, insofar as most actualistic studies are necessarily carried out in modern settings (Dunnell 1984; Trigger 1984).

2. Some researchers question the relevance of many middle range studies to substantive archaeological problems. The average working field archaeologist has little use for the "Mickey Mouse laws" that make up much middle range theory (Flannery 1982; Thomas et al. 1983; Courbin 1987).

3. There is fundamental confusion over what constitutes middle range research. While some equate it with the study of site formation processes, others would prefer to see middle range theory developed to address more complex interpretive problems (Willey and Sabloff 1980; Deal 1985).

4. There is further uncertainty about the degree to which middle range propositions should be generalizing or specific. Must all such principles be nomothetic ones or can middle range theories be developed that are relevant only for particular culture areas (Watson et al. 1984)?

5. It is becoming increasingly clear that there are epistemic limits to middle range research as it is currently defined and that all aspects of the

past are not accessible through actualistic research (Wylie 1989). Critics maintain that middle range research is only concerned with defining the effects of ecological constraints on human behaviour. It is thus rather difficult to interpret many phenomena of primarily social or cultural significance through the application of middle range methods (Hodder 1982a, 1982b, 1986; Wylie 1985).

The first two observations reflect the current division between the development of interpretive theory and its application to practical archaeological situations. This situation is a consequence of the more specific problems outlined above. In other words, the split between theory and practice is a product of the way that middle range theory has been developed along nomothetic, functional lines, with a primary concern for site formation processes rather than for more complex cultural behaviour. Archaeologists engaged in research in areas with a rich ethnohistorical record or a lengthy archaeological tradition that provides a ready body of accepted (but often untested) interpretive knowledge are unwilling to dismiss their present methodology of interpretation for an interpretive method that ignores the effects of culture. For these researchers, middle range theory is of little use as long as it is limited to general nomothetic principles involving functional interpretations.

Those researchers who have disputed the equation of middle range theory with the study of formation processes, maintain that the middle range concept should be reserved for studies conducted at a higher level of theoretical abstraction (Raab and Goodyear 1984; Deal 1985). Willey and Sabloff share this view, arguing that the identification of site formation processes should be viewed as low level theory while middle range theory is concerned with "why a dynamic system of the past produced the static archaeological record" (1980:250). This viewpoint would seem to suggest that middle range theory should play a role in the explanation of human behavior. Yet Binford asserts that it is concerned with the simple identification of the processes that have shaped the archaeological record:

Much of the time, use of a paradigm [a middle range frame of reference] is

viewed as an act of identification. Can we identify a habitation, a hide scraper, a matrilineage, a base camp, agriculture? Or can we diagnose the functions of a site, tool, or element of debris? In most cases we are seeking an unambiguous definition... All such interpretations are dependant on a general, accurate, and unambiguous knowledge of the relationship between statics and dynamics, the formal consequences for organized matter that derive from the operation of a dynamic system (Binford 1983b:415).

Even within the limits set by Binford, there is scope for expanding the concept of middle range theory to include more than site formation processes. It can be argued that the recognition of a social entity such as an extended family in the archaeological record involves more than understanding site formation processes. Such an interpretation would have to be based on ethnographic or historical knowledge of such groups and the archaeological products of their organization. For example, it may be possible to infer an Iroquoian extended family from the archaeological remains of an Iroquoian longhouse, but this inference depends upon the demonstrated relationship between extended families and longhouse structures in historic Iroquoian society. Such a middle range proposition is certainly less secure than an interpretive principle based on a simple site formation process because it cannot be verified experimentally. Yet, at the same time, it offers more socially significant information than one could hope to acquire from any site formation study.

Colin Renfrew (1984:9) has stressed the need to develop middle range theory for the express purpose of understanding prehistoric social behaviour. Renfrew views the different concerns of social archaeology, such as population dynamics, settlement patterns, trade, warfare, and social structure, as distinct subject areas each requiring a separate body of interpretive theory:

...each avenue of inference requires systematic consideration, and the development of what Binford and others have termed 'middle range theory' (e.g. Binford 1977, 7) so that sound principles of archaeological inference can be established (Renfrew 1984:9).

It is clear from this discussion that many archaeologists expect middle range theory to address interpretive problems beyond the technological and subsistence level. However, as we turn to problems of social and cultural interest, the general applicability of interpretive principles decreases and inferences may become less secure.

Most archaeologists engaged in actualistic studies are attempting to discover general principles of site formation that may be widely applied across time and space. These studies are premised on the belief that there is significant uniformity in human behaviour cross-culturally, making it possible to employ general comparative analogies to aid our understanding of past behaviour (Gould and Watson 1982; Watson et al. 1984). Little consideration has been given to the possibility that highly specific bodies of middle range theory may be developed to address the interpretive problems of specific sets of archaeological sites. Watson, Leblanc and Redman (1984:264) have suggested that it may be necessary to develop separate middle range models for different types of societies (i.e. all tribal horticulturalists or all Arctic hunter-gatherers). These would still be of a very general nature, consistent with the view of archaeology as a nomothetic social science. In a similar vein, Renfrew has argued that the principles he develops in addressing social issues are meant to have general applicability, even though they do not achieve the status of universal laws (1984:18).

Binford's emphasis on the generalizing nature of middle range research and, indeed, the entire thrust of his processual paradigm, has always been at odds with the view that explanation of the past in culture-historical terms should be a principal aim of the discipline (Trigger 1978b). Although general middle range principles will certainly illuminate important aspects of culture-historical situations (Trigger 1978b:26-27), it cannot be denied that much patterning in human behaviour is unique to particular cultural contexts (Gellner 1982). These

phenomena are not amenable to explanation using nomothetic "covering law" type principles. Instead, they require the development of bodies of middle range theory that are aimed at solving more culturally specific archaeological problems, leading inevitably to a more idiographic view of middle range research. Working with ethnographic and ethnohistorical data relating to specific cultures, it is possible to derive middle range propositions that may be applicable only to the interpretation of the archaeological record of one or more historically related cultures. Such propositions draw heavily on the strength of direct historical analogy (Gould and Watson 1982) and are premised on the belief that some aspects of human behaviour are culturally specific. As Wylie has stated:

> ...there is tremendous scope for idiosyncratic variability at a cultural or individual level... Indeed, there is a strong case to be made that this variability is the distinctively human and cultural feature of the archaeological subject; hence it should be the special interest of an anthropological archaeology (1985: 90).

This brings us to the most serious charge against the middle range research program, namely that it is dismissive of culture. Ethnoarchaeological studies have shown that cultural variability plays a crucial role in structuring the archaeological record, not only through expression in material culture but also through its effect on domestic life (Hodder 1982a, 1985). Despite his ethnoarchaeological experiences, Binford has repeatedly repudiated this point of view, arguing that we must rid ourselves of "the silly equation of artefacts with fossilized ideas" (1983b:62). Binford maintains that archaeologists are ill-equipped to study mental phenomena since they must work with material remains. Yet this position entirely ignores the potential for material remains to be patterned in meaningful ways by culturally determined behaviour and dismisses any hope of understanding the basis of such patterning. This is not a defensible anthropological perspective (Deetz 1971:3). While Binford's general middle range principles of interpretation may have explanatory power for a limited range of activities and processes, especially those that are causally related to ecological factors, such principles fail to explain and are in fact dismissive of much ideationally based behaviour.

It is clear from this discussion that the current development and application of middle range theory in archaeology is highly limiting for the majority of archaeologists. Nonetheless, there are strengths in the middle range interpretive method that make it attractive. Foremost among these is the security of knowledge that comes from a clear understanding of the relationship between archaeological residues and the processes known to have produced them. The difficulty is that many social and cultural processes may intervene in the formation of archaeological statics, and these processes are difficult to generalize about. Moreover, the archaeological signatures of social and cultural processes will most certainly be more ambiguous and less verifiable than physical and ecological processes governing site formation.

What is called for, is a broadening of the concept of middle range theory to incorporate all the social and cultural processes that condition the archaeological record (see also Trigger 1995). The result will be a more flexible approach to archaeological interpretation that makes use of a broader range of source-side data. Because the present formulation departs substantially from Binford's original concept of middle range theory, that term has been abandoned in this study in favour of the more inclusive term, **interpretive theory**. Interpretive theory may be defined as "a body of archaeological principles employing analogical reasoning to relate archaeological residues to the natural processes or cultural behaviours inferred to have produced them".

It must be pointed out that my concept of interpretive theory represents a broadening of the term as applied by David Clarke (1979:100). It subsumes much of the predepositional, postdepositional, retrieval and analytical theory Clarke envisioned. Similarly, interpretative theory plays a role in each of the several domains of archaeological theory recently described by Schiffer in the realms of social, reconstruction and methodological theory (1988:465).

Interpretive theory shares with middle range theory a basic concern with obtaining a secure knowledge of the past and a recognition that all archaeological interpretation must have analogical referents to known natural and cultural processes that have shaped the archaeological record. However, it differs from middle range research in a number of important ways.

First, interpretive theory may be general or particular. In many cases the most useful bodies of interpretive theory are those which pertain to a particular cultural or ethnic group, although generalizing cross-cultural correlations are not excluded.

Second, it follows that the source side data base for interpretive theory must be expanded. Ethnohistoric and ethnographic data become of prime importance in developing interpretive theory for particular culture areas. Thus textual sources become as relevant as actualistic data for forming interpretive principles.

Third, as we have seen in the above discussion, interpretive propositions may vary in complexity and in the degree of security they offer. This is a natural consequence of the effort to use interpretive theory to understand social and cultural phenomena. While security of inference is sought, we must acknowledge that it cannot always be obtained.

Finally, the interpretive method proposed here departs from middle range theory in that it recognizes existing bodies of interpretive theory as valid sources of archaeological interpretations, with the proviso that the integrity of such interpretive principles must be evaluated. Every tradition of archaeological research has built up a corpus of knowledge that is used in archaeological interpretation. Such knowledge is shared, learned, and accepted by participants within the tradition, yet it is rarely questioned. These bodies of interpretive knowledge are primarily concerned with the identification and interpretation of patterns in the archaeological record, whether the patterns take the form of sets of post moulds, sets of tool attributes, or sets of decorative elements that make up ceramic motifs. In the field of Iroquoian archaeology, accepted interpretive principles include the recognition of hearths, longhouse structures, sweat bath structures, and so on. These interpretations have been supported experimentally or ethnographically, and they are accepted as "warranted" within the tradition of Iroquoian archaeology. The interpretive method advocated here encourages examination of where such interpretations come from, but it does not advocate their rejection for the simple reason that they are accepted inferences. It is possible to use present knowledge to support further inferences, provided that existing interpretations are securely documented. Interpretive theory critically evaluates and builds upon current states of knowledge.

## Analogy and Interpretive Theory

The most important methodological link between Binford's middle range theory and the interpretive method proposed here involves the rigorous use of analogical reasoning. The relationship between archaeological statics and dynamic processes is an analogical one, with the archaeological remains forming the subject side and the natural or cultural processes forming the source side of the interpretive equation. Wylie has stated the rationale for the use of analogical reasoning in archaeology, which is similar to the rationale for interpretive theory outlined here:

> The point and value of such [analogical] arguments is, after all, precisely that they are a means of using background knowledge about more accessible, familiar contexts to reach beyond the archaeological record and provide an account of how, and for what purposes the surviving materials might have been generated (Wylie 1985:80).

The recognition that analogical reasoning is implicit in the application of interpretive theory makes relevant the ongoing theoretical debate concerning the role of analogy in archaeological interpretation.

Some archaeologists have long maintained that analogy is the basis of archaeological interpretation (Chang 1967; Charlton 1981; Watson in Gould and Watson 1982; Wylie 1985). All interpretation must proceed from the familiar to the obscure, and we must draw upon our own

experience to make sense of archaeological remains. Although analogy has been employed in archaeological interpretation for several centuries, there recently has been growing concern about how we can evaluate the strength of competing arguments from analogy (Ascher 1961; Binford 1967; Salmon 1982; Gould and Watson 1982; Wylie 1985). Critics have maintained that the use of analogy limits our archaeological interpretations to phenomena that are observable in the modern world. These researchers maintain that a dependence on analogy can be both misleading and limiting, and some have gone so far as to suggest that analogy should be eliminated from the context of archaeologcial interpretation (Gould 1980). At the same time, other scholars have risen to the defense of analogy, arguing that interpretive arguments from analogy can be evaluated in probabilistic terms, that they need not be misleading, and that analogy should remain a central concept in archaeological interpretation (Watson in Gould and Watson 1982; Wylie 1985).

In outlining her view of the role of analogy, Watson maintains that we must build "interpretive bridges" from the present to the past (Gould and Watson 1982:362). Such bridges take the logical form of analogies and, together, they form what I have termed interpretive theory - an expanded form of middle range theory. With respect to the question of strength and relevance, Watson proposes a two stage testing procedure similar to that outlined by Binford (1967) and implemented by Hill (1968). First, one examines the number and nature of similarities in form between subject and source; second, one checks the implications of the analogy in the archaeological context to see what observed patterns may be associated with the positive analogy (Gould and Watson 1982:362-363). This latter aspect of analogical argument, whereby one examines the relationships of the analogical subject to other aspects of the archaeological context, has been taken up by Alison Wylie in her discussions of the importance of **relational** analogy.

Wylie goes beyond previous researchers in isolating **causality** as a crucial criterion for assessing relevance. Causality, is used here in the Humean sense, where certain conditions (A) give rise to similar effects (B) and A always precedes B. She distinguishes the formal analogy, based on simple correspondences of form, from the relational analogy, in which there are causal conditions common to both sides of the analogy that structure both the source and the subject (1985:94). If these causal conditions can be identified, a connection is made between the source and subject and the relevance of the analogy is established.

The search for causal agency in the archaeological record leads back to an exploration of the interrelatedness of things both in the ethnographic/experimental context and in the archaeological context. This requires a more holistic or contextual approach to ethno-archaeological and actualistic studies:

> ...the object of such research must be to establish ...the principles of connection necessary for relational reasoning and ... to go beyond the documentation of detail and pattern in potential (ethnographic or experimental) sources; they must specifically seek an understanding of the causal or other relations of dependence that determine manifest structure - the detail and pattern - of cultural, behavioral contexts and their material record (Wylie 1985:104).

Wylie responds to the charges concerning the inherently limiting and distorting nature of analogical inference with the assertion that analogy can be a creative and expansive type of interpretive argument (1985:105). Through appeal to a variety of sources, each of which may illuminate a different aspect of the archaeological subject, it is possible to construct an interpretive model that is substantially different from any single known contemporary analogue (ibid:106). However, for such arguments to be viable the analogies employed must share some common element of causality. In this manner, multiple analogue models can be constructed to explain complex archaeological situations without relying upon facile ethnographic analogies or sacrificing analytical rigour. Wylie has also argued that the analogical reasoning processes she advocates provide an appropriate methodology for understanding the symbolic and ideational

components of past societies (1982). Hodder has also adopted the concept of relational analogy as an integral part of his structural/contextual approach (1982b, 1985). Within his theoretical frame of reference, historical structuring principles may serve to organize archaeological residues in meaningful ways (Hodder 1986:116-117). Such principles form the underlying conditions that lend relevance to the transfer of a structural analogy from the present to the past. Hodder rejects middle range theory precisely because historical contexts differ cross-culturally, and he denies that middle range theory can exist independently of cultural context. Yet I have argued that the logical structure of middle range theory can be recast with a much broader mandate, including the development of culturally specific bodies of interpretive theory. This logical structure is based on relational analogy, and when interpretive theory of this kind is employed in archaeology the cultural (social, symbolic, and ideational) aspects of the past do indeed become accessible.

In sum, it is suggested that the recent arguments in support of analogical inference are directly relevant to our attempts to develop interpretive theory by expanding the scope of middle range research as it is presently understood. Binford's notion that analogy should lead to the recognition of "new forms of order" in archaeological data and Wylie's demonstration of the the the importance of identifying the causal connections on both sides of the analogy imply a new kind of expansive argument for interpretive theory. The use of relational analogy in interpretive theory requires that we flex the bounds of our interpretive propositions to explore further related correspondences in the archaeological record. This will serve to expand our knowledge of the archaeological subject by accessing new regularities, while at the same time, strengthening the credibility of our interpretive propositions by contributing to the establishment of relevance.

Finally, it has been suggested that interpretive theory, based on the analogical relationships between known processes and archaeological residues, can be formulated to address the entire range of interpretive problems from technology and economy through to social organization and ideology. The following section

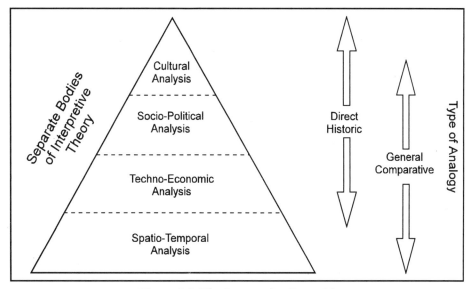

Figure 1.1. The Interpretive Pyramid.

explores the relationship of this interpretive methodology to various levels of archaeological inference.

## The Interpretive Pyramid

The role of interpretive theory in archaeological inference is most easily illustrated using the conceptual framework of an "interpretive pyramid". The interpretive pyramid, outlined in Figure 1.1, is a schematic representation showing the relationship between different categories of archaeological information and the interpretive method proposed here.

Most archaeologists would agree that certain types of information about the past are more easily recovered than others. This point of view was succinctly stated many years ago by Christopher Hawkes (1954), who proposed the well known ladder of archaeological inference beginning with technology as the type of information most easily recovered, and rising through subsistence and socio-politics to religion, on a scale of increasing difficulty of understanding.

In the early 1960s, Lewis Binford challenged this view of archaeological inference with the

assertion that information at all levels should be equally accessible. He coined the terms "technomic", "sociotechnic", and "idiotechnic" to describe the specific artifact characteristics that could be analyzed to understand these different aspects of society. In the succeeding two decades, however, Binford's own research program has focussed on technological and economic problems at the expense of the social and ideational aspects of past societies. When faced with choices between social/cultural explanations or ecological/economic ones, he has consistently opted for the latter. Binford's studies of Mousterian assemblage variability and his work on the interpretations of faunal deposits from early hominid sites are excellent examples of this trend towards ecological/economic explanation (Binford and Binford 1966; Binford 1981a).

The majority of American archaeologists influenced by the "new archaeology" have shared this primary interest in ecological and economic interpretations of the past (B. Smith 1978; Thomas et al. 1983; Schiffer 1976). Much of the middle range research conducted in recent years has contributed directly to the study of prehistoric technology and economy with an emphasis on lithic reduction and use-wear, subsistence strategies, and domestic activities, such as hearth use and refuse disposal. Such studies are generally linked to bio-physical properties that can be independently studied (i.e., the fracture properties of stone, the cutting efficiency of stone axes, the relationship between soil, climate, and agricultural potential). Given their connection to natural properties and environmental conditions, the middle range principles developed on this level have greater scope for generalization using propositions derived from the physical and biological sciences. It is not surprising then, that in the search for universal principles of interpretation many processual archaeologists have adopted this ecological position. It is, in fact, the only theoretical position from which they can substantiate their belief in the role of archaeology as a nomothetic social science. Unfortunately, this position has contributed to a tendency to ignore the social and cultural implications of archaeological data to the extent that social or cultural behaviour is sought in the archaeological record only when it is apparent or easily accessible. For the most part, this is where such behaviour reflects the "principle of least effort".

Wylie has reviewed the problem of epistemic limits in relation to actualistic research (1989). She concludes that archaeologists should work toward developing "an empirically specified 'ladder of inference', one in which the relative degrees of security attainable by different sorts of interpretive inference are assessed against the background knowledge on which it necessarily depends" (Wylie 1989:108). Such a ladder of inference may be similar to the interpretive pyramid proposed here.

The dimensions of space and time form the broad base of the interpretive pyramid (Figure 1.1), a level at which there are various law-like principles used in archaeological interpretation. Examples include the laws of stratigraphy, the principles of radiocarbon dating, and the principles of dendrochronology. Inferences based on these well grounded principles are applicable on a world-wide basis and have a very high degree of interpretive security.

The ecological, economic, and technological sub-systems of society form the next level, at which there is still much potential for cross-cultural generalization and the development of general interpretive theory (Figure 1.1). Both direct historic and general comparative analogical arguments may be employed in such theoretical propositions.

As one moves into the realm of interpretation on the societal level, bio-physical and ecological conditions have a less constraining effect and it becomes more difficult to draw generalisations from the data. Trigger (1978b) has advocated a synthetic approach to archaeological interpretation that seeks to integrate the functional concerns of processual archaeology with his view that society is the dynamic entity that archaeologists should attempt to understand. Colin Renfrew has likewise argued that we must achieve a better balance between our consideration of social factors and that of subsistence and technology (1984). Within American archaeology a number of students of the processual school have recognized the limitations of a functional approach and have begun to develop a range of methods for the investigation of social behaviour (Redman et al. 1978). Explicit models based on decision making, locational analysis, multivariate systems models, quantitative simulation models, and middle range research dealing with social behaviour have all made substantial contributions in this area. Thus a distinctive social archaeology has begun to develop in both the Old and New Worlds (Renfrew 1984; Redman et al. 1978).

As noted earlier, Renfrew maintains that a social archaeology should be concerned with the development of general principles of social behaviour, although such principles might only apply under certain conditions and not constitute universal laws (Renfrew 1984:18). Insofar as particular ecological and economic conditions may impose constraints on societal factors such as group size and mobility, it can be argued that there are some general principles relating to similar social strategies that may occur cross-culturally under specified boundary conditions.

Within the interpretive pyramid then, the social realm holds an intermediate position in which there is still scope for generalisation in the interpretive theories developed. At the same time, however, much of the social behaviour inferred may be limited in its applicability to a particular cultural context. Thus, in employing analogy to infer social behavior, a combination of direct historic and general comparative analogies will be useful.

At the top of the interpretive pyramid we find the symbolic and ideational component of society. This is the realm of belief systems, ritual, ceremonialism, ideology, and the unspoken grammar of culture that guides the behaviour of individuals and the use of material culture. Despite the traditional difficulty that archaeologists have experienced in seeking this information, there is renewed interest in the symbolic and ideational aspects of the past. The current interest in symbolic and contextual archaeology has developed largely in Britain as a reaction to the American processual school and its techno-economic interests (Hodder 1982a,b, 1986).However, there are important precedents for an interest in culture and ideas in American archaeology. Deetz (1967, 1971, 1977) has long argued that archaeologists must attempt to understand the cultural information encoded in artifacts. He has also stressed the need to explore the cultural context of material things, in both present and past societies. Deetz's work owes a debt to the insights of Taylor's (1948) *A Study of Archeology* in which Taylor advocated his "conjunctive approach", stressing the relationships among artifacts and their role as parts of an integrated cultural whole (Redman et al. 1978:3). It is apparent that the new frontiers presently being pursued in contextual archaeology have deep roots in the American tradition.

When dealing with cultural and ideational behaviour there is little scope for generalization. Gellner has noted that cultural variability occurs most often in the realms of ideology, symbolism, mythology, ritual, and art; areas where ecological constraints do not impinge significantly on human expression, as they do at the lower levels of the pyramid (Gellner 1982:104). Consequently, interpretive theory developed at this level is heavily reliant upon direct historical analogy. Yet there are cases where cultural or ideational phenomena are shared by several cultures or ethnic groups. In these cases general comparative analogies may be relevant, especially if the causal factors underlying the cultural phenomena are established (von Gernet and Timmins 1987).

The interpretive pyramid outlined above forms a comprehensive framework for archaeological interpretation. It is a general model, but it may be adapted for individual situations. We have recognized separate bodies of interpretive theory for dealing with spatio-temporal, techno-economic, societal, and ideational components of past societies. As we move up the pyramid, these bodies of theory become increasingly culturally specific and the analogical reasoning processes that underlie our interpretations change with respect to source data. For example, a significant part of the body of interpretive theory required to understand Iroquoian agriculturalists is largely independent of the interpretive theory that is relevant to Arctic hunter-gatherers. Interpretive theory in Iroquoian archaeology will draw upon extant knowledge of historic and prehistoric Iroquoian culture as source data for interpretive principles.

The spatio-temporal, techno-economic, societal, and cultural levels are each broad categories of anthropological concern. In recent years preferences concerning which category of information should be given primacy have developed into conflicting paradigmatic positions, each with its own goals and methods (Binford 1983a, 1983b; Redman et al. 1978; Renfrew 1984; Hodder 1982b, 1986). The paradigmatic posturing occurring among these positions is unproductive and reflects the differing goals and methods of each approach (cf. Binford 1983a; Hodder 1986). The interpretive pyramid is proposed as a step towards the integration of these positions. The methodological link that facilitates such an integration lies in the recognition of analogy as the underlying logical process in archaeological interpretation. Interpretive theory at any level seeks to identify causality in the archaeological record and such knowledge can only be gained through analogical reasoning between past and present contexts.

As an interpretive model, the pyramid can also be used to structure archaeological inquiry at the analytical level. It provides a logical approach to archaeological analysis by proceeding from fundamental questions concerning space and time, to economy and technology, and finally to more complex social and cultural issues. At each level of the analysis some questions are answered, but new questions emerge that require access to

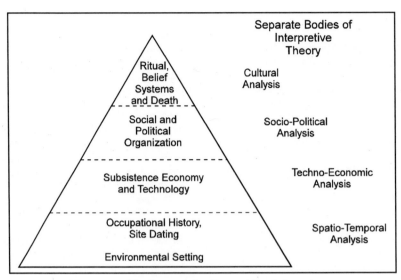

Figure 1.2. The Interpretive Pyramid and the structure
of the Calvert site inquiry.

different types of source data for the construction of our interpretive propositions.

The substantive chapters of this study, dealing with the analysis and interpretation of the Early Iroquoian Calvert site, are organized within the framework of the interpretive pyramid. Figure 1.2 illustrates the structure of the Calvert inquiry.

The inquiry begins with a review of past Early Iroquoian archaeology presented in Chapter 2. This discussion provides important background information on the current state of knowledge of the Early Iroquoian period and focuses on the interpretations proposed by past researchers. Well grounded interpretations and background information act as source data for the Calvert analysis.

We enter the interpretive pyramid at the spatio-temporal level (Figure 1.2). The analysis begins with a reconstruction of the environmental setting of the Calvert site, presented in Chapter 4. A variety of sources are used to understand the prehistoric environment of the Calvert locale, setting the stage for later catchment and subsistence analyses.

In Chapter 5 the occupational history of the site is analyzed and chronometric evidence is considered to provide a temporal placement of the site on the calendrical time-scale. Much of the success of this study depends upon the development of a reliable procedure for separating the Calvert data into sub-samples corresponding to occupational phases. This separation requires an understanding of how the Calvert site was formed. An important methodological contribution of the study lies in the analysis of site formation processes as they relate to occupational history.

In Chapter 6 we move up the pyramid to consider the evidence for the economy of the Calvert community. The results of floral and faunal analyses are summarized and interpreted in terms of subsistence, site function, and season of occupation.

Still at the techno-economic level, Chapter 7 is concerned with technology and change within the Calvert community. In this chapter the ceramic, lithic, and bohe artifacts are analyzed and the settlement pattern data are described. Changes in the domestic life of the Calvert community are addressed through a comparative analysis of data from different phases in the occupation of the site.

Chapter 8 moves into the socio-political realm with interpretations of the Calvert settlement pattern data and their change through time. Demographic trends in the site occupation are discussed and the spatial and functional organization of the village is considered. In this chapter we also place the Calvert community within the broader context of Early Iroquoian society through a comparative examination of other sites in the region.

With Chapter 9 we move to the symbolic and ideational realm of the Calvert community, the highest level of the interpretive pyramid. The evidence for ritual behaviour is considered, based on Calvert and relevant source data. This is the most inaccessible realm of the Calvert community and interpretations are limited.

The interpretations offered at each level of the analysis draw upon specific bodies of interpretive theory that either are derived from previous research or have been developed for the present analysis. In all cases an attempt is made to be explicit about where interpretations are coming from, by citing the interpretive correlation or analogue model that is being used. Chapter 10 reviews the interpretative model developed here and summarizes the application of interpretive theory and the use of the interpretive pyramid in the analysis of the Calvert data.

# Chapter 2

# An Historical Overview of Early Iroquoian Research

This chapter summarizes current knowledge about Early Iroquoian society and culture history through a review of past research. The purpose of this review is to examine the types of problems addressed by previous researchers and the interpretations they have offered. This overview leads to the identification of a series of ongoing research problems in Early Iroquoian studies.

Investigations of Early Iroquoian sites have been conducted in Ontario and New York State since the turn of the century. During this time, the interests, concerns, and methods of Iroquoianists have changed substantially. These developments have been summarized by Bruce Trigger (1985b), who has defined three sequential periods in the history of Iroquoian archaeology (ethnographic, chronological, and spatial) from the time of David Boyle (the 1880s) to the present. Trigger's scheme provides a convenient framework for the organization of this review.

For the purposes of the following discussion the term "Early Iroquoian" is adapted from J.V. Wright's "Early Ontario Iroquois" (1966) and its usage expanded to include the Glen Meyer culture of southwestern Ontario, the Pickering culture of south-central Ontario, "Pickering-like" manifestations in eastern Ontario, southern Quebec, and northeastern New York State, and the Owasco culture of upper central, eastern, and western New York State. All of these archaeological manifestations are believed to be ancestral to later Iroquoian populations and are thought to be essentially coeval, dating to between ca. A.D. 900 and ca. A.D. 1300, with the possibility of some slight temporal variations between regions (Timmins 1985).

Also included in this discussion are a number of transitional sites that date to either the beginning or the end of the Early Iroquoian period. These include sites of the Princess Point Complex (Stothers 1977) at the early end of the continuum, and sites that have been variously categorized as late Glen Meyer or Uren sub-stage components at the recent end of the sequence (J. Wright 1966; M. Wright 1986).

## Early Iroquoian Ethnographic Archaeology

Iroquoian archaeology at the turn of the century was concerned with the functional interpretation of artifacts as an aid to the reconstruction of past Indian ways of life (Trigger 1985b:7-8). An essentially static view of native prehistory prevailed in which Indian societies were thought to have little time depth and to have undergone minimal change prior to European contact (Trigger 1980). As a result, early ethnographic and ethnohistorical sources were used as guides to the interpretation of most archaeological remains.

The initial Early Iroquoian investigations in New York State were conducted within this ethnographic framework and the resulting archaeological interpretations were profoundly affected by it. A.C. Parker, the first New York State archaeologist to excavate an Owasco site, recognized distinctive differences among New York assemblages. Yet rather than attributing these differences to internal change within a single society, he invoked a series of population migrations in and out of the region. Thus Parker's *Archaeological History of New York* (1922) proposed an early pre-ceramic occupation of Eskimo-like peoples, who were displaced northward by an intrusive race of Moundbuilders from the south (Parker 1922). This was followed by an Algonkian occupation that lasted until the

Iroquoian speaking peoples migrated into the area from the south in fairly recent times (Parker 1916, 1922). Accordingly, when Parker excavated the first known Early Iroquoian assemblage from the Owasco Lake site (also known as Lakeside Park) in 1915, he judged it to be distinct from known Iroquoian material and assigned it to an Algonkian occupation of central New York (Parker 1922:342; Ritchie 1969:272).

Parker's work was an early influence on that of his successor, William Ritchie, who took up the study of Early Iroquoian archaeology and became the major architect of our present understanding of New York State prehistory (Ritchie 1944, 1969). Between 1927 and 1935, Ritchie conducted major excavations on the Levanna, Castle Creek, Sackett (Canandaigua), and Bainbridge sites, all Owasco components (Ritchie 1944). During this early stage of his career, Ritchie shared with Parker and other archaeologists of the day a keen interest in the functional study of artifacts and archaeological features and the reconstruction of prehistoric cultural life (Taylor 1948:78).

In 1920, William Wintemberg conducted major excavations at the Uren site, a transitional Early to Middle Iroquoian village that he regarded as "proto-Neutral," with "Algonkian" influences apparent in the ceramics (Wintemberg 1928). Like most of his other reports, Wintemberg's Uren monograph exemplifies the functional/ethnographic concerns of the time. Data were described in terms of functional or economic categories such as "food procurement" and "tool use," the explicit goal being to infer the way of life of the site's inhabitants (Trigger 1985b:8). Because of the artifact-based orientation of Wintemberg's work, his excavation strategies focussed on midden excavation, and structural data (i.e. post moulds) were neither sought nor recorded (M. Wright 1986).

The final contribution to Early Iroquoian studies in terms of the style of the ethnographic period was W. Wilfrid Jury's 1947-1948 excavation of the Early to Middle Iroquoian Crawford site, near the Ausable River in southwestern Ontario. Much of Jury's career was devoted to learning about Indian ways, through historical research, archaeological investigations, and material culture experiments (Timmins

1982). As a non-academic archaeologist, he was largely isolated from the influence of McKern's (1939) Midwestern Taxonomic Method; thus his work at the Crawford site, although conducted in the 1940s, may be seen as a survival of the period of ethnographic archaeology.

Jury worked, for a time, as Wintemberg's field assistant and correspondence between the two illustrates that Wintemberg was a major influence in his archaeological training (E. Jury and R. Pearce: personal communication). Indeed, Jury's brief Crawford site report is organized in the Wintemberg format, with sections devoted to categories such as "Foodstuffs," "Procuring of Food," and "Preparation of Food". However, unlike Wintemberg, Jury claimed to recognize house patterns on the Crawford site. Significantly, these were said to be of longhouse form, 6.1 m in width and ranging from 17.7 to 25.9 m in length, with central hearths (Jury 1948:3-4). A single circular structure was also found. Yet despite his recognition of the Iroquoian longhouse form, Jury was not convinced that the site was Iroquoian, since the crudity of the pottery suggested Algonkian authorship (Jury 1948:8). Noting ceramic affinities to Wintemberg's Uren site he concluded, "If the Crawford site is not Algonkian, it is proto-Neutral, as Wintemberg concluded of the Uren site,..."(1948:8).

It is apparent that Parker's early cultural-chronological scheme had a profound effect on archaeological interpretation during the ethnographic period of research. Since the Iroquoians were thought to be recent arrivals in the Northeast, only sites yielding ceramics similar to historic Iroquoian material were accepted as Iroquoian. Early Iroquoian sites, with their distinctive ceramics, were assigned to the period of Algonkian occupation or seen as subject to strong Algonkian influences. The identification of Owasco sites as Algonkian also may have influenced the interpretation of Owasco house patterns at this time. Prior to the 1960s, post mould patterns on Owasco sites were consistently interpreted as circular structures that were analogous to the Algonkian wigwam or lodge (Ritchie 1944; Ritchie 1969:215-216). More recent research has demonstrated that the most common Owasco structure is indeed a longhouse or proto-longhouse form. However, no houses of this type were clearly identified on Owasco sites until after the establishment of the Iroquois *in situ* theory during the chronological-classificatory period.

## Early Iroquoian Chronological-Classificatory Archaeology

Iroquoian archaeologists began to take a greater interest in the cultural classification of their data and the development of cultural chronologies in the 1930s. This interest was slow to develop in the Northeast, where the southern hypothesis of Iroquoian origins and a lack of stratified sites indicated little time depth for the Iroquoians and seemed to preclude the possibility of significant internal change. Thus the chronology of Iroquoian development was not a major issue in Parker's time, although Alanson Skinner made an early distinction between Archaic Iroquois and later Iroquoian peoples (Trigger 1985a:10).

W.J. Wintemberg was the first archaeologist to recognize major developmental trends within an Iroquoian group and grant them additional time depth on this basis (Wintemberg 1931; Pearce 1984). Drawing on ceramic comparisons among southwestern Ontario sites that he had excavated, Wintemberg proposed sequential Archaic, Transitional, Pre-European, and Post-European periods spanning Uren to historic times (Wintemberg 1931). Although the cultural designations have changed, his chronology remains valid today (Pearce 1984:30).

With the publication of *The Pre-Iroquoian Occupations of New York State* in 1944, William Ritchie adopted the Midwestern Taxonomic Method (MWTM). He assigned the earlier Owasco Aspect to the Woodland Pattern and the later Iroquois Aspect to the Mississippian Pattern. The Woodland and Mississippian Patterns were distinguished by a number of basic cultural differences, including settlement and subsistence patterns, artifact types, and burial practices (McKern 1939:309). Each was viewed as a basic, widely distributed cultural pattern and an evolutionary or developmental relationship between the two was not implied (McKern 1939:309; Willey and Sabloff 1980; Pearce

1984). Yet some Owasco sites showed clear Iroquoian traits, while some Iroquoian ones included Owasco materials, leading Ritchie to suggest, as Wintemberg had done for Ontario, that the Algonkians and the Iroquoians had coexisted for some time and had influenced one another (Ritchie 1944). Thus, the adoption of the MWTM did not substantially alter Ritchie's interpretation of Owasco-Iroquoian development; it simply changed the cultural designations.

Taylor (1948:77-80) has argued that Ritchie's adoption of the MWTM eroded his early interest in functional studies and the reconstruction of cultural life. *The Pre-Iroquoian Occupations of New York State* consists mainly of detailed trait lists and straightforward artifact descriptions with limited interpretation (Ritchie 1944). Of 288 items on Ritchie's Owasco trait list, 269 deal with artifact observations, seven pertain to burials, six deal with features and settlement data, and only two involve subsistence data (Ritchie 1944:46, 351). These figures may accurately reflect the general distribution of the interests of most northeastern American archaeologists during the 1940s when artifact typologies were the building blocks for cultural chronologies.

Despite a growing interest in culture chronology, the Early Iroquoian Owasco sites had still not been drawn into the Iroquoian continuum by the late 1940s. At this time Richard MacNeish began his substantial influence on Iroquoian archaeology with a study of so called "Pre-Iroquoian" pottery from New York State, which he conducted with Ritchie (Ritchie and MacNeish 1949). In their report Ritchie and MacNeish constructed a ceramic typology for Point Peninsula and Owasco ceramics and presented a seriation illustrating the probable development of Owasco out of Point Peninsula (Ritchie and MacNeish 1949:119-121). They also suggested the possibility that at least part of the Owasco Aspect might have been ancestral to the Mohawk Iroquois, but did not elaborate upon this idea (Ritchie and MacNeish 1949:122).

MacNeish's introduction to Owasco ceramics led him to study the pottery of later Iroquoian groups. This research culminated in the publication of *Iroquois Pottery Types*, in which he claimed to demonstrate an *in situ* development of Iroquoian culture from Middle Woodland Point Peninsula times through to the historic period, effectively replacing the southern hypothesis of Iroquoian origins (MacNeish 1952).

MacNeish recognized four areal divisions of the Owasco culture, all of which were believed to have developed from a widespread, culturally homogenous Middle Woodland base (1952:81, 83). One of these divisions was a poorly defined "Ontario Owasco", identified by Tom Lee during archaeological surveys conducted in southwestern Ontario in 1949 and 1950 (Lee 1951, 1952). Lee's Ontario Owasco is not wholly identical to the Glen Meyer Focus, which he also defined at this time, although some recent studies have assumed that this is the case (Pearce 1984; Williamson 1985). Using the Midwestern Taxonomic System, Lee organized the Owasco Aspect in Ontario into four foci: Point Pelee, Port Royal, Kreiger, and Glen Meyer (1952:76). However, he was dissatisfied with the MWTM, partly because he anticipated considerable time depth within foci as well as temporal differences between them. In both his 1951 and 1952 reports he treated Glen Meyer as a development **out of** the Ontario Owasco (1951:45; 1952:65). Similarly, MacNeish mentions Lee's discovery of numerous key (Glen Meyer) sites connecting Uren with an Owasco type of culture in the lower Ontario region (1952:83). Although Lee did not describe his Ontario Owasco components in any detail, Stothers believes that they can be broadly correlated with the Princess Point Complex (Stothers 1977:23). Lee's recognition of Glen Meyer, and the earlier Ontario Owasco, together with MacNeish's demonstration of cultural continuity, had major implications for the future understanding of Iroquoian prehistory. It indicated that Iroquoian development in Ontario and New York State had occurred over a lengthy period and had proceeded along similar lines in both areas. MacNeish's work, in particular, destroyed the myth that the Owasco were ancestral to later Algonkian peoples, clearing the way for a better understanding of Early Iroquoian culture through the use of the Direct Historic Approach.

The *in situ* theory effectively quickened the pace of Iroquoian research during the 1950s and 1960s as researchers sought to substantiate MacNeish's sequence and elucidate specific parts of it (Ritchie 1961; Lenig 1965; Wright 1966; Kenyon 1968; Noble 1969). At the same time, however, concern began to be expressed that the wholesale adoption of MacNeish's dendritic developmental scheme contributed to a sense of cultural isolation for the Iroquoians and ignored processes of diffusion that are crucial for an understanding of cultural change (Guthe 1960:203-205; Trigger 1970:30; Pearce 1984:46). In an early paper on this subject, Alfred Guthe (1960) pointed out that not all Iroquois culture traits could be derived from Owasco. Among the non-artifactual Iroquoian traits that he cited as possible evidence of diffusion from adjacent groups were the Iroquoian longhouse form, ossuary burial, earthworks, and village size (Guthe 1960:205). While recent research has demonstrated that some of these traits evolved within the Iroquoian continuum, Guthe nevertheless indicated that Iroquoian development could not be viewed in isolation from adjacent cultures.

Between 1958 and 1961, Walter Kenyon conducted excavations on the Miller site near Toronto, a project that resulted in a major contribution to Early Iroquoian research in Ontario (Kenyon 1968). The Miller excavations were designed to investigate the possibility of an Owasco variant in south central Ontario, as suggested by earlier work by Ritchie along the Trent waterway (1949) and by Ridley at the Boys site (1958). Kenyon's primary aim was to collect a large artifact sample for analytical and comparative purposes (Kenyon 1968:8).

Approximately 75% of the .42 ha Miller village was opened to view and thousands of post moulds, outlining six houses and many problematic structures, were mapped. Kenyon described the houses as being "flattened oval" in form and stated that "there can be little doubt that the Miller houses are ancestral to the Long House of the later Iroquois periods" (Kenyon 1968:53). This was the first recognition of the longhouse form on an accepted Early Iroquoian site. Kenyon also recognized the possibility that the site might have had an extended occupation, judging from evidence of structure rebuilding and hearths that appeared to have been used repeatedly (1968:16, 20). He even tested for the possibility of changes in ceramic style during the duration of the Miller occupation:

> The sample of artifacts from a single pit was assumed to represent a shorter time-span than that occupied by the entire village. If, therefore, there had been any significant changes in ceramic styles during the period that the village was occupied, our only hope of detecting change lay in the comparison of the artifact contents of the various pits. Such a comparison was made, and with totally negative results (Kenyon 1968:24).

Negative results aside, this was the first attempt to separate the deposits on an Early Iroquoian site temporally, on the basis of stylistic criteria, rather than simply treating the assemblage as an homogenous sample.

The culture-chronological goals of Kenyon's Miller site research were realized with the establishment of the Pickering culture and the demonstration, contrary to Guthe (1960), of the early existence of longhouse forms and ossuary-type burial. Kenyon's insights into Early Iroquoian settlement patterns foreshadowed the concerns of later researchers.

J.V. Wright's *Ontario Iroquois Tradition* was the final major contribution to the culture-chronological phase of Early Iroquoian studies. Wright presented the first systematic description of the Glen Meyer culture and also drew together available information on the Pickering culture, which Walter Kenyon was in the process of defining (J. Wright 1966; Kenyon 1968). Adopting the concept of a cultural tradition from Willey and Phillips (1958), Wright proposed that the Ontario Iroquois tradition developed through successive Early, Middle, and Late stages, each of which was characterized by a different cultural process (J. Wright 1966:14). Thus Early Iroquois, consisting of the Pickering and Glen Meyer "branches," was seen to undergo a process of cultural "convergence" leading ultimately to a cultural "fusion," as the Pickering branch purportedly conquered and absorbed the Glen Meyer people, initiating the Middle stage (ibid.).

While Wright's framework continues to be a useful working model for the classification of archaeological material, the validity of the Pickering/Glen Meyer conquest has long been questioned (Noble 1975a; M.J. Wright 1986). As data accumulate and studies become more detailed, some archaeologists have argued that Iroquoian prehistory may best be viewed in terms of a number of distinct communities developing through time within circumscribed geographical areas (Pearce 1984). From the perspective of the community sequence model proposed by Robert Pearce, the broad cultural processes defined by Wright are less useful for understanding Iroquoian development.

## Early Iroquoian Spatial Archaeology

As cultural chronologies became better established, archaeologists were able to turn their attention once again to the study of Iroquoian behaviour and the reconstruction of various aspects of Iroquoian life (Trigger 1985b:11). This research was influenced by two important trends in field methods: 1) the implementation of regional site surveys; and 2) the large-scale excavation of Iroquoian sites. Both types of investigation yielded important spatial data concerning Iroquoian settlement and subsistence patterns, demography, socio-political organization, community organization, and domestic life. These studies have contributed to an increased awareness of the Early Iroquoian period as a time of both economic and socio-political transition. They have also demonstrated that the archaeology of the Early Iroquoian village is, for various reasons, more complex than that of later Iroquoian sites.

William Ritchie was among the first to implement a program of excavation that was specifically designed to recover settlement pattern data from Iroquoian sites. During the 1950s and 60s, he excavated substantial portions of the Maxon-Derby, Sackett (Canandaigua), Bates, Roundtop, and Kelso sites, recovering a partial site plan in each case (Ritchie and Funk 1973). Although inspired by a widespread American interest in settlement archaeology, this work displays a natural continuity with his earlier research, in that much of the analysis continued to involve the construction of detailed trait lists and typological classifications of artifacts. Occasionally, entire living floors were exposed, but broad-scale areal excavation was not part of the overall research strategy. Usually only a small portion of the site was completely excavated, with other structures being inferred with the aid of extensive slit trenching (Ritchie and Funk 1973).

Despite these limitations, Ritchie was able to demonstrate the central problem of Early Iroquoian settlement archaeology - namely, the overwhelming complexity of settlement patterns. Overlapping structures and high post mould densities made structure definition extremely difficult, especially when only small areas had been exposed. The most telling example of this occurred at the Sackett site, where a series of highly speculative circular houses were defined while central lines of hearths flanked by wall lines of typical longhouse form were overlooked (Ritchie and Funk 1973:215, 216; Snow 1980:313; Trigger 1981:12).

Ritchie developed a typology of settlement types that was largely based on the presence or absence of structural remains. A single house represented a hamlet (i.e. the Bates site), while a site with two or more houses was defined as a village (Ritchie and Funk 1973:359). Both were assumed to have been occupied year-round. Other sites, presumably without structural remains, were classified as temporary or recurrent camps or workshops.

Ritchie appears to have believed that the adoption of agriculture and concomitant sedentism occurred very rapidly. Although cultigens had not been identified on Middle Woodland sites, the presence of corn, beans, and squash at the Early Owasco Roundtop site led him to infer that the Roundtop people were "sedentary farmers" (Ritchie and Funk 1973:193). Yet the site was built on a river terrace that showed evidence of flooding, indicating that occupation was probably seasonally recurrent rather than year-round. Ritchie's belief that early Owasco sites were occupied year-round may be seen as an expression of the older uniformitarian view that the prehistoric Iroquoians were essentially similar to historically documented groups in both their economy and settlement patterns.

An alternative to Ritchie's views about the development of Iroquoian horticulture was offered by Marian White in her interpretation of the Oakfield site, a thirteenth-century village located in western New York (White 1963). At Oakfield, indications of winter occupation were lacking although cultigens were abundant, prompting her to suggest that Oakfield had been occupied by early farmers who did not yet produce the necessary agricultural surplus to see them through the winter (1963:9). She proposed that "...as agriculture was adapted and increased in efficiency, the settlement pattern changed from Recurrent to Semi-Sedentary to Semi-Permanent Sedentary" (1963:11). This long-ignored paper contained the first suggestion that the development of agriculture by the Early Iroquoian peoples might have been a lengthy, gradual process involving many minor shifts in settlement patterns.

Evidence of Iroquoian occupation in northern Pennsylvania came to light in the mid-1960s as a result of salvage excavations conducted in the area of the Allegheny Reservoir (Dragoo 1977). Since that time additional research in the region has resulted in the definition of a chronological sequence of Iroquoian occupation extending from late Middle Woodland to Middle Iroquoian times (Johnson 1976:71), the approximate time that the Iroquoian sequence in the Niagara frontier begins.

The Allegheny Iroquoian sequence has received little attention from Ontario Iroquoianists, despite the fact that the sites share strong similarities with Early and Middle Iroquoian components in Ontario. A prime example is the Glen Meyer-like Kinzua site that has produced a variety of Glen Meyer ceramic types, together with settlement features that show affinities to Early and Middle Ontario Iroquoian sites (Dragoo 1977).

The Kinzua site is a small (1 ha.) village with a single row palisade encircling several structures and pit features. Both incipient longhouse and circular structures are represented. The houses were tightly packed within the stockade, creating narrow walkways between structures. According to Dragoo, "refuse was deposited in small pits near the houses and stockade walls rather than being left to clutter the village area" (1977:43-44). Of particular interest is the presence of large, shallow "turtle pits", a distinctive feature type also known to occur on many Early and Middle Ontario Iroquoian village sites, where they have been interpreted as sweat lodges (MacDonald 1988). Given the obvious parallels between Early Iroquoian settlements in southwestern Ontario and the Upper Allegheny valley, it would seem appropriate for Ontario Iroquoianists to pay greater attention to the role of this Iroquoian population in the overall development of Iroquoian prehistory.

During the mid-1960s, James Tuck conducted important research in central New York, where he traced the sequential village movements of two Iroquoian communities from Late Owasco through to historical times. Tuck's most extensive Owasco excavation was at the Chamberlin site, a ca. A.D. 1300 village where at least two phases of rebuilding were indicated by overlapping house structures (Tuck 1971:24). The major contribution of Tuck's research lay not with his Owasco work, but with his demonstration that the concept of community could be successfully employed to reconstruct lengthy sequences of local development.

Additional data on Pickering settlement patterns became available in 1969, when J.V. Wright and J.E. Anderson published their monograph on the Bennett site. Wright described the archaeology of this late Pickering village and Anderson summarized the osteology of the 13 human burials found on the site. The Bennett excavations, conducted in 1962, exposed approximately 10% of the 1.0-1.2 ha village (Wright and Anderson 1969:8). Wright's excavation strategy was designed to maximize the recovery of settlement data and resulted in the documentation of three definite and four tentative house structures, surrounded by a double row palisade (Wright and Anderson 1969:10, 12). The inferred structures were described in detail by Wright and a brief distributional study was made of the pit features which were classified according to size but not function (Wright and Anderson 1969:13-23). Unfortunately, structural post mould patterns were difficult to interpret due to a combination of variable soil conditions and structure overlapping, which occurred in at least two areas (Wright and Anderson 1969:15,

19, 20). Although the Bennett settlement patterns were adequately described, the fact that only 10% of the village was excavated limited interpretations. It was not possible to say much about community organization, population estimates were not attempted, and the possible implications of the overlapping house patterns were not discussed. Instead, analysis was focussed on a comparative artifact study in an attempt to substantiate Wright's Pickering/Glen Meyer conquest hypothesis (Wright and Anderson 1969:62-79). Thus Wright's Bennett site work was closely linked to his earlier *Ontario Iroquois Tradition* (1966) in an effort to support the controversial conquest hypothesis.

A more comprehensive attempt to reconstruct some social aspects of Early Iroquoian behaviour was made by William C. Noble in the mid-1960s (Noble 1969). Rather than concentrating on pottery analysis, Noble studied settlement, burials, subsistence patterns, and pipe data to look for trends in Ontario Iroquoian development. His interpretations concerning the Early Ontario Iroquoians are of particular interest to this study.

Using as ethnographic analogies the historic Iroquoians, Noble equated the archaeological longhouse with the "sociological lineage household" (Noble 1969:18). On the basis of this assumption, he was able to draw inferences about Early Iroquoian social organization from archaeological house patterns. Thus the "proto-longhouses" found on Early Iroquoian sites were interpreted as evidence of extended family households (probably matrilineal), while the smaller circular houses found on some Owasco sites were taken to be the houses of non-lineage, probably non-matrilineal, social groups (Noble 1969:18). That these lineages were in a developmental state until about A.D. 1200 was further suggested by the internal organization of Early Iroquoian houses, which according to Noble did not become standardized with central hearths and bunk lines until after A.D. 1200 (ibid.).

Noble also sought to infer aspects of Early Iroquoian political organization by postulating a relationship between community organization and political structure. He concluded that Iroquoian houses prior to A.D. 1300 were randomly arranged throughout the village, implying that "community planning by a village council was either nonexistent or unnecessary" (Noble 1969:19).

Turning to subsistence practices, Noble viewed agricultural surplus as an impetus to settlement and argued that the large pits found on Early Iroquoian sites may have been used for corn storage (Noble 1969:21). He cited Chang (1958:300) with respect to the causal relationship between agriculture and semi-sedentary life, and shared with Ritchie the uniformitarian view that Early Iroquoian settlements were occupied year round and were fully agricultural, like their historic Iroquoian counterparts (Noble 1969, 1975a). In the face of new data, many of Noble's interpretations of Early Iroquoian life have had to be revised (Williamson 1985). Yet his synthesis marks a crucial juncture in the development of Early Iroquoian studies, inasmuch as it exerted a major influence on research conducted during the next decade.

The 1970s witnessed a flurry of research on Early Iroquoian sites in Ontario. During this period Noble and Kenyon investigated the early Glen Meyer Porteous site (1972); C.S. Reid conducted excavations at the Pickering Boys site (1975); William Fox investigated the Glen Meyer Dewaele site (1976); Noble conducted a major excavation at the Van Besien site, a large Glen Meyer village (1975a); David Stothers re-investigated Porteous and used it, along with several other sites, to define the ancestral Glen Meyer Princess Point Complex in southwestern Ontario (1977); Milton Wright re-investigated the Uren site (1986); R.J. Pearce dug the Pickering branch Richardson site (1978); and Robert Rozel excavated the late Pickering Gunby village (1979). Taken together, these investigations greatly advanced our understanding of the Early Iroquoian period in Ontario.

The Porteous site, located within the City of Brantford, is a crucial early link in the Glen Meyer developmental sequence. Initially investigated by Thomas and Ian Kenyon, the site was excavated by Noble in 1969, with additional salvage work being conducted under Stothers. These combined excavations resulted in the exposure of approximately 70% of the .1 ha village (Stothers 1977:126). Noble and Kenyon's

(1972) initial examination of the Porteous village focussed on it as an early expression of Glen Meyer village life, in contrast to the seasonally occupied, riverine oriented camps of earlier times (1972:30). The site was dated ca. A.D. 700 on the basis of two divergent radiocarbon dates; however, this date has repeatedly been adjusted later as additional dates from Porteous and earlier Princess Point sites have become available (Stothers 1977; Timmins 1985:71; MacDonald 1986:20). A date in the ninth or tenth century A.D. is now favoured (Timmins 1985; MacDonald 1986).

David Stothers' re-investigation of the Porteous site occurred as part of his doctoral research and contributed to his formulation of the Princess Point Complex, an early Late Woodland manifestation that is ancestral to Glen Meyer (Stothers 1977). Stothers viewed Porteous as a late Princess Point component that demonstrated a shift from the riverine floodplain encampments occupied during earlier Princess Point times to elevated sand knoll locations during the terminal Princess Point phase (Stothers 1977). However, other researchers have tended to agree with Noble and Kenyon's identification of Porteous as the earliest Glen Meyer village documented to date (Fox 1982c; Williamson 1990:308). This disagreement is of minor concern since it involves an arbitrary break in the Princess Point-Glen Meyer continuum and it is clear that Porteous is a transitional site.

Porteous displays much of the complexity in settlement patterns that is typical of the Early Iroquoian village (Stothers 1977:125). Five structures were exposed, as well as portions of a double walled palisade (ibid.). Middens occurred **outside** this palisade, an unusual situation for an Early Iroquoian village. The structures include three "proto-longhouses," two of which overlap, a circular structure with a central hearth, and a complex rectanguloid structure with an undisturbed living floor (Stothers 1977:124-134). Careful excavation of this living floor allowed Stothers to make inferences concerning its interior spatial organization, including the definition of food processing, cooking, stone tool making, and sleeping areas (ibid.).

With his definition of the Princess Point Complex, Stothers addressed the problem of agricultural origins in southern Ontario. The early Princess Point sites, located on river mudflats, low-lying peninsulas, and lakeshores near river mouths, were viewed as seasonal, spring-summer camps that were conducive to the development of limited maize horticulture in the context of a diffuse hunting and fishing economy (Stothers 1977:117-118). Maize has been identified at the Princess Point type site and the Grand Banks site (Stothers 1977:117; Fecteau 1985:126). The association of maize with Princess Point has been questioned due to the multi-component nature of these sites (Fox 1990:178). However, recent research by David Smith and Gary Crawford has confirmed the presence of maize on the Grand Banks site (Smith and Crawford 1995:68) and most researchers now agree that Princess Point groups were at least experimenting with maize horticulture.

As Stothers worked to define the Princess Point Complex, excavations of Glen Meyer sites on the Norfolk Sand Plain began to flesh out a developmental continuum for the Early Iroquoians along the north shore of Lake Erie (Noble 1975a; Fox 1976). Based, in part, on their excavations at the Van Besien and Dewaele sites respectively, both Noble and Fox began to postulate a westerly population movement out of the Grand River Valley and onto the Norfolk sand plain around A.D. 1000.

The Van Besien site, excavated by William Noble (1975a), is an early Glen Meyer village dated to the mid-eleventh century by two mutually supportive radiocarbon dates (Timmins 1985:72). Noble's excavations exposed approximately 6.5% of the 1.2 ha village, revealing a complex settlement pattern involving at least two village expansions as indicated by palisade lines (Noble 1975a:43). Three houses were defined and described in detail, including a 2.5 m long structure that contained no less than 128 interior pits, suggesting "intensive occupation" (ibid:10). Such evidence, combined with the indications of village growth, suggested a lengthy occupation of the site, perhaps spanning "two or three generations" (Noble 1975a:43). Time depth was also reflected in the spatial distribution of ceramics, with all earlier cord-wrapped stick decorated rim sherds coming from middens in the core area of the village rather than the later "expansion area" (Noble

1975a:7). Yet, despite his recognition of these temporal differences, Noble treated the Van Besien ceramics as a homogeneous sample in comparative analyses.

With only a fraction of the village settlement pattern exposed, and none of the core area investigated, it is difficult to understand the spatial organization and construction sequence of the Van Besien village. Nonetheless, Noble drew substantial conclusions concerning the spatial organization of the three exposed houses. He suggested that their absence of parallel alignment indicated a lack of "conscious village planning" (Noble 1975a:43). The settlement pattern was characterized as an example of "formal village life," with semi-permanent residence and a fully agricultural economy that provided a stable subsistence base for population growth (ibid.). Noble had not altered his earlier view that the ready adoption of agriculture and creation of an agricultural surplus had spurred both a population increase and the establishment of village life at the beginning of the Early Iroquoian period (Noble 1969, 1975a, 1975b).

Further insight into Glen Meyer life on the Norfolk sand plain was gained from William Fox's extensive excavations at the Dewaele site, a small twelfth century village located about 1.6 km northwest of Van Besien. Fox excavated approximately 25% of the .32 ha. village, exposing all or part of eight structures. Four of these were of the traditional longhouse form, three were rectangular, and one was ovate (Fox 1976:178). Following Noble, Fox suggested that the smaller structures might have been occupied by "neolocal" rather than extended families (ibid:186). However, one small rectangular structure contained ten large pits distributed primarily around the periphery of the living floor. This structure was interpreted as a communal storage house, with enough storage capacity to see the village through most of a winter (Fox 1976:185).

As part of the Dewaele study, Fox undertook an innovative analysis of the pit features excavated within the storage house and defined two distinct pit types that varied in both form and function. Type I pits are large, usually stratified, and flat-bottomed. Fox suggested that they were originally lined with bark and used for food storage, and subsequently were infilled with refuse over an extended period (1976:182). Smaller Type II pits are more variable in cross-section, are generally shallower, and are rarely stratified. They may have been used primarily for disposal of floor debris (ibid.).

Fox proposed a regional Glen Meyer subsistence pattern in which agricultural production at inland village sites was augmented by aquatic resources from small fishing stations along the Lake Erie shore in the vicinity of Long Point (1976:169). Recent investigations of one of these sites (Varden) has confirmed their importance in the Glen Meyer subsistence cycle (MacDonald 1986). The contribution of agriculture at sites such as Dewaele has been downplayed and greater emphasis placed on the faunal evidence for hunting and fishing activities, indicating a diffuse agricultural economy (Fox 1976:176).

During the mid 1970s, additional evidence of Pickering settlement and subsistence patterns came to light through the research of C.S. Reid (1975), R.J. Pearce (1978), and R. Rozel (1979). This research suggested that Pickering settlement and subsistence practices might have been substantially different from those established for Glen Meyer.

Reid (1975) excavated approximately 20% of the .5 ha Boys site, exposing two houses and a single row palisade. The settlement patterns from this Pickering village are strikingly different from Owasco and Glen Meyer sites. Post mould patterns are relatively clear, there is no structure overlapping, and both pit and post densities are low, producing a much less complex community pattern (see Reid 1975:63, 64, 72). The Boys palisade was also less substantial than most others, leading Reid to suggest that it might have been built mainly as a windbreak or snow fence rather than for defense (1975:40). Reid proposes "year round semi-permanent occupation" for this site (Reid 1975:54); however, the overall settlement evidence suggests that the occupation was neither as intensive nor as lengthy as on contemporaneous Glen Meyer and Owasco sites.

R.J. Pearce's (1978) investigations of a regional Pickering expression in the Rice Lake area have provided additional grounds to differentiate Pickering adaptive patterns from those of other Early Iroquoian groups. Pearce excavated the early Pickering Richardson village, exposing a portion of one longhouse, a single wall of a possible second house, and a rather flimsy palisade (1978:18). As at Boys the density of posts and pits was relatively low and the sporadic nature of the palisade suggests that defense was not a major concern.

Pearce also documented eight multi-component campsites along the shore of Rice Lake, each of which yielded Pickering remains (ibid:20). Noting the diverse range of aquatic resources available around these sites, Pearce postulated a regional Pickering subsistence pattern involving semi-permanent, year round occupation at inland village sites such as Richardson, complemented by the use of shoreline base camps for the exploitation of a wide variety of food resources (1978:21, 22).

Robert Rozel's excavation of the Gunby site in 1977, provided much needed additional information concerning late Pickering settlement patterns. Rozel excavated about 10% of the 1.1 ha village, which is located only 1.6 km from the Bennett site (Rozel 1979:3). Two house structures were completely excavated and eight others outlined by slit-trenching along house walls (Rozel 1979:16). Two rows of palisade were uncovered, one of which ran through the end of a house pattern, indicating that at least one village expansion had occurred (1979:49). In another area two house structures were found to overlap, confirming that the Gunby site occupation had involved two periods of construction. No attempt was made to determine the sequence of use of the two overlapping houses. Contemporaneity of all other houses appears to have been assumed and the construction sequence at the site received little attention. The Gunby houses ranged from very long (45 m) traditional structures to smaller rectangular cabins (Rozel 1979:35, 126). Their size and internal organization foreshadow houses of the Middle Ontario Iroquois period and, in this sense, the Gunby settlement patterns were said to be "transitional to later Iroquoian patterns" (Rozel 1979:125).

Milton Wright undertook a re-investigation of the Uren site in 1977 in an effort to clarify the nature of the Uren horizon and further test J. Wright's Pickering-Glen Meyer conquest hypothesis (M. Wright 1986). Although Wintemberg had conducted excavations at Uren in 1920 he did not identify structural remains and encountered few subsoil features (M. Wright 1986:9-10). Wright recorded 11 houses, a 2-5 row palisade, and over 1000 pit features, which suggested that Wintemberg had not excavated to subsoil levels. The substantial palisade at Uren was viewed as evidence **against** the conquest hypothesis, since, under a scenario of Pickering conquest and amalgamation with Glen Meyer, the resultant Uren population would not be expected to have needed defensive facilities (M. Wright 1986:62-63). Both traditional longhouses and smaller rectangular houses were found at Uren, together with one small oval structure.

A large number of the 1089 pit features documented at Uren occurred outside houses, presenting a new interpretive problem. Wright speculated that some of these features indicated exterior activity areas and suggested the existence of workshop areas around pits located between palisade lines (M. Wright 1986:16).

By comparing the 1977 Uren collection with Wintemberg's 1920 assemblage, Wright was able to demonstrate major differences in the composition of the samples. These differences, attributed to intra-site assemblage variability, were most apparent in ceramic decorative techniques and motifs, which indicated a higher percentage of Glen Meyer rather than Pickering traits in the 1977 sample (M. Wright 1986:33-45). Given the preponderance of Glen Meyer traits at Uren, J.V. Wright's proposed conquest of Glen Meyer by Pickering peoples to initiate the Uren sub-stage was called into question. M. Wright argued that the concept of a Uren horizon should be set aside until further data became available (1986:67).

One important adjustment to our understanding of Iroquoian development in southern Ontario has been a reorientation of ideas concerning the spatial and temporal placement of the Princess Point Complex (Fox 1982c; 1990). On the basis of new data William Fox suggested that the sites of the westerly Point Pelee focus of Princess Point were more closely related to the Western Basin Tradition and should be considered as components of the Riviere aux Vase phase of that tradition. This proposal has been accepted by researchers working in the area (Murphy and Ferris 1990), while the position of the Ausable focus remains problematic (Fox 1990:174). Since it is generally agreed that the Porteous site is an early Glen Meyer component, it has been suggested that the latest phase of Princess Point as defined by Stothers (1977) should be dropped from the Complex (Fox 1982c). When these data are considered, the Princess Point Complex is reduced to only the Grand River Focus sites, most of which seem to date between A.D. 700 and 900, although the early part of this chronology remains poorly understood (Fox 1990:182; Smith and Crawford 1995:63). These people were incipient agriculturalists and may have been related to similar groups in central and eastern Ontario who are even more poorly known (Fox 1990:182-183).

Recent Pickering research conducted by Mima Kapches led to the suggestion that the Pickering chronology may be extended as early as ca. A.D. 775, making early Pickering coterminous with Princess Point (Kapches 1987, 1990). Kapches conducted excavations at the early Pickering Auda site, a small village with ten elliptical structures that averaged seven metres in length by four metres in width (ibid:155). She has argued that Auda dates ca. A.D. 775, on the basis of a single radiocarbon date of 885 ± 110, which she accepts at the earliest end of its one sigma range (ibid:168). Calibration of this date using the Stuiver and Becker (1986) calibration program yields a calibrated age of A.D. 984 and a one sigma range of A.D. 783-1147. Researchers have rejected Kapches claim for an eighth century inception of Pickering, opting instead for an initial date of A.D. 850-900 which is better supported by the calibrated radiocarbon evidence (Timmins 1985:83-92; Williamson 1990:308-310; Snow 1995:67-68).

The early Late Woodland sites in central and eastern Ontario that Fox has identified as "Princess Point-like" are the same sites that Kapches has interpreted as early or incipient Pickering (Fox 1982c; Kapches 1987). Kapches recognizes a combination of late Point Peninsula, New York State Owasco, and early Pickering attributes in the Auda ceramics (ibid:164).

Regardless of the taxonomic label used for sites like Auda, they appear to be transitional between the Middle and Late Woodland periods in this area.

Floral and faunal data from Auda suggest that the site was occupied during the spring and summer when subsistence activities focused on fishing, hunting, and limited maize agriculture (Kapches 1987:168). During the cold season the Auda villagers may have dispersed to single family camps, or moved as a group to a winter village (ibid:173).

Gary Warrick's investigation of Iroquoian village organization drew upon a wide range of ethnographic and ethnohistoric data to explain the changes observed in Ontario Iroquoian community patterns from the tenth century to the historic period (Warrick 1984a). He focused on internal socio-political forces within villages (i.e. social cohesion, formation of residential wards) as major determinants of community organization, and downplayed the effects of external forces such as warfare. Yet many of his conclusions may not be applicable to an Early Iroquoian society in which village populations were small and both internal and external socio-political realities probably differed from later periods. Warrick's "model" Early Iroquoian village (1984a:61) is the complex aggregate of overlapping structures with which we have become familiar, rather than the single phase in the occupational history of such a village that more accurately portrays the prehistoric reality.

The most ambitious study of an Early Iroquoian settlement-subsistence system undertaken to date is Ronald Williamson's doctoral research on the Glen Meyer population of the Caradoc Sand Plain in southwestern Ontario (Williamson 1985). Between 1979 and 1983 Williamson conducted archaeological surveys and excavations on the sand plain, recording five Glen Meyer villages, and 20 hamlets or special activity sites. One village and five of the hamlets were partially excavated.

Williamson adopted an ecological approach in his research, first reconstructing the prehistoric environment as much as possible, and then defining a schedule of resource exploitation that allowed prediction of the locations of different types of sites (Williamson 1985:159-161). Specifically, he was able to demonstrate a strong correlation between maple-beech forest micro-environments and village locations (usually also associated with swamps) and between oak forest environments and smaller special activity sites (Williamson 1985:161-163).

Williamson's major contribution was his evidence that Early Iroquoian subsistence, at least in the Caradoc area, involved major dependence upon naturally occurring local resources that were exploited from a wide variety of special purpose sites. Among the non-village sites investigated, the Yaworski site proved to be a fall-winter hunting camp; the Berkmortel site was interpreted as a fall hunting/spring fishing camp; the Kelly site was a spring/fall/summer plant and animal processing camp; the Little site was a unique deer drive/kill and butchering site; and the Crowfield site and two other small stations were interpreted as temporary hunting camps (Williamson 1985:214, 215, 224, 245, 256, 263).

Distinct types of intra-site settlement patterns were discovered at each functional variant within the regional settlement framework. The Roeland village contained the expected complex mass of post moulds and pit features indicating long-term occupation, while settlement features at the other sites were generally less complex as a result of their intermittent or short-term use. At the Kelly site clusters of exterior features allowed the definition of distinct activity areas, while the ratio of in-house to exterior house features demonstrated the probability of a warm weather occupation (Williamson 1985:231-232). The Yaworski site showed evidence of distinct occupational episodes in different areas probably involving different social groups. This interpretation is based on the discovery of different types of structures (longhouse and circular) in association with ceramic cross-mend patterns that did not overlap, indicating their lack of contemporaneity (Williamson 1985:203).

Williamson's ceramic analysis indicated a high degree of homogeneity among the Caradoc sites (1985:344). As radiocarbon dates suggest a 150 year occupation of the sand plain, he concluded that ceramic change must have occurred very slowly. Noting significant differences between the Caradoc ceramics and those from other Early Iroquoian sequences, he suggested that matrilocal residence may have contributed to the formation of regional ceramic micro-traditions during the Early Iroquoian period (1985:344).

In sum, Williamson's research demonstrated that Early Iroquoian settlement-subsistence patterns were much more complex than originally believed. He negated the notion that Early Iroquoian village life was necessarily coincident with a fully agricultural economy (cf. Noble 1969, 1975b) and showed that the transition to agriculture occurred slowly, probably over a period of several centuries.

Two other recent contributions to Glen Meyer research are the result of large scale salvage operations conducted on the Calvert and Elliott sites by William Fox of the Ontario Ministry of Citizenship and Culture. As the Calvert site is the subject of this dissertation, it will not be discussed in detail here. Suffice it to say that the Calvert investigations revealed approximately 80% of a small Glen Meyer village, which exhibited at least three periods of village construction (Fox 1982a).

The Elliott site excavations likewise documented a multiple phase village occupation. That site consists of three distinct but partially overlapping villages, two of which were surrounded by a single row palisade. These two were designated Village II and Village III and were almost completely excavated by Fox, while Village I was only minimally investigated (Fox 1986a,b). Settlement patterns show a range of structural types from small longhouses to smaller rectanguloid and squarish structures, many of which appear to be associated with specific longhouses (Fox:personal communication 1992). A total of 22 structures was exposed, 14 in Village II and 8 in Village III (Fox 1986a:14). It has been suggested that there was a temporal hiatus of several years between the occupation of these villages (Fox:personal communication 1992).

Mary Ann Niemczycki's (1986) recent work in the Genesee River Valley of New York State has important implications for Early Iroquoian studies. Owasco sites in this region are generally

much smaller than those reported by Ritchie (Ritchie 1969; Ritchie and Funk 1973), and the settlement system is considered to be more similar to a Middle Woodland pattern, involving the use of seasonally reoccupied base camps (Niemczycki 1987:personal communication). One such site is Markham Pond, a Middle Owasco station located on the Genesee floodplain. Of three discrete occupational loci at this site, one was thoroughly investigated, exposing a "rectangular oblong" structure associated with a number of exterior storage pits. Noting a lack of overlapping features, Niemczycki argued for an extremely brief use of this site (five years), despite the existence of a ceramic collection that typologically spans two centuries (1986:27). She concludes that the variability of the ceramic assemblage constitutes a typical "ceramic profile" for sites of this time period in the Genesee Valley (ibid:36). However, we are given no data on the dating of the occupations of the other two loci at Markham Pond, leaving open the possibility that they may have contributed earlier or later ceramic material to the locus investigated.

Niemczycki attributes the appearance of incised pottery on Owasco sites in the Genesee area ca. A.D. 1250 to interaction with Ontario Iroquoian populations living west of the Genesee River at this time. Based on ceramic comparisons and village locational data, she proposes an easterly movement of Ontario Iroquoian peoples, involving some of the Niagara frontier sites investigated by White (1961) (i.e. Oakfield) and other recently documented villages that have produced Ontario Iroquoian ceramics. This incursion is thought to have contributed to the formation of the Seneca tribe, with Ontario Iroquoian cultural traits, and perhaps people, being incorporated into indigenous Owasco populations (Niemczycki 1986:41). This provocative hypothesis adds a new dimension to the discussion of Early Iroquoian development.

In 1990, Mima Kapches published the results of a spatial analysis of Iroquoian longhouses that documented changes in internal longhouse organization from Early Iroquoian to historic times (Kapches 1990). Using longhouse floor plans from several Pickering sites, the fifteenth century Draper site, and the ca. A.D. 1600 Ball site, Kapches demonstrated an increase in the degree of longhouse spatial organization from early to late Pickering times. This change in the amount of organized interior space is interpreted as a result of a developing matrilocal residence pattern during the Early Iroquoian period (ibid:64-65).The amount of organized space peaked at the Draper village, which is seen as a result of strong social (matrilocal) control. Organized space declined somewhat at the Ball site, apparently in response to the stress of European contact (ibid). This study is important because it provides a clear demonstration of the link between archaeological house patterns and developing matrilocal residence patterns in an Early Iroquoian context.

In a recent summary of the Early Iroquoian period in southern Ontario, Ronald Williamson (1990) reviewed the status of the Pickering-Glen Meyer conquest theory proposed by J.V. Wright (1966). Williamson noted that most Ontario Iroquoianists "have not accepted the idea of a conquest because there is no direct evidence of large-scale military operations or disruptions in the archaeological record of southwestern Ontario...nor is there any evidence that Early Iroquoian regional populations had any kind of pan-regional cultural or political organization necessary to carry out such a conquest" (Williamson 1990:311). Wright countered with a reassessment of the theory in which he argued that radiocarbon, settlement pattern, artifactual and mortuary evidence have accumulated to support the conquest theory (Wright 1992). The proposed Pickering-Glen Meyer conquest and the role of warfare in Early Iroquoian development in general are discussed in greater detail in Chapter 8 of this study.

Another significant development in recent years has been the re-affirmation of the Uren substage of the Middle Iroquoian stage as a legitimate taxonomic entity (Dodd et al. 1990). During the 1970s and 1980s, there was a trend to eliminate the use of the Uren substage as a taxonomic construct because of questions about its validity and usefulness (Noble 1975b; M. Wright 1986; Pearce 1984; Timmins 1985). However, in a recent review of the Middle Iroquoian period, Dodd and others have noted that there are now several known sites that can be readily classified as Uren, and they have argued that the substage is still useful as an evolutionary stage in Iroquoian prehistory (Dodd et al. 1990:

322). They also proposed a revision of the chronological placement of the Uren substage from the A.D. 1300-1350 period proposed by J. Wright (1966) to A.D. 1280-1330. This revision was based on a series of calibrated radiocarbon dates; however, they admitted that it is difficult to use radiocarbon dates to refine such a short-term chronology, and they stressed that the chronology of the period remains problematic (Dodd et al. 1990: 359).

The debate concerning Iroquoian origins has recently been reopened by American archaeologists (Starna and Funk 1994; Snow 1995). William Starna and Robert Funk have called attention to several assumptions underlying the *in situ* hypothesis that have not been adequately tested. Foremost among these is the "fundamental assumption ... that each Iroquoian tribe had distinctive and distinguishable pottery types" (1994:47). They also highlighted several other research questions that have been inadequately addressed by Iroquoianists, including the relationship between language and culture, the effects of trade on material culture, the duration of site occupations, and our understanding of rates of culture change (ibid:49-52). While stopping short of rejecting the *in situ* hypothesis, Starna and Funk urged researchers to test the implications of the *in situ* hypothesis with archaeological data.

In his recent work Dean Snow has explicitly rejected the *in situ* hypothesis in favour of a migration hypothesis to explain Iroquoian origins (1995). Arguing that the hypothesis has become a controlling model in Iroquoian archaeology, he suggested that Iroquoianists have ignored or overlooked major anomalies in linguistic evidence, cultural theory, ceramic technology and site distributions in their blind adherence to MacNeish's *in situ* construct (Snow 1995:70-72). In brief, he noted that recent linguistic evidence suggests that the separation of Northern Iroquoian languages from a single proto-Northern Iroquoian language occurred only about 1000 years ago (ibid:70). He also argued that matrilocal residence patterns and horticulture appeared suddenly rather than gradually in Iroquoia and that the Iroquoian method of manufacturing pottery by modelling shows a discontinuity with the Middle Woodland method of coil manufacture. Finally, in proposing discontinuity between the Middle Woodland Point Peninsula culture and Iroquoian culture, Snow pointed out that the distribution of Point Peninsula sites does not correspond well with the known distribution of Iroquoian sites (ibid:72).

As an alternative to the *in situ* hypothesis, Snow hypothesized that Iroquoian culture developed from the Clemson's Island culture of Pennsylvania, and postulated a northward migration of Clemson's Island people into New York State and southern Ontario after A.D.900 (ibid:73-74). One of the problems with the derivation of Iroquoian culture from Clemson's Island is that it discounts the role of the Princess Point culture in southwestern Ontario. The Clemson's Island culture began around A.D. 775 in central Pennsylvania, whereas Princess Point developed by ca. A.D. 700-750 (Timmins 1985:68; Fox 1990:180). Moreover, there is substantial evidence of continuity in material culture and settlement/subsistence patterns between Princess Point and Glen Meyer (Fox 1990:182; Smith and Crawford 1995:68). Snow's hypothesis has heightened awareness of some of the discontinuities between Middle and Late Woodland cultures in the northeast and re-asserted migration as a viable explanation for Iroquoian origins. However, the derivation and role of the Princess Point Complex in Iroquoian development must be addressed if the issue is to be resolved.

## Discussion

The last two decades have seen a re-orientation of Early Iroquoian research to include ecological and spatial approaches to archaeological interpretation. These studies have focussed on three major areas of inquiry: 1) the Middle to Late Woodland transition and the introduction of agriculture; 2) the investigation of Early Iroquoian communities on the regional level and the documentation of variability in their settlement-subsistence patterns; and 3) the documentation and explanation of intra-site settlement patterns and their implications for the understanding of Early Iroquoian socio-political organization and domestic life. The last of these topics is of greatest relevance to our investigation of the Calvert site and is further discussed below.

While broad areal excavations of Middle and Late Iroquoian villages such as Nodwell (Wright 1974) and Draper (Finlayson 1985) have produced a wealth of new data concerning late prehistoric Iroquoian village life, the major excavations of Early Iroquoian villages have not provided information of comparable quality. This is partly due to the extreme complexity of most Early Iroquoian village sites, where numerous overlapping structures and features complicate interpretation. Most archaeologists have not attempted to draw out the internal chronologies of Early Iroquoian villages, primarily because they have lacked the techniques to do so. This failure has, in turn, limited our understanding of Early Iroquoian behaviour since the assemblage of settlement data encoded in every site plan is, to use Binford's terms, very "coarse-grained," with "low resolution," as a result of the extended occupation of the site. This study seeks to redress this deficiency by developing a methodology for reconstructing the occupation history of Early Iroquoian villages and applying this method to the interpretation of a Glen Meyer site.

While there has been no comprehensive study of Early Iroquoian settlement patterns at the intra-site level, Iroquoianists have not wholly neglected the study of early community patterns. In the preceding review we have described the nature of the settlement data gathered through past research and the interpretations of that data offered by archaeologists. These studies have not, however, allowed archaeologists to reconstruct the internal history of sites or their nature at a single point in time. Thus the analysis and interpretation of intra-site settlement data forms a substantial portion of the problem orientation of this thesis. Our review has helped to isolate four ongoing interpretive problems in Early Iroquoian intra-site studies. These problems are outlined below.

1. Feature Analysis: Iroquoianists have sorely neglected the analysis of archaeological features as domestic facilities. While many researchers have undertaken limited distributional analyses of features, these are often little more than observations, with little attention being paid to the determinants of feature location. As facilities (i.e. hearths, storage pits, refuse pits), Iroquoian features were certainly as important as pots or other tools. Yet they are generally

subjected to minimal analysis, and little attention is paid to their role in domestic life. There is a need to employ experimental, ethnographic, and ethnohistoric information on feature formation processes to interpret the form, function, and distribution of Early Iroquoian features.

2. Structure Analysis:    As our overview has amply demonstrated, a wide variety of types of structures have been documented on Early Iroquoian sites. The most common of these is the longhouse or proto-longhouse, unequivocally identified in the ethnohistoric literature as a multifamily dwelling. More problematic, however, is the consistent appearance of small round, oblong, or rectangular structures in Early Iroquoian villages. Most researchers have opted to call them nuclear family dwellings (Williamson 1985; Pearce 1984), while others have suggested their use as granaries (Tuck 1971). Other options for the function of these small structures include charnel-houses (Fox: personal communication), sweat baths, wood sheds, and storage houses. The advantage of studying structure use within a nearly fully excavated village lies in being able to examine individual structures in relation to other contemporaneous ones, such that the archaeological features of the village can be viewed as an integrated whole.

3. Analysis of Occupational History: While Iroquoianists have recognized that many Early Iroquoian sites were occupied over the long term, there have been few attempts to explore the internal chronology of these sites. This is a serious shortcoming of previous research, since the failure to break down Early Iroquoian villages into occupational phases is directly related to our inability to derive meaningful behavioral information from the data.

There have been some attempts to reconstruct internal village chronologies, but no systematic approach has yet been applied to a large data set. Walter Kenyon (1968) made an innovative effort to seriate the Miller site pits on the basis of their ceramics and there have been a few cases involving the straightforward interpretation of small numbers of superimposed house structures. Yet at the same time there has been a tendency to treat the ceramic assemblages from these sites as homogeneous samples, even in

cases where considerable time depth in the ceramics has been recognized (i.e. Noble 1975a).

A prime methodological goal of the present study is to develop a systematic procedure for separating the data from Early Iroquoian villages into contemporaneous units. This will be done in stepwise fashion using stratigraphic and superpositional data, spatial logic, ceramic cross-mend data, and general and specific principles of Iroquoian site formation. It is anticipated that the methodology so developed will be widely applicable to other sites with a similar level of depositional and structural complexity.

4. Analysis of Community Organization and Change: As discussed above, our interpretations of Early Iroquoian village organization depend upon our success in unravelling the occupational histories of these sites. Since success in the latter endeavour has been limited, current views of Early Iroquoian village planning, socio-political organization, demography, and community development have been without a firm basis. For example, the confusing community patterns found on Glen Meyer villages continue to be interpreted as displaying a lack of village planning, which is perhaps indicative of weak political organization and leadership (Noble 1969, 1975a; Warrick l984a; Ferris and Spence 1995:107). Yet when the occupational histories of these villages are reconstructed, the organization of the individual occupational phases may not be so random, thus calling into question the notion that Early Iroquoians lacked communal political institutions.

Our inability to reconstruct the occupational histories of Early Iroquoian villages has also precluded any attempts to study short term change within the Early Iroquoian community. The archaeological deposits of such sites may represent the accumulated residue of many decades and even generations of domestic life. As such, comparative analysis of the deposits from different periods of occupation should yield valuable insights into the nature of sociocultural change within the community.

In sum, when the Early Iroquoian village is viewed in diachronic perspective as a dynamic and constantly changing community, a more accurate understanding of Early Iroquoian village life will emerge. Approached in this manner, it should be possible to gain insight into some of the social and political dimensions of Early Iroquoian communities that have eluded us in the past.

## Conclusion

In this chapter we have reviewed more than half a century of Early Iroquoian research, focussing on the interpretations of Early Iroquoian society offered by past researchers.

While this exercise has provided the contextual background to the present study, it has also revealed gaps in our current understanding of an important phase in the development of Iroquoian culture and isolated the methodological problems inherent in Early Iroquoian archaeology. In short, the Early Iroquoian village constitutes a methodological challenge that has not been met by previous researchers. It is suggested that the solution to this dilemma lies in the development of a rigorous methodology explicitly formulated for the interpretation of Early Iroquoian sites.

# Chapter 3

# An Introduction to the Calvert Site

## Location and Physical Setting

The Calvert site (AfHg-1) is located 10 km east of the City of London, Ontario, within the Village of Dorchester, on land that was formerly part of Lot 18, Concession A, in North Dorchester Township (Figure 3.1). The site is situated on a sandy plateau that today overlooks the Dorchester Mill Pond to the east and the large wetland area of the Dorchester Swamp to the southeast. The sand plateau continues to the north for 400 m and at that point drops abruptly down to the floodplain of the Thames River.

The Mill Pond was created by the damming of Dorchester Swamp Creek around the year 1800. At that time a sawmill was built at the mouth of the creek, where it empties into the Thames River just 1 km north of the Calvert site. Prior to the creation of the Mill Pond, the creek would have had a small floodplain in this area. A reconstruction of the prehistoric environment of the Calvert locale is presented in Chapter 4.

The property on which the Calvert site is located has seen an interesting sequence of land use since the occupation of the village by an Early Iroquoian Glen Meyer community between 800 and 900 years ago. After the Indians abandoned the area, their village and cornfields were succeeded by the growth of a substantial stand of white pine, although there is evidence to suggest that much white pine existed in the locality prior to the Calvert occupation as well. In any case, the Dorchester pinery was the principal attraction for the establishment of the sawmill on Dorchester Swamp Creek (Upper Thames River Conservation Authority 1986). The site area and much of the surrounding upland was subsequently logged in the early 1800s. The cleared land was then put to agricultural use and remained as farmland until the 1980s.

The Mill Pond, however, became a focus of recreational activity for residents of Dorchester and London during the late nineteenth century. In 1892 the London Gun Club built a club house on the west side of the pond that was used until it burned down in 1913. Recreational use continued into the 1930s and 1940s with the establishment of a dance hall, known locally as "Dreamland," also on the west side of the pond. The Mill Pond area remains an important natural and recreational area today. The pond supports a moderate sport fishery and a series of nature trails have been constructed around its perimeter. Most recently, residents of Dorchester have undertaken a program of reforestation within the Mill Pond lands, which are now managed by the Upper Thames Conservation Authority.

This sequence of land use attests that the Calvert locale has long been an attractive area to live in or visit, and it may have been inevitable that residential development would eventually come to the area. Somewhat ironically, it was the construction of a new subdivision of palatial modern homes that led to the excavation and ultimate destruction of the Calvert site and the writing of a new chapter in the history of the Dorchester area.

## History of Investigation of the Calvert Site

Prior to the subdivision development, the property on which the Calvert site is located was owned and farmed by the Tiner family. The existence of the site was well known locally. Current and former residents of Dorchester have indicated that it was common knowledge that Tiner's field was the best place in the area to find Indian artifacts (C. Hale 1990: personal communication).

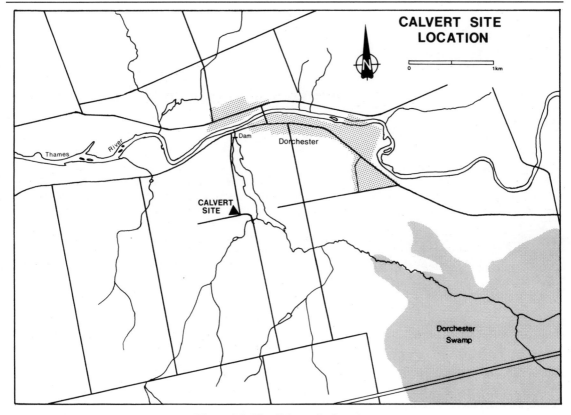

Figure 3.1. The Calvert site location.

Intensive surface collection and some digging on the site was apparently done by a Mr. Eugene "Red" Williams, who was an artifact collector from Dorchester active in the 1950s and 1960s. Mr. Williams is reported to have compiled a fairly detailed map of his work on the site (H. Hale: personal communication); however, he has lived out of the province since the 1960s and the location of his data is not known.

More surface collecting was done by Mr. Robert Calvert, another amateur archaeologist from the London area for whom the site is named. Robert Calvert was responsible for bringing the site to the attention of the archaeological community and arranging to have it registered with the Ontario Ministry of Citizenship and Culture. Calvert's collecting activity on the site was limited, and he has donated his small artifact collection from it to the Ministry of Citizenship and Culture, Heritage Branch (London Office).

In early 1981, Mr. James Keron, a volunteer Archaeological Conservation Officer for the Ministry of Citizenship and Culture, discovered that topsoil stripping had begun on the Calvert site in preparation for the subdivision development. Subsequent negotiations between the developer, Mr. Keith Davidson, and officials of the Ministry led to a six week (April 15 to May 31) mitigative excavation of the site under the direction of Mr. William Fox, then Regional Archaeologist for Southwestern Ontario. A depressed housing market allowed Fox to return for another four weeks in 1982 (May 11 to June 8) to complete the excavations. With the help of over 1300 man-hours of labour contributed by over 60 volunteers, 70% of the .28 ha village was excavated. In total, about .2 ha (2000 square m) were opened to view. The resulting data base is one of the largest and most complete ever recovered from an Early Iroquoian site.

The excavation followed methods that are now standard in Ontario for the archaeological salvage of plough-disturbed Iroquoian sites. The plough zone was removed using power equipment and the subsoil surface was then shovel-shined to look for post moulds and archaeological features. In the end, a complex mass of over 5000 post moulds and 333 features was uncovered and mapped (Figure 3.2). Two hundred and twenty-two of the features were excavated and 108 were sampled for flotation analysis.

Since many Glen Meyer features are large and complex, feature excavation and recording techniques were adopted that allowed for efficient excavation, yet detailed recording. Pit features were cross-sectioned, with the first half being excavated in a single unit. Detailed profile drawings were then made before the second half of the feature was excavated in natural levels. Separation of these natural excavation units was maintained throughout cataloguing and analysis, so that material from different layers of a feature could be assigned to different periods of the occupation, if warranted.

Upon returning from the field, approximately two thirds of the artifacts were catalogued and all the flotation samples were processed by volunteers from the Ontario Archaeological Society. A large-scale map of all features and post moulds was plotted by Ministry staff, and William Fox published a brief report describing the excavations and the results of his preliminary analysis (Fox 1982a). In this report Fox defined three construction phases for the Calvert village and proposed a change in site function from village to hunting camp in the final phase. The latter interpretation was suggested by the presence of large quantities of deer bone in what were interpreted as late phase refuse pits.

The writer initially became involved in the Calvert analysis as a Master's study research project in the summer of 1983. During the fall of 1983 it became apparent that the Calvert analysis was too large a task for an M.A. thesis and a decision was made to use the material for a Ph.D. project. The doctoral research leading to this monograph thus began in 1985.

# The Calvert Data Base

The selection or creation of a particular type of archaeological data base is an important part of archaeological inquiry. As Thomas (1976:7) has pointed out, archaeologists purposefully create their data bases, both in the field, where they select certain data for observation and recording, and in the lab, where they further specify attributes of the archaeological material for analysis. In all cases, whether consciously or not, data are retrieved and selected with a concept of relevance in mind. The observed data are perceived to be relevant to an interpretive problem, and the selection of data is based on some prior knowledge of the relationship between the archaeological residue and the behaviours or processes that may have produced it. Thus, most archaeologists operate within an implicit middle-range interpretive framework.

The Calvert data base consists of artifactual, ecofactual, and settlement pattern data. These data form the subject side of the interpretive equation. They are what needs to be explained.

Of equal importance are the data that form the source side of the interpretive equation, for these are the data that permit explanation. Such data are generated through middle-range research, past archaeological research, and other sources that lie outside the archaeological record. The interpretive data used in this study are discussed in the appropriate sections of the monograph. This section describes the archaeological data base only. Each of the basic data classes is briefly discussed below.

## Artifactual Data

The artifactual data from Calvert include 31,847 items of material culture recovered from the site through either excavation or flotation. Table 3.1 presents the breakdown of these artifacts into specific categories. As this table shows, 16,735 (52.6%) of the artifacts are ceramic, 15,021 (47.2%) are lithic, and only 91 (0.3%) are made of bone, antler, or shell. These percentages do not accurately reflect the relative numbers of tools in the collection as the ceramic and lithic values include all pot sherds and lithic detritus and do not represent the actual numbers of vessels or stone tools used at the site.

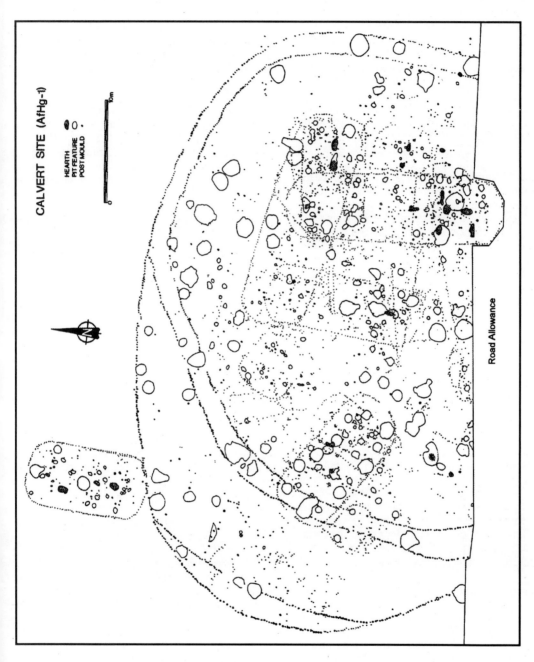

Figure 3.2. The Calvert site.

Table 3.1. Calvert site artifact inventory.

| Artifact Category | n | Totals |
|---|---|---|
| Ceramics | | |
| Rim Sherds | 447 | |
| Fragmentary Rim Sherds | 31 | |
| Neck Sherds | 1836 | |
| Body Sherds | 3053 | |
| Microsherds and Split Sherds | 11283 | |
| Pipe Fragments | 18 | |
| Juvenile Rim Sherds | 45 | |
| Other Juvenile Ceramics | 17 | |
| Miscellaneous Ceramic Objects | 5 | |
| Total Ceramics | | 16735 |
| Lithics | | |
| Bifaces | 154 | |
| Scrapers | 56 | |
| Celts and Celt Blanks | 21 | |
| Other Rough and | | |
|    Ground Stone Tools | 46 | |
| Utilized Flakes | 374 | |
| Wedges | 9 | |
| Gravers | 25 | |
| Drills | 4 | |
| Fire Cracked Rock | 1850 | |
| Chipping Detritus | 12446 | |
| Cores and Nodules | 36 | |
| Total Lithics | | 15021 |
| Bone and Antler Tools | | |
| Bone Artifacts | 46 | |
| Antler Artifacts | 43 | |
| Shell Artifacts | 2 | |
| Total Bone, Antler and Shell Tools | | 91 |
| Grand Total | | 31847 |

A computerized version of the Calvert catalogue was prepared to facilitate the tabulation and manipulation of artifactual data. A detailed analysis of the various artifact classes is presented in Chapter 7.

## Settlement Data

The 5,021 post moulds and 333 features mapped at Calvert comprise the settlement pattern data base. Fourteen house structures and up to four rows of palisade may be identified in the overall village pattern. As mentioned above,

the pattern is extremely complex, with several overlapping structures evident. Unfortunately, there is no continuous stratigraphy present on the site. Nevertheless, it is one of the aims of this research to show that the settlement data can be successfully separated into distinct periods or "phases" in the site occupation.

This reconstruction of occupational history is largely based on a specialized analysis of "key features" within the settlement data base. These are features that involve the intersection or superposition of post moulds and/or pits, such that it is possible to determine their stratigraphic sequence even though there is no comprehensive stratigraphy. Other types of data that contribute to the reconstruction of occupational history are ceramic cross-mends between features, feature spatial distributions, and feature formation data. These data are detailed in the discussion of occupational history presented in Chapter 5.

Once the Calvert settlement pattern is dissected into separate occupational phases, it essentially becomes three separate, but sequential, community patterns that we will argue are probably attributable to the same group of people. At this point the more traditional settlement analysis may be conducted relating to the spatial organization of the village, the function of the various structures and features, the population of the community, and its social organization. In the Calvert case there is the added opportunity to examine short term change within the community as reflected in the changes manifested in successive settlement patterns. This analysis is presented in Chapters 7 and 8.

### Ecofactual Data

The ecofactual data base from Calvert consists of large collections of faunal and floral material, both of which have been analyzed by specialists. Table 3.2 presents a summary of the floral and faunal material.

The entire collection of 47,648 bones has been analyzed by Rosemary Prevec (1984a) resulting in the identification of 22% of the faunal sample to order or lower taxa. Prevec's report also includes a consideration of butchering marks evident on the bones, food resources, notes on non-human and artifactual alteration of the bones, a study of features that are of special interest in terms of their faunal content, and a consideration of seasonality indices.

Floral analysis has been completed by Glenna Ounjian of Erindale College, University of Toronto, on 58 flotation light fraction samples from 38 features. Her analysis has resulted in the identification of 18,119 seeds from the site. Ounjian's (1988) report describes these plant remains, discusses their uses, habitats, distribution across the site, and value as indicators of seasonality. In addition to Ounjian's analysis, samples of carbonized wood from two features were identified by Rudy Fecteau (1992).

Detailed analyses of the floral and faunal data are presented in Chapter 6.

## Conclusion

This chapter has introduced the Calvert site through a discussion of the sequence of land use in the Calvert area and a review of the history of investigations of the site. It has also summarized the raw data recovered from Calvert, setting the stage for the detailed analysis of these data in subsequent chapters.

Table 3.2. Inventory of Calvert site ecofacts.

| Ecofact Category | Weight | Number |
|------------------|--------|--------|
| Floral Remains | | |
|   Seeds* | | 18119 |
|   Carbonized Wood | 3597.3 g | |
| Faunal Remains | | 47648 |
| Soil Samples | | 12 |
| Total Ecofacts | | 65779 |

* includes excavated and floated seeds

Table 3.3. Summary of the Calvert site data.

| Category | Number |
|----------|--------|
| Artifacts | 31847 |
| Ecofacts | 65779 |
| Settlement Data | 5354 |
| Total Data Base | 102980 |

# Chapter 4

# The Environmental Setting of the Calvert Site

## Introduction

In this chapter the environmental setting of the Calvert site is described with reference to the glacial history of the region, its physiography, topography, drainage systems, soils, and climate. These data are then combined with modern and historic data concerning the flora and fauna of the Dorchester area to define a series of distinct micro-environments around the site that could have been exploited by the Calvert villagers on a day to day basis. The purpose here is to describe the natural resources that were routinely available to the Calvert people and lay the groundwork for later discussions of their subsistence practices (Chapter 6).

Site catchment analysis is a method of examining archaeological site location in relation to surrounding resources (Roper 1979:135). It assumes that human settlements are normally located in proximity to natural resource zones that may be economically exploited (Vita-Finzi and Higgs 1970). For the purposes of this discussion it is necessary to establish a study area that will encompass the local hinterland of the Calvert village. Catchment studies suggest that a circular area around the site with a radius of five km would encompass the area that is likely to have been exploited from the site on a daily basis, without establishing special purpose camps (Vita-Finzi and Higgs 1970; Flannery 1976). This study area is shown in Figure 4.1. My purpose in defining this study area is simply to create geographic limits for a general description of the local environment and available resources. Actual catchment areas are usually irregular in size and shape due to variations in topography and resource availability (Roper 1979; Jamieson 1986). More detailed discussion of the catchment area that was actually used by the Calvert people is based on empirical data from the site (floral and faunal remains) and is presented in Chapter 6.

## Physiography

The Calvert site lies on the edge of an easterly extension of the Caradoc Sand plain, which Chapman and Putnam call the London Annex (1984:146). This extension occupies a shallow basin of irregular shape extending from the Dorchester area east as far as Ingersoll and north beyond Thamesford, where an arm of the plain extends into West Nissouri Township (see Figure 4.2).

In the vicinity of the Calvert site, the sand plain narrows rapidly, following the Thames valley west toward London. As a result, the site is sandwiched between two other physiographic zones, the Mount Elgin Ridges to the south and a southerly extension of the Stratford Till Plain to the north (Figure 4.2). Less than two km south of the site the well-defined Ingersoll Moraine forms the northerly limit of the Mount Elgin Ridges in this area. This terminal moraine consists of a series of prominent ridges formed of silty clay till that skirt the Calvert site and the Dorchester Swamp to the south. North of the Thames River, but still less than three km from Calvert, the Dorchester Moraine forms a similar series of upland clay hills that level off somewhat as one moves north onto the Stratford Till Plain.

## Glacial History

The present natural landscape of North Dorchester Township has been shaped by the advance and retreat of continental ice sheets. The most significant glacial activity in the region took place during the Port Bruce Stadial of the Late Wisconsinan Substage, about 15,000 to 14,000 years ago.

Late Wisconsinan glacial events in the Dorchester area are complicated by the fact that both the Huron and Erie ice lobes were active in

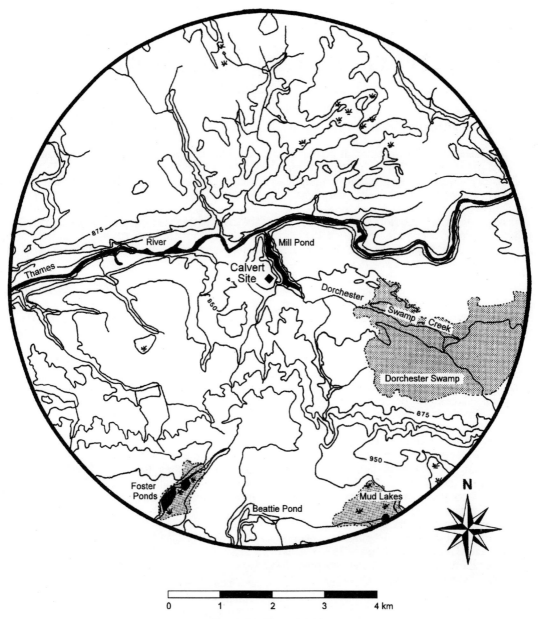

Figure 4.1. The study area.

this region. During the Port Bruce Stadial the Erie ice lobe advanced from the Lake Erie basin northward, overriding earlier tills and depositing the Port Stanley Till, a brown clay silt till that makes up the Ingersoll and Westminster Moraines. North of the Thames valley the Huron ice also advanced, overriding the older Dorchester Moraine and depositing the Tavistock Till, which varies from gritty clay to sand (Ontario Ministry of Natural Resources 1982a:10).

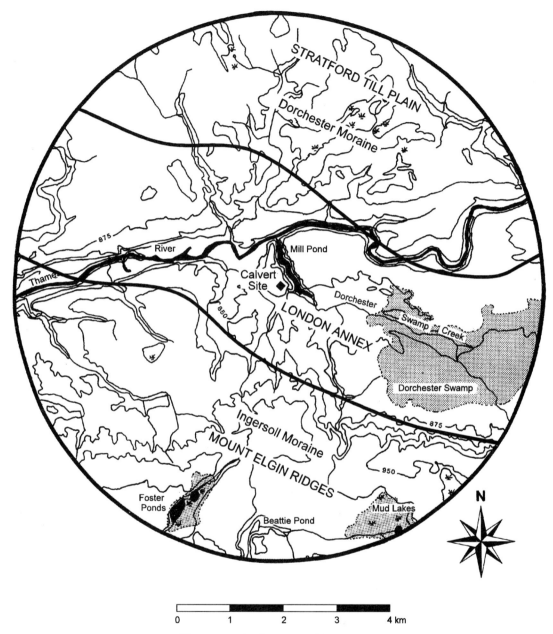

Figure 4.2. Physiography of the study area.

The edges of the Huron and Erie ice lobes met at the Ingersoll Moraine. As the ice in this interlobate zone retreated, huge quantities of meltwater emptied into the Thames valley spillway. The muddy glacial waters pooled in the shallow basin between London and Thamesford, where they deposited the sands found in the area today. This small lake had its shoreline at the 277 m a.s.l. level, thus most of the study area was submerged at this time. Farther west the spillway

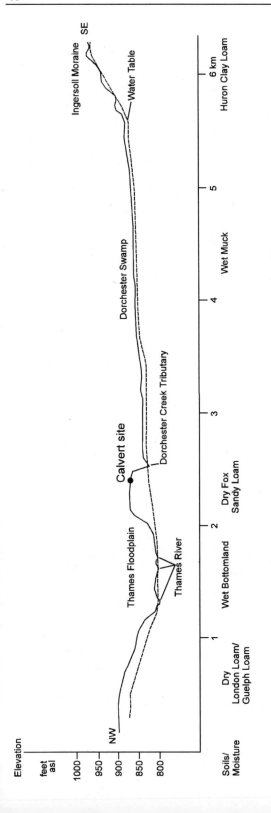

Figure 4.3. Northwest-southeast relief profile through the study area.

eventually broke through a series of terraces in the Komoka area, discharging the meltwater into pro-glacial Lake Maumee, leading to the formation of the Komoka delta and the Caradoc Sand Plain (Chapman and Putnam 1984:146). In sum, most of the surface materials in the upper Thames valley, including the sands on which the Calvert site was built, are outwash products of this period of Late Wisconsinan glacial retreat.

Another important product of the glacial events of this period are the swamps, bogs, and kettle ponds that may be seen in the area today. These features were formed by the settling of stagnant ice blocks in former meltwater channels. The Mud Lakes and Foster Ponds to the south of Calvert are the result of this process.

## Topography

The general topography of the study area is determined by the character of the different physiographic regions within its limits. Most of North Dorchester Township, including the southern half of the study area, is characterized by the morainic ridges and valleys of the Mount Elgin Ridges that run parallel to the Lake Erie shore. Maximum relief on these gently rolling hills is about 30 m, with elevations ranging from 244 to 305 m a.s.l., and slopes rarely exceeding 10 degrees (Chapman and Putnam 1984:144-145). The well-drained ridges form divides for the region's drainage systems and the intervening valleys are often poorly drained, containing swampy areas and bogs.

One such area is the Dorchester Swamp, which occupies the southeast quarter of the study area lying at the base of the Ingersoll moraine. The topography of the area is basically flat with surface elevations ranging from 257 m a.s.l. in the northwest section to 265 m a.s.l. in the southeast. This is clearly illustrated in Figure 4.3, which is a relief profile drawn through the study area from northwest to southeast.

North of the Thames River, on the Dorchester Moraine, a series of gently rolling hills rises to elevations of 280 m a.s.l.. The topography in this area is generally less rugged than along the ridges to the south and local relief does not exceed 10 to 15 m.

Within the Thames basin itself topography has been shaped by the glacial and more recent history of the river, as witnessed by the presence of a broad flood plain and associated sand and gravel terraces, as well as lake plains, all of which are products of glacio-fluvial activity. Elevations within the basin range from 244 to 274 m a.s.l.. The Thames floodplain just north of the Calvert site lies at 245 m a.s.l., while the site itself occurs at an elevation of about 263 m a.s.l. (Figure 4.3).

The topography in the immediate vicinity of the Calvert site is dominated by the small sandy plateau on which the village is situated. This plateau rises gently to the north where it forms the crest of a east-west trending ridge, approximately 200 m north of the site. This ridge terminates about 500 m to the northwest and drops down to a broad swampy section of the Thames floodplain as shown in Figure 4.3. At least three other Early Iroquoian sites have been found along this ridge.

To the east of the site the terrain slopes down into the narrow valley now occupied by the Dorchester Mill Pond. Prior to the damming of Dorchester Swamp Creek in the early 1800s, the creek would have formed a flood plain in this valley. The Mill Pond is less than one m deep at both the north and south ends, and it reaches a maximum depth of about 2.5 m in the centre and along the west side. These depths indicate that the valley floor was fairly level and suggest the former existence of a floodplain in the valley. The pond has an average width of 66 m but reaches 100 m at its widest point. The width of the pond probably approximates the width of the former floodplain. The valley walls on the west side, adjacent to the site, are long and moderately inclined with slopes between 15 and 20 % (Upper Thames River Conservation Authority 1986). This slope cannot be considered an important defensive feature of the site location, since the village itself was set back from the break in slope. A similar topographic situation holds to the south of the village where the terrain drops down into a shallow gully formed by a small tributary of Dorchester Swamp Creek (Figure 4.3).

## Drainage

The study area lies wholly within the Thames River drainage basin which encompasses a large portion of inland southwestern Ontario (Figure 4.4). The upper Thames consists of three main branches, the North Branch, which originates near Mitchell, and the Middle and South Branches which rise farther east near Tavistock. The latter two converge near Putnam just east of Dorchester, while the North Branch joins the main channel in the City of London. From London the Thames continues to flow to the southwest draining much of Middlesex, Kent, and Essex Counties, until it eventually discharges into Lake St. Clair.

Within the study area there are three main watercourses, the Thames River South Branch, Dorchester Swamp Creek, and Dingman Creek.

The South Branch of the Thames passes just 900 m north of the Calvert village; thus the Calvert people had easy access to this major river for both transportation and fishing. The river provides a wide variety of differing habitats for aquatic plants and animals, while its floodplain supports distinct plant communities. The specific resources available in this riverine micro-environment are discussed later in this chapter.

During Early Iroquoian times the Thames would have been an important travel route linking the Calvert community to another Glen Meyer group 25 km downstream in the Byron area and a third community located about 45 km downstream on the Caradoc Sand Plain. The river would have also provided a link to people of the Western Basin Tradition living farther west along the lower Thames.

Dorchester Swamp Creek is a small tributary of the South Branch of the Thames River. It is the only viable source of drainage for the large area covered by the Dorchester Swamp. The watershed drained by this creek is shown in Figure 4.5. Dorchester Swamp Creek is classed as a coldwater stream. Its total length, including its three tributaries, is 20.5 km; however, the main branch is only 8.9 km long. The elevation of the creek drops from 282 m a.s.l. at the source to 250 m a.s.l. at its mouth, giving it an average

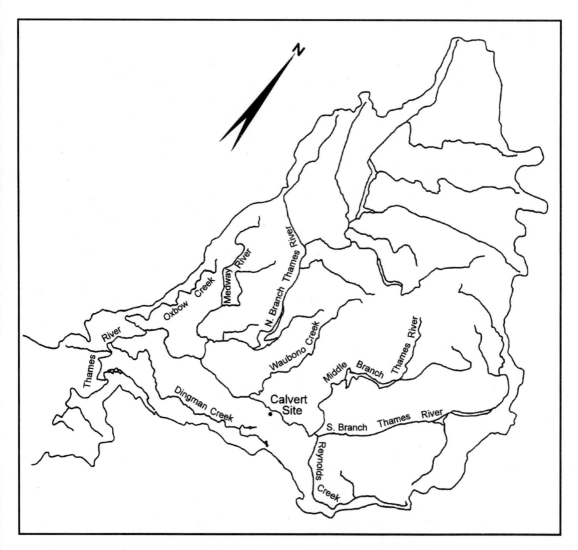

Figure 4.4. The Upper Thames River watershed.

gradient of 3.55 m/km. Most of it is still a permanent stream that discharges year-round.

The creek was evaluated by the Ontario Ministry of Natural Resources in July, 1981, in part to determine its potential as a trout fishery (Ontario Ministry of Natural Resources 1982b). A total of seven different habitat types within the creek were identified at that time, each of which supported a slightly different range of aquatic resources. The types of fish available in the creek are discussed later in this chapter.

In July, 1981, the average depth of Dorchester Swamp Creek (including all tributaries) was only 13.7 cm, although it reached a depth of 40.1 cm within the main branch. The average water temperature at that time was 24.2 degrees Celsius. The coolness of the water is attributed to the fact that the Dorchester Swamp is fed by numerous springs that rise on the northern slopes of the Ingersoll moraine. The swamp is the second largest water storage area in the entire Thames watershed.

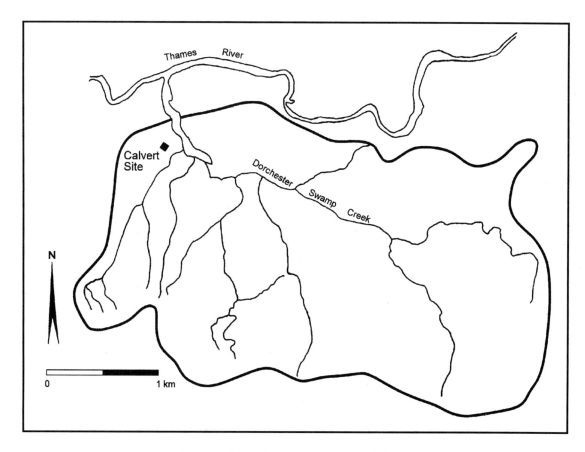

Figure 4.5. Dorchester Swamp Creek drainage.

Recent mapping of wetland areas in southwestern Ontario has highlighted the fact that such areas are diminishing at an alarming rate. Wetland loss is primarily a recent phenomenon related to forest clearance and agricultural drainage, among other factors. In this regard, the Dorchester Swamp has lost considerable area in the past century. Most of the contraction of the swamp has occurred along its western boundary, which is the area closest to the Calvert site. As Figure 4.6 shows, prior to 1967 an arm of Dorchester Swamp extended down the creek to within 300 m of the Calvert site. This suggests that the Calvert site was located much closer to the swamp at the time of occupation than it is today.

If, indeed, the Dorchester Swamp was larger in the past, the volume of water stored in it would have been greater. It follows that the volume of water flowing into Dorchester Swamp Creek would have been greater as well, and the creek would have been wider and deeper on average than it is today. However, the relatively steep gradient of the creek and the narrowness of its channel throughout most of its course suggest that it did not have great channel storage. Water flow would have been greatest at spring run-off, at which time the swamp would have received large quantities of meltwater from the surrounding higher land. This seasonal flow probably inundated the floodplain occupied by the Mill Pond today. The gradient of the creek decreases in this area, suggesting that a natural slowdown of water flow would have contributed to a flood situation.

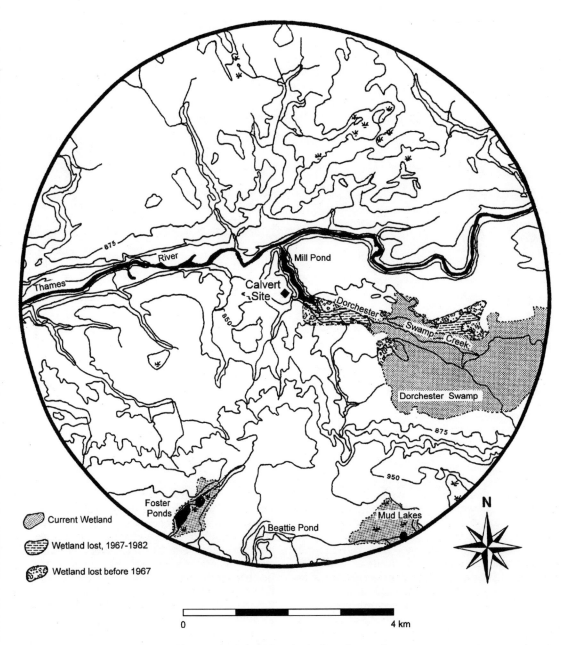

Figure 4.6. Wetland loss in the Dorchester Swamp.

The other drainage system of relevance to the Calvert site is that of Dingman Creek, located about 4 km south of the site. The Foster, Beattie, and Dingman Lakes (all kettle ponds) form the headwaters of Dingman Creek, which flows in a westerly direction draining a broad, flat-bottomed valley between the Ingersoll and Westminster moraines, eventually emptying into the Thames just north of Delaware. Dingman may have provided an alternative travel route to the

Thames in prehistoric times, yet its channel is not wide and it contains numerous meanders. The distance along Dingman from the Calvert site to the Caradoc Sand Plain is about 50 km. Many archaeological sites have been located along the creek and its tributaries. These sites, however, relate primarily to later Iroquoian and earlier Middle Woodland and Archaic occupations (Timmins 1983; Keron 1984, 1986).

## Climate

The study area lies entirely within the South Slopes climatic zone, which is a long, narrow, inland region extending from southeastern Huron County on the west to the Kingston area on the east. The region has no contact with any of the Great Lakes and climatic conditions within it are slightly more severe than in areas immediately adjacent to the lakes.

Average daily temperatures in the region range from a high of -2 degrees Celsius to a low of -11 degrees Celsius in January and from a high of 27 degrees Celsius to a low of 14 degrees Celsius during July (Ontario Ministry of Natural Resources 1986:26). The area has an average of 152 frost free days each year and a growing season of about 205 days. The frost free period usually lasts from late April to mid to late October. The average annual precipitation in the area is 92.5 cm, of which 73.5 cm occur as rain. The remaining 19 cm fall as snow and amount to approximately 200 cm (Pearce 1984:116).

Unfortunately, the data presented above are based on recent climatic measurements and are not necessarily representative of the palaeo-climatic situation in the study area. A generalized series of palaeo-climatic shifts has been defined for central and eastern North America, based primarily on palynological records, and these are relevant to the study area. One of the laminated cores used in reconstructing regional palaeo-climate has been taken from the Pond Mills pond, located just 11 km west of the study area (McAndrews 1981).

The period between A.D. 700 and A.D. 1200 has been described as a time of favourable conditions that were both warmer and more moist than at present (Griffin 1960; Baerreis and Bryson 1965). This trend was originally suggested by Griffin who, in part, based his hypothesis on historical records which indicate that the period of Norse settlement in Greenland between the late tenth century and ca. A.D. 1200 occurred during a warm climatic period, while the decline of the colony coincided with the onset of cooler temperatures after A.D. 1200.

Recent revisions of palaeo-climatic data have indicated that there was greater regional variation in past climates than previously realized (Baerreis, Bryson and Kutzbach 1976). It appears that the warm trend for the period prior to A.D. 1200 is basically correct; however, there are indications that the degree of moisture varied from region to region and the transition to cooler weather may have begun as early as A.D. 1100 in some areas (ibid.). More precise interpretations for the Calvert area are not possible at this time. We can only suggest that climatic conditions were slightly warmer, and possibly more moist, during the Calvert occupation than they are in the study area today.

The significance of a slightly warmer and wetter climate is difficult to gauge. We would expect water flows in creeks and rivers to be increased and the growing season to be prolonged. Yet the growing season was already more than adequate for maize horticulture. It is possible that the increased precipitation would have affected the flooding of the Thames River, yet these effects may have been muted by greater vegetation cover which would have reduced runoff compared to today.

The low-lying Dorchester Swamp also experiences microclimatic effects that are important to the floral and faunal species found within it. These effects derive primarily from the high water table, the presence of permanently standing water, and the dense vegetation within the swamp, which result in increased humidity and slightly cooler temperatures during the growing season. During the winter, the dense vegetation also lowers the wind speed along the ground. This can have significant effects, especially in flat areas, resulting in substantially warmer temperatures than are found in more open and elevated locations. The warmer temperatures permit a slightly earlier start to the growing season for some understory and ground level plants and have the effect of extending the

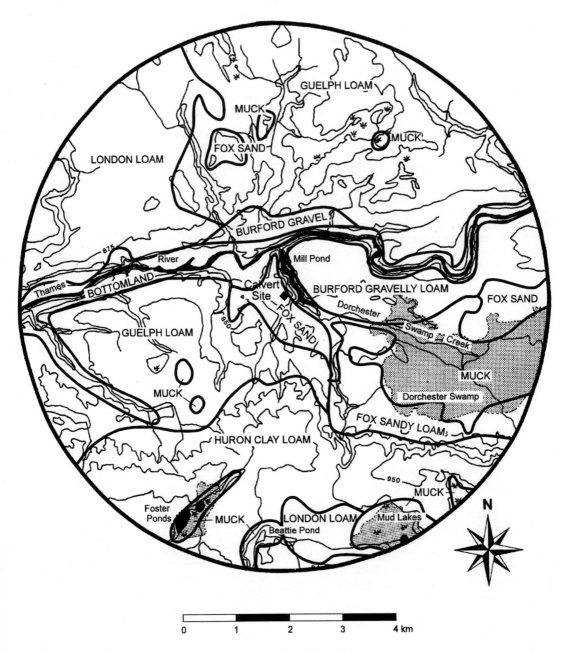

Figure 4.7. Soils of the study area.

growing season into late fall for many species (Ontario Ministry of Natural Resources 1986). These micro-climatic effects obviously create more favourable conditions for animal species that winter in the swamp. In particular, the warmer winter temperatures and extended growing season for browse vegetation would be important for deer yarding within the swamp.

# Soils

Recent detailed mapping of the soils in the study area has been undertaken by the Ontario Geological Survey of the Ontario Ministry of Natural Resources for the purpose of compiling an inventory of sand and gravel deposits suitable for extraction (Ontario Ministry of Natural Resources 1982a). This ministry has also mapped the soils of the Dorchester Swamp in detail (Ontario Ministry of Natural Resources 1986).

The majority of the soils present are of glacio-fluvial or morainic origin. Soils of the Guelph, London, Huron, and Burford series are most common in the study area. Muck soils and soils of the Fox series occur in smaller quantities but they are probably of greater significance with regard to the prehistoric occupation considered here. Figure 4.7 shows the distribution of the various soil types in the study area.

The Calvert site itself is situated on a pocket of Fox Sandy Loam that is an outwash deposit of the Thames spillway. These soils are well drained, deep, and stone free, and generally occur on level to undulating land. In the immediate vicinity of the site this sand deposit has a depth of at least 15 m. The Fox sands are the finest-grained sands found in North Dorchester Township and were the preferred soil type for most Early Iroquoian settlement in the area.

To the west of the site soils change rather abruptly to the heavier Guelph Loams. These soils are fairly stony, generally well drained, and normally found on elevated rolling terrain. Within the study area, they form a broad band running south of the Thames River and west of the Calvert site to a point just west of the village of Nilestown. In the London area Guelph Loam may be a preferred soil type for Middle and Late Iroquoian settlement, and there are a number of Late Iroquoian sites situated on it in the Nilestown area (Keron 1986).

East of the site, on the opposite side of the Mill Pond, the soils grade into Burford Gravelly Loam. These soils are common in this portion of the Thames spillway and occur on undulating to rolling land with good drainage. The deposit within the study area parallels the Thames to the east for several kilometres. It encompasses most

of the old Village of Dorchester and extends to the north side of the river within the village. Although these soils are classed as gravelly loam, the recent surveys by the Ontario Geological Survey indicate that they are predominantly sand and less than 35% gravel (Ontario Ministry of Natural Resources 1982a).

To the north of the Thames River the dominant soil types are Guelph and London Loam. The former, described above, is the constituent material of the Dorchester Moraine; the latter extends over a broad area to the northwest. London Loam occurs on level to undulating terrain and may have poor to good drainage.

The Dorchester Swamp to the southeast of the Calvert site is composed primarily of muck soils (82%). These consist of black, well decomposed organic material and are usually found on nearly flat land with very poor natural drainage. During the spring thaw, when meltwaters flood the swamp, the water table rises above the level of muck soil. By late summer, however, the water table lies just below the surface, although standing water may still be found in some low depressions. Consequently, the muck soils of the Dorchester Swamp are wet through most of the year (Ontario Ministry of Natural Resources 1986:25).

Around the edges of the swamp, but still within it, there is a band of Fox Sandy Loam. These sands are part of the same glacial outwash formation as the Fox sands on which the Calvert site is located. In fact, when one examines the distribution of Fox sand around the Muck as shown in Figure 4.7, the glacio-fluvial origin of the entire basin becomes more apparent. The Fox Sandy Loam constitutes about 16% of the peripheral area of the Dorchester Swamp (ibid:24).

The final important soil type found in the study area is the Huron Clay Loam which occurs on the Ingersoll moraine, where it rises to the south of the swamp. Huron Clay is usually found in such rolling upland areas and exhibits fair to good drainage.

For agricultural purposes the soils of the Fox and Burford series are regarded as Class 2s soils, having moderate limitations that restrict the range

Table 4.1. Mammals of the Study Area.

| Order/Family/Species | | English Name |
|---|---|---|
| Order Insectivora | | |
| Family Soricidae | | |
| *Sorex cinereus* | | Masked Shrew |
| *Blarina brevicauda* | * | Short-tailed Shrew |
| Family Talpidae | | |
| *Parascalops breweri* | | Hairy-tailed Mole |
| Order Lagomorpha | | |
| Family Leporidae | | |
| *Sylvilagus floridanus* | * | Eastern Cottontail |
| *Lepus americanus* | | Snowshoe Hare |
| Order Rodentia | | |
| Family Sciuridae | | |
| *Tamias striatus* | * | Eastern Chipmunk |
| *Marmota monax* | * | Woodchuck |
| *Sciurus carolinensis* | * | Grey/Black Squirrel |
| *Tamiasciurus hudsonicus* | * | American Red Squirrel |
| *Glaucomys sabrinus* | | Northern Flying Squirrel |
| *Glaucomys volans* | | Southern Flying Squirrel |
| Family Castoridae | | |
| *Castor canadensis* | * | American Beaver |
| Family Muridae | | |
| *Peromyscus maniculatus* | * | Deer Mouse |
| *Peromyscus leucopus* | | White-footed Mouse |
| *Synaptomys cooperi* | | Southern Bog Lemming |
| *Ondatra zibethicus* | * | Muskrat |
| *Microtus pennsylvanicus* | * | Meadow Vole |
| Family Dipodidae | | |
| *Zapus hudsonius* | * | Meadow Jumping Mouse |
| Family Erethizontidae | | |
| *Erethizon dorsatum* | E | American Porcupine |

Table 4.1 (continued).

| Order/Family/Species | | English Name |
|---|---|---|
| Order Carnivora | | |
| Family Canidae | | |
| *Canis latrans* | * | Coyote |
| *Vulpes vulpes* | * | Red Fox |
| *Urocyon cinereoargenteus* | | Grey Fox |
| Family Ursidae | | |
| *Ursus americanus* | E | American Black Bear |
| Family Procyonidae | | |
| *Procyon lotor* | * | Raccoon |
| Family Mustelidae | | |
| *Martes americana* | E | American Marten |
| *Martes pennanti* | E | Fisher |
| *Mustela erminea* | * | Ermine |
| *Mustela frenata* | | Long-tailed Weasel |
| *Mustela vison* | * | American Mink |
| *Mephitis mephitis* | * | Striped Skunk |
| *Lontra canadensis* | | River Otter |
| Family Felidae | | |
| *Lynx lynx* | | Lynx |
| *Lynx rufus* | | Bobcat |
| Order Artiodactyla | | |
| Family Cervidae | | |
| *Rangifer tarandus* | | Caribou |
| *Odocoileus virginianus* | * | White-tailed Deer |
| *Alces alces* | E | Moose |
| *Cervus elaphus canadensis* | E | Elk |

* Found in Dorchester Swamp; E Extirpated
(Ontario Ministry of Natural Resources 1986;
Banfield 1974)

of crops that may be grown. Adverse soil characteristics around the Calvert site, as judged by modern standards, might include undesirable structure, low natural fertility, and low moisture-holding capacity. Yet these light soils would have been easily worked with hoes and digging sticks and may have been well suited to Early Iroquoian agricultural technology.

Most of the heavier soils in the Calvert study area, including those of the Huron, Guelph, and London series, are Class 1 soils with no significant limitations. These soils are usually deep, hold moisture well, and are nutrient rich.

## Flora and Fauna

The foregoing discussion of soils, topography, drainage, and palaeo-climate is essential for any attempt to reconstruct the prehistoric floral and faunal resources of the study area. Of equal importance are historical accounts of the natural environment of the area at the time of European settlement as well as present day ecological studies of natural areas in the vicinity. The following section draws together data from these sources to reconstruct, as accurately as possible, the prehistoric environment of the Calvert site ca. A.D. 1100-1250. This analysis permits the definition of a series of distinct micro-environments within the study area.

Table 4.2. Fish found in the Thames River watershed.

| Family/Species | | Common Name |
|---|---|---|
| Family Petromyzontidae | | |
| Ichthyomyzon fossor | * | Northern Brook Lamprey |
| I. unicuspis | | Silver Lamprey |
| Petromyzon marinus | | Sea Lamprey |
| Family Acipenseridae | | |
| Acipenser fulvescens | E | Lake Sturgeon |
| Family Lepisosteidae | | |
| Lepisosteus oculatus | | Spotted Gar |
| L. osseus | | Longnose Gar |
| Family Amiidae | | |
| Amia calva | | Bowfin |
| Family Salmonidae | | |
| Salvelinus fontinalis | * | Brook Trout |
| Family Hiodontidae | | |
| Hiodon tergisus | | Mooneye |
| Family Umbridae | | |
| Umbra limi | * | Central Mudminnow |
| Family Esocidae | | |
| Esox lucius | | Northern Pike |
| Esox masquinongy | | Muskellunge |
| Family Cyprinidae | | |
| Chrosomus eos | * | Northern Redbelly Dace |
| C. neogaeus | | Finescale Dace |
| Hybognathus hankinsoni | * | Brassy Minnow |
| Nocomis biguttatus | * | Hornyhead Chub |
| N. micropogon | * | River Chub |
| Notemigonus crysoluecas | * | Golden Shiner |
| Notropis atherinoides | | Emerald Shiner |
| N. cornutus | * | Common Shiner |
| N. heterolepis | | Blacknose Shiner |
| N. hudsonius | | Spottail Shiner |
| N. volucellus | | Mimic Shiner |
| Pimephales notatus | | Bluntnose Minnow |
| P. promelas | * | Fathead Minnow |
| Rhinichthys atratulus | * | Blacknose Dace |
| R. cataractae | | Longnose dace |
| Semotilus atrolaculatus | * | Creek Chub |
| S. margarita | | Pearl Dace |
| Family Catostomidae | | |
| Carpiodes cyprinus | | Quillback |
| Catostomus catostomus | | Longnose Sucker |
| C. commersoni | * | White Sucker |
| Moxostoma anisurum | | Silver Redhorse |
| M. duquesnei | | Black Redhorse |
| M. erythrurum | | Gold Redhorse |
| M. macrolepidotum | | Shorthead Redhorse |

Table 4.2 (continued).

| Family/Species | | Common Name |
|---|---|---|
| Family Ictaluridae | | |
| Ictalurus melas | * | Black Bullhead |
| I. natalis | | Yellow Bullhead |
| I. nebulosus | | Brown Bullhead |
| I. punctatus | | Channel Catfish |
| Noturus flavus | * | Stonecat |
| Family Gasterosteidae | | |
| Culaea inconstans | * | Brook Stickleback |
| Family Percopsidae | | |
| Percopsis omiscomaycus | | Trout-Perch |
| Family Percichthyidae | | |
| Morone chrysops | | White Bass |
| Family Centrarchidae | | |
| Ambloplites rupestris | * | Rock Bass |
| Lepomis cyanellus | * | Green Sunfish |
| L. gibbosus | * | Pumpkinseed |
| L. macrochirus | | Bluegill |
| Micropterus dolomieui | | Smallmouth Bass |
| M. salmoides | | Largemouth Bass |
| Family Percidae | | |
| Perca flavescens | | Yellow Perch |
| Stizostedion vitreum | | Walleye |
| Ammocrypta pellucida | | Eastern Sand Darter |
| Etheostoma blennioides | | Greenside Darter |
| E. caeruleum | * | Rainbow Darter |
| E. exile | | Iowa Darter |
| E. flabellare | | Fantail Darter |
| E. microperca | | Least Darter |
| E. nigrum | * | Johnny Darter |
| Percina caprodes | | Log Perch Darter |
| P. maculata | | Blackside Darter |
| Family Sciaenidae | | |
| Aplodinotus grunniens | | Freshwater Drum |
| Family Cottidae | | |
| Cottus bairdi | | Mottled Sculpin |

* also found in Dorchester Swamp Creek; E Extirpated (Williamson 1985; Ward 1982; Upper Thames Conservation Authority 1952; Scott and Crossman 1973)

## Mammals

The study area was home to a diverse range of mammals prior to the encroachment of the Europeans. The Dorchester Swamp remains a rich habitat for numerous species and continues as a favoured hunting and trapping area to the present day. Table 4.1 lists the mammals known to have occupied the Thames River watershed and indicates those that are known to occupy the Dorchester Swamp today (Ontario Ministry of Natural Resources 1986). It is likely that all of the species listed would have been available either within or near the study area.

Of particular interest to the present study is the fact that the Dorchester Swamp is classed as an area of white-tailed deer range and concentration (Ontario Ministry of Natural Resources 1986:85). The vegetation found within the swamp provides excellent shelter and abundant browse for the deer population during the winter months. There is evidence to indicate that it was also an important deer yarding area in historic times. In November 1820, while surveying the Muncey Indian Reserve west of London, Mahlon Burwell noted that most of the Indians were absent from the reserve, having gone to Dorchester to hunt. Apparently, they were not expected to return until they had killed enough animals to see them through the winter (Findlay 1978). Although neither the swamp nor the deer are mentioned specifically, it is probable that the yarding deer were the main target of this "harvest".

Based on modern studies, Williamson estimated the fall density of deer on the Caradoc Sand Plain at 19 individuals/square km; higher in swamp areas during the winter (1985:33). If we adopt this figure for the Dorchester Swamp and use White's (1953) figure of 20.6 kg of dressed meat per individual, we arrive at a harvest potential of 2,144 kg of deer meat for the 5.48 square km Dorchester Swamp. This estimate is probably conservative inasmuch as prehistoric deer densities within the swamp are likely to have been higher than they are today.

Table 4.3. Birds found in the study area.

| Genus/Species | Common Name | Seasonal Occurrence |
|---|---|---|
| Gavia immer | Common Loon | M |
| Ardea herodias | Great Blue Heron | S |
| Butorides striatus | Green-backed Heron | S |
| Branta canadensis | Canada Goose | S |
| Aix sponsa | Wood Duck | S |
| Anas platyrhynchos | Mallard | P |
| Cathartes aura | Turkey Vulture | S |
| Buteo jamaicensis | Red-tailed Hawk | P |
| Aquila chrysaetos | Golden Eagle  E | M |
| Falco sparverius | Sparrow Hawk | P |
| Bonaasa umbellus | Ruffed Grouse | P |
| Meleagris gallapavo | Wild Turkey  E | P |
| Charadrius vociferus | Killdeer | S |
| Actitus macularia | Spotted Sandpiper | S |
| Gallinago gallinago | Common Snipe | S |
| Scolopax minor | American Woodcock | S |
| Columba livia | Rock Dove | P |
| Zenaidura macroura | Mourning Dove | P |
| Ectopistes migratorius | Passenger Pigeon  Ex | S |
| Bubo virginianus | Great Horned Owl | P |
| Strix varia | Barred Owl | P |
| Chordeiles minor | Common Nighthawk | S |
| Archilochus culubris | Ruby-throated Hummingbird | S |
| Ceryle alcyon | Belted Kingfisher | S |
| Melanerpes erythrocephalus | Red-headed Woodpecker | S |
| Picoides pubescens | Downy Woodpecker | P |
| Picoides villosus | Hairy Woodpecker | P |
| Colaptes auratus | Northern Flicker | S |
| Contupus virens | Eastern Wood-Pewee | S |
| Empidonax traillii | Willow Flycatcher | S |
| Empidonax minimus | Least Flycatcher | S |
| Myiarchus crinitus | Great Crested Flycatcher | S |
| Tyrannus tyrannus | Eastern Kingbird | S |
| Eremophila alpestris | Horned Lark | P |
| Tachycineta bicolor | Tree Swallow | S |
| Riparia riparia | Bank Swallow | S |
| Hirundo pyrrhonota | Cliff Swallow | S |
| Hirundo rustica | Barn Swallow | S |
| Cyanocitta cristata | Blue Jay | P |
| Corvus brachyrhynchos | American Crow | P |
| Parus atricapillus | Black-capped Chickadee | P |
| Sitta canadensis | Red-breasted Nuthatch | M |
| Sitta carolinensis | White-breasted Nuthatch | P |
| Certhia americana | Brown Creeper | P |
| Troglodytes aedon | House Wren | S |
| Troglodytes troglodytes | Winter Wren | W |
| Regulus satrapa | Golden-crowned Kinglet | M |

Table 4.3 (continued).

| Genus/species | Common name | Seasonal Occurrence |
|---|---|---|
| Regulus calendula | Ruby-crowned Kinglet | M |
| Polioptilla caerulea | Blue-gray Gnatcatcher | S |
| Sialia sialis | Eastern Bluebird | S |
| Catharus fuscescens | Veery | S |
| Hylocichla mustelina | Wood Thrush | S |
| Turdus migratorius | American Robin | S |
| Dumetella carolinensis | Gray Catbird | S |
| Toxostoma rufum | Brown Thrasher | S |
| Bombycilla cedrorum | Cedar Waxwing | P |
| Vireo flavifrons | Yellow-throated Vireo | S |
| Vireo gilvus | Warbling Vireo | S |
| Vireo olivaceus | Red-eyed Vireo | S |
| Vermivora pinus | Blue-winged Warbler | S |
| Vermivora chrysoptera | Golden-winged Warbler | S |
| Dendroica petechia | Yellow Warbler | S |
| Dendroica coronata | Yellow-rumped Warbler | M |
| Dendroica virens | Black-throated Green Warbler | M |
| Dendroica castanea | Bay-breasted Warbler | M |
| Setophaga ruticilla | American Redstart | S |
| Seiurus aurocapillus | Ovenbird | S |
| Seiurus novaboracensis | Northern Waterthrush | S |
| Geothlypis trichas | Common Yellowthroat | S |
| Wilsonia pusilla | Wilson's Warbler | M |
| Piranga olivacea | Scarlet Tanger | S |
| Cardinalis cardinalis | Northern Cardinal | P |
| Pheuticus ludovicianus | Rose-breasted Grosbeak | S |
| Passerina cyanea | Indigo Bunting | S |
| Pipilo erythrophtalmus | Rufous-sided Towhee | S |
| Spizella arborea | American Tree Sparrow | W |
| Spizella passerina | Chipping Sparrow | S |
| Spizella pusilla | Field Sparrow | S |
| Pooecetes gramineus | Vesper Sparrow | S |
| Passerculus sanwichensis | Savannah Sparrow | S |
| Melospiza melodia | Song Sparrow | S |
| Melospiza georgiana | Swamp Sparrow | S |
| Zonotrichia albicollis | White-throated Sparrow | S |
| Junco hyemalis | Dark-eyed Junco | W |
| Agelaius phoeniceus | Red-winged Blackbird | S |
| Sturnella magna | Eastern Meadowlark | S |
| Quiscalus quiscula | Common Grackle | S |
| Molothrus ater | Brown-headed Cowbird | P |
| Icterus galbula | Northern Oriole | S |
| Carduelis tristis | American Goldfinch | P |
| Passer domesticus | House Sparrow | P |

Ex, extinct; E, Extirpated; P, permanent resident; S, summer resident;
W, winter resident; M, migrant; (Ontario Ministry of Natural Resources 1986;
Upper Thames River Conservation Authority 1952; Godfrey 1966)

## Fish

Table 4.2 lists the various species of fish that have been recorded in the upper Thames River, excluding introduced species. Many of these species are very small and of limited economic importance, except as forage fish for larger predators. Many of these larger species were, in fact, exploited by the Calvert people. A discussion of the role of fish in the subsistence regime is reserved for Chapter 6.

Twenty-seven fish have been recorded in Dorchester Swamp Creek in a recent study (Ontario Ministry of Natural Resources 1982b). These are also listed in Table 4.2. Most of these species are very small, suggesting that the fishery in the creek was probably of minor economic importance to the Calvert people. The biomass potential of small cold water trout streams is generally very low (M. Bisson: personal communication).

## Birds

Numerous species of birds were present in the study area at the time of the Calvert occupation and 87 different species have been recorded in the Dorchester Swamp. The majority of these, however, were not of economic importance to the prehistoric Iroquoians. Table 4.3 lists the avian species found in the study area. Included in the list are the passenger pigeon, which in now extinct, and the wild turkey and golden eagle, both of which have been extirpated from the study area.

## Reptiles and Amphibians

Table 4.4 lists the reptiles and amphibians that have been observed in the study area. Of the species listed, the turtles were probably of greatest economic importance.

Table 4.4. Reptiles and Amphibians in the study area.

| Genus/species | Common Name |
|---|---|
| Reptiles | |
| Chelydra s. serpentina | Common Snapping Turtle |
| Emydoidea blandingi | Blanding's Turtle |
| Chrysemys picta marginata | Midland Painted Turtle |
| Clemmys guttata | Spotted Turtle |
| Nerodia s. sipedon | Northern Water Snake |
| Storeria d. dekayi | Northern Brown Snake |
| Thamnophis s. sirtalis | Eastern Garter Snake |
| Lampropeltis t. triangulum | Eastern Milk Snake |
| Amphibians | |
| Necturus maculosus | Mudpuppy |
| Ambystoma maculatum | Yellow-spotted Salamander |
| Notophthalmus v. viridescens | Red-spotted Newt |
| Plethodon cinereus | Eastern Redback Salamander |
| Bufo a. americanus | Eastern American Toad |
| Hyla c. crucifer | Northern Spring Peeper |
| Hyla versicolor | Tetraploid Gray Treefrog |
| Pseudacris t. triseriata | Midland Chorus Frog |
| Rana catesbeiana | Bullfrog |
| Rana clamitans melanota | Green Frog |
| Rana sylvatica | Wood Frog |
| Rana pipiens | Northern Leopard Frog |

(Ontario Ministry of Natural Resources 1986)


## Flora

The study area lies within the Niagara section of the Deciduous Forest Region defined by Rowe (1972). This forest is composed primarily of broad-leafed trees, including sugar maple, American beech, red maple, basswood, and red, white, and bur oak. White cedar and tamarack may be found on wet soils in the region and hemlock and white pine occur in some upland areas (Ontario Ministry of Natural Resources 1986).

The northern boundary of the Carolinian forest passes just 10 km south and west of the study area, and some more southerly species occur within the study area. These include black cherry, hickories, silver maple, and blue beech (ibid.).

Most of the land within the study area has been cleared for agricultural activity, with the exception of the Dorchester Swamp, the area around the Foster and Beattie Ponds, and the Mud Lakes. Fortunately, the ecology of these remaining natural areas has been studied to varying degrees in recent years. The swamp has been the focus of a major study conducted by the

Ontario Ministry of Natural Resources (1986) and the overstory vegetation of the Foster Ponds and Mud Lakes has been examined by Small (1978). Such data do not exist for the other portions of the study area (the cleared agricultural land). However, it is possible to reconstruct the pre-European vegetation in general terms on the basis of recent ecological studies conducted in the area. This reconstructed vegetation pattern may then be compared to historic vegetation records compiled by early 19th century land surveyors (Findlay 1978).

Small (1978) has studied the overstory vegetation in many of the remaining natural areas of Middlesex County. In his work he classified forest communities empirically, relating tree species present to other factors such as soil type, soil moisture, and topography or slope. As a result, he was able to generate model communities for different combinations of soils, moisture, and topography. While there is admittedly a high degree of variation within the different community types, the definition of the model communities allows one to predict what the pre-European forest cover would likely have been if the underlying factors are known. Therefore, this ecologically based method of reconstructing prehistoric vegetation provides a line of evidence that is independent of the historic forest data. Small's work was influenced by that of Maycock (1963), who studied southwestern Ontario forests with regard to soil and moisture requirements for specific tree species. Yet, because Small's data are all derived from Middlesex County, they are of greater relevance to this study.

For the present environmental reconstruction, data from recent studies of surviving natural areas, such as the Dorchester Swamp, the Foster Ponds, and Mud Lakes, have been used to reconstruct the prehistoric environment of these specific areas, since they have seen limited change since European settlement. In upland areas where land has been mostly cleared, Small's method of predicting plant communities on the basis of existing soil, moisture, and topographic conditions has been employed. Finally, as an independent check of the

Table 4.5. Plant communities within Dorchester Swamp.

| Plant Community | |
|---|---|
| Scientific Name | Common Name |
| *Upland Deciduous Forest* | |
| Acer saccharum | Sugar Maple |
| Prunus serotina | Black Cherry |
| *Upland Mixed Forest* | |
| Tsuga canadensis | Eastern Hemlock |
| Acer saccharum | Sugar Maple |
| Betula alleghaniensis | Yellow Birch |
| Acer rubrum | Red Maple |
| Pinus strobus | Eastern White Pine |
| Thuja occidentalis | Eastern White Cedar |
| Betula caerulea-grandis | Blueleaf Birch |
| Prunus serotina | Black Cherry |
| Fraxinus americana | White Ash |
| *Hardwood-Conifer Swamp* | |
| Thuja occidentalis | Eastern White Cedar |
| Acer rubrum | Red Maple |
| Betula alleghaniensis | Yellow Birch |
| Populus tremuloides | Trembling Aspen |
| Pinus strobus | Eastern White Pine |
| Ulmus americana | White Elm |
| *Conifer-Hardwood Swamp* | |
| Thuja occidentalis | Eastern White Cedar |
| Betula alleghaniensis | Yellow Birch |
| Tsuga canadensis | Eastern Hemlock |
| Acer rubrum | Red Maple |
| Larix laricina | Tamarack |
| Fraxinus nigra | Black Ash |
| *Hardwood Swamp* | |
| Acer saccharinum | Silver Maple |
| Acer rubrum | Red Maple |
| Fraxinus nigra | Black Ash |
| Ulmus americana | White Elm |
| Betula alleghaniensis | Yellow Birch |
| Populus sp. | Poplar |
| Salix sp. | Willow |
| *Tall Shrub (Thicket)* | |
| Cornus sp. | Dogwood |
| *Swamp* | |
| Salix sp. | Willow |
| *Cat-tail Marsh* | |
| Typha sp. | Cat-tail |
| *Low Shrub-Herb Community* | |
| Gaylussacia sp. | Black Huckleberry |
| Carex sp. | Sedge |
| Vaccinium macrocarpus | Large Cranberry |
| Class Musci | Moss |
| *Pond Vegetation* | |
| Nymphaea sp. | Yellow Pond Lily |
| Potamogeton sp. | Variable Pondweed |

(Ontario Ministry of Natural Resources 1986)

results of this exercise the historic vegetation maps prepared by Findlay (1978) have been analyzed and compared with the results of our environmental reconstruction.

While it is recognized that none of these methods of environmental reconstruction accounts for either past climatic change or forest succession, it is nonetheless believed that these methods provide the best assessment of the late prehistoric environment of the study area. The effects of slightly warmer and more moist climatic conditions during the Calvert occupation have not been estimated as detailed palaeo-environmental data are simply not available at this time.

# Natural Areas

## Dorchester Swamp

The Ontario Ministry of Natural Resources (1986) has defined nine natural plant communities within the swamp. The composition of these communities is listed in Table 4.5, which clearly shows that the swamp provides a diversity of vegetation types. Of the nine plant communities, two are classed as Upland Forest (Deciduous and Mixed). These occur primarily on the sandy loams around the perimeter of the area. The remaining communities are lowland (wetland) vegetation types and include various combinations of Hardwood and Conifer Swamp, together with Tall Shrub Swamp, Cat-Tail Marsh, a Low Shrub-Herb Community, and Pond Vegetation. The four swamp communities cover the largest area.

## Foster Ponds and Mud Lakes

Small (1978) reports a White Oak-Beech-Sugar Maple community and a Silver Maple Swamp Forest around the Foster Ponds. There is also a large Swamp Thicket community consisting of buttonbush, elderberry, dogwood, buckthorn, and nannyberry surrounding the ponds, a Marsh Community dominated by bur-reed, and a Bog Community with tamarack, willow, dogwood, blueberry, poison sumac, and a variety of other typical bog plants.

Around the Mud Lakes, Small has recorded a Beech-Sugar Maple-White Ash community in the

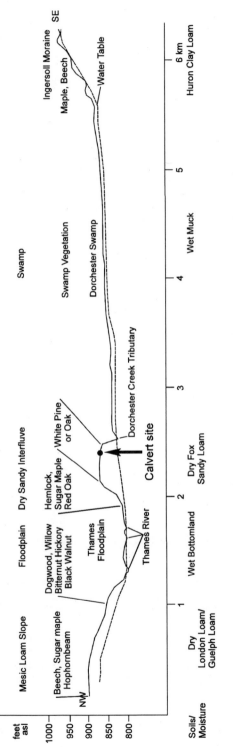

Figure 4.8. Relief profile showing relationship of soils, moisture, slope and vegetation.

elevated areas and a pure stand of Silver Maple Swamp Forest. There is also a bog consisting of a floating sphagnum mat which supports a variety of grasses together with cat-tails, dogwood, willow shrubs, and other bog species.

In sum, these ponds each provide the only bog environment within the study area, although other bogs do occur along the Ingersoll Moraine.

Based on our foregoing analysis of soils, drainage, and topography, it is possible, using Small's method, to predict the various forest communities that may have occurred within the deforested portions of the study area (1978). Figure 4.8 demonstrates the relationship between soils, soil moisture, slope, and forest cover along a relief profile that runs through the Calvert site from northwest to southeast.

This figure shows how the vegetation would be expected to change from a Dry Loam Slope Community dominated by beech, sugar maple, and hophornbeam to a Sandy Loam or Loam Floodplain Community dominated by dogwood, willow, bitternut hickory, black walnut, and ninebark. Moving up the steep bank of the sandy ridge we would probably have a Dry Sandy Slope community composed of hemlock, sugar maple, and red oak.

Small was unable to define a model community for a Dry Sandy Interfluve area, such as the one on which the Calvert site is situated, since there were few such communities in his database. However, other data indicate that the most likely forest types for such well drained sandy loam soils would be white pine or oak (Maycock 1963; Hilborn 1970; Upper Thames River Conservation Authority 1952).

Following this method, it has been possible to construct the forest cover map shown in Figure 4.9 for the entire study area. As would be expected, given the diversity of soils, drainage, and topography of the area, there is considerable variation in the predicted vegetation. However, most of the upland forest communities, with the exception of those on the sand, show a definite dominance of the maple-beech association. The sandier areas south of the Thames and around the swamp were probably dominated by either white pine or oak.

Figure 4.9. Predicted prehistoric vegetation of the study area.

## Historic Vegetation

Historical records indicate that the land surrounding the Dorchester Mill Pond and Dorchester Swamp Creek supported hardwood forests and large tracts of white pine at the time of European pioneer settlement. White pine was the most sought after timber in eastern North America from the seventeenth century through the early nineteenth century, initially because of

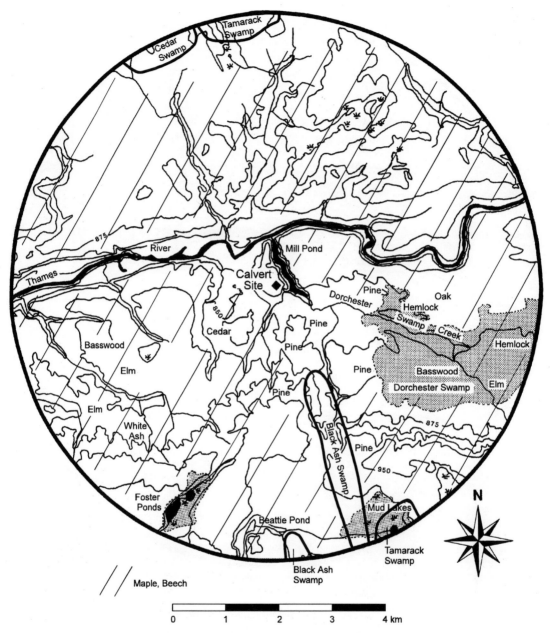

Figure 4.10. Historic vegetation of the study area.

the suitability of its long, straight trunks for masting (Bowman 1979:51). During the 1800s at least six saw mills were established in North Dorchester Township, and there was a mill operating at the Dorchester Mill Pond as early as 1800 (Upper Thames River Conservation Authority 1986:3).

The most useful source of information about historic forest cover comes from the notes of the land surveyors who conducted the original township surveys in the early 1800s. For southwestern Ontario these data have been compiled by Findlay (1978), resulting in a generalized mapping of the historic forest cover of the region.

Findlay's map for the Dorchester area, reproduced in Figure 4.10, shows large pure stands of pine on the two lots adjacent to the Calvert site to the south. The surrounding area is dominated by a maple-beech forest both north and south of the Thames. Pine, hemlock, basswood, and elm are shown intermixed with the dominant maple-beech community around the perimeter of the Dorchester Swamp.

Surprisingly, the swamp itself is not shown on the historic vegetation map. This is unusual since swamps were usually noted by the surveyors. It is understandable that shrub/thicket communities would not be recorded; yet there is no mention of cedar or birch trees despite the fact that they must have been present in large numbers as they are today. It is certainly difficult to believe that the surveyors missed a swamp that covers over 500 ha. This anomaly is cause for some concern when archaeologists rely too heavily and uncritically on these historical vegetation records.

Putting aside the absence of the swamp, the rest of the general pattern of historic vegetation corresponds with our predicted vegetation pattern. The dominance of the maple-beech association throughout most of the study area is as expected. Further, the historical data confirm the presence of pine rather than oak on the sandy soils both east and west of the Mill Pond. While the Dorchester Swamp is not shown, there is certainly a diversity of species in that area. Around the Mud Lakes a tamarack swamp is shown that is not present today, and the historic data show maple-beech in the vicinity of the Foster Ponds where tamarack is present today. These discrepancies may simply be because the forests surrounding the ponds are now in another stage of succession.

## Definition of Microenvironments

On the basis of our environmental reconstruction, it is possible to define five distinct micro-environmental zones within the study area.

These zones are depicted in Figure 4.11 and are briefly described below.

### The Sandy Upland Plateau

This is a narrow zone running between the Dorchester Swamp and the Thames River. It conforms fairly closely to the distribution of Burford Gravelly Loam south of the Thames, but also includes the section of Fox Sandy Loam on which the Calvert site is located. Prehistoric vegetation within this zone was probably dominated by white pine stands and a maple-beech community. It is in this area that the Calvert people would have had their corn fields and it is likely that some land clearance may have taken place, perhaps through the controlled use of fire (Day 1953; Hilborn 1970:43). This also would have created a disturbed forest edge environment that would have been attractive to certain plants, such as strawberry, sumac, chenopod, knotweed, and elderberry and forest edge animals, including deer, fox, woodchuck, and porcupine.

Although there is some evidence for white pine succession on abandoned Indian corn fields (Bowman 1979), it seems unlikely that the extensive white pine stands recorded in the area historically are wholly the result of native agricultural activities. This species is discussed in the Conservation Report of the Upper Thames River Conservation Authority:

"White pine typically occurs on fresh, sandy loam upland but also on clay in swampy areas and on loamy sand. On sandy soils on the moraines it tends to be permanent... It was never very abundant on the watershed but now [1952] occupies only 77 areas of the wooded area, mostly in North Dorchester Township" (Upper Thames River Conservation Authority 1952:22).

### The Thames River, Dorchester Swamp Creek, and Associated Floodplains

The aquatic environment offered by the river and the creek is another distinctive resource zone within the study area. While Dorchester Swamp Creek was probably not a prime fishery, the nearby Thames supported a rich and varied fish population. Shallow areas with rapids occur along the Thames near the mouth of the creek and

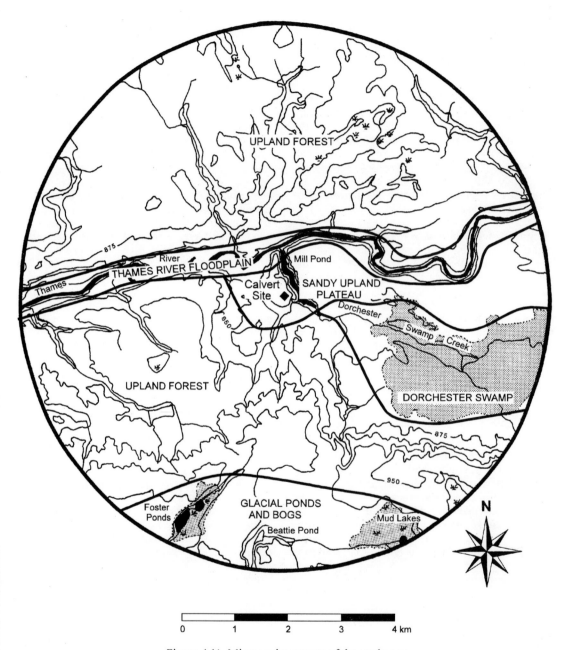

Figure 4.11. Microenvironments of the study area.

may have been excellent fishing spots. It is likely that the larger species (i.e. walleye and catfish) would have been prime fishing targets.

Another important component of the riverine zone would have been the riparian and floodplain environment adjacent to the watercourses. This area would have supported a distinctive floodplain community that probably included stands of black walnut, bitternut hickory, willow, and dogwood. Both the black walnut and hickory could have been used by the Calvert people for food, medicine, dye, and technology (Ounjian 1988).

### The Dorchester Swamp

The swamp is probably the most important micro- environmental zone within the study area and is perhaps the prime strategic factor in the location of the Calvert site. As Figure 4.6 shows, it was much larger in the past than it is today and may have extended to within 200 m of the site. The swamp is home to a broad range of plant communities, including upland deciduous and mixed forests and lowland swamp forests and thickets. It would have been an important source of cedar poles and bark for building construction. Furthermore, it supports a rich understory vegetation involving over 600 plant species, many of which native people may have exploited for food or medicinal purposes.

The swamp also provides a suitable habitat for numerous species of birds, mammals, and reptiles. Of special significance are the favourable conditions for deer yarding within the swamp, which attracted a large deer population during the winter months.

### The Upland Forests

Extending in a wide ring around the sand and swamp zones of the study area (Figure 4.11), the Upland Forest was the characteristic climax maple-beech community that dominated most of Middlesex County in historic times. These forests would have been home to animals that prefer a timbered environment, such as bear, bobcat, and raccoon. Their distribution within the forest would have been more generalized and less concentrated than that of animals living in the swamp.

### The Glacial Ponds

This zone includes the Mud Lakes and the Foster and Beattie Ponds along the southern edge of the study area (Figure 4.11). These are unique bog communities that do not occur elsewhere within the study area and that prehistorically may have been used for the collection of specific plant species. They would also have attracted a variety of birds and animals for feeding, which would have made the ponds excellent hunting areas. Recent archaeological research around other pond/bog complexes on the Ingersoll Moraine indicates that they were occupied as hunting camps for several thousand years (Finlayson et al. 1990).

## Conclusions

As this review demonstrates, the Calvert site, is strategically located to provide easy access to five distinct micro-environments within the study area. Each of these micro-environments offers a different range of resources that could have been exploited by the Calvert people, although we have not attempted to quantify these resources. The use of these micro-environmental zones by the Calvert villagers will be empirically assessed in Chapter 6 through an examination of floral and faunal remains recovered from the site.

# Chapter 5

# The Occupational History of the Calvert Site

## Introduction

This chapter describes the procedures used to reconstruct the occupational history of the Calvert site, outlines their implementation, and summarizes the resulting interpretations. The term occupational history as used here refers to the sequence of construction and use of structures and facilities on the site and the timing and duration of these activities. This analysis yields three chief products:

1. four distinct sets of settlement pattern data represented by the sequential community patterns at Calvert;

2. four sub-samples of feature, artifactual, and ecofactual data corresponding to the separate community patterns; and

3. an estimate of the dating of the site on the calendrical time-scale, estimates of the duration of the entire occupation, and estimates of the duration of individual phases of the occupation.

## Analytical Method

The analysis of occupational history is conducted within the framework of interpretive theory outlined in Chapter 1. This approach seeks to provide solid, well-grounded interpretations of archaeological data by relating them to causal behaviour patterns or natural processes. That requires an examination of the integrity of source side premises that provide interpretive arguments for archaeological subjects. As discussed in Chapters 1 and 3, source side premises form the interpretive data that facilitate explanation through their correlation with specific types of archaeological data that require explanation.

In analyzing occupational history, it is necessary to select certain types of archaeological data that are perceived to be relevant to the specific problem at hand. In the present study five different categories of archaeological data inform the analysis. These are outlined below together with a discussion of the source side premises (interpretive data or principles) that permit the interpretation of each data type:

1. Stratigraphic evidence resulting from the superposition of structures, features, and other deposits can provide a relative chronology of such deposits. On Iroquoian sites, where horizontal stratification is rarely encountered, stratigraphic analysis may be limited to obvious cases of feature and post superposition. In many cases houses may overlap but not display any instances of feature/post superposition that show the chronology of the structures. Yet such cases at least allow a stratigraphically and spatially based inference that the structures are not contemporaneous.

Unfortunately, cases of feature/post and post/feature superposition on Iroquoian sites are not always obvious in the field. This is because post mould and pit feature fills are often similar in colour and texture, making it easy to overlook post/feature superpositions. If post moulds intrusive to pit features are not recorded in the field, these data are lost and cannot be used to reconstruct structure sequence. At the same time, it is dangerous to infer that a pit post-dates a structure wall even if it appears to be superimposed on a wall in a site plan, since wall posts may be obscured in the pit fill. Fortunately, **clear cut** cases of post/feature superposition are frequently recorded and the resulting site plan will show the posts running through the feature. These cases may be taken as reliable stratigraphic data, since there can be no confusion that the superposition was observed and documented in the field.

Interpretations of relative chronology based on stratigraphic evidence are generally highly reliable, as they are founded on the Law of Superposition, which is the source side principle in this case.

2. Spatial data can provide important information concerning the arrangement of the community pattern at any given point in time. The spatial organization of features and structures is culturally and functionally determined. Drawing upon previous research concerning community patterns and spatial organization within similar or related groups (i.e., on other Glen Meyer sites), it may be possible to predict culturally based spatial patterns of structure and feature distribution and use these patterns to interpret the spatial arrangements of structures at Calvert and to assign features to specific structures.

3. Cross-mend evidence involving co-joining fragments of artifacts excavated from different deposits is another method of linking contemporaneous features or deposits. The cross-mend data base must be actively constructed by the investigator, insofar as it is necessary to match artifact fragments in order to create the data base. The interpretation of these data is also more difficult, since numerous scenarios may result in the deposition of parts of an artifact in two different areas of a site. Regardless of the precise formation processes involved, we tend to conclude that deposits linked by cross-mends are likely to have been in use at the same time. This is not always a reliable inference, since it is possible that features may fall into disuse for some time and then be reused, resulting in a transfer of refuse from older contexts to more recent ones (Schiffer 1987).

4. Chronometric data derived from radiocarbon determinations provide the best means for establishing the dating of the Calvert occupation on the calendrical time-scale. Five dates are available for the Calvert site. In this case, the source side premises are grounded in the processes involved in radiocarbon production, decay, and sample measurement. The reliability of inferences based on radiocarbon dates depends on the precision of the dating method and the integrity of the sample and its archaeological context (Timmins 1985). When these factors are assessed systematically, we can conclude that, in probabilistic terms, the dated event falls within the one sigma time range two times out of three.

5. Post mould density data provide the final important type of information for the reconstruction of occupational history. Past studies have identified a relationship between wall post densities and length of occupation (Finlayson 1985), and recently attempts have been made to quantify such data based on actualistic studies of post decay (Warrick 1988). While the radiocarbon dates serve to provide the general time range of the Calvert occupation, post density data may provide a more accurate estimate of the actual length of occupation in each phase.

## Analysis of Occupational History

In analyzing the occupational history data from the Calvert site an attempt was made to proceed from the most obvious and secure deductions to the least secure. Since there are no known precedents for this type of analysis on an Iroquoian site, much of the procedure was initially attempted on a trial and error basis. The systematization of this procedure was only developed after much experimentation.

Prior to beginning this analysis, all structures and palisade segments that could be visually defined were assigned numbers. The house structures were numbered from 1 to 14 and the palisade segments were numbered from 101 to 104, as shown in Figure 5.1. A number of problematic structures also shown in Figure 1 were labelled from A to L.

### Stratigraphic Analysis

The first step in the stratigraphic analysis was to eliminate from consideration all combinations of structures that could not be contemporaneous because of superposition. These structure combinations are listed in Table 5.1.

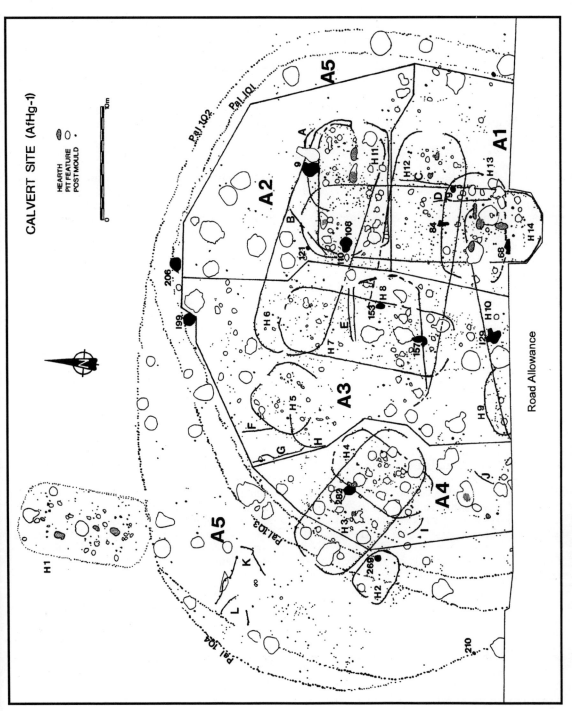

Figure 5.1 House numbers, palisade numbers, key features, and site areas.

Table 5.1. Non-contemporaneous structures due to overlap.

1. Houses 11, 14, and 6
2. Houses 13, 14, and 10
3. Houses 7, 8, and 12
4. Houses 6 and 7
5. Houses 3 and 4
6. Houses 14 and 12
7. Houses 11 and 12
8. Houses 3 and 2 and Palisade Segments 101 and 103
9. House 1 and Palisade Segment 104

The next step was to examine all cases of clear superpositions involving features or post moulds and tabulate the inferences from such data to determine the relative chronology among different structures. Working from large-scale settlement pattern maps and detailed profile and plan view drawings of individual features, a list of all stratigraphic superpositions was prepared (Table 5.2). Each case was assigned a record number and the chronological implications of each superposition were recorded as comments (i.e. "House 9 post-dates Feature 400").

The interior of the site was then subdivided into four areas of maximum house overlap and high feature density (Figure 5.1). The palisades and peripheral features associated with them were treated as a fifth distinct area. The site was sub-divided into these smaller areas to facilitate stratigraphic analysis, since it is easier to sort out a few superpositions from a small area than to sort over 50 superpositions from the complete site. Each area was analyzed with reference to the stratigraphic documentation that had been compiled in Table 5.2. Many of the superpositions proved to be meaningless with regard to determining structure sequence; however, a small number of **key features** were identified that provided important stratigraphic information. These key features are shown in Figure 5.1, and the stratigraphic relationships they demonstrate are indicated with an asterisk (*) on the record numbers in Table 5.2. In many cases, inferences drawn from these stratigraphic situations involved the use of spatial information as well.

As Table 5.2 (Record 1) shows, the stratigraphic data in Area 1 indicate that House 13 postdates House 14, largely on the basis of the superposition of the north wall of House 13 over Feature 84, which is a central hearth associated with House 14. This overlap is illustrated in Figure 5.2. Similarly, Feature 68 is a central hearth undoubtedly associated with House 10 that cannot be attributed to either of the overlapping Houses 13 or 14 on the basis of its spatial position (Figure 5.1). Further, it can be argued that a well documented intrusive post in Feature 68 is part of a poorly defined south wall of House 13. This wall may be traced across House 14, running 6 m south of the better defined north wall of House 13 (Table 5.2, Record 15). In sum, Records 1 and 15 demonstrate that House 13 postdates both Houses 10 and 14. The sequence of the latter two houses cannot be ascertained from the stratigraphic data in Area 1.

Turning to Area 2, Table 5.2, Record 25 indicates that Feature 121 postdates the end wall of House 14 (see Figure 5.3). This further implies that House 6 postdates House 14, if we assign Feature 121 to House 6 on spatial grounds. The temporal position of House 11 remains unclear. House 11 and problematic Structure A both postdate Feature 9, indicating that neither of these structures pertains to the initial occupation (Figure 5.1 and 5.2).

In Area 3 the most important stratigraphic observation is Record 37, in which the south wall of House 8 passes through Feature 157, a central hearth in House 7, demonstrating that House 8 postdates House 7. This is shown in Figures 5.1 and 5.2. Further evidence for the early dating of House 7 comes from Feature 153, which is superimposed on the east wall of House 7 (Record 33, Table 5.2, Figure 5.2).

Within Area 3, we find that there are no stratigraphic records demonstrating the chronological relationship of Houses 7 and 8 to Houses 6 and 12. The north wall of House 10 at the south edge of the site appears to be superimposed on Feature 129, indicating that it postdates this feature (Record 36, Table 5.2). This suggests that House 10 does not belong to the earliest occupation of the site, while Record 15 from Area 1 demonstrates that House 10 is postdated by House 13. These data suggest that House 10 must pertain to an intermediate or 'middle' period.

Table 5.2. Structure, Feature and Post Superpositions.

| Record Number | Area | Observation | Source | Comments |
|---|---|---|---|---|
| *1 | 1 | H.13 postdates F.84 | Plan | H.13 postdates H.14 (F.84 is spatially assoc. with H.14) |
| 2 | 1 | PM 1206 & 1207 postdate F.80 | Plan | |
| 3 | 1 | PM 1249 postdates F.65 | Plan | |
| 4 | 1 | F.64 postdates F.65 | Plan | |
| 5 | 1 | F.73 postdates F.71 | Plan | F.73 is assoc. with H.13 |
| 6 | 1 | PM "A" postdates F.71 | Plan | |
| 7 | 1 | F.71 postdates F.74 | Plan | F.71 may postdate H.14 if F.74 is a H.14 support post |
| 8 | 1 | PM 1241,1266,1270 postdate F.65 | Plan | |
| 9 | 1 | PM 900 postdates F.57 | Plan | |
| 10 | 1 | Support post postdates F.75 | Plan | H.10 is not final phase if F.75 is assoc. with H.10 |
| 11 | 1 | F.32 postdates F.31 | Plan | |
| 12 | 1 | F.39 postdates F.38 | Plan | |
| 13 | 1 | Hearth portion of F.65 postdates F.65 pit | Plan | |
| 14 | 1 | PM 1267 & 1266 postdate F.66 | Plan | |
| *15 | 1 | PM 1254 postdates F.68 | Plan | H.13 postdates H.10 |
| *16 | 2 | H.11 postdates F.9 | Plan | If F.9 is assoc. with H.6, H.11 postdates H.6 |
| 17 | 2 | Structure A postdates F.9 | Plan | |
| 18 | 2 | F. 101 postdates 2 PM | Plan | |
| 19 | 2 | F.103 postdates F.101 | Plan | |
| 20 | 2 | PM 1735 postdates F.96 | Plan | |
| 21 | 2 | Un-numbered PM postdates F.14 | Plan | |
| 22 | 2 | F.15 postdates F.14 | Plan | F.14 is assoc. with H.6; F.15 is assoc. with H.11 |
| 23 | 2 | F.131 postdates un-numbered post | Plan | |
| 24 | 2 | PM 1731 postdates F.95 | Plan | |
| *25 | 2 | F.121 postdates PM 154 | Plan/ Profile | F.121 is assoc. with H.6; PM 1524 is assoc. with H.14, so H.6 postdates H.14 |
| 26 | 2 | F.117 postdates F.119 | Plan | |
| *27 | 2 | F.110 postdates F.108 | Profile | |
| 28 | 2 | F.112 postdates F.113 | Plan | |
| 29 | 3 | F.177 postdates F.178 | Plan | |
| 30 | 3 | PM 2782 postdates F.178 | Plan | |
| 31 | 3 | PM 2343 postdates F.167 | Plan | |
| 32 | 3 | PM 2028 & 2030 postdate F.130 | Plan | If PM 2028 & 2030 are assoc. with H.9, H.9 postdates F.130 |
| *33 | 3 | F.153 postdates 3 un-numbered posts | Plan | F.153 postdates H.7, if posts are H.7 wall |
| 34 | 3 | F.250 postdates 1 un-numbered post | Plan | F.250 postdates Structure B |

Table 5.2 (continued).

| Record Number | Area | Observation | Source | Comments |
|---|---|---|---|---|
| 35 | 3 | Un-numbered post postdates F.169 | Plan | |
| 36 | 3 | H.10 postdates F.129 | Plan | H.10 is not early |
| *37 | 3 | H.8 postdates F.157 | Plan | F.157 is a H.7 hearth, so H.8 postdates H.7 |
| 38 | 3 | F.159 postdates F.157 | Plan | |
| 39 | 4 | F.283 postdates F.282 | Plan | |
| *40 | 4 | H.4 postdates F.282 | Plan | If F.282 is assoc. with H.3, H.4 postdates H.3 |
| 41 | 4 | F.283 postdates F.284 | Plan | |
| 42 | 4 | F.276 postdates F.282 | Plan | |
| 43 | 4 | PM 4416 postdates F.294 | Plan | Suggests F.294 is associated with H.3 |
| 44 | 4 | F.267 postdates un-numbered post | Plan | |
| 45 | 4 | Un-numbered post postdates F.265 | Plan | |
| 46 | 4 | PM 4442, 4443, & 4444 postdate F.282 | Plan | |
| 47 | 4 | PM 4418 & 4210 postdate F.295 | Plan | PM 4210 is assoc. with Structure C; F.295 is assoc. with H.3; so Structure 3 postdates H.3 |
| 48 | 4 | PM 4668 postdates F.305 | Plan | |
| 49 | 4 | F.305 postdates F.309 | Plan | |
| 50 | 4 | F.292 postdates F.290 | Plan | |
| *51 | 5 | Pal.101 postdates F206 | Profile | Palisade 101 is late |
| *52 | 5 | Pal.101 postdates F.269 | Plan | F.269 is assoc. with H.2; Pal.101 postdates H.2 |
| 53 | 5 | PM 413 postdates F.199 | Plan | PM 413 is assoc. with Pal.101; Pal.101 postdates F.199 |
| *54 | 5 | F.210 postdates underlying post | Profile | Post used as pit after palisade removal; Pal.101 is early |
| 55 | 5 | PM 4013 postdates F.263 | Plan | PM 4013 is assoc. with Pal.101; Pal.101 postdates F.263 |

* Key Feature; PM Post Mould; F Feature; H House

Moving on to Area 4, the complex mass of features in the area of overlap of Houses 3 and 4 can be at least partially unraveled by the stratigraphic analysis. The most important observation is Record 40 (Table 5.2) which shows the superposition of the west wall of House 4 over Feature 282, a large pit that can be assigned to House 3 on spatial grounds. This superposition, shown in Figure 5.2, demonstrates that House 4 postdates House 3.

Area 5 encompasses the entire peripheral area of the site, including all palisade rows and their associated features. The most important

data occur along the western half of the site, where superpositional data indicate the sequence of Palisade Segments 104, 103, and 101 (Figure 5.1).

Palisade segments 103 and 104 share a common root in Palisade 102, indicating that they are either contemporaneous or sequential, with continuity between them. However, Houses 2 and 3 overlap Palisades 103 and 101 which suggests that they are associated with the outer Palisade 104. This suggests that Palisades 101/103 and 104 cannot be contemporaneous. Feature 210, located within Palisade 104, is a

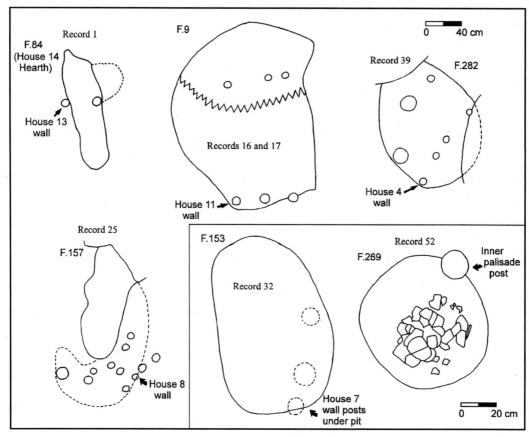

Figure 5.2. Key features, plan views.

small pit that is superimposed upon a former palisade post (Record 54, Figure 5.3). This superposition suggests that Palisade 104 was dismantled at some point in the occupation, while the formation of Feature 210 demonstrates that the area remained in use after the palisade was removed.

Stratigraphic data indicate that the inner Palisade 101 dates late in the sequence of palisade construction. Records 51 and 53 show the superposition of the inner Palisade 101 on Features 206 and 199 respectively (Figure 5.1). This evidence indicates that Palisade 101 postdates the formation of these features. Similarly, another Palisade 101 post is superimposed on Feature 269 within House 2

(Record 52, Table 5.2 and Figure 5.2) indicating that House 2 predates Palisade 101. Finally, the spatial relationship of Palisade 103 to Palisade 101 suggests that they are contemporaneous. Palisade 101 is built uniformly 2-2.5 metres inside the combined Palisades 103 and 102, suggesting that the two rows of palisade were meant to function together, presumably as a defensive unit.

Taken together, the combined stratigraphic and spatial evidence support a sequence of palisade construction beginning with the outer Palisade 104 and followed by the contraction of the palisade with the construction of Palisade 103 and 101. Continuity in the use-life of Palisades 104 and 103 is suggested by the fact that they

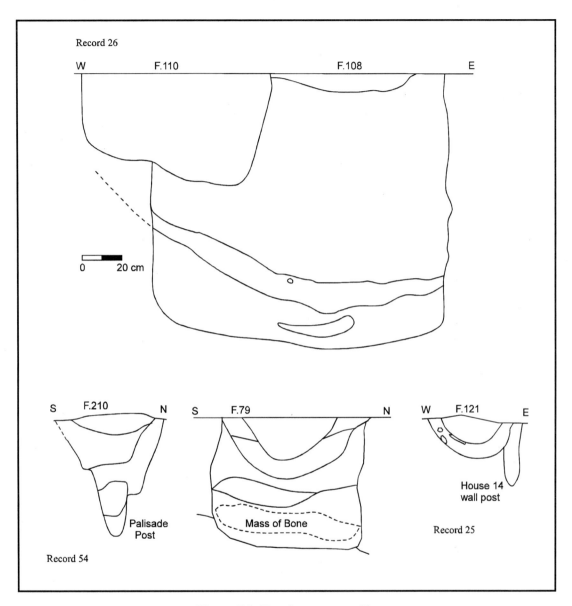

Figure 5.3. Key features, profiles.

share a common root in Palisade 102 (Figure 5.1).

One final point of interest concerns the intersection of Palisade 104 with the southern end of House 1 (Figure 5.1, Table 5.1). The house posts can be distinguished from those of the palisade on the basis of size. Upon close examination, it is evident that the end of Structure 1 passes **inside** the palisade rather than abutting or being intertwined with it. Hence, the two are not contemporaneous.

Table 5.3. Summary of structure sequence by area using stratigraphic evidence.

| Phase | Area 1 | Area 2 | Area 3 | Area 4 | Area 5 |
|---|---|---|---|---|---|
| Early | House 14 | House 14 | House 7 | House 3 | Pal. 104 House 2 |
| Middle | | House 6 | House 10 | | |
| Middle or Late | | | | House 4 | Pal. 101 House 5 |
| Late | House 13 | House 11 | House 8 | | |

In summary, analysis of feature/structure superpositions has helped to determine the sequence of some of the overlapping structures at Calvert. A summary of the relative sequence of structures in each area is presented in Table 5.3. Yet, these sequences are based on stratigraphic data within each sub-area only. To this point we have not examined which structures may be contemporaneous across the entire site. This problem can be partially addressed by examining the spatial organization of structures and features within the village.

## Spatial Organization of Structures and Features

We have already had recourse to some interpretations based on spatial data in the preceding discussion. Before proceeding with further such interpretations, it is necessary to justify our use of spatial data for this purpose.

The spatial organization of structures and features within Iroquoian villages often follows predictable patterns (Warrick 1984a). Recognition of these patterns has evolved from the often implicit use of source side interpretive analogies based on historic accounts of Iroquoian villages and longhouses. Discovery of these patterns has not usually involved complex quantitative methods of spatial analysis (i.e., Carr 1984).

A number of generalizations can be drawn regarding the spatial organization of facilities and structures in Glen Meyer villages. If these generalizations can be adequately documented, it follows that this information will be useful for determining the occupational history at Calvert, insofar as it may aid in determining which structures and features were contemporaneous. I would add that this is an example of past knowledge of the archaeological record informing current interpretations of the record without recourse to actualistic or ethnoarchaeological data. For the present analysis it does not matter what the observed feature and structure patterns mean in terms of their function. It is enough to demonstrate that they occur as a culturally significant pattern, which means that they may be expected to occur at Calvert as well.

The most important spatial observations concerning Early Iroquoian (Glen Meyer) sites are as follows:

1. Parallel, non-overlapping houses are likely to be contemporaneous. This is a trend that begins to develop in the Early Iroquoian period and becomes more pronounced during Middle and Late Iroquoian times. The parallel layout of Iroquoian longhouses may be functionally related to social factors (Warrick 1984a), defensive considerations, wind patterns (Norcliffe and Heidenreich 1974), or space conservation. Such patterns appear on Glen Meyer sites as early as Van Besien (Noble 1975a), and are also apparent on the Elliott site (Fox 1986a) and the Dewaele site (Fox 1976).

2. Large exterior features are often associated with palisades. This pattern has been observed at the Roeland site on the Caradoc Sand Plain (Williamson 1985). It has also been observed at the slightly later Uren site (M. Wright 1986), where the features have been interpreted as the foci of exterior activity areas.

3. Small interior features are often associated with centrally located hearths. This observation was initially made by Fox (1976) at the Dewaele site and it has since been confirmed at all Glen Meyer sites excavated to date (Williamson 1985; Fox 1986a; Stothers 1977; Noble 1975a).

4. Large interior features are usually found under bunklines along the sides of longhouses. This spatial attribute is less consistent in its occurrence, but has been observed by Williamson at the Roeland site (1985) and by Fox at the Dewaele and Elliott sites (1976, 1986a).

5. Exterior clusters of small features appear to represent exterior activity areas. Although this proposition has not been explored by other researchers, exterior clusters of small features may be observed on several Glen Meyer sites, including Elliott and Roeland.

6. A final important spatial observation is that small houses often occur on Glen Meyer sites in apparent association with larger structures. This has been noted on the Elliott and Dewaele sites (Fox 1976, 1986a).

With the foregoing trends in mind we may turn to the next step in unraveling the Calvert data, which involves combining the stratigraphic and spatial data.

Houses 2 and 3 represent perhaps the most obvious large structure/small structure association at Calvert and also conform to the trend towards parallelism among contemporaneous Iroquoian houses. We have already seen that House 2 predates Palisade 101 on stratigraphic grounds, and Palisade 103 by association. If we conclude that Houses 2 and 3 are contemporary on the basis of their spatial association, it follows that they both predate Palisades 101 and 103 and are likely contemporary with exterior Palisade 104, occurring early in the structural sequence.

Moving on to other structure groups that share similar orientation, we conclude that Houses 7 and 14 are contemporary and also early in the occupational history, as indicated by their early stratigraphic placement in Areas 1, 2, and 3 (Table 5.3). We also suspect that Houses 2, 3, 7, and 14 and Palisade segments 102 and 104 may all be contemporary, but at present lack sufficient evidence to link the structures on the west side of the site (Houses 2 and 3) to those on the east side (Houses 7 and 14).

Another obvious set of parallel structures that may be contemporary involves Houses 6, 12,

and 10, all east-west oriented structures of similar size. The stratigraphic data reviewed above indicate that Houses 6 and 10 share an intermediate or middle placement in terms of the structural sequence (Table 5.3). House 6 also may be spatially related to House 5, which is situated near the west end of House 6 in a manner similar to the placement of such small structures at Uren and Elliott. Further, House 5 appears to be attached to the inner palisade 101 by a house-to-palisade wall, indicating that these structures must be contemporary. We have also suggested that Palisade 101 and the combined Palisade Segments 102 and 103 were built to function as a double-rowed unit. In sum, we may conclude that Palisades 101, 102, 103, and Houses 5, 6, 10, and 12 are all contemporary and associated with a middle phase of the site occupation.

The final set of parallel structures that are likely to be contemporary includes Houses 11, 13, and 8. These are small structures that share an east-west orientation. Stratigraphic analysis indicates that each of them occurs late in the structural sequence within their respective areas (Table 5.3). We may therefore conclude that Houses 8, 11, and 13 are associated with a late phase in the site occupation.

The sequential placement of three structures remains unresolved in the analysis conducted thus far. These are:

- House 1, which occurs outside the village and intersects Palisade Segment 104,
- House 4, which overlaps and postdates House 3, and
- House 9, represented only by a partial house end exposed at the south end of the site.

House 1 cannot be assigned to any phase of the occupation at this point, although we know that it was not contemporary with the early phase since it overlaps Palisade 104. House 9 shows no convincing superpositions or spatial associations and cannot be assigned to any period at this time. House 4 postdates the early phase but could relate to either the middle or late construction stages (or both).

Spatial data can also help in assigning specific features to structures, based on the

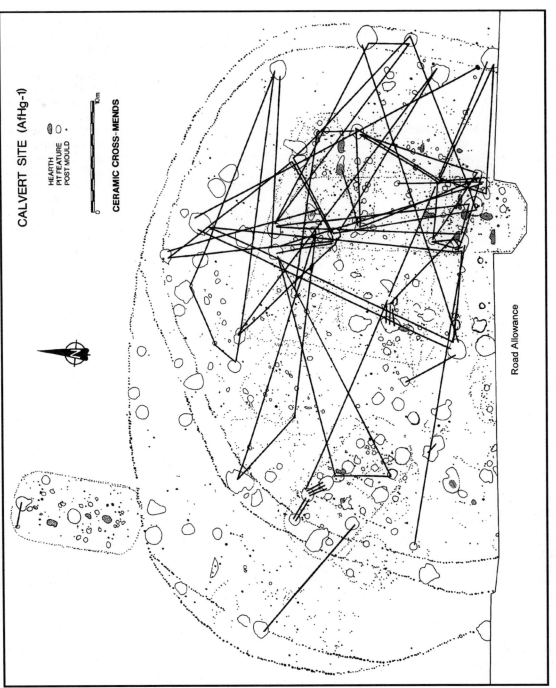

Figure 5.4. Ceramic cross-mends.

generalizations discussed above concerning the spatial organization of features on Glen Meyer sites. Many of the Calvert features were assigned to structures on spatial grounds, following a set of general rules.

For interior house features, in areas where no feature or structure overlapping was observed, features were assigned to the house that they were in. In areas of structure overlap, features within the overlapping area usually could not be assigned to a specific structure on spatial grounds. There were some exceptions to this rule, usually involving hearths, which have a predictable spatial distribution within houses. One example is the case of Feature 84, a central hearth assigned to House 14. This feature also falls within House 12, but is located off the central corridor in an area where hearths are not normally found.

Following these general rules, and adhering to the known patterns of Glen Meyer feature distribution, it was possible to assign 147 of the Calvert site features to specific structures on spatial or spatial/stratigraphic grounds. These results are summarized in Timmins (1992:Appendix B) which provides lists of the features assigned to each structure in each phase of site occupation, together with a notation of the type of evidence used to support each decision.

## Ceramic Cross-mend Analysis

While the stratigraphic and spatial analysis described above linked many interior features to specific structures and phases, few exterior features were yet assigned to a specific structure or phase. One remaining method of establishing a relationship between contemporaneous features was through the use of ceramic cross-mends. This analysis proved to be particularly useful in relating the large exterior features around the periphery of the site to specific structures and phases in the site occupation. It also revealed a number of large stratified features that were apparently used during more than one phase of the site occupation. In some cases it was possible to assign strata within features to specific occupational phases, based on the cross-mend data.

To begin the cross-mend analysis the rim and neck sherds of the ceramic collection were subjected to an intense vessel search, which was initiated by the London Chapter of the Ontario Archaeological Society and completed by the author. The ceramics were grouped by decorative technique, re-grouped by decorative motif, and grouped again by provenience in an attempt to identify all possible matches. Each feature-to-feature cross-mend was mapped and lists were compiled documenting which sherds were involved in each case, their provenience, and whether the cross-mend was in an inferred or a physical match.

Physical mends were those in which two sherds actually fitted together, while inferred mends involved pottery fragments that were assigned to the same vessel on the basis of similarities in form, decorative technique, motif, paste, and temper characteristics. The use of inferred mends in the cross-mend analysis was facilitated by the fact that most of the Calvert vessels are distinct in their decorative motifs and techniques. A total of 54 ceramic cross-mends were discovered through this procedure, 40 of which were feature-to-feature matches.

All cross-mends were physically re-checked by the author to ensure consistency in interpretation, especially in cases of inferred matches.

The resulting cross-mend pattern, when mapped in its totality as shown in Figure 5.4, presents a bewildering mass of lines linking features. Like the Calvert settlement pattern in general, the total pattern appears chaotic. The next task was to see if this pattern had any underlying order, by attempting to break it down into groups or sub-samples of cross-mends relating to different phases in the site occupation. To do this it was necessary to "anchor" the cross-mend analysis in the stratigraphic and spatial analysis conducted previously. Consequently, only cross-mends involving at least one previously assigned feature could be used to extend the inference to the contemporaneous features linked through the mend. Once features were assigned a phase association based on a cross-mend to a feature of known association, they could be used to link other features through additional cross-mends. Cross-mends involving

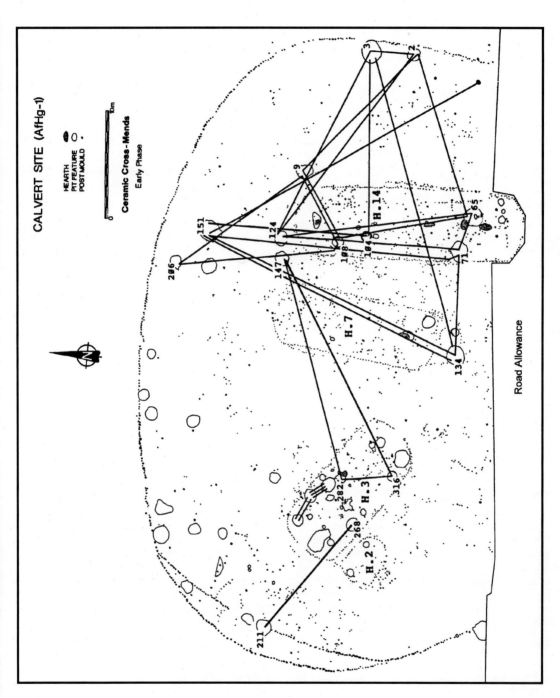

Figure 5.5. Ceramic cross-mends - Early Phase.

Table 5.4. Summary of ceramic cross-mend data.

| Phase | Feature to Feature X-Mends | Number of Features Involved | X-Mends with Known Strat/ Spatial Assoc. | X-Mends with Feature/Phase Conflict | X-Mends with No Feature/ Phase Conflict |
|---|---|---|---|---|---|
| Early | 17 | 22 | 13 | 6 | 11 |
| Middle | 7 | 17 | 4 | 3 | 4 |
| Late | 16 | 21 | 13 | 6 | 10 |
| Totals | 40 | 60 | 30 | 15 | 25 |

features of unknown structure or phase association provided no useful data. Of the 40 feature-to-feature cross-mends tabulated, 30 involved a feature with a known structure or phase assignment.

Timmins (1992:Appendix B) provides a list of all feature-to-feature cross-mends showing the features involved in each mend and the phase assignment of each feature according to spatial, stratigraphic, or cross-mend data.

Analyzing the cross-mends by working from known stratigraphic and spatial feature associations, it was possible to check the validity of using cross-mends to establish contemporaneity among features. The cross-mend pattern was expected to duplicate the results of the stratigraphic analysis, in that early features were expected to be linked to other early ones, late to late, and so on. Since the stratigraphic/spatial interpretations were believed to be well-grounded, a high degree of disagreement from feature/phase assignments resulting from the cross-mends would indicate that the cross-mends may not be valid indicators of contemporaneity.

To test the validity of the working hypothesis that cross-mended ceramics indicate contemporaneity among the vessels involved, we can compare the feature-phase associations for each ceramic cross-mend (Timmins 1992: Appendix B). Of the 40 cross-mends employed, 15 (37%) involve at least one feature with a phase association that disagrees with the phase association of the other features in that cross-mend. However, all of the problematic cross-mends come from only eight features, while a total of 60 features are involved. Upon closer examination, these eight features (104, 108, 110, 134, 72, 71, 147, 273) all show evidence of multi-phase use, involving either disturbance of

an original deposit by a later one or superposition of deposits. These features have been used in more than one phase of the occupation. In such cases it is necessary to exclude the contents of all or part of these features from further phase-by-phase analysis. The majority of the features involved in cross-mends display only single phase use. If we exclude those features in which admixture of deposits has obviously occurred, the features involved in the cross-mends display a remarkable degree of agreement in their phase associations. This suggests that most of the Calvert cross-mends **are** strong indicators of contemporaneity.

Table 5.4 provides a summary of the number of cross-mends on a phase-by-phase basis. It shows that the majority of the cross-mends pertain to the Early and Late Phases, while few are associated with the Middle Phase. There are no cross-mends linking the exterior House 1 to the village proper.

Figures 5.5, 5.6, and 5.7 illustrate the cross-mend patterns for each phase. These figures reveal some important differences between phases in the distribution of cross-mends and in the types of features involved. Cross-mends in the Early and Middle phases occur primarily between exterior features or between interior and exterior features. In contrast, Late Phase cross-mends tend to occur within houses and in many cases provide links between houses. The behavioural implications of these observations are discussed in Chapter 7.

The Early Phase cross-mend pattern shown in Figure 5.5 displays an important cross-mend between Feature 268 in House 3 and Feature 211 along the westerly palisade. This mend establishes the contemporaneity of the outer Palisade 104 with House 3, both Early structures. Of equal

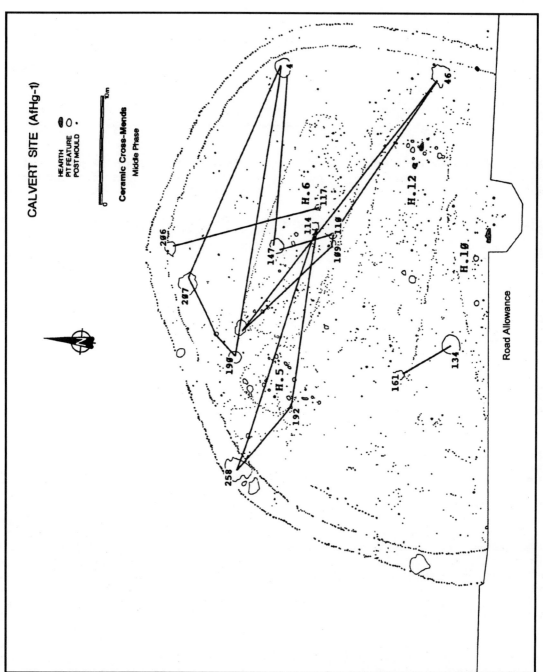

Figure 5.6. Ceramic cross-mends - Middle Phase.

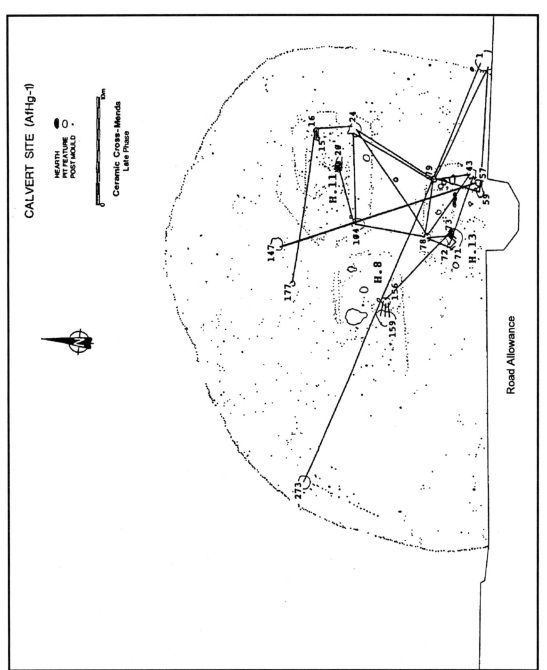

Figure 5.7. Ceramic cross-mends - Late Phase.

Table 5.5. Calvert site radiocarbon dates.

| Lab. No. | Provenience | Phase | Radiocarbon Years BP | Calibrated Range BP* (1 sigma) | Calibrated* Age(s) AD |
|---|---|---|---|---|---|
| I-12176 | F.241-4 | House 1 | 900 ± 80 | 927-732 | AD 1133 |
| | | | | | AD 1136 |
| | | | | | AD 1156 |
| I-12174 | F.147-5 | Early | 860 ± 80 | 914-690 | AD 1191 |
| I-12173 | F.126 | Early | 820 ± 80 | 819-673 | AD 1219 |
| I-12175 | F.151-3, 4, 5 | Early | 800 ± 80 | 790-671 | AD 1230 |
| | | | | | AD 1243 |
| | | | | | AD 1256 |
| I-12476 | F.216 | Early | 740 ± 75 | 730-666 | AD 1277 |
| Average | 4 samples | Early | 803 ± 39 | 741-687 | AD 1228 |
| | | | | | AD 1249 |
| | | | | | AD 1255 |

All dates are on carbonized wood extracted from flotation of pit fill.
* Dates have been calibrated using the University of Washington, Quaternary Isotope Lab,
Radiocarbon Calibration Program, Rev. 2.0. Calibrated ranges summarize all ranges obtained
for dates yielding multiple intercepts and ranges (Stuiver and Becker 1986).

importance is the link established by the cross-mend between Features 282 and 316 in House 3 and Feature 147 between Houses 7 and 14. This link helps to demonstrate the contemporaneity of Houses 3, 7, and 14.

The Middle phase cross-mend pattern (Figure 5.6) likewise provides strong evidence of the contemporaneity of the inner Palisades 101, 102, and 103 and associated exterior Features 258, 207, 46, and 4, with Middle Phase House 6.

The Late Phase cross-mend pattern shown in Figure 5.7 provides abundant evidence for the contemporaneity of Houses 8, 11, and 13, as shown by the many cross-mends between them. In-house cross-mends are also more common than in the earlier phases, with House 13 showing the highest occurrence of interior cross-mends on the site.

In summary, the ceramic cross-mend analysis has successfully linked at least 20 exterior features to specific structures on the premise that the cross-mends themselves indicate feature contemporaneity. This assumption has been strongly supported by the observation that a very high proportion of the cross-mends mirror or duplicate the structure and phase associations of features based on the stratigraphic and spatial

evidence. Quite clearly, the analysis demonstrates that there is an underlying order to the cross-mend pattern. We have yet to explain what these cross-mends mean in terms of the lateral transfer of material within the site in systemic context. This problem is pursued in Chapter 7.

## Chronometric Dating

Five radiocarbon dates have been processed for the Calvert site. The radiocarbon samples were selected prior to the detailed analysis of occupational history and, unfortunately, do not provide representation of all phases in the site occupation. Of the five dated features, four have been assigned to the Early Phase. The fifth is from Feature 241 in House 1, the exterior house that does not have a phase association at present.

Table 5.5 summarizes the radiocarbon data and provides contextual information for each sample. As this table shows, the Early Phase dates show reasonable correspondence, falling between 860 ± 80 and 740 ± 75 BP. The dates were calibrated using the University of Washington's Quaternary Isotope Lab program, Calib Version 2.0 (Stuiver and Becker 1986). The calibrated ages and ranges for each date are also shown in Table 5.5.

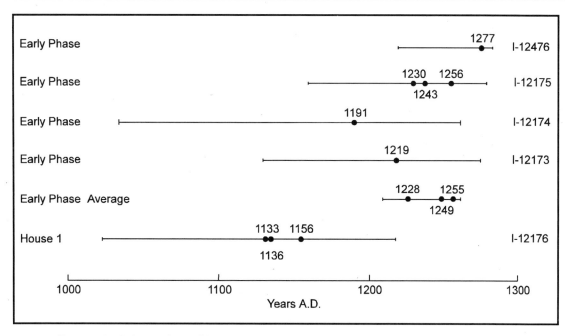

Figure 5.8. Calvert site calibrated radiocarbon dates (see Stuiver and Pearson 1986).

The four Early Phase dates may be averaged since they all relate to the same target event, namely the Early Phase. The average date is 803 ± 39 BP. Upon calibration this average date yields three calibrated ages (A.D. 1228, 1249 and 1255) and a one-sigma range of 741-687 BP. Calibration of the House 1 date of 900 ± 80 BP also gives three calibrated ages (A.D. 1133, 1136, and 1156) and a one-sigma error range of 927-732 BP. Multiple calibrated ages occur when an uncalibrated date intersects an irregular area of the calibration curve so that there are multiple intercepts of the curve (Timmins 1985: 41). The reader will note that, in contrast to uncalibrated radiocarbon dates, the uncertainty range is not symmetrical around the calibrated age. This is a result of the incorporation of the uncertainty of the calibration curve into the uncertainty of the calibrated date. It should also be noted that the probability that the calibrated age matches the sample age is highest around the intercept of the calibration curve and lowest at the outer edges of the uncertainty range (Stuiver and Pearson 1986:808). Efforts are currently underway to develop more precise probabilistic calibration methods that take into account the Gaussian distribution of non-calibrated dates (Bowman 1990:48).

The calibrated ages and ranges for all the Calvert dates and the Early Phase average are plotted on Figure 5.8. Although the one-sigma ranges for the House 1 date and the Early Phase average date overlap by about 10 years, it is probable that House 1 predates the Early Phase. Stratigraphic evidence (the house/palisade overlap) indicates that they cannot be contemporary, and given the ranges shown in Figure 5.8, it is highly unlikely that House 1 could postdate the Early Phase.

Ceramic data, discussed in detail in Chapter 7, provide an independent line of inquiry. The House 1 ceramics are quite distinct from those of the main village, showing a very high occurrence of suture stamped decoration. It can (and will) be argued that suture stamping is an early decorative technique, thus the House 1 ceramics support an earlier rather than a later chronological placement of House 1 in relation to the main village occupation. It is also possible that the people who lived in House 1 were unrelated to the occupants of the later phases of the village. This possibility is also explored in Chapter 7.

A mid-twelfth century date (A.D. 1130-1160) for House 1 is consistent with all three calibrated ages for the single House 1 date (Figure 5.8). The Early Phase must post-date this period, perhaps with a temporal gap occurring after House 1 was abandoned. As a baseline for further discussion, an initial date for the Early Phase in the early thirteenth century (ca. A.D. 1210) is suggested here. In view of the dating of other Early Iroquoian sites, these dates seem surprisingly late. However, most previous researchers have not calibrated radiocarbon dates and this has the effect of moving the Calvert dates forward by 50-100 years. Similar adjustments are required for the entire Iroquoian chronology (Timmins 1985).

## House Wall Post Densities as an Index of Length of Occupation

The radiocarbon dates for House 1 and the Early Phase have given us the approximate time of the initial occupation of the Calvert site; yet they provide no information about the duration of the site occupation or the individual construction phases. To obtain a measure of the relative lengths of each occupational phase, we must turn to other types of data.

A number of researchers have demonstrated a correlation between the densities of wall posts and length of occupation on Iroquoian sites (Dodd 1984; Finlayson 1985). The underlying assumption is that Iroquoian houses required repair over time and such maintenance activity involved the installation of additional posts in house walls. This behaviour would be reflected in the archaeological record by an increase in post mould density on houses that remained in use for longer periods. To my knowledge, there is no source side ethnohistoric documentation of such activity, although it could be shown experimentally that the addition or replacement of posts is a viable method for repairing house walls. Such an experiment would not necessarily demonstrate a causal relationship between rebuilding and post density, since there may be other cultural factors that could explain variations in post density.

Calculations of wall post density on Early Iroquoian sites is complicated by the common occurrence of overlapping structures. While we have demonstrated that the structures at Calvert can be separated successfully into their various phases, it is often difficult to assign posts to specific houses in areas where walls overlap. This must be done through comparison of the nature and orientation of the intersecting walls, and many of the decisions made are rather arbitrary. A more troublesome problem is encountered when analyzing walls running through other structures and trying to determine whether additional posts near a wall are evidence of repair or simply interior posts associated with the underlying or overlying house. For this reason, Early Iroquoian post densities are less reliable than similar data from later Iroquoian sites.

Gary Warrick (1988) has attempted to quantify the relationship between wall post density and length of occupation. Using wood decay curves for different wood types and estimates of original house post densities, Warrick has translated post densities into time, within a specified error range. In constructing his model, Warrick calculated original post densities for a number of Iroquoian longhouses from Prehistoric, Protohistoric, and Historic Huron and Neutral sites. Average original post densities were then calculated for each group (Warrick 1988:44-45).

Application of this method requires knowledge of the type of wood used in house construction (i.e., cedar, pine, elm, oak, or hickory), and an accurate measurement of wall post density. To determine the length of occupation for any particular house, the wall post density is divided by the average post density for that group and the resulting ratio is plotted on the abscissa of the wood decay graph. The elapsed time is read off the ordinate at the intercept with the appropriate wood decay curve (ibid:38).

Warrick's results provide some confirmation of early historic accounts of Iroquoian village duration. He determined that most prehistoric Iroquoian village occupations lasted between 10 and 40 years, which agrees well with the early reports of Champlain (Sagard 1939). Using the Calvert site as one example, he also demonstrated that Early Iroquoian sites with multiple occupations may have been occupied for

Table 5.6. House post density data.

| House | Side/End | Wall Length | No. of Posts | Posts/metre |
|---|---|---|---|---|
| **Early Phase** | | | | |
| 14 | N | 5.8 | 35 | 6.03 |
| | S | 4.9 | 20 | 4.08 |
| | E | 17.9 | 83 | 4.64 |
| | W | 16.5 | 83 | 5.03 |
| | Total | 45.1 | 221 | 4.90 |
| 7 | N | 5.7 | 23 | 4.04 |
| | S | 4.4 | 20 | 4.55 |
| | E | 12.6 | 57 | 4.52 |
| | W | 13.3 | 55 | 4.14 |
| | Total | 36.0 | 155 | 4.31 |
| 3 | N | 10.0 | 52 | 5.20 |
| | S | 9.1 | 54 | 5.93 |
| | E | 6.9 | 42 | 6.09 |
| | W | 6.6 | 33 | 5.00 |
| | Total | 32.6 | 181 | 5.55 |
| 2 | N | 3.1 | 12 | 3.87 |
| | S | 3.3 | 14 | 4.24 |
| | E | 3.5 | 15 | 4.29 |
| | W | 3.6 | 15 | 4.17 |
| | Total | 13.5 | 56 | 4.15 |
| Early Total | | 127.2 | 613 | 4.82 |
| **Middle Phase** | | | | |
| 5 | N | 3.7 | 15 | 4.05 |
| | S | 1.7 | 12 | 7.06 |
| | E | 1.6 | 8 | 5.00 |
| | W | 5.3 | 27 | 5.09 |
| | Total | 12.3 | 62 | 5.04 |
| 6 | N | 15.8 | 77 | 4.87 |
| | S | 14.2 | 80 | 5.63 |
| | E | 5.6 | 25 | 4.46 |
| | W | 7.7 | 45 | 5.84 |
| | Total | 43.3 | 227 | 5.24 |
| 10 | N | 13.0 | 54 | 4.15 |
| | S | | | |
| | E | 2.4 | 13 | 5.42 |
| | W | | | |
| | Total | 15.4 | 67 | 4.35 |
| 12 | N | 9.1 | 28 | 3.08 |
| | S | 14.7 | 70 | 4.76 |
| | E | 9.5 | 23 | 2.42 |
| | W | 1.6 | 7 | 4.38 |
| | Total | 34.9 | 128 | 3.67 |
| Middle Total | | 105.9 | 484 | 4.57 |

Table 5.6 (continued).

| House | Side/End | Wall Length | No. of Posts | Post/metre |
|---|---|---|---|---|
| **Late Phase** | | | | |
| 8 | N | 4.9 | 18 | 3.67 |
| | S | 8.7 | 52 | 5.98 |
| | E | 3.3 | 15 | 4.55 |
| | W | | | |
| | Total | 16.9 | 85 | 5.03 |
| 11 | N | 8.3 | 34 | 4.10 |
| | S | 5.6 | 23 | 4.11 |
| | E | 8.0 | 36 | 4.50 |
| | W | 5.0 | 25 | 5.00 |
| | Total | 26.9 | 118 | 4.39 |
| 13 | N | 5.9 | 27 | 4.58 |
| | S | | | |
| | E | 5.1 | 21 | 4.12 |
| | W | | | |
| | Total | 11.0 | 48 | 4.36 |
| Late Total | | 54.8 | 251 | 4.58 |
| **Unknown Phase** | | | | |
| 1 | N | 7.1 | 41 | 5.77 |
| | S | 7.0 | 32 | 4.57 |
| | E | 9.1 | 62 | 6.81 |
| | W | 9.3 | 57 | 6.13 |
| | Total | 32.5 | 192 | 5.91 |
| 4 | N | 4.2 | 14 | 3.33 |
| | S | 3.7 | 15 | 4.05 |
| | E | 4.0 | 18 | 4.50 |
| | W | 5.8 | 21 | 3.62 |
| | Total | 17.7 | 68 | 3.84 |
| 9 | N | 7.6 | 37 | 4.87 |
| | Total | 7.6 | 37 | 4.87 |
| A | N | 4.6 | 19 | 4.13 |
| B | N | 7.9 | 31 | 3.92 |

about 50 years (Warrick 1988:51). Historic Iroquoian sites, in contrast, were shown to have occupation spans of 10-20 years, which are more in line with observations in the Jesuit Relations.

Warrick's research represents an important advance in the task of achieving temporal control over village occupations. One problematic aspect of his model, however, concerns the derivation and use of average original post densities. He recognizes staggered and straight walled structures and notes that, with staggered walls,

Table 5.7. House post densities and estimated length of occupation.

| Phase | House | Posts/ metre | Original Posts/m | Length of Occupation | Standard Deviation |
|-------|-------|--------------|------------------|----------------------|--------------------|
| Early | 14 | 4.90 | 3.60 | | |
| | 7 | 4.31 | 3.40 | | |
| | 3 | 5.55 | 4.20 | | |
| | Mean | 4.82 | 3.73 | 20 | 18-21 |
| Middle | 6 | 5.24 | 4.20 | | |
| | 10 | 4.35 | 3.70 | | |
| | 12 | 3.67 | 3.70 | | |
| | Mean | 4.57 | 3.83 | 17 | 16-19 |
| Late | 8 | 5.03 | 3.40 | | |
| | 11 | 4.39 | 4.00 | | |
| | 13 | 4.36 | 3.30 | | |
| | Mean | 4.58 | 3.57 | 19 | 17-21 |
| Unknown | 1 | 5.91 | 3.70 | 26 | |
| | 4 | 3.84 | 3.50 | 16 | |
| | 9 | 4.87 | 3.70 | 19 | |
| | A | 4.13 | 3.70 | 16 | |
| | B | 3.92 | 3.70 | 15 | |

original post patterns are easily determined by simple inspection. When walls are straight he opts to use the house with the lowest post density in the village, or the post density of the most recently constructed house, to determine original post density. The latter method may be a source of error, since considerable variation in house post density that is not related to occupation duration may be observed within any one village. However, much of this variation is captured by the standard deviation of Warrick's average original post densities.

Wall post densities for the Calvert site structures were calculated only for those areas in which the post pattern was reasonably clear and there were no obvious gaps in the walls. Care was taken not to assign any post to more than one structure. Each structure was analyzed individually and separate densities were calculated for each side wall and each end. The total wall length and total number of posts were then used to derive a mean post density per metre for each house side, for each house end, and for each house overall. These data are summarized in Table 5.6. Figures 5.9, 5.10, and 5.11 accurately depict the actual assignment of posts to structures.

The average wall post density calculated for each phase is presented in Table 5.6. The Early Phase has the highest density at 4.85 posts/m and the Middle and Late Phases are almost identical at 4.57 and 4.58 posts/m respectively. The values for all phases are so similar that they suggest that there

are no significant differences in the length of occupation of any of the phases at Calvert.

However, if we examine the range in post densities among the houses in each phase we will note significant variability. This is surprising, since we would expect houses of the same phase to have been occupied for a similar length of time and thus to have similar post densities. In fact, they do not. In the Early Phase, Houses 3 and 14 have a significantly higher post density than Houses 7 and 2. Likewise, Houses 6, 10, and 12 in the Middle Phase show divergent values, although they are believed to have been con-temporaneously occupied. These unexpected differences in post density suggest that other variables related to house design may be responsible for some of the observed variation in post densities. These include soil conditions, season of construction, labour available for construction, different structural plans, the planned function of the structure, and the economic or political status of the family for whom the house was built. It is also possible that some houses were simply occupied longer than others in the same phase.

Since the Calvert house post densities display some variability that we believe is not related to length of occupation, it would be inappropriate to employ the average original post density calculated by Warrick for prehistoric Neutral sites to determine estimates of occupation length for the Calvert houses. As an alternative, an attempt was made to calculate the original post density for each Calvert house. This was done by visual inspection of each house to determine if there was a section of low density, evenly spaced posts that could be interpreted as the original post pattern. In this manner, it was possible to derive original post

Table 5.8. Palisade post densities and estimated use-lives.

| Palisade Segment | Posts/ metre | Original Posts/m | Estimated Use-Life |
|---|---|---|---|
| 101 | 4.59 | 3.96 | 16-19 |
| 102 | 4.48 | 4.22 | 15-17 |
| 103 | 4.45 | 4.01 | 15-18 |
| 104 | 4.28 | 3.95 | 15-18 |

densities for eight of the Calvert houses (see Table 5.7). Houses for which individual post density could not be determined were assigned the average value of 3.7 ± .3 calculated for the first eight houses.

The original post density values for each house were then used to derive the estimates of occupation duration shown in Table 5.7. The cedar wood decay curve was used, based on the plausible assumption that most of the Calvert poles were cedar ones taken from the nearby Dorchester Swamp. A one sigma standard deviation was calculated for each mean length of occupation.

As expected, the resulting occupation spans are similar for all three phases of the site. The Early Phase range of 18-21 years is almost identical to the Late Phase range of 17-21 years, and the Middle Phase range of 16-19 years is only slightly shorter. Taken together, all phases suggest a cumulative occupation span of up to 60 years.

Using original post densities specific to the Calvert houses has effectively decreased the variation in use-life of houses within the same phase by recognizing that some houses had a higher original post density to begin with. House 3 in the Early Phase is a good example of this.

House 1, located outside the palisade, indicated the longest occupation span (21-30 years) as a result of its evidence for extensive repair. If it preceded the construction of the Early Phase it may have been used as a seasonally occupied cabin site, which may have required repairs after each period of abandonment. This noncontinuous pattern of occupation would result in a high post density that should not be attributed to a long term occupation.

Finally, Table 5.7 also provides occupation spans for problematical structures A and B. It is not known whether these are portions of houses or some other type of structure and they do not appear to be specifically associated with any of the three main occupations. Their post densities indicate that they have seen little repair and suggest maximum use-lives of only 15 years.

Palisade post densities were also calculated to determine if any substantial differences existed among palisade segments. Although palisade maintenance may be manifested archaeologically by the presence of replacement posts and thus may serve as a temporal index similar to house post densities, there is the added complication of defensive considerations in palisade construction. Increased defensive concerns could lead to construction of stronger palisades, with extra or larger posts, a phenomenon that is unrelated to time or maintenance.

These concerns aside, it was anticipated that Palisade Segment 104 might have the lowest post density, since the village contracted after the Early Phase, while Segment 102 was expected to have the highest density since it existed during both the Early and Middle Phases. The inner palisade 101 was expected to have a relatively high density since it was established during the Middle Phase and may have remained in use throughout the Late Phase.

Table 5.8 presents the actual post densities, estimated original post densities, and elapsed time for each palisade segment calculated using Warrick's cedar wood decay curve. All time estimates range between 15 and 18 years, suggesting that there are no significant differences in the use-lives of palisade segments. This is unexpected, since the sequence of palisade construction and use suggests that there **are** differences in the use-lives of some palisade segments (especially 102, 103, and 104). While the estimated duration of Palisades 104, 103, and 101 coincide well with the estimated duration of the Early, Middle, and Late Phases, Palisade Segment 102 would appear to be anomalous in not reflecting a longer use-life. Alternatively, these results may indicate that palisade post densities are not reliable indices of length of occupation. As palisades are generally built of larger poles than house walls, and are sturdier

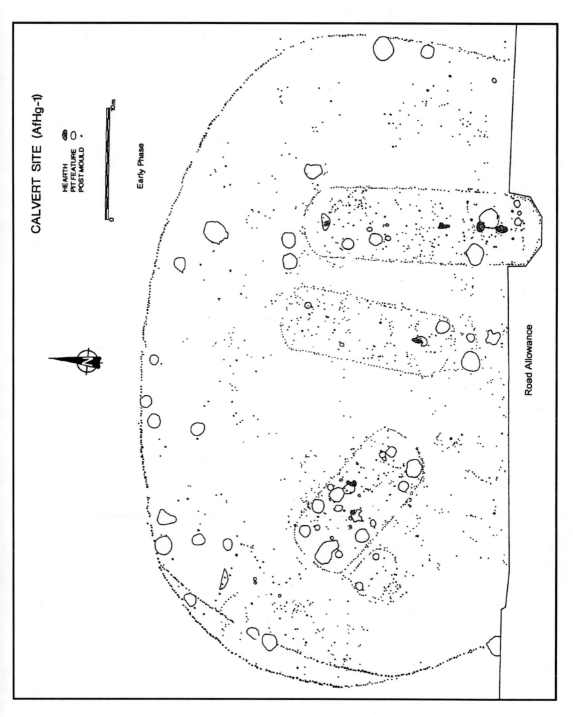

Figure 5.9. Early Phase settlement pattern.

structures to begin with, they may have required little maintenance.

# Summary of Occupational History

On the basis of the data analyzed in this chapter, it is possible to present a general reconstruction of the chronology of structure and feature use at the Calvert site. The sequence of construction phases is detailed in Figures 5.9, 5.10, and 5.11.

## House 1

The combination of stratigraphic, chronometric, and ceramic evidence strongly suggests that House 1 predates the main village occupation. If this interpretation is correct, the Calvert site may have been first used as a cabin site that was seasonally occupied on a short term basis for hunting, gathering, or tending crops. The post densities in this house indicate either a long period of use or seasonal re-use characterized by abandonment and repair.

The possibility remains that House 1 was occupied during the Middle and/or Late Phases. The alternate interpretations of House 1 are testable hypotheses that will be explored further in subsequent chapters through comparison of the House 1 data with data from the main village.

## The Early Phase

Figure 5.9 depicts the settlement pattern of the Early Phase of the Calvert site as reconstructed here. Stratigraphic evidence indicates that only the outer palisade, comprising Segments 102 and 104, existed during the Early occupation. This is a single row palisade, with the exception of a 25 metre section along its westerly boundary where it branches into a double row. The five metre long line of small posts at the south end of this doubled section is interpreted as a former entrance way. The posts in this area are uniformly 6.5 cm smaller in diameter than the other palisade posts in this wall, suggesting that this section was closed off at some point after the original palisade was built. Various other apparent gaps appear in the northern and eastern sections of the palisade, any of which may have served as alternate entrances.

Within this single row palisade stood at least four structures, Houses 7, 14, and 3, as well as the small Structure 2, which was probably not a dwelling. All of these structures may be placed early on stratigraphic grounds, as shown in Figure 5.3. A link between the westerly House 3 and Houses 7 and 14 on the east side of the site has been established through a ceramic cross-mend (Figure 5.5; Timmins 1992:Appendix B).

Houses 7 and 14 have been linked by cross-mends to a number of large exterior features located to the north and east of them. Other exterior features were surely in use during this phase, but we lack physical evidence to demonstrate this. On spatial grounds, all of the features lying between Palisade Segments 103 and 104 have been included in the Early Phase, although it is conceivable that some of them continued to be used in later phases of the site occupation. However, the fact that there are no ceramic cross-mends extending into this outer area from Middle or Late phase features does suggest that it was little used during the Middle and Late Phases.

House post densities for the Early Phase structures suggest that this period lasted for about 20 years, while a series of three averaged radiocarbon dates indicates a calendrical date in the late twelfth to early thirteenth century.

## The Middle Phase

The beginning of the Middle Phase is marked by the dismantling of Houses 2 and 3 and the construction of Palisade Segment 103, a modification to the community plan that resulted in a substantial contraction of village space (see Figure 5.10). Continuity in the occupation is suggested by the fact that Palisade 103 was built to join with the older Palisade 102. It is possible that Palisade 104 remained standing or the poles from Palisade 104 may have been pulled out and used to build Palisade 103.

The dismantling of Houses 2 and 3 was probably closely followed by the simultaneous dismantling of Houses 7 and 14 to make room for the construction of a series of three east-west oriented structures. Houses 6, 10, and 12 were built in a radial pattern with their west ends

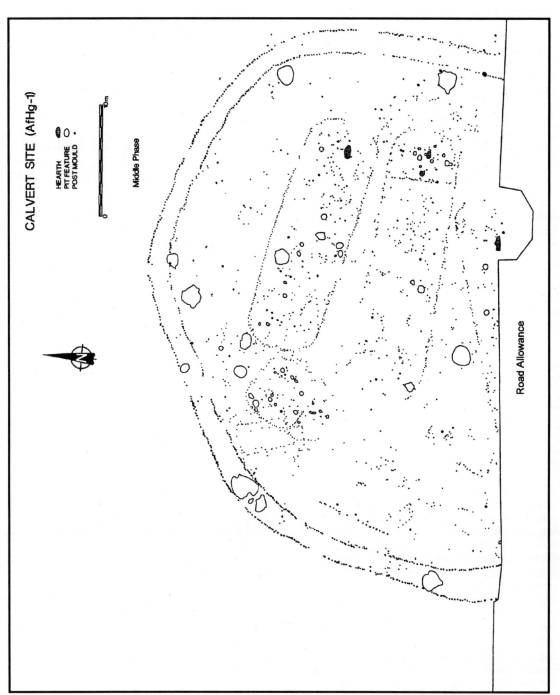

Figure 5.10. Middle Phase settlement pattern.

diverging and their east ends converging to within one metre of each other.

The wholesale rebuilding of all structures within the village could be viewed as evidence of a temporal gap between the Early and Middle Phases, during which the original houses had deteriorated to the point where they had to be torn down. However, no evidence of any substantial period of abandonment has been discovered in our analysis of the large stratified pit features, which appear to have been used over the long term. Specifically, the three features that have yielded cross-mended artifacts from different levels corresponding to the Early and Middle Phases do not display any sterile or low artifact density strata between the Early and Middle Phase deposits which might indicate a period of abandonment.

House 6 appears to be spatially associated with the small House 5, just slightly offset from its west end. These structures are also linked by ceramic cross-mends. This small structure/large structure association is almost identical to cases observed at the Glen Meyer Elliot and Dewaele sites (Fox 1976; 1986a), as well as the slightly later Uren site (M. Wright 1986).

House 5 also appears to be linked to the inner Palisade 101 by a house-to-palisade wall, which establishes the inner palisade as a Middle Phase structure. Some of the small structures at Elliot were rebuilt several times and there is some evidence to indicate that House 5 at Calvert may have been rebuilt as well. A curved line of posts overlapping the south end of House 5 can be easily discerned (Figure 5.10). This structure is also connected to the inner palisade with a house-to-palisade wall. The southern and eastern portions of this proposed structure are missing; they occur in that portion of the site where much settlement pattern was lost because of poor soil conditions (Fox: personal communication).

Stratigraphic and cross-mend evidence suggests that Palisade 101 was not built at the beginning of the Middle Phase but rather was constructed some time later during the Middle Phase. This is indicated by the superposition of the palisade on Feature 206, which, judging from the cross-mend evidence, appears to have distinct

strata that relate to both the Early and Middle Phases.

In sum, the Middle Phase community pattern involves a major contraction of the westerly palisade, together with the construction of three large east-west oriented houses. At some time during this period a second palisade was added parallel to and just inside the first one, and the small House 5 was constructed between House 6 and the new palisade. Post mould densities indicate that the houses of the Middle Phase were occupied for about 20 years. Continuity with the Early Phase occupation would place the Middle Phase in the early thirteenth century.

### The Late Phase

The large east-west oriented structures of the Middle Phase were eventually removed to make way for a series of smaller structures with a similar spatial orientation, marking the beginning of the Late Phase. Houses 8, 11, and 13 occupy the central and eastern portions of the site and all are placed late in the occupation sequence on the basis of strong stratigraphic evidence. The Late Phase settlement pattern is shown in Figure 5.11.

There is some evidence to support the presence of a single row palisade in the Late Phase. The post densities of Palisade 101 and Palisade 102/103 are quite similar, suggesting that they had use-lives of similar duration. However, we have noted that Palisade 101 was probably built after Palisade 102/103. If it was constructed midway through, or towards the end of, the Middle Phase it would certainly have lasted into the Late Phase, but perhaps not throughout it. It is also possible that House 5, or perhaps the rebuilt version of it, was present in the Late Phase as well. There is no evidence for any major discontinuity in occupation between the Middle and Late periods.

Unlike the earlier houses, the Late Phase structures are strongly interconnected by house-to-house cross-mends. On the other hand, there are few cross-mends in the final phase that link structures to large exterior features. The possible behavioural implications of these patterns are discussed in the following chapter.

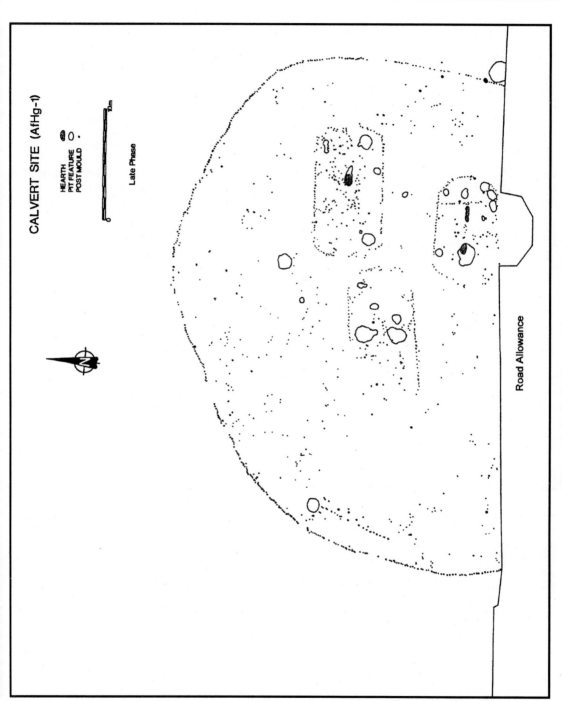

Figure 5.11. Late Phase settlement pattern.

In summary, the Late Phase of the Calvert site consisted of at least three small houses (8, 11, and 13), probably surrounded by a single row palisade for at least part of the occupation. House post densities suggest that the duration of this occupation was about 20 years. If there was continuity with the Middle Phase occupation, we would expect the Late Phase to date to the early to mid-thirteenth century.

## Problematic Structures

A number of structures, including House 4 and problematic Structures A and B, have not been assigned to a specific phase for various reasons. In the case of House 4, we know that it does not date to the Early Phase because of its superposition over House 3, yet there is no strong evidence to place it in either the Middle or Late period.

Structures A and B are both straight walls that could be sides of small houses, but, they are very incomplete, lacking opposite walls and ends. Unfortunately, they both occur in an area where three houses (14, 6, and 11) pertaining to all three phases already overlap, but they cannot be interpreted as intra-structural walls. This suggests that they cannot be contemporaneous with any of these structures. Structure B is superimposed on Early Phase Feature 9, suggesting that it, at least, probably postdates the Early Phase.

## Conclusions

The analysis presented in this chapter has been an attempt to impose order on a data base that resists such order. Insofar as the formation of the Calvert site was probably a fluid, ongoing process occurring over several decades, the attempt to structure the resulting archaeological data into a series of temporal phases may be at odds with the nature of the data.

The Calvert site represents the residue of the daily activities and decisions made by at least one and possibly two or three communities over the course of 50 to 60 years. During this time, pits were dug, used, abandoned, and sometimes reused, structures were modified, torn down, and rebuilt, and the village was entirely reorganized on at least three occasions. We have documented and discussed evidence to show that within a single phase certain structures or features were dismantled or abandoned in a complex sequence. To attempt to identify even the major episodes in the formation of a such a site is a daunting task, and it would be impossible to determine the precise sequence of every structure and deposit.

Nonetheless, we believe that we have struck a middle ground with the definition of the Early, Middle, and Late Phases at Calvert. The evidence suggests that these groupings of structures and features represent an authentic level of order within the conflated database. We have created a stratified sequence of structures and features from a largely unstratified deposit, and in doing this have formed distinct sets of settlement pattern, artifactual, and ecofactual data that represent subsets of the total Calvert data base.

Through the combination of chronometric data and indices of occupation duration we have estimated the position of the Calvert site on the calendrical time scale and the time spans involved in each occupational phase. The end result of the occupational history analysis is the realization that the Calvert site saw massive change in the course of its occupation. The reasons for this change have not yet been explored in detail. In the next two chapters we attempt to explain the observed changes through the analysis of the artifactual and ecofactual evidence relating to the economy and technology of the Calvert community.

# Chapter 6

# Domestic Life in the Calvert Community: Economy

## Introduction

Our analysis of occupational history has shown that the Calvert site underwent a series of dramatic changes over a span of several decades. We must now ask why these changes took place and whether they are reflected in other aspects of the Calvert data, including artifacts and ecofacts. This chapter examines the changing economy of the Calvert people through the description and interpretation of ecofactual remains.

The economic analysis involves the study of floral and faunal remains and catchment analysis. The aim is to describe the subsistence activities of the Calvert people during each phase and to determine if there is any substantive evidence of change in these activities through time. In doing this I will also attempt to resolve the questions of seasonality and site function for each occupational phase. It has been hypothesized that the Early and Middle phases at Calvert represent a semi-permanent year round village occupation while the Late phase represents a hunting camp (Fox 1982a). This proposal must be tested against the floral and faunal data. The role of House 1 also remains in question and the floral and faunal analysis may provide some insight into its function. Finally, the results of the analyses will be integrated with the environmental data presented in Chapter 4, leading to a discussion of the Calvert catchment area and how it may have changed through time.

## Faunal Analysis

A thorough analysis of the Calvert faunal material has been completed by Rosemary Prevec (Prevec 1984a). Prevec examined all of the bone excavated from all features as well as that recovered by flotation. Her report provided detailed information on faunal identifications, food resources, and human alterations such as heat exposure, butchering, and artifactual alteration. My discussion will emphasize the economic aspects of the faunal material using data drawn from Prevec's report.

## Faunal Identifications and Taxonomic Abundance

The faunal identifications resulting from Prevec's analysis of the entire faunal sample are summarized in Tables 6.1 through 6.6. Table 6.1 provides the distribution by class which shows the dominance of mammalian elements (92.3%), followed by fish (3.77%), and very small samples of avian, reptilian, pelecypoda, and gastropoda elements. Table 6.2 provides the breakdown of the mammalian specimens by taxon. These data clearly reveal the dominance of white-tailed deer (90.81%) and the significant occurrence of other medium to large mammals, including raccoon (2.27%), bear (1.67%), and beaver (1.06%). Among the fish the sucker family (Catostomidae) was the clear favourite. Suckers of the genus *Catostomus* made up 46.08% of the sample, while an additional 34.92% were identified only to the sucker family (Table 6.3). Wild turkey (73.79%) appears to be the most common avian species represented but the sample is skewed by the presence of a nearly complete individual (Table 6.4). All percentages given above are the percentage of the total number of specimens identified to below class (the sub-totals in Tables 6.2 to 6.4). While these data give us an indication of the fauna exploited by the Calvert people, they do not tell us what we want to know, namely, whether the subsistence activities at Calvert changed from phase to phase.

For the purposes of the present study it was necessary to sub-divide the faunal sample into smaller aggregates corresponding to each occupational phase. At the time the faunal analysis was conducted the separation of features into occupational phases was not complete and these data could not be included in Prevec's report. The separation was done by the writer and involved entering the faunal data into a

Table 6.1. Faunal findings by zoological class.

| Class | House 1 | Early | Middle | Late | Unassigned | Total |
|---|---|---|---|---|---|---|
| Mammalia | 868 | 6886 | 5746 | 10864 | 19617 | 43981 |
| Osteichthyes | - | 274 | 345 | 25 | 1153 | 1797 |
| Aves | 1 | 41 | 56 | 16 | 68 | 182 |
| Reptilia | - | 3 | 9 | 8 | 51 | 71 |
| Pelecypoda | - | - | - | - | 19 | 19 |
| Gastropoda | - | - | - | - | 1 | 1 |
| Class uncertain | - | - | - | - | 1597 | 1597 |
| Total | 869 | 7204 | 6156 | 10913 | 22506 | 47648 |

Table 6.2. Mammalian specimen identification.

| Taxon | House 1 | Early | Middle | Late | Unassigned | Total |
|---|---|---|---|---|---|---|
| Short-tailed Shrew | - | - | - | 1 | - | 1 |
| Hairytail Mole | - | - | - | 6 | - | 6 |
| Eastern Cottontail | - | - | 3 | - | 10 | 13 |
| Family Leporidae | - | 3 | 1 | - | 7 | 11 |
| Eastern Chipmunk | - | 17 | 6 | 4 | 25 | 52 |
| Woodchuck | 2 | 1 | 3 | 3 | - | 9 |
| Grey/Black Squirrel | - | - | - | 1 | 15 | 16 |
| Red Squirrel | - | - | - | 1 | 1 | 2 |
| American Beaver | - | 12 | 14 | 5 | 65 | 96 |
| Mouse | - | - | 1 | - | 6 | 7 |
| Muskrat | - | 1 | - | 2 | 2 | 5 |
| Meadow Vole | - | 2 | 1 | - | 9 | 12 |
| American Porcupine | - | 2 | - | 1 | - | 3 |
| Family Canidae | - | - | - | - | 2 | 2 |
| Grey Fox | - | - | - | 1 | - | 1 |
| American Black Bear | 3 | 9 | 9 | 95 | 36 | 152 |
| Raccoon | 7 | 31 | 14 | 129 | 25 | 206 |
| American Marten | - | - | 3 | - | 16 | 19 |
| Fisher | - | - | - | - | 1 | 1 |
| Striped Skunk | 1 | - | - | - | - | 1 |
| River Otter | - | - | 2 | 15 | 2 | 19 |
| Family Mustelidae | - | 3 | - | - | - | 3 |
| Bobcat | - | - | 1 | 35 | 1 | 37 |
| Order Carnivora | - | 1 | 2 | 9 | 10 | 22 |
| White-tailed Deer | 47 | 2119 | 1020 | 1919 | 3153 | 8258 |
| Family Cervidae | - | 14 | 60 | 20 | 46 | 140 |
| Sub-total | 60 | 2215 | 1140 | 2247 | 3432 | 9094 |
| Unidentified Mammal | 808 | 4671 | 4606 | 8617 | 16185 | 34887 |
| Total | 868 | 6886 | 5746 | 10864 | 19617 | 43981 |

Table 6.3. Fish specimen identification.

| Taxon | House 1 | Early | Middle | Late | Unassigned | Total |
|---|---|---|---|---|---|---|
| Lake Sturgeon | - | - | - | - | 2 | 2 |
| Bowfin | - | - | 2 | - | - | 2 |
| Lake Whitefish | - | - | 2 | 4 | 22 | 28 |
| Salvelinus sp. | - | 1 | - | - | - | 1 |
| Family Salmonidae | - | 4 | - | 1 | 1 | 6 |
| Family Cyprinidae | - | 1 | - | - | 6 | 7 |
| Longnose Sucker | - | - | - | - | 1 | 1 |
| Catostomus sp. | - | 12 | 124 | - | 281 | 417 |
| Golden Redhorse | - | - | 56 | - | 21 | 77 |
| Family Catostomidae | - | 181 | 20 | 8 | 107 | 316 |
| Brown Bullhead | - | 1 | - | - | 3 | 4 |
| Channel Catfish | - | 1 | 1 | - | 1 | 3 |
| Family Ictaluridae | - | 7 | - | - | 4 | 11 |
| Yellow Perch | - | 2 | - | - | - | 2 |
| Rock Bass | - | - | - | - | 9 | 9 |
| Largemouth Bass | - | 1 | - | - | - | 1 |
| Micropterus sp. | - | - | 4 | - | 2 | 6 |
| Walleye | - | 1 | - | - | 5 | 6 |
| Stizostedion sp. | - | 1 | - | - | 2 | 3 |
| Family Percidae | - | - | - | - | 1 | 1 |
| Pike | - | - | - | 2 | - | 2 |
| SUB-TOTAL | 0 | 213 | 209 | 15 | 468 | 905 |
| Unidentified Fish | 0 | 61 | 136 | 10 | 685 | 892 |
| TOTAL | 0 | 274 | 345 | 25 | 1153 | 1797 |

approach circumvents the major problem of specimen interdependence that plagues NISP counts, but detailed studies of the characteristics of MNI counts in archaeological analyses have indicated that they are potentially more problematic than NISP counts (Grayson 1984:17-92). The major difficulty with the use of the MNI is that it is closely related to sample size. These problems become particularly acute when a faunal sample is sub-divided into smaller samples for comparative analysis, as I propose to do with the Calvert sample. As Grayson states:

"The simple operational definition of minimum numbers glosses over the crucial stage in defining those numbers: the definition of the clusters of faunal material from which minimum numbers are defined. ...the numerical values of minimum numbers of individuals vary with the way in which faunal material from a given site is divided into those smaller aggregates. Not only will the use of different approaches to aggregation change the calculated minimum numbers, but these changes in abundance will probably occur differentially across taxa. ...There are no such difficulties with specimen counts" (Grayson 1984: 29).

DBASE III+ file, sorting it by phase, and translating the data into a Lotus format for further numerical manipulation. The primary purpose of this analysis was to attempt to quantify taxonomic abundance among the different phases and thus enable their comparison. For this reason, only information on species and the number of identified specimens (NISP) was recorded.

The problems of quantifying taxonomic abundance using NISP have been recognized for several years. They include the 'schlepp' effect, which results from the differential transport of body parts from the kill site to the base camp (White 1953), the fact that the number of identifiable elements varies from species to species (Grayson 1984), the effects of butchering and processing techniques and of differential preservation (Chaplin 1971), and the lack of independence among the units being counted (Grayson 1984). The latter problem refers to the fact that we have no way of knowing how many bones in any given assemblage came from the same individual, yet the assumption is made that NISP is representative of the entire population.

Faunal analysts responded to these problems by calculating the minimum number of individuals (MNI) represented in the assemblage, a measure that is usually based on counting the most abundant single element for each species in the faunal sample (White 1953). This

Grayson's analysis of the relationship between

Table 6.4. Avian specimen identification.

| Taxon | House 1 | Early | Middle | Late | Unassigned | Total |
|---|---|---|---|---|---|---|
| Family Anatidae | - | - | 5 | 1 | - | 6 |
| Family Accipitridae | - | - | - | - | 2 | 2 |
| Family Tetraonidae | - | 4 | - | - | 2 | 6 |
| Wild Turkey | 1 | 13 | 40 | 11 | 11 | 76 |
| Passenger Pigeon | - | - | 1 | 1 | 1 | 3 |
| Barred Owl | - | - | - | - | 1 | 1 |
| Sapsucker | - | - | - | - | 1 | 1 |
| Carolina Parakeet | - | - | - | - | 3 | 3 |
| Bunting | - | 1 | - | - | 4 | 5 |
| SUB-TOTAL | 1 | 18 | 46 | 13 | 25 | 103 |
| Unidentified Avian | 0 | 23 | 10 | 3 | 43 | 79 |
| TOTAL | 1 | 41 | 56 | 16 | 68 | 182 |

Table 6.5. Reptilian specimen identification.

| Taxon | House 1 | Early | Middle | Late | Unassigned | Total |
|---|---|---|---|---|---|---|
| Snapping Turtle | - | - | 3 | 3 | 21 | 27 |
| Spotted Turtle | - | - | - | - | 1 | 1 |
| Painted Turtle | - | 1 | 1 | 1 | 14 | 17 |
| Blanding's Turtle | - | - | - | 1 | 1 | 2 |
| Pond or Marsh Turtle | - | - | 2 | 2 | 11 | 15 |
| Turtle, unidentified | - | 2 | 3 | - | 3 | 8 |
| Garter Snake | - | - | - | 1 | - | 1 |
| TOTAL | 0 | 3 | 9 | 8 | 51 | 71 |

Table 6.6. Pelecypod specimen identification.

| Taxon | No. of Identified Shells | % of Identified Shells | % of Total Excavated Shells |
|---|---|---|---|
| *Elliptio dilatatus* | 1 | 5.3 | 5.3 |
| *Elliptio* sp. | 1 | 5.3 | 5.3 |
| *Lampsilis radiata* | 1 | 5.3 | 5.3 |
| *Lampsilis ventricosa* | 1 | 5.3 | 5.3 |
| Spheridae | 1 | 5.3 | 5.3 |
| Unionidae | 14 | 73.6 | 73.6 |
| Total | 19 | 100.1 | 100.1 |

NISP and MNI demonstrates that MNI can be 'tightly predicted' from NISP counts and concludes that the number of identified specimens per taxon (NISP) is not only more easily obtained, but is also the best unit available for measuring the relative abundance of taxa in faunal assemblages (1984:62,92). Accordingly, the following comparison of taxonomic abundance among the phases at Calvert is based on NISP counts.

As the MNI was not used, no attempt was made to estimate meat weights for any of the faunal classes. As Prevec notes, meat weight

based on the MNI yields a minimal amount of information, and there is no doubt that "deer was the main meat of the Calvert people" (Prevec 1984a:-22).

## Faunal Remains by Zoological Class

Table 6.1 presents the phase by phase breakdown of faunal remains by zoological class and Tables 6.2 through 6.5 present the phase by phase frequencies of individual species within each class. The data summarized in these tables are crucial to understanding the subsistence economy of the Calvert people. Figure 6.1 shows the location of the features discussed in the faunal and floral analyses.

Based on the figures presented in Table 6.1, mammals make of 95.6% and 93.3% of the Early and Middle phase samples respectively. These figures contrast with the Late phase which has mammalian representation of 99.6% and House 1, where mammals make up 99.9% of the sample. The difference between the Early and Middle phase samples compared to those from House 1 and the Late phase lies mainly in the quantity of fish present. Fish comprise 3.8% and 5.6% of the Early and Middle phase samples, respectively, but make up only .2% of the Late phase sample and are absent in House 1.

Birds also appear to be under-represented in House 1 and the Late phase, yet

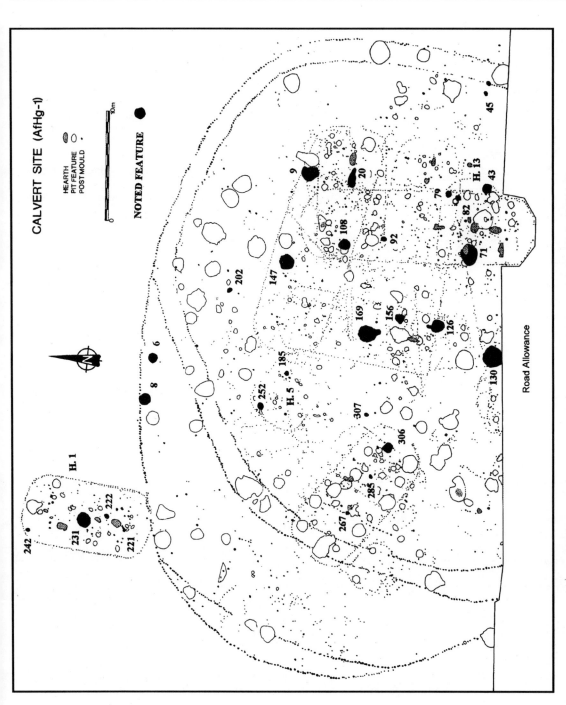

Figure 6.1. Location of features discussed in floral and faunal analyses.

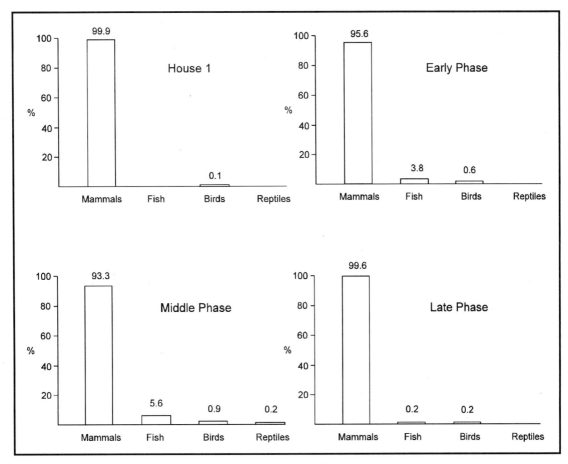

Figure 6.2. Comparison of faunal remains by class.

sample sizes are small, exerting a negative effect on the use of NISP counts. For example, 40 of the Middle phase avian bones are from a single wild turkey. Given the small sample size, they have the effect of tripling the NISP count for the Middle phase, giving the impression that there are many more birds represented in the Middle phase than in the Late phase. In fact, the Middle and Late phase counts for birds are similar, while the Early phase appears to have a genuinely higher percentage of birds.

The differences in the faunal samples among the three phases and House 1 are shown in Figure 6.2, which is a series of histograms based on faunal percentages by class. The changes from House 1 through the Early, Middle and Late phase samples indicate changes in subsistence patterns. House 1 is dominated by mammal remains, suggesting a focus on mammal hunting. The Early and Middle phases show a shift to a 'broad spectrum' pattern of hunting and fishing, while the Late phase faunal remains indicate a return to a focus on mammal hunting augmented by very limited fishing. These data lend strong support to the interpretation of a hunting camp function for both House 1 and the Late phase. This interpretation is strengthened when we examine the range of species within each class.

## Mammals

Table 6.2 shows the breakdown of identified mammal taxa on a phase by phase basis. The number of identified taxa increases from a low of 5 in House 1, to 13 in the Early phase, 15 in the Middle phase, and 17 in the Late phase. However, this apparent increase in diversity may be misleading, as the low number of identified taxa in House 1 is undoubtedly related to the small sample size. Moreover, the 17 Late phase taxa include short-tailed shrew and hairytail mole, neither of which were economically important.

While there do not seem to be great changes in species diversity from phase to phase, there is some variation in the frequency of white-tailed deer. The percentage of white-tailed deer is only 78.3% in House 1, increases to 95.7% in the Early phase, drops to 89.5% in the Middle phase, and decreases again, to 85.4%, in the Late phase. While the House 1 percentage may again reflect the small sample size, the decrease in deer in the Late phase may relate to increased hunting of other mammals. As Table 6.2 shows, bear, raccoon and bobcat are all well represented in the Late phase sample.

Several large refuse pit features assigned to the Late phase occur within houses (Figures 6.1 and 7.15). Many of these pits yielded large quantities of faunal material, and some produced a surprising variety of species. Feature 156 in House 11 contained deer, raccoon, muskrat, and otter, as well as a range of non-mammals, including garter snake (burnt), turtle, and sucker. Feature 79, in House 13, contained the almost complete skeletons of a deer, a bear, a bobcat, and two raccoons (Prevec 1984a:44). Prevec notes that it is unusual to find such complete skeletons and speculates about a possible ceremonial function for the animals in this feature (ibid:45). It did, however, contain a normal range of artifactual debris and may simply represent the remains of a highly successful hunting expedition. Two of the bobcat bones showed evidence of skinning and a number of the bear bones had been butchered. While the presence of these nearly intact skeletons has doubtless inflated the NISP count for the Late phase, this does not make their appearance less culturally significant, and the focal emphasis on mammal hunting cannot be denied.

More evidence of successful Late phase hunting expeditions comes from Feature 169, which is located across from Feature 156 in House 8 (Figure 6.1). This pit yielded one of the largest faunal assemblages on the site - 1,936 pieces, including parts of at least seven deer mainly represented by leg bones and vertebrae (Prevec 1984a:44). This may be evidence of the schlepp effect, whereby deer were initially butchered at the kill site, with the legs, meat, and hide brought back to the camp for processing. A similar pattern was noted by Williamson at the Yaworski site, a fall-winter hunting camp (1985:206).

Feature 20, in the centre of House 11 (Figure 6.1), yielded 1,311 bone fragments most of which were calcined. It is significant that all of the Late phase structures containing Features 156, 169, 79, and 20 are connected through ceramic cross-mends, indicating their contemporaneous use (Figure 7.15).

Late phase features were not the only ones that yielded large faunal samples. Several Early and Middle phase pits contained evidence for more than one deer. These are listed in Table 6.7 together with the NISP of deer, the minimum number of deer represented, and the element used for determining MNI.

## Fish

Turning to identified fish taxa, there are no fish identified from House 1 and we find the greatest variety of fish in the Early phase, where 12 taxa are represented. This drops to seven taxa in the Middle phase, and to four taxa in the Late phase. These changes in diversity may well be a function of sample size, since diversity increases with sample size and the Early and Middle phases have much larger samples of fish remains than the other phases (Grayson 1984:166). Overall, the data indicate the dominance of the sucker family (Catostomidae) during the Early and Middle phases. Suckers make up 90.6% of the identified Early phase sample and 95.7% of the Middle phase sample.

Some of the fish remains are from very small fish that would probably have been caught by netting (Prevec 1984a). They are primarily found in Early phase features and would likely have

Table 6.7. Features with multiple deer.

| Feature | Phase | NISP | MNI | Determining Element |
|---------|-------|------|-----|---------------------|
| 31 | Middle | 88 | 2 | Right Talus |
| 117 | Middle | 28 | 2 | Left Talus |
| 130 | Unassigned | 103 | 2 | Right Tarsal |
| 148 | Unassigned | 344 | 2 | Right Talus |
| 151 | Early | 519 | 2 | Right Talus |
| 161 | Middle | 121 | 2 | Right Metatarsal |
| 207 | Middle | 367 | 2 | Left Talus |
| 258 | Middle | 207 | 2 | Left Tibia |
| 312 | Middle | 131 | 2 | Right Tibia |
| 71 | Early | 53 | 2 | Left Talus |
| 190 | Middle | 140 | 2 | Right Talus |
| 147 | Early | 256 | 3 | Axis |
| 156 | Late | 262 | 3 | Right Talus |
| 209 | Early | 371 | 3 | Right Talus |
| 236 | Early | 39 | 3 | Left Tibia |
| 306 | Early | 106 | 3 | Right Ulna |
| 315 | Unassigned | 163 | 3 | Left Humerus |
| 169 | Late | 660 | 7 | Left Humerus, Right Femora |

been available both in the Thames River and Dorchester Swamp Creek throughout the warm months of the year.

Fishing was obviously not a crucial subsistence activity for the Calvert people, although it provided variety in the diet, especially in the Early and Middle phases (Prevec 1984a:22). The higher percentage of fish in the Early and Middle phases is an important aspect of the broad spectrum subsistence strategy associated with a more sedentary, full-fledged village settlement. In short, the Calvert people would have been present in the spring and fall when certain fish made their spawning runs up the Thames River and possibly into Dorchester Swamp Creek. If occupations were intermittent, and the economic focus was on mammal hunting, these fish runs would not have been exploited, which appears to be the case with House 1 and the Late phase.

## Birds

As noted previously, birds are poorly represented at Calvert and must have formed a very small part of the diet. As Table 6.4 shows, only one taxon is represented in House 1 and there are three taxa represented in each of the Early, Middle and Late phases.

The overall sample, which includes those features not identified to a specific phase, contains the remains of two unusual avian species (Table 6.4). The first of these

is a bald or golden eagle (Family Accipitridae), which is rarely seen during its spring-fall migrations in southwestern Ontario today (Prevec 1984a:53). A single middle phalanx from a foot was recovered.

The second unusual find was from Feature 285 and included parts of the head, wing, and tail of a Carolina parakeet in association with a complete stone pipe bowl, a slate knife, and an antler prong tool. The Carolina parakeet has been extinct since the 1930s and is found far north of its usual range on the Calvert site. It was North America's only breeding parrot and was widely sought for its colourful plumage and for use as a caged bird (Prevec 1984b). The discovery of the Carolina parakeet at Calvert has been discussed in detail by Prevec (1984b), and the symbolic implications of the parakeet bones and associated artifacts have been reviewed by von Gernet and Timmins (1987 - see also Chapter 9).

## Reptiles

Table 6.5 summarizes the reptilian taxa that occur at Calvert. In economic terms, the turtles were obviously the most important species and would have augmented the food supply. Of the several species represented, the snapping turtle is the most common. It is the largest of these species and may have been sought more often for this reason. Reptiles are absent in House 1, but there are no notable differences in reptilian representation among the three later phases.

## Butchering Evidence

Butchering evidence is summarized here in the hope that it may aid in the later interpretation of features and activity areas. According to Prevec, evidence of cutting, chopping, or scraping was located on 295 bones. The assemblage of butchered elements includes 276 white-tailed deer bones, six raccoon bones, five bear bones, two bobcat bones, one otter bone, one of the deer family, and three

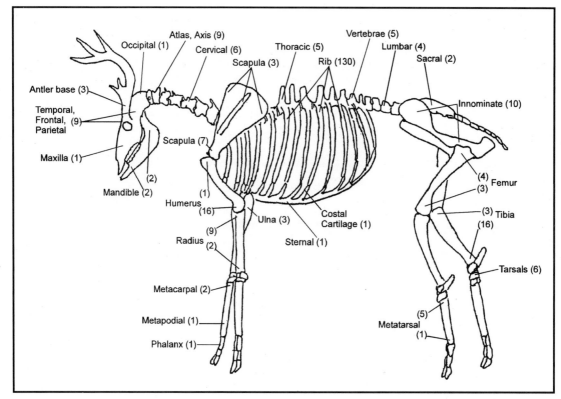

Figure 6.3. Location and number of butchering marks on white-tailed deer skeleton (after Prevec 1984a).

bones that were identified only as mammal (Prevec 1984a:26).

Figure 6.3 shows the location and number of butchering marks found on white-tailed deer. Many of these cuts are located near joints and were for disarticulation, but some (n=17) were for skinning (Prevec 1984a:26-30). Interestingly, the largest number of marks (n=130) were striae found on the inner surface of deer rib bones, running parallel to the rib length. They may be from scraping the inside of the chest cavity during cleaning (ibid.). Alternatively, it may be that deer rib bones served some function that is not presently understood and that these marks are in fact a wear pattern.

Prevec notes that two of the butchered raccoon bones are tail vertebrae indicating that tails were cut off, probably to be used as decoration.

Several features produced bones from specific body parts and these may be indicative of the spatial distribution of butchering activities. We have already discussed the dominance of leg bones in Feature 169 and the indications of major butchering events in the Late phase houses. Of particular interest is the distribution of features that contain only deer foot or head and foot bones. These would normally be removed early in the butchering sequence and might be expected to be deposited near the location of the initial processing (if they were not removed at the kill site). Features yielding head and foot bones, or foot bones only, are listed in Table 6.8 and their locations are shown in Figure 6.1. They include Early phase Feature 6, located near Palisade 104, Features 219, 221, 222, 231, and 241 in House 1, and Features 252 and 185 in the enigmatic House 5. These data indicate that initial butchering activities were probably carried out within Houses 1 and 5. There is also a tendency for head

Table 6.8. Features with deer
head and foot, or deer foot bones.

| Head and Feet | Feet |
|---|---|
| Feature 5 | Feature 82 |
| 6 | 165 |
| 24 | 185 |
| 65 | 219 |
| 71 | 221 |
| 88 | 231 |
| 116 | 286 |
| 137 | 307 |
| 182 | |
| 202 | |
| 217 | |
| 222 | |
| 241 | |
| 252 | |
| 267 | |

These features lack other identified deer elements
but may contain other species.

or foot bones to be found alone in very small pits
associated with other features (i.e., Features 221,
222, 252, 185, 202, 267, 82). The reason for
differential treatment of deer head and foot bones
is not known.

### Summary

In sum, a phase by phase analysis of the
faunal remains from Calvert indicates a strategy
based primarily on mammal hunting in House 1,
followed by a shift to a broad spectrum hunting
and fishing pattern in the Early and Middle
phases, and a return to a focus on mammal
hunting in the Late phase. The main evidence for
these changes is the lack of fish remains in House
1 features and the scarcity of fish in the Late
phase. A decrease in the intensity of deer hunting
in the Late phase was also inferred. Thus, while
hunting was a dominant activity in the final phase
and white-tailed deer continued to be the
principal prey, other species were taken more
often. Further evidence for the Late phase
hunting focus is found in several features that
yielded large faunal samples, a diversity of
mammals, and some almost complete butchered
animals. Other features appeared to have been
affected by the schlepp effect.

The presence of five features containing deer
head and foot elements in House 1 strongly
suggests that deer were being butchered in the
house, and the meat taken elsewhere. This
supports the specialized hunting camp
interpretation of House 1 and also has seasonality
implications, as deer would only be butchered
inside during cold weather. Similarly, the
presence of two features with only deer head and
foot bones in House 5 suggests the presence of a
special butchering area within this small structure.

## Floral Analysis

### Methodology and Sampling

Unlike the faunal assemblage which was
analyzed in its entirety, only a portion of the
flotation residue could be analyzed for floral
remains due to cost constraints. Of the 222
features excavated at Calvert, flotation samples
were taken from 102. These were initially
processed by volunteers from the Ontario
Archaeological Society. On the advice of Dr.
Gary Crawford of Erindale College all samples
were re-processed by the writer using a solution
of sodium bicarbonate and water to increase the
recovery of carbonized remains. This procedure
effectively doubled the light fraction residue
weight from most samples and is recommended
as a useful method of increasing flotation
recovery rates.

A total of 58 light fraction samples were
submitted to Glenna Ounjian for paleoethnobotanical analysis. Two samples were
submitted to Rudy Fecteau, specifically for
carbonized wood analysis. Twenty-nine samples
were initially submitted as data for Ounjian's
Master's thesis and an additional 29 were
analyzed for the writer at a later date. The results
of the latter analysis were summarized in a report
by Ounjian (1988), while raw data on the first 29
samples were made available to the writer in table
form. For the present analysis I have integrated
both data sets and broken the data down on a
phase by phase basis.

The initial set of Ounjian's samples was
selected based mainly on the quantity of
carbonized material since past experience had
demonstrated that large samples were likely to
contain the most floral remains. When the second
set of samples was chosen, I departed from this
procedure and selected samples from a variety of

Table 6.9. Plant remains in numbers by phase.

| Taxon | House 1 | Early | Middle | Late | Total |
|---|---|---|---|---|---|
| Cultigens | | | | | |
| Maize kernels (*Zea mays*) | 15 | 477 | 69 | 282 | 843 |
| Maize cupules (*Zea mays*) | 16 | 894 | 165 | 124 | 1199 |
| Bean (*Phaseolus vulgaris*) | - | - | 1 | - | 1 |
| Squash (*Cucurbita pepo*) | 2 | 6 | 1 | 17 | 26 |
| Sunflower (*Helianthus annuus*) | - | 3 | - | 3 | 6 |
| Tobacco (*Nicotiana rustica*) | - | 10 | 2 | 7 | 19 |
| Sub-total | 33 | 1390 | 238 | 433 | 2094 |
| Grains/Greens | | | | | |
| Maple-leaved Goosefoot (*Chenopodium hybridum*) | - | 2 | - | 1 | 3 |
| White Goosefoot (*Chenopodium berlandieri*) | - | 18 | 2 | 5 | 25 |
| Crabgrass (*Digitaria* sp.) | - | 1 | - | 105 | 106 |
| Knotweed (*Polygonum* sp.) | - | 15 | 14 | 9 | 38 |
| Waterpepper (*Polygonum hydropiper*) | - | - | 1 | - | 1 |
| Panic Grass (*Panicum* sp.) | - | 13 | 6 | 17 | 36 |
| Purslane (*Portulaca oleracea*) | - | 32 | 9 | 22 | 63 |
| Wheat Grass (*Agropyron* sp.) | 3 | 6 | 4 | - | 13 |
| Wild Rye (*Elymus* sp.) | - | 2 | - | - | 2 |
| Unidentified Grasses | 10 | 14 | 10 | 1 | 35 |
| Unknown Grass | - | 7 | 1 | 5 | 13 |
| Sub-total | 13 | 110 | 47 | 165 | 335 |
| Fleshy Fruits | | | | | |
| Black Nightshade (*Solanum nigrum*) | - | 45 | 96 | 23 | 164 |
| Blueberry (*Vaccinium* sp.) | - | - | - | 1 | 1 |
| Bramble (*Rubus* sp.) | 8 | 49 | 43 | 60 | 160 |
| Elderberry (*Sambucus canadensis*) | - | - | 2 | - | 2 |
| Grape (*Vitis* sp.) | - | - | - | 1 | 1 |
| Hawthorn (*Crataegus* sp.) | - | 7 | 2 | 9 | 18 |
| Strawberry (*Fragaria* sp.) | 6 | 44 | 5 | 33 | 88 |
| Sub-total | 14 | 145 | 148 | 127 | 434 |

feature types and from different areas of the village to get full spatial and chronological representation. It was difficult to get equal representation from all phases since there were, by chance, few features from the Middle phases and House 1 from which flotation samples had been taken. In the end, the analyzed sample included:

1. fourteen Early phase samples from 13 features with an aggregate weight of 349.60 g;
2. five Middle phase samples from five features, with an aggregate weight of 108.29 g;
3. nine Late phase samples from nine features, with an aggregate weight of 430.39 g;
4. two samples from two House 1 features, with a total weight of 186.17 g; and
5. single samples from House 1 and the Early phase that were analyzed for wood charcoal.

Since the variety and quantity of floral remains recovered is affected by differential preservation and sample size, it is extremely difficult to compare the different phases and to estimate their dietary composition. The quantification and interpretation of floral remains in terms of their contribution to the overall subsistence economy is an ongoing problem in paleoethnobotany (Ford 1982; Munson et al. 1971; Yarnell 1982; Miksicek 1987). For the

Table 6.9 (continued).

| Taxon | House 1 | Early | Middle | Late | Total |
|---|---|---|---|---|---|
| Other Taxa | | | | | |
| Cleavers (*Galium* sp.) | 6 | 32 | 9 | 5 | 52 |
| Buttercup family (Ranunculaceae) | - | 1 | - | - | 1 |
| Composite family (Compositae) | - | 6 | - | 1 | 7 |
| Sedge (*Carex* sp.) | - | 3 | - | 1 | 4 |
| Sedge family (Cyperaceae) | - | 1 | 2 | 1 | 4 |
| Milkweed (*Asclepias* sp.) | 1 | 7 | - | 6 | 14 |
| Flax (*Linum* sp.) | 1 | 1 | 1 | - | 3 |
| Sumac (*Rhus typhina*) | 6 | 83 | 40 | 555 | 684 |
| Vervain (*Verbina* sp.) | - | - | - | 1 | 1 |
| Violet (*Viola* sp.) | - | - | - | 1 | 1 |
| Foamflower (*Tiarella cordifolia*) | - | - | 1 | 1 | 2 |
| Sea Lavender (*Limonium nashii*) | - | - | - | 1 | 1 |
| Cat-tail (*Typha* sp.) | 43 | 773 | 326 | 2162 | 3304 |
| Evening Primrose (*Oenothera* sp.) | - | 1 | - | - | 1 |
| Miterwort (*Mitella* sp.) | - | 1 | - | - | 1 |
| Rose family (Rosaceae) | - | 3 | - | - | 3 |
| Vetch (*Vicia* sp.) | - | 1 | - | - | 1 |
| Unidentified Seeds | 12 | 117 | 37 | 78 | 244 |
| Unknown Seeds | 1 | 15 | 9 | 7 | 32 |
| Sub-total | 70 | 1045 | 425 | 2820 | 4360 |
| Other Plant Remains | | | | | |
| Bud (unknown woody plant) | - | 2 | - | - | 2 |
| Horsetail stem (*Equisetum* sp.) | - | 4 | 3 | 1 | 8 |
| Peduncle (unknown) | 1 | 1 | - | - | 2 |
| Thirn (unknown) | - | 1 | - | 1 | 2 |
| Tuber (unknown) | 2 | - | 14 | 1 | 17 |
| Whole Dried Fruit (unknown fleshy fruit) | - | 1 | - | - | 1 |
| Sub-total | 3 | 9 | 17 | 3 | 32 |
| Total Plant Remains | 133 | 2699 | 875 | 3548 | 7255 |
| Total Sample Volume (litres) | 72 | 402 | 88 | 247 | 809 |

purpose of the present study, both plant and seed counts were used as guides to relative abundance, although plant food weight is taken to be a better measure of economic importance. The plant remains in each phase may be compared by reducing them to seeds per litre of soil (Miksicek 1987:238), but even this method can be unreliable without a systematic method of sampling all types of features. Suffice it to say that while the foregoing analysis provides information concerning the floral remains in each phase, caution must be used in drawing conclusions about the phase by phase use of plant resources based on these data. As Miksicek noted

in a recent discussion of this problem, "general trends will be much more meaningful than absolute numbers" (ibid:239).

Ounjian's analysis followed standardized laboratory procedures described in Crawford (1982). Light fraction residues were sieved and separated into fractions for ease of sorting. A binocular microscope (7x to 30x) was used for identifications, which were made with the aid of identification guides and reference collections at Erindale College and the Royal Ontario Museum.

Table 6.10. Cultigens and nut remains in gram weights by Phase.

| Taxon | House 1 | Early | Middle | Late | Total |
|---|---|---|---|---|---|
| Cultigens | | | | | |
| Maize Kernels (*Zea mays*) | 0.88 | 38.86 | 6.20 | 23.91 | 69.85 |
| Maize Cupules (*Zea mays*) | 0.18 | 8.70 | 1.82 | 1.40 | 12.10 |
| Bean (*Phaseolus vulgaris*) | - | - | 0.02 | | 0.02 |
| Squash (*Cucurbita pepo*) | 0.02 | 0.09 | 0.01 | 0.21 | 0.33 |
| Sunflower (*Helianthus annuus*) | - | 0.01 | - | 0.02 | 0.03 |
| Sub-total | 1.08 | 47.66 | 8.05 | 25.54 | 82.33 |
| Nuts | | | | | |
| Beech Husk (*Fagus grandifolia*) | - | - | - | 0.01 | 0.01 |
| Black Walnut Meat (*Juglans nigra*) | - | 0.03 | 0.01 | 0.07 | 0.11 |
| Black Walnut Shell (*Juglans nigra*) | - | 0.01 | - | | 0.01 |
| Butternut Meat (*Juglans cinerea*) | - | - | - | 0.01 | 0.01 |
| Butternut Shell (*Juglans cinerea*) | - | - | 0.01 | 0.14 | 0.15 |
| Sub-total | 0.00 | 0.04 | 0.02 | 0.23 | 0.29 |
| Total | 1.08 | 47.70 | 8.07 | 25.77 | 82.62 |
| Total Sample Volume (litres) | 72.00 | 402.00 | 88.00 | 247.00 | 809.00 |
| Plant Food Weight/litre | 0.02 | 0.12 | 0.09 | 0.10 | 0.10 |

Fecteau's wood charcoal analysis was accomplished by breaking each specimen to obtain a fresh cross-section. Charred wood was classified into 13 categories using wood anatomy texts and by comparison with reference specimens (Fecteau 1992:2).

## Results

A total of 7,255 seeds representing 37 identified taxa were extracted from all samples with phase associations. Table 6.9 presents a breakdown of the seed data on a phase by phase basis, while Table 6.10 provides total weights for cultigens and nuts in the sample. Data on the uses, seasonality, and habitats of the plants found at Calvert have been provided by Ounjian (1988) and are summarized in Timmins (1992:Appendix C).

## Cultigens

Cultigens recovered from Calvert include maize, squash, bean, sunflower, and tobacco. Maize kernels and cupules account for 98.78% of the plant food weight; thus we may conclude that maize was the main plant food of the Calvert people. Metric measurements on the maize sample may be found in Ounjian (1988). Based on these measurements, Ounjian concludes that the Calvert maize is likely Northern Flint.

There are no cob fragments in the samples with phase associations, although a small number were extracted from samples of unknown phase. The lack of cob fragments suggests that most of the corn was shelled for storage (Ounjian 1988:5). This interpretation was supported by the fortuitous recovery of several hundred carbonized corn kernels that appeared to have undergone spontaneous combustion in Layer 3 of Feature 126 within House 7 (Fox 1982a) (Figure 6.1).

Of the remaining cultigens, sunflower, squash, and tobacco are present in small amounts while bean is represented by a single specimen from the Middle phase (Table 6.9). More bean was recovered from other samples of unknown phase. These data suggest that squash and bean may have been cultivated at Calvert, but they were likely of minor economic importance.

## Nuts

As Table 6.10 shows, the quantity of nut remains recovered from Calvert is very small. Only black walnut is represented in the Early phase; black walnut and butternut are present in trace amounts in the Middle phase; while the Late phase has small quantities of black walnut, butternut, and beech nut. Hickory is possibly represented from one feature of unknown phase; acorn is conspicuous in its absence (Ounjian 1988:7). It is difficult to say if the increase in diversity from Early to Late is meaningful, given the small sample sizes.

The scarcity of nuts at Calvert is unusual as they normally form a significant component of the plant food at other Early Iroquoian sites. One obvious conclusion is that the Calvert site may not have been located in proximity to many nut-producing trees. Our environmental reconstruction suggests that the site was located in a maple/beech or pine dominated forest (Chapter 4), however, beech nuts were obviously not heavily exploited.

### Grains and Greens

Over 100 crabgrass seeds were recovered from one Late phase feature, making it the most abundant taxon in this category. Their presence is probably not important, as this plant is not known to have any economic value. Purselane, a pot herb, is the second most abundant taxon, followed by goosefoot (two varieties), which may have been eaten, used for medicine, or smoked. Both of these taxa are most abundant in the Early phase (Table 6.9). Of the remaining taxa in the grains/greens group, panic grass and wheatgrass may have been used medicinally (Ounjian 1988:13).

### Fleshy Fruits

The most common fleshy fruits are black nightshade, strawberry, and bramble (Table 6.9). Black nightshade, which is most common in the Middle phase but present in all major phases, has recorded medicinal uses but would probably not have been eaten (ibid.). Strawberry and bramble would normally have been eaten whole and raw, although they may have been added to other foods for flavour (ibid.).

Blueberry, elderberry, grape, and hawthorn are present in smaller quantities and would also have been used as food. Surprisingly, parts of most of these fleshy fruits, including their roots and leaves, had medicinal as well as food uses (Ounjian 1988:13-14).

All of the major fleshy fruits are found in each phase, although House 1 contains only bramble and strawberry. The implications of these finds in relation to site seasonality are discussed in the following section.

### Other Taxa

The most numerous taxa in this residual category are cat-tail and sumac, both of which are present in all phases, but most common in the Late phase (Table 6.9). Sumac and cat-tail were both multiple use plants. Cat-tail root stalk was used as a food, while the leaves, fibres, ripe flowers, down, and stems were used for a variety of medicinal, ritual, and technological purposes (Ounjian: personal communication, 1991). According to Ounjian "Sumac berries were reportedly used as a beverage and medicine, the bark and leaves for tannin, the leaves for smoking and medicine, and the wood for technological purposes" (1988:14). Within the Late phase both cat-tail and sumac are common in House 13, Features 79, 78, and 43 and House 11, Feature 20 (Figure 6.1). All of these features are linked by ceramic cross-mends and most contain impressive faunal assemblages as well. These features are interpreted elsewhere as showing evidence of a successful communal hunt. It may be that the presence of the sumac and cat-tail is related to other communal activities such as ritual, food processing, or hide tanning conducted in these houses.

Cleavers are most common in the Early phase, but drop in frequency in the Middle and Late phases (Table 6.9). The only recorded native use for this plant is medicinal (Ounjian 1988:14). Several of the other seeds included in the "Other" group had medicinal uses as well. They include: the sedges, violet, horsetail, milkweed, and mountain ash (Timmins 1992:Appendix C). Among these, the sedges and violet are rare finds on Ontario archaeological sites (Ounjian 1988:11-14).

### Carbonized Wood

A total of 72.9 g of charred or carbonized wood was identified by Fecteau (1992:6). The results, presented in Table 6.11, indicate that beech and sugar maple are most common, forming 55% and 22% of the sample weight respectively. Although the analyzed sample is

Table 6.11. Carbonized wood in gram weights.*

| Taxon | Weight (g) | Percent |
|---|---|---|
| Deciduous | | |
| Beech (*Fagus grandifolia*) | 40.37 | 55.38 |
| Sugar Maple (*Acer saccharum*) | 16.14 | 22.14 |
| White Elm (*Ulmus americana*) | 11.18 | 15.34 |
| Ash (*Fraxinus* sp.) | 1.93 | 2.65 |
| Birch (*Betula* sp.) | 1.04 | 1.43 |
| Maple (*Acer* sp.) | 0.37 | 0.51 |
| Ironwood (*Ostrya virginiana*) | 0.07 | 0.10 |
| Elm (*Ulmus* sp.) | 0.05 | 0.07 |
| Butternut or Black Walnut (*Juglans* sp.) | 0.16 | 0.22 |
| Indeterminate | | |
| Diffuse porous | 0.72 | 0.99 |
| Indeterminate | 0.64 | 0.88 |
| Coniferous | | |
| Pine (*Pinus* sp.) | 0.09 | 0.12 |
| Indeterminate | 0.14 | 0.19 |
| Total | 72.90 | 100.00 |

* These data are based on analysis of samples from Feature 242 (House 1) and Feature 126, Level 5, Early Phase (Fecteau 1992).

very small, these data tend to confirm the predicted presence of a maple/beech community in the Calvert area. White pine, which was also a predicted species, represents only .12% of the total sample. Rather than suggesting its scarcity in the area, this may only indicate that pine was not normally selected for firewood. While pine wood ignites easily, it also produces much spark and heavy smoke. Moreover, it has the lowest heating value of all the wood species present at Calvert making it an inefficient fuel (Fecteau 1992:10, 11).

## Summary

In sum, our analysis of the Calvert floral data has demonstrated that maize was the major plant food of the Calvert people, comprising over 98% of the total plant food weight. Squash, bean, and sunflower are present in small quantities, were likely cultivated on a minor scale, and were probably of little economic importance. The recovery of a small sample of tobacco seeds indicates that tobacco was likely cultivated and smoked. This is corroborated by the presence of a small sample of pipes in the artifact collection.

Fleshy fruits are common in the three major occupational phases and would have provided variety in the diet during the spring, summer, and fall. They are relatively rare in the House 1 samples.

The major species identified in the wood charcoal analysis are beech, maple, and white elm. These may simply represent the species favoured for firewood.

The diversity of archaeobotanical assemblages may be directly related to the length of site occupation (Miksicek 1987:229), although season of occupation may affect diversity as well. There are no notable changes in the diversity of floral species among the three main phases. Fewer taxa were noted in the House 1 samples, and there is a significant decrease in plant food weight per litre in this house (Figure 6.10). This supports the notion that House 1 functioned, primarily , as a hunting camp.

If the Late phase also represents a hunting camp, occupied repeatedly on a short-term basis, it is possible that corn was brought to the village to augment the food supply. Yet, while hunting may have been the main economic activity during such occupations, the floral data indicate that plant collecting was carried out as well. This problem is further explored in the following discussion of seasonality.

## Seasonality

The evidence of season of occupation is derived from floral and faunal indices. These are discussed in sequence below.

### Faunal Seasonality Indices

Several general and specific indices of seasonality are present in the faunal sample. The large amount of deer bone recovered from Calvert strongly suggests that the site was occupied during the cold season, since deer yarding in the nearby Dorchester swamp would have concentrated the resource and created optimal hunting conditions in the fall and winter months. Specifically, Prevec noted two deer skulls with shed antlers from Late phase Feature 71-1 (House 13). Antlers fall off in December or January and bud in the early spring, so these deer were taken in mid to late winter (Prevec 1984a:51).

Winter occupation in the Early phase is confirmed by deer dentition. Mandibles from immature deer were recovered in Features 306 and 130-4. Judging by tooth development (deciduous premolars and un-erupted second molar), they were taken between November and February, assuming that they were born in May as is usual for white-tailed deer in southwestern Ontario (ibid.).

Fish provide strong evidence for a spring occupation during at least the Early and Middle phases when sucker is most common. Sucker (Catostomus sp. and Family Catostomidae) spawn in the spring and would have been available not only in the Thames River but likely in Dorchester Swamp Creek as well (ibid.). Some Early phase features (306, 147-5) produced masses of matted sucker scales suggesting that large numbers were caught at once, as is possible during the spawning season. Whitefish spawn in the late fall (November/December) and are present in the Middle and Late phase samples. Small fish that would have been caught by netting during the warm season were found in Early phase Features 9, 306, 92, and 108-3.

The remaining fauna provide less specific seasonality information. Turtle and woodchuck, which occur in all phases, are available in spring, summer, and fall. Of the birds, the passenger pigeon, which is present in the Middle and Late phases, would not have been available in the winter.

As noted above, the presence of five features containing deer head and foot elements in House 1 suggests that initial butchering activities took place within that house. Since deer would probably only be butchered inside a house during the cold season, this pattern may be a cold weather seasonality indicator for House 1. With the exception of the woodchuck, the fauna found in House 1 would have been available year round (Table 6.2).

In sum, the faunal data provide some evidence for cold season occupation of House 1 and strong evidence for occupation in all seasons during the Early and Middle phases. The faunal remains show little evidence of spring or summer occupation during the Late phase.

**Floral Seasonality Indices**

The floral data are of great help in addressing seasonality issues, and specifically, the question of whether the Late phase was occupied during the spring and summer. Plants found at Calvert were apparently collected from the early spring through to the very late fall. Some plants, especially cultigens, were stored through the winter months as well.

The earliest available plant found at Calvert is the violet, which is available in March and is represented by one seed in the Late phase. Strawberry is available in April and is represented in all phases, including the Late phase. It occurs in all of the Late phase features but one. As a seasonality indicator strawberry can be problematic, since it may either be eaten when picked or dried and stored for winter use.

Panic grass, cleavers and sedge become available in May and are also represented in all phases. Summer occupation for all phases is indicated by the presence of bramble, milkweed, sumac, and wheatgrass. A wide variety of well represented plants become available in the fall. They include purselane, hawthorn, goosefoot, knotweed, and of course, nuts and cultigens.

Thus the floral data leave little doubt that the Calvert site was occupied in the spring, summer, and fall during all phases. The evidence is weaker for a summer occupation in House 1, but strawberry, elderberry, and sumac are represented, indicating some warm weather use. The floral evidence does not negate the hypothesis that the Calvert site functioned as a hunting camp in the Late phase; it simply demonstrates that the site was used, to some extent, during the warm seasons. Semi-permanent (shifting every 10 to 30 years) year-round occupation in all phases has not been demonstrated.

## Catchment Analysis

As discussed in Chapter 4, the catchment of the Calvert site is the area around the village that was likely to have been exploited on a daily basis without establishing special purpose camps (Vita-Finzi and Higgs 1970). Through comparison of archaeological evidence with resource availability within the region, it is now possible to determine how large an area was required to meet subsistence needs (Flannery 1976). In this section I will briefly examine the Calvert site catchment in relation to the archaeological floral and faunal data from the site.

In Chapter 4 a series of five distinct micro-environmental zones were defined within a 5 km radius around the Calvert site. These zones were:
1. the sandy upland plateau on which the site is located;
2. the riparian environment of the Thames River, Dorchester Swamp Creek, and associated floodplain;
3. the Dorchester Swamp;
4. the upland maple/beech forest; and
5. the glacial ponds and bogs.

Figure 6.4 shows that even a small circular catchment of one km radius around the site intersects four of the five micro-environments. Thus the Calvert site was strategically placed in a true ecotonal situation.

The results of the floral and faunal analyses indicate that these environmental zones were not exploited on an equal basis in each occupational phase. The zones of greatest economic importance were the sandy upland plateau around the site proper, and the Dorchester Swamp to the southwest. Data concerning the habitats of the plants found at Calvert are given in Timmins (1992:Appendix C) and Ounjian (1988). These data were used to predict which plants might have been available in the different micro-environments around the site.

The agricultural fields of the Calvert people would have been located in the sandy plateau zone surrounding the site. Cultivated maize, squash, beans, tobacco, and perhaps sunflower would have come from this zone during the Early and Middle phases. During the Late hunting phase cultigens may or may not have been grown here and the sandy plateau may have had less economic importance.

Forest clearance and cultivation on the upland plateau would also have created ideal conditions for plants that adapt well to disturbed soil and animals that prefer a forest edge environment. Such plants include goosefoot, knotweed, purselane, cleavers, and strawberry, all of which are found in each of the Calvert phases. Animals that would be attracted to such an environment include white-tailed deer, woodchuck, fox, and porcupine.

It was suggested, in Chapter 4, that overstory vegetation on the sandy plateau was likely dominated by a permanent white pine stand. As such, few nuts would be available in this zone. This is certainly reflected by their low occurrence in the floral sample.

The Dorchester Swamp zone was likely as important to the Calvert economy as the upland plateau, and may have been more important in the Late phase. Although no agricultural activities would have been carried out in this zone, a wide variety of the plants exploited by the Calvert people were readily available in the swamp. Of the 37 plant taxa documented at Calvert, 19 may occur in wet, moist soils or swamps (Timmins 1992:Appendix C). These include a variety of fleshy fruits (blueberry, elderberry, bramble) used for food and medicine, and some plants with medicinal uses that may not have been available in other zones (the sedges). In addition, the swamp would have been an excellent source of the cedar poles and bark required for village construction.

There is little question that the swamp was the most important environmental zone for hunting. Cedar swamps are a preferred habitat for deer during the winter, since they provide shelter and abundant browse. Depending on the severity of the weather and the depth of the snow, the deer may congregate in groups or 'yard'. This creates an optimal hunting situation in which the deer are concentrated in large numbers and have restricted mobility. Historical records indicate that the swamp was an important hunting area in the nineteenth century and it continues to support

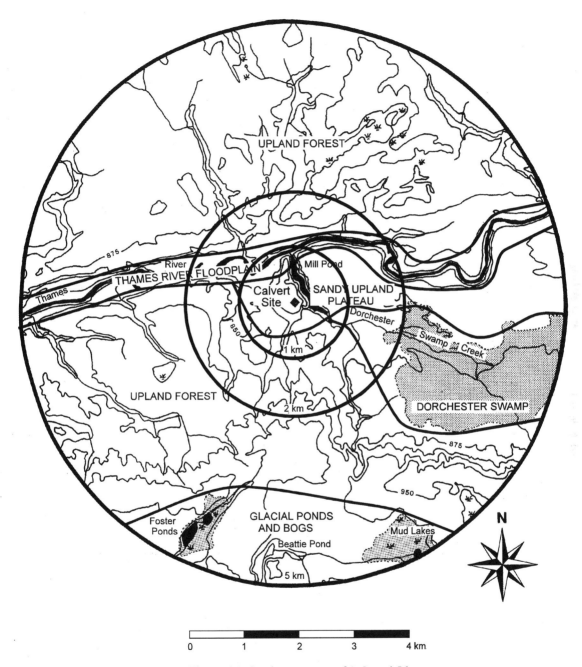

Figure 6.4. Catchment areas of 1, 2, and 5 km.

a large white-tailed deer population today (Upper Thames River Conservation Authority 1986).

Other mammals found in the swamp, and represented at Calvert, include raccoon, beaver, woodchuck, eastern cottontail, and the striped skunk. All varieties of turtle recovered at Calvert are present in the Dorchester Swamp as well. As most of these animals are represented in all of the Calvert samples, the swamp was obviously heavily utilized during the occupation of House 1 and all three phases.

The riverine environment offered by the Thames River and Dorchester Swamp Creek was most heavily utilized for fishing in the Early and Middle phases as we have seen. With the exception of lake whitefish, all of the fish species identified at Calvert occur in the Thames watershed today; however, only dace and brook trout are found in Dorchester Swamp Creek. Even if the creek held more water in the past, it is unlikely that, as a small trout fishery, it would have been a significant contributor to the resource base. Most of the fishing would have been done in the Thames River. The whitefish found at Calvert may have come from a different watershed, perhaps one to the south draining into Lake Erie, where the whitefish are available year round. The fact that whitefish is most common in the Late phase may indicate that it was brought in from elsewhere by a hunting group.

Floral resources associated with the riverine zone may have included some mast producing trees that favour river bank or valley locations (black walnut, butternut, hickory), as well as elderberry, bramble, panic grass, mountain ash, and knotweed (Tables 6.9 and 6.10). Mammals found in this zone include river otter, muskrat, and beaver. The latter are most common in the Early and Middle phases, but are represented in the Late phase as well, together with a significant occurrence of otter. In sum, the riverine zone appears to have been most heavily exploited in the Early and Middle phases, while the lack of fishing evidenced for both House 1 and the Late phase suggests that it was of less economic importance during those periods of occupation.

The upland beech-maple forest zone located north and south of Calvert was likely the preferred habitat for a small number of mammals

represented at Calvert, including black bear, bobcat, chipmunk, raccoon, marten, and fisher. Three of these species are most common in the Late phase (Table 6.2). The diversity in mammalian species noted in the Late phase can probably be attributed to an expansion of hunting activities into the upland forests. Beech and other nuts that may have been available in this zone do not appear to have been utilized by the Calvert people. Further, it is unlikely that there were many small plant species available in the upland forest that were not more conveniently available on the sand plateau, in the Dorchester Swamp, or in the Thames River valley.

The dominance of beech and maple in the carbonized wood sample may indicate that the beech-maple zone was a preferred source of firewood (Fecteau 1992). However, it is unlikely that beech and maple were confined to this zone. As the most common climax forest association in southwestern Ontario these species probably occurred in other environmental zones as well, including the sandy upland plateau.

The zone of glacial ponds and bogs, located 3-4 km south of Calvert, would have supported plant and animal communities similar to those found in the Dorchester Swamp, perhaps with the addition of more migratory fowl. There are no plant or animal species in the Calvert assemblage that are unique to these ponds and bogs and that could not have been taken or collected closer to home. It is likely, therefore, that the ponds and bogs lay outside the regular Calvert catchment.

It is difficult to determine the catchment area of House 1, given the small size of both the floral and faunal samples. Most of the species recovered probably came from either the sandy upland plateau or Dorchester Swamp, although species like bear and raccoon could have been taken in the upland forests as well. If hunting was the main activity conducted at Calvert during the House 1 occupation, the catchment area was probably oriented towards the Dorchester Swamp.

During the Early and Middle phases the catchment analysis indicates that the sandy upland plateau immediately surrounding the site and Dorchester Swamp were the most heavily exploited environmental zones. The riverine environment of the Thames and Dorchester Swamp Creek ranked third in economic importance during these phases.

The vast majority of the plants and animals found at Calvert during the House 1, Early and Middle phases could have been obtained from a catchment area that was probably ovate in shape (to include more of Dorchester Swamp) and 4 to 5 km in length. While the Calvert people surely ranged beyond this zone, particularly to acquire chert, most of their economic needs could have been met within it.

Apparent changes in subsistence strategy led to concomitant changes in the catchment area during the occupation of the Late phase. While the Dorchester Swamp was still heavily utilized, the evidence shows a decrease in white-tailed deer and an increase in the representation of other mammals such as bear, bobcat, and raccoon. This pattern suggests that the hunting range was expanded to include the upland forests, creating a more circular catchment, like the 5 km catchment shown in Figure 6.4.

## Conclusions

In summary, our analysis of the floral and faunal data from Calvert together with a consideration of the site catchment leads to a number of conclusions regarding the economic function and seasonality of the site in each period of occupation.

With regard to site function, the data indicate a heavy reliance on hunting during the occupation of House 1, with no evidence for fishing, and little evidence for agriculture. If House 1 functioned as a hunting camp it is possible that the very small amounts of cultigens and other plant foods found within the house were transported there as stored food. The only seasonality indicator from House 1 is the presence of deer head and foot bones in several features, which hints at indoor butchering practices and a probable cold weather occupation.

The ecofactual evidence for the Early and Middle phases suggests a "broad-spectrum" subsistence strategy involving a combination of agriculture, hunting, fishing, and plant collecting. Seasonality indices for these periods also suggest a semi-permanent, year-round occupation of the village.

In contrast, the faunal data from the Late phase quite clearly demonstrate an increased reliance on the hunting of mammals and a concurrent drop in the importance of fishing. A wide variety of plants were still collected indicating that the site was occupied during at least part of the warm season. In view of these data, the Late phase is interpreted as a hunting/gathering camp that was occupied intermittently, primarily in the cold season, but occasionally during the warm season as well. Artifactual, refuse disposal, and settlement pattern data, discussed in the following chapter, add further support to this interpretation.

# Chapter 7

# Domestic Life in the Calvert Community: Technology

## Introduction

In this chapter we examine the technology of the Calvert people through an analysis of all major artifact categories in the collection. Where possible, we will also examine the evidence for technological or stylistic change in these artifact categories, through a comparative analysis of data from successive phases. The technological categories described include:

1. Lithic Technology
2. Ceramic Technology
3. Bone, Antler, and Shell Technology
4. Feature Function and Formation
5. Refuse Disposal Technology
6. Building Technology and Structure Function (Settlement Pattern Analysis)

The question of group identity will also be dealt with in this chapter. We are interested in determining whether the different occupations at Calvert represent one or more communities. It is possible that as many as four different groups are represented at Calvert. If different communities occupied the site this will be reflected in the artifact assemblages and should be particularly apparent through comparison of the ceramics from each occupation.

Finally, the technological analysis is expected to yield additional evidence to either corroborate or modify the conclusions regarding economy and seasonality derived in Chapter 6.

## Lithic Technology

A total of 622 chert tools, 67 rough and ground stone tools, and 12,446 pieces of lithic debitage were recovered in the Calvert excavations. In the following analysis, lithic debitage and individual stone tool categories are

described separately, followed by a discussion of assemblage variability in relation to lithic raw materials, occupation span, and site function. This approach attempts to understand the lithic assemblage as a tool kit, recognizing that changes in the composition of tool kits may indicate significant changes in the activities they were used to conduct. In this study, comparisons are sought to determine if there were any significant differences in the assemblages from each phase that could be related to the proposed shifts in site function from a hunting camp to a semi-permanent village and back to a hunting camp. There has been a decided lack of such integrated assemblage analysis in past studies of Iroquoian lithics.

With the exception of a single experiment involving utilized flakes, no attempt was made to create interpretive data through experiments in lithic reduction or tool use. Such a study lies beyond the scope of this project. Instead, traditional tool typologies with traditional functional interpretations were employed (i.e., projectile points, scrapers) and extant experimental data were used when available to provide interpretative data (i.e., Callahan 1981; Magne 1985).

### Lithic Raw Materials (Cherts)

Cherts were visually identified with the aid of hand samples on the basis of attributes such as colour, lustre, translucency, and the presence of inclusions. The four most common chert types represented in the Calvert sample are Onondaga, Kettle Point, Selkirk, and local pebble cherts.

Onondaga chert is a mottled light to dark grey chert that often displays a brown patina (Eley and von Bitter 1989). It occurs in Middle Devonian Onondaga Formation limestone and is exposed along beaches and in creek beds and quarries north of Lake Erie between Port Dover

Table 7.1. Debitage chert types by phase.

| Phase | House 1 | | Early | | Middle | | Late | | Total | |
|---|---|---|---|---|---|---|---|---|---|---|
| Chert Type | f | % | f | % | f | % | f | % | f | % |
| Onondaga | 258 | 70.9 | 354 | 33.6 | 458 | 39.0 | 525 | 37.5 | 1595 | 40.0 |
| Kettle Point | 7 | 1.9 | 344 | 32.7 | 141 | 12.0 | 500 | 35.7 | 992 | 24.9 |
| Selkirk | 15 | 4.1 | 9 | 0.9 | 116 | 9.9 | 60 | 4.3 | 200 | 5.0 |
| Local | 59 | 16.2 | 222 | 21.1 | 102 | 8.7 | 103 | 7.4 | 486 | 12.2 |
| Unknown Chert | 25 | 6.9 | 124 | 11.8 | 357 | 30.4 | 212 | 15.1 | 718 | 18.0 |
| Total | 364 | 100.0 | 1053 | 100.0 | 1174 | 100.0 | 1400 | 100.0 | 3991 | 100.0 |

and Fort Erie. In the London area it is also found in pebble form along stream beds and in till deposits associated with the Ingersoll moraine.

Kettle Point chert is found at the interface between the Middle Devonian Ipperwash Formation limestones and the Upper Devonian Kettle Point formation shales (Eley and von Bitter 1989:15). It is translucent with a waxy lustre and varies in colour from a dark blue-grey or black to a distinctive mauve. Kettle Point chert outcrops at Kettle Point on the Lake Huron shoreline near Port Franks. The outcrops are presently under shallow water and would have been inaccessible during periods of high lake levels in the past.

Selkirk chert is a medium grey to grey-brown material occurring in Dundee Formation limestone outcrops of Middle Devonian age (ibid:16). This chert usually contains many small fossils. It occurs in quarries in the Selkirk to Nanticoke area, and may have been available in pebble deposits and beach outcrops in the vicinity as well. It may also have been available in pebble deposits in the London area.

Local pebble cherts are common in the Dorchester area and through much of southern Middlesex County. As noted above, some of this chert can be assigned to the Onondaga or Selkirk type. Like other archaeologists (i.e. Keron 1986:140), I have found that it is extremely difficult to distinguish local Onondaga from quarried Onondaga unless a nodular, cortical surface is present. Therefore such a distinction was not attempted in this study and the local Onondaga material was simply classed as Onondaga. Most of the material classed as Local chert is light brown to whitish grey and was

probably derived from the Lower Devonian Bois Blanc Formation.

Cherts that could not be identified were assigned to the Unknown category.

## Debitage Analysis

Lithic debitage was analyzed in terms of raw materials and flake morphology. A sample of 3991 pieces of chert debitage comprising 32.1% of the debitage collection was analyzed for chert type. Table 7.1 presents the chert type frequency data for all phases and House 1. A number of pertinent observations can be drawn from these data.

The Early and Late phases appear to be broadly similar, especially with respect to their frequencies of Kettle Point and Onondaga cherts, which range between 33 and 38%. Selkirk chert is poorly represented in the Early phase (.9%), but increases to almost 10% in the Middle phase.

The Middle phase is the most unusual of the three phases in terms of lithic raw materials. It has a relatively low percentage of Kettle Point material (12%), the highest occurrence of Selkirk chert (9.9%), and a very high percentage of Unknown chert (30.4%). This phase thus exhibits the greatest variability in lithic raw materials among the three phases.

House 1 is also aberrant with respect to lithic materials when compared to the three major occupational phases. Over 70% of the chert in House 1 is Onondaga, while Kettle Point material is barely present, at only 1.9%.

Table 7.2. Flake types by phase.

| Phase | House 1 | | Early | | Middle | | Late | | Total | |
|---|---|---|---|---|---|---|---|---|---|---|
| Flake Types | f | % | f | % | f | % | f | % | f | % |
| Primary | 21 | 5.8 | 135 | 12.7 | 121 | 10.3 | 122 | 8.3 | 399 | 9.8 |
| Secondary | 58 | 16.0 | 190 | 17.9 | 252 | 21.4 | 320 | 21.8 | 820 | 20.1 |
| Biface Thinning | 68 | 18.7 | 254 | 23.9 | 242 | 20.5 | 314 | 21.4 | 878 | 21.6 |
| Resharpening | 0 | 0.0 | 51 | 4.8 | 6 | 0.5 | 9 | 0.6 | 66 | 1.6 |
| Fragments | 187 | 51.5 | 348 | 32.8 | 449 | 38.1 | 632 | 43.0 | 1616 | 39.7 |
| Shatter | 29 | 8.0 | 83 | 7.8 | 110 | 9.3 | 72 | 4.9 | 294 | 7.2 |
| Total | 363 | 100.0 | 1061 | 100.0 | 1180 | 100.0 | 1469 | 100.0 | 4073 | 100.0 |

The implications of these differences in raw material are discussed in the concluding section on assemblage variability.

## Flake Morphology and Reduction Sequences

Over 4000 pieces of chipping detritus constituting 32.7% of the total debitage sample were classified according to morphological flake types. This analysis was done to characterize the lithic reduction stages represented at the site and to permit a comparison of reduction technologies among occupational phases.

The debitage sample was obtained by the systematic selection of features from each phase. The sample was selected to achieve representation of all types of features located both within and outside longhouses.

The morphological flake types employed in the analysis generally follow those used by Keron (1986) and are thought to relate to the stages of primary flaking, secondary flaking and margin production, thinning, and retouching (Ellis 1979). These flake types are described below.

Primary Flakes are a by-product of the initial core reduction stage and normally display cortex on their striking platforms. They are generally produced by hard hammer percussion and have a platform to ventral surface angle of about 90 degrees. As defined here, primary flakes will include cortical flakes detached by direct freehand percussion as well as bipolar flakes with cortical striking platforms (Crabtree 1982).

Secondary Reduction Flakes are usually produced by direct freehand percussion but in all cases they lack cortical striking platforms. They

are larger than biface thinning flakes and may result from the secondary trimming of cores or the initial shaping of bifacial tools. Secondary reduction flakes may be indicative of the use of prepared cores or cores from which the cortex has been previously removed. Dorsal flake surfaces exhibit a few scars from previous flake removals and the platform to ventral surface angle may vary from near 90 degrees to obtuse.

Biface Thinning Flakes result from the final shaping and thinning of bifacial tools and thus occur late in the reduction sequence. They are characterized by obtuse platform to ventral surface angles and are generally thinner and smaller than secondary flakes. Most biface thinning flakes were produced by pressure flaking. They have small striking platforms and often display diffuse bulbs of percussion. Dorsal flake surfaces display evidence of several earlier flake removals.

Resharpening Flakes result from tool maintenance activity, namely the removal of small flakes from the working edges of unifacial and bifacial tools. They are normally produced by pressure flaking and always exhibit use-wear on their striking platforms. Resharpening flakes were identified in this analysis with the aid of a small 30x microscope used to verify the presence of use-wear.

Flake fragments are distal portions of flakes lacking striking platforms. Despite Magne's (1985) demonstration that such flakes can be classified by flake scar counts, this was not attempted in the present analysis.

Shatter flakes are angular, usually thick fragments of chert that lack striking platforms

Table 7.3. Core types and raw materials.

| Phase | House 1 | Early | Middle | Late | Unknown | Total |
|-------|---------|-------|--------|------|---------|-------|
| | | Core Type | | | | |
| Uni-Directional | - | - | - | - | 2 | 2 |
| Bi-Directional | - | 3 | 1 | 2 | 3 | 9 |
| Random Block | - | 6 | 1 | 6 | 4 | 17 |
| Bi-polar | 1 | 2 | 2 | - | 3 | 8 |
| Total | 1 | 11 | 4 | 8 | 12 | 36 |
| | | Chert Type | | | | |
| Onondaga | - | 3 | 1 | 5 | 2 | 11 |
| Kettle Point | 1 | 1 | 1 | 1 | 1 | 5 |
| Local | - | 6 | 1 | 1 | 5 | 13 |
| Selkirk | - | - | 1 | - | - | 1 |
| Unknown | - | 1 | - | 1 | 4 | 6 |
| Total | 1 | 11 | 4 | 8 | 12 | 36 |

and morphological consistency. These types of flakes result from the breakage of cores along natural fault lines during initial core reduction (Ellis 1979).

## Results

Table 7.2 shows the frequency and percentage of each of the flake types on a phase by phase basis. These data indicate that all stages in the lithic reduction sequence are present in each phase. Primary reduction flakes are poorly represented in House 1 (5.8%). They increase to almost 13% in the Early phase and then show a small but steady decline in percentage occurrence through the Middle and Late phases. Although this trend is not pronounced, it may indicate that the Early phase chert knappers had greater access to primary chert sources. However, it was observed that the majority of the primary flakes showed rounded cortical surfaces characteristic of pebble cores rather than tabular cortical surfaces indicative of quarried chert.

The occurrence of secondary flakes remains relatively consistent throughout the three phases, as does the frequency of biface thinning flakes. However, when we consider resharpening flakes, we find that they attain a significantly higher percentage in the Early phase than in any other. This suggests that more tool maintenance activity was occurring in the Early phase which may reflect a longer period of occupation. This

possibility is discussed further in our consideration of assemblage variability.

House 1 again appears anomalous in having lower percentages of primary, secondary, and biface thinning flakes and an unusually high percentage of flake fragments.

In sum, with the exception of House 1, the debitage analysis indicates that very similar lithic reduction sequences were followed in each of the three phases.

### Cores

The cores were classified into four categories based on direction and mode of flake removal. Cores resulting from direct freehand percussion dominate the assemblage, while cores produced by the bipolar technique form a minority of the sample. It should be noted that these techniques are not necessarily mutually exclusive and that hand held cores are sometimes further reduced by the bipolar technique.

Uni-directional cores are those that have had flakes removed in one direction, working from a single end or platform area. Bi-directional cores have had flakes removed from two opposite platform areas, and random cores have been rotated and struck from several different platform areas around the perimeter of the core. Bipolar cores have been placed on an anvil and struck, resulting in the application of force to both the

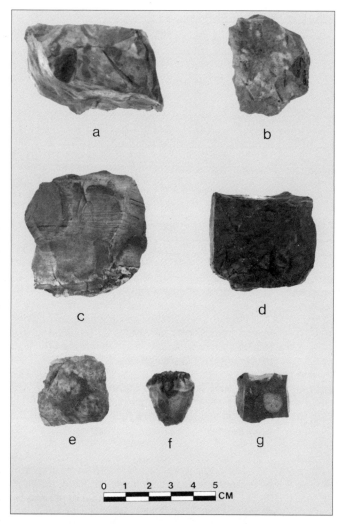

Figure 7.1. Cores and wedges: a-b, random cores;
c-d, bi-directional cores; e-g, wedges.

indicate that Kettle Point cores were being extensively curated rather than discarded, or it could indicate that Kettle Point material arrived at the site as preforms.

The cores are separated by phase in Table 7.3, however, the small sample size makes phase by phase comparisons difficult. It is noted that the scarcity of cores from House 1 parallels the low frequency of primary flakes, indicating that initial core reduction was uncommon during the House 1 occupation.

## Chipped Stone Tool Analysis

Table 7.4 presents a breakdown of the Calvert chipped stone tool assemblage organized by tool type and phase. Informal flake tools obviously dominate the assemblage with utilized flakes (UFLs) comprising 65.8% of the total sample. Some tool forms are poorly represented and sample sizes become very small when the sample is broken down on a phase by phase basis, making comparisons difficult.

### Bifaces

Summary data for the bifaces are provided in Table 7.5. Of the 154 bifaces analyzed, only 87 could be attributed to a specific occupational phase. Many of these were fragmentary, effectively decreasing the sample size for many attributes.

As Table 7.5 shows, there are no major differences in biface size or form among the three main phases. There is only one small complete biface from House 1, so the mean biface length and width given for House 1 is based on a single example (Table 7.5). The majority (89%) of the bifaces are triangular in form, with concave or straight bases (Figure 7.2,a-i). Four side-notched specimens were recovered (Figure 7.3, g-h). These may represent variants of the Dewaele type, which is a minority form on Glen Meyer sites (Fox 1982e). The triangular bifaces that dominate the Calvert

top and the bottom of the core. A selection of these cores is shown in Figure 7.1.

The breakdown of core types is shown in Table 7.3. This analysis clearly shows that random and bi-directional cores dominate the small assemblage. The cores are also separated by chert type in Table 7.3, which shows that Onondaga and Local cherts are about equally represented (n=11 and 13 respectively). Kettle Point chert appears to be under-represented in relation to debitage frequencies (n=5). This may

Table 7.4. Lithic tool frequencies by phase.

| Phase | House 1 | | Early | | Middle | | Late | | Total | |
|---|---|---|---|---|---|---|---|---|---|---|
| Tool type | f | % | f | % | f | % | f | % | f | % |
| Utilized flake | 15 | 65.2 | 87 | 66.9 | 85 | 70.8 | 76 | 59.8 | 263 | 65.8 |
| Biface | 4 | 17.4 | 25 | 19.2 | 23 | 19.2 | 35 | 27.6 | 87 | 21.8 |
| Scraper | 2 | 8.7 | 11 | 8.5 | 7 | 5.8 | 10 | 7.9 | 30 | 7.5 |
| Graver | 2 | 8.7 | 5 | 3.8 | 2 | 1.7 | 6 | 4.7 | 15 | 3.8 |
| Wedge | 0 | 0.0 | 2 | 1.5 | 3 | 2.5 | 0 | 0.0 | 5 | 1.3 |
| Total* | 23 | 100.0 | 130 | 100.0 | 120 | 100.0 | 127 | 100.0 | 400 | 100.0 |

* excludes tools with unknown phase

assemblage generally conform to the Glen Meyer type as defined by Fox (1982d); however, many of the Calvert points differ from the Glen Meyer type in minor ways. Most Glen Meyer points are asymmetrical and sometimes spurred, with concave bases. Yet many of the Calvert points are symmetrical, few are spurred, and straight bases occur with regularity. These differences may reflect regional stylistic patterns.

Many of the Calvert bifaces may have functioned both as projectile points and knives. In the present analysis the presence or absence of polish and/or microflaking on the lateral edges of bifaces was recorded to determine if these tools had been used as knives. Only nine bifaces in total displayed polish, but six of these came from the Late phase. Similarly, 12 Late phase bifaces showed evidence of microflaking compared to five and one for the Early and Middle phases respectively (Table 7.5). Although the phase by phase samples are small, the results indicate that a disproportionate number of Late phase bifaces display polish and microflaking. This suggests more use of bifaces as knives and scrapers in the final phase.

Notable differences also occur in chert frequencies. While Onondaga chert bifaces occur consistently at about 60% through all main phases, Kettle Point bifaces increase steadily from 4% in the Early phase to 26% in the Late phase. Another anomaly lies

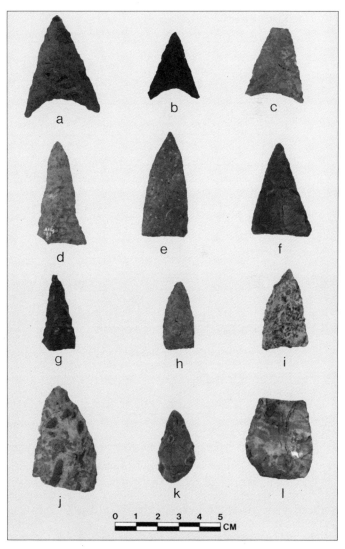

Figure 7.2. Projectile points and bifaces:
a-i, projectile points; j-l, bifaces.

Table 7.5. Biface data by phase.

| Phase | | House 1 | Early | Middle | Late | Unknown | Total |
|---|---|---|---|---|---|---|---|
| Number | f | 4 | 25 | 23 | 35 | 67 | 154 |
| Percent | % | 2.6 | 16.2 | 14.9 | 22.7 | 43.5 | 100.0 |
| Metrics | | | | | | | |
| Mean Length | | 22.5 | 31.0 | 33.7 | 34.3 | 39.2 | 34.6 |
| Mean Width | | 17.7 | 22.5 | 23.9 | 23.6 | 23.9 | 23.5 |
| Mean Thick | | 4.0 | 5.0 | 5.8 | 4.7 | 5.5 | 5.3 |
| Chert types | | | | | | | |
| Onondaga | f | 3 | 16 | 14 | 21 | 37 | 91 |
| | % | 75.0 | 64.0 | 60.9 | 60.0 | 55.2 | 59.1 |
| Kettle Point | f | 1 | 1 | 3 | 9 | 9 | 23 |
| | % | 25.0 | 4.0 | 13.0 | 25.7 | 13.4 | 14.9 |
| Selkirk | f | 0 | 5 | 1 | 2 | 8 | 16 |
| | % | 0.0 | 20.0 | 4.3 | 5.7 | 11.9 | 10.4 |
| Local | f | 0 | 1 | 0 | 0 | 2 | 3 |
| | % | 0.0 | 4.0 | 0.0 | 0.0 | 3.0 | 1.9 |
| Unknown | f | 0 | 2 | 5 | 3 | 11 | 21 |
| | % | 0.0 | 8.0 | 21.7 | 8.6 | 16.4 | 13.6 |
| Total | f | 4 | 25 | 23 | 35 | 67 | 154 |
| | % | 100.0 | 100.0 | 100.0 | 100.0 | 100.0 | 100.0 |
| Basal Form | | | | | | | |
| Straight | f | 1 | 2 | 1 | 6 | 6 | 15 |
| Convex | f | 0 | 1 | 0 | 1 | 1 | 3 |
| Concave | f | 0 | 4 | 3 | 4 | 18 | 29 |
| Stemmed | f | 0 | 1 | 0 | 0 | 1 | 2 |
| Side-Notch | f | 0 | 0 | 1 | 1 | 2 | 4 |
| Total | f | 1 | 8 | 5 | 12 | 28 | 53 |
| Other attributes | | | | | | | |
| Burnt | f | 1 | 2 | 2 | 10 | 6 | 21 |
| | % | 4.8 | 9.5 | 9.5 | 47.6 | 28.6 | 100.0 |
| Reworked Tip | f | 0 | 0 | 0 | 5 | 0 | 5 |
| | % | 0.0 | 0.0 | 0.0 | 100.0 | 0.0 | 100.0 |
| Polish | f | 0 | 0 | 0 | 6 | 3 | 9 |
| | % | 0.0 | 0.0 | 0.0 | 66.7 | 33.3 | 100.0 |
| Microflaking | f | 2 | 5 | 1 | 12 | 16 | 36 |
| | % | 5.6 | 13.9 | 2.8 | 33.3 | 44.4 | 100.0 |
| Basal Grind | f | 0 | 2 | 0 | 5 | 4 | 11 |
| | % | 0.0 | 18.2 | 0.0 | 45.5 | 36.4 | 100.0 |

in the high percentage of Selkirk chert bifaces attributed to the Early phase (20.0%). Few bifaces are made of local chert, although it forms a significant portion of the debitage in each phase. The implications of these data are discussed later.

In addition to the typical Glen Meyer bifaces discussed above, the Calvert excavations yielded two pre-Iroquoian projectile points. These are stemmed bifaces, one of which is made of Selkirk chert, the other of an unidentified, pinkish, heat altered chert (Figure 7.3, e-f). These points are interesting because they appear to be of a similar

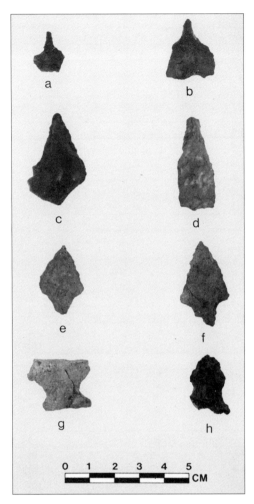

Figure 7.3. Drills and projectile points: a-b, unifacial narrow bit drills; c-d, bifacial drills; e-f, contracting stemmed projectile points (Morrow Mountain?); g-h, side-notched projectile points.

type, characterized by a contracting stem. Further, they were found close together, in Early phase Features 319 and 134. Typologically they resemble Morrow Mountain points, a Middle Archaic form usually found in the southeastern United States and to the north along the eastern seaboard (Justice 1987:107). These points are rarely found in Ontario, but the Middle Archaic period is generally poorly understood in the region. Their presence at Calvert may indicate an Archaic occupation of the site; however, the fact that they were found in Early Iroquoian features suggests that they may be curios collected by a Calvert resident.

## Scrapers

Unlike other Glen Meyer sites, such as Kelly and Roeland on the Caradoc Sand Plain (Williamson 1985), chert scrapers are not a highly developed artifact class at Calvert. Only 56 scrapers are present in the entire site assemblage (Figure 7.4, a-f). Of these, two come from House 1 while 11, seven, and ten are assigned to the Early, Middle and Late phases respectively. With such small samples it is not possible to draw reliable conclusions from a phase by phase comparison. We will therefore confine our comments to the total sample.

Attribute data for scrapers are provided in Table 7.6. As this table shows, end, side, and combination scrapers are about equally common at Calvert. Most of the combination scrapers are end/side scrapers. Average scraper edge angles fall between 63 and 67 degrees in the Early, Middle and Late phases, indicating that the majority of scrapers were used as scraping tools rather than knives (Wilmsen 1968:156). Polish is present on 84% of the scrapers and 57% display edge rounding from use.

## Utilized Flakes

With 374 chert flakes classified as utilized flakes (UFLs), this category of informal tools is by far the largest lithic tool form represented at the Calvert site. The utilized flake is also the simplest and most common lithic tool form represented on the majority of Iroquoian sites. The characteristic attribute of this tool is evidence of modification from use on at least one flake edge. Use modification usually consists of a continuous series of very small flake scars on the working edge of the flake, although in some cases only edge polish and edge rounding are present.

The high frequency of UFLs at Calvert is quite surprising; however, it has been my experience that these tools are often overlooked during cataloguing. Many of the UFLs in the Calvert collection were reclassified from chipping detritus during the debitage analysis.

Table 7.6. Scraper data by phase.

| | House 1 | Early | Middle | Late | Unknown | Total |
|---|---|---|---|---|---|---|
| Sample Size | 2 | 11 | 7 | 10 | 26 | 56 |
| Metrics | | | | | | |
| Mean Length (mm) | 21.9 | 34.3 | 27.4 | 30.6 | 29.5 | 29.8 |
| Mean Width (mm) | 19.5 | 22.8 | 20.2 | 20.3 | 20.0 | 20.6 |
| Mean Thickness (mm) | 5.3 | 7.9 | 4.6 | 7.6 | 6.0 | 7.7 |
| Scraper Type | | | | | | |
| End | 1 | 4 | 2 | 1 | 8 | 16 |
| Side | 0 | 3 | 2 | 5 | 4 | 14 |
| Spokeshave | 0 | 2 | 2 | 1 | 1 | 6 |
| Combination | 1 | 0 | 1 | 3 | 13 | 18 |
| Fragmentary | 0 | 2 | 0 | 0 | 0 | 2 |
| Chert Type | | | | | | |
| Onondaga | 1 | 5 | 3 | 6 | 18 | 33 |
| Kettle Point | 1 | 2 | 2 | 1 | 6 | 12 |
| Selkirk | 0 | 0 | 0 | 1 | 1 | 2 |
| Local | 0 | 2 | 2 | 0 | 0 | 4 |
| Unknown | 0 | 2 | 0 | 2 | 1 | 5 |
| Heat and Cortex | | | | | | |
| Number Heated | 0 | 3 | 1 | 2 | 3 | 9 |
| Cortex Present | 0 | 3 | 1 | 3 | 3 | 10 |
| Number of Scraping Surfaces | | | | | | |
| One | 1 | 10 | 6 | 5 | 6 | 28 |
| Two | 1 | 1 | 1 | 5 | 15 | 22 |
| Three | - | - | - | - | 2 | 3 |
| Four | - | - | - | - | 3 | 3 |
| Scraping Edge Attributes: First Scraping Surface | | | | | | |
| Mean Edge Angle | 79.5 | 63.9 | 62.9 | 65.0 | 66.9 | 66.0 |
| Mean Wear Length | 17.0 | 25.8 | 18.2 | 20.1 | 24.4 | 21.8 |
| Rounded Wear Pattern | 2 | 6 | 4 | 5 | 16 | 32 |
| Angular Wear Pattern | 0 | 4 | 3 | 5 | 10 | 22 |
| Dorsal Wear Location | 2 | 8 | 6 | 9 | 27 | 51 |
| Ventral Wear Location | 0 | 3 | 1 | 1 | 0 | 5 |
| Polish Present | 2 | 8 | 6 | 8 | 23 | 47 |
| Scraping Edge Attributes: Second Scraping Surface | | | | | | |
| Mean Edge Angle | 46.0 | - | - | 59.8 | 62.2 | 61.1 |
| Mean Wear Length | 13.0 | - | - | 22.8 | 21.0 | 20.9 |
| Rounded Wear Pattern | 0 | 1 | 0 | 4 | 16 | 21 |
| Angular Wear Pattern | 1 | 0 | 1 | 1 | 5 | 8 |
| Dorsal Wear Location | 0 | 1 | 1 | 6 | 18 | 26 |
| Ventral Wear Location | 1 | 0 | 0 | 0 | 3 | 3 |
| Polish Present | 1 | 1 | 0 | 4 | 19 | 25 |

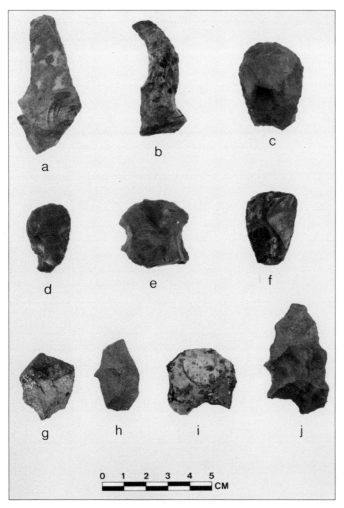

Figure 7.4. Scrapers and gravers: a, side scraper; b, spokeshave; c-f, end scrapers; g, utilized flake; h-i, gravers; j, experimental graver.

were also measured. These attributes were selected with specific problems in mind. It was felt that chert type could be relevant to native perception of chert quality, assuming that favoured cherts would be selected for use more often than less favoured ones (Keron 1986). If Kettle Point chert was used for UFLs more often than its percentage occurrence in the debitage sample, this could indicate a preference for Kettle Point material. The number of utilized edges may reflect the availability of chert, with greater utilization indicating that chert was in low supply (Schiffer 1987). Edge form (rounded or angular) is possibly related to duration of use (Williamson 1985), although it may also relate to the type of material worked and the task performed. Flake type was examined simply to determine whether specific stages in the reduction sequence yielded flakes that were more suitable for use. Once compiled, these data were entered into a DBASE III+ file and a comparative analysis was conducted between phases.

The results are presented in Table 7.7. In examining these data, few trends are apparent among the occupational phases. The mean metric measurements of utilized flakes in each phase are similar. Trends do occur with respect to chert type, yet these are difficult to interpret. Onondaga is the favoured raw material for UFLs during all phases and exceeds the percentage occurrence of Onondaga in the debitage sample in all phases except House 1 (Table 7.1). Kettle Point shows a steady increase in popularity from House 1 to the Late phase, rising from 13% to over 35%. If we compare these percentages to the occurrence of Kettle Point chert in the debitage sample we find an inverse relationship in the Early and Middle phases (Figure 7.5). In the Early phase, Kettle

Experimental studies conducted by Callahan (1981:197-201) indicate that flakes may be hafted and used to perform a wide variety of functions, including cutting, scraping, sawing, and planing various plant and animal materials. Given their several uses, and ease of production, it is not surprising that they dominate the tool assemblage.

All utilized flakes were hand examined to determine chert type, presence or absence of evidence of heat treatment, number of utilized edges, edge form, and flake type. Complete UFLs

Table 7.7. Utilized flake data by phase.

| | | House 1 | Early | Middle | Late | Unknown | Total |
|---|---|---|---|---|---|---|---|
| Number | f | 15 | 87 | 85 | 76 | 111 | 374 |
| Percent | % | 4.0 | 23.3 | 22.7 | 20.3 | 29.7 | 100.0 |
| | | | **Metrics** | | | | |
| Mean Length | | 20.2 | 26.2 | 26.3 | 25.8 | 25.9 | 25.7 |
| Mean Width | | 14.1 | 17.8 | 18.8 | 17.5 | 17.8 | 17.8 |
| Mean Thick | | 4.4 | 4.9 | 4.8 | 4.3 | 4.5 | 4.6 |
| | | | **Chert Type** | | | | |
| Onondaga | f | 7 | 57 | 41 | 36 | 75 | 216 |
| | % | 46.7 | 65.5 | 48.2 | 47.4 | 67.6 | 57.8 |
| Kettle Point | f | 2 | 14 | 24 | 27 | 22 | 89 |
| | % | 13.3 | 16.1 | 28.2 | 35.5 | 19.8 | 23.8 |
| Selkirk | f | 1 | 2 | 2 | 2 | 2 | 9 |
| | % | 6.7 | 2.3 | 2.4 | 2.6 | 1.8 | 2.4 |
| Local | f | 2 | 7 | 4 | 1 | 4 | 18 |
| | % | 13.3 | 8.0 | 4.7 | 1.3 | 3.6 | 4.8 |
| Unknown | f | 3 | 7 | 14 | 10 | 8 | 42 |
| | % | 20.0 | 8.0 | 16.5 | 13.2 | 7.2 | 11.2 |
| Total | f | 15 | 87 | 85 | 76 | 111 | 374 |
| | % | 100.0 | 100.0 | 100.0 | 100.0 | 100.0 | 100.0 |
| | | | **Flake Type** | | | | |
| Primary | f | 2 | 22 | 14 | 16 | 21 | 75 |
| | % | 13.3 | 25.3 | 16.5 | 21.1 | 18.9 | 20.1 |
| Secondary | f | 6 | 28 | 28 | 23 | 47 | 132 |
| | % | 40.0 | 32.2 | 32.9 | 30.3 | 42.3 | 35.3 |
| Biface Thin | f | 3 | 7 | 10 | 14 | 13 | 47 |
| | % | 20.0 | 8.0 | 11.8 | 18.4 | 11.7 | 12.6 |
| Fragmentary | f | 4 | 28 | 32 | 23 | 27 | 114 |
| | % | 26.7 | 32.2 | 37.6 | 30.3 | 24.3 | 30.5 |
| Bipolar | f | 0 | 2 | 0 | 0 | 2 | 4 |
| | % | 0.0 | 2.3 | 0.0 | 0.0 | 1.8 | 1.1 |
| Shatter | f | 0 | 0 | 1 | 0 | 1 | 2 |
| | % | 0.0 | 0.0 | 1.2 | 0.0 | 0.9 | 0.5 |
| Total | f | 15 | 87 | 85 | 76 | 111 | 374 |
| | % | 100.0 | 100.0 | 100.0 | 100.0 | 100.0 | 100.0 |
| | | | **Edge Form** | | | | |
| Rounded | f | 8 | 50 | 48 | 41 | 63 | 210 |
| | % | 53.3 | 57.5 | 56.5 | 53.9 | 56.8 | 56.1 |
| Angular | f | 7 | 37 | 37 | 35 | 47 | 163 |
| | % | 46.7 | 42.5 | 43.5 | 46.1 | 42.3 | 43.6 |
| | | | **Utilized Edges** | | | | |
| Mean Number | | 1.27 | 1.60 | 1.47 | 1.45 | 1.36 | |
| | | | **Heat Treatment** | | | | |
| Burnt | f | 5 | 25 | 31 | 27 | 29 | 117 |
| | % | 33.3 | 28.7 | 36.5 | 35.5 | 26.1 | 31.3 |

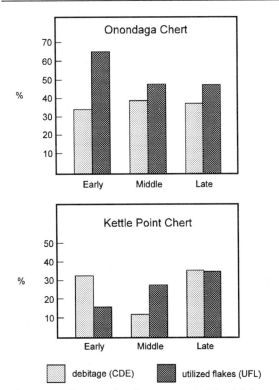

debitage (CDE)    utilized flakes (UFL)

Figure 7.5. Comparative frequency of utilized flakes and debitage of Onondaga and Kettle Point Chert.

Point chert forms 32% of the debitage sample but only 16% of the UFLs. Over 65% of the UFLs are on Onondaga chert in the Early phase. In the Middle phase the occurrence of Kettle Point drops to 12% in the debitage, but its use for UFLs increases to 28%. This clearly reflects a change in the management of Kettle Point material - although it is less common in raw form, it is being more heavily utilized for informal tools. In the Late phase the occurrence of Onondaga and Kettle Point cherts is quite similar when the debitage and UFL samples are compared. The relationship between chert types for debitage and UFLs among the three main phases is graphically illustrated in Figure 7.5.

Turning to the data on the types of flakes that are utilized, we find that secondary flakes are consistently most commonly used in all phases (Table 7.7). There is an unexplained increase in the use of biface thinning flakes in the Late phase

that is not paralleled by any similar increase in the production of Late stage debitage.

The data on edge form are remarkably consistent among the phases, with an average of 56% of the UFLs displaying rounded edges while the remainder are angular (Table 7.7). The mean number of utilized edges is highest in the Early phase at 1.6 edges compared to 1.47 and 1.45 for the Middle and Late phases respectively. This is the only indication that Early phase utilized flakes may have seen greater use than UFLs from the later phases, but it is probably too small to be considered significant.

Gravers

Gravers are single or multi-pointed flake tools that have been recognized on Palaeo-Indian, Early Archaic, and Glen Meyer sites (Ellis and Deller 1988; Fox 1976). Their function is poorly understood and interpretations of their uses include borers, tattooing needles, and specialized wood working tools (Deller: personal communication).

In past analyses, the points of these tools have been assumed to be the working edges, and some Palaeo-Indian gravers do indeed exhibit polish on their points (Ellis and Deller 1982). In examining the points on the Calvert gravers, it was determined that the extreme tips of these tools often bore little evidence of use in the form of polish or edge rounding. Yet the sides of the points possessed microflake scars identical to those observed on utilized flakes.

A simple half hour experiment using a large flake of Kettle Point chert to shave a wooden arrow shaft demonstrated at least one activity that can produce a tool with a form and use pattern that is identical to that observed on most gravers. Repeated working of an initially straight flake edge on the convex surface of the arrow shaft resulted in the removal of a series of small microflakes from the flake edge, as with any utilized flake. As this working motion was repeated, however, the flake edge began to form a concave surface, adapting itself to the shape of the shaft. The scraping action became more efficient as this concavity grew more pronounced from use, allowing the worker to apply more pressure without fear of tool slippage. If the

Table 7.8. Graver summary data.

| Metrics | | |
|---------|------|------|
| Mean Length | | 22.6 |
| Mean Width | | 17.4 |
| Mean Thickness | | 13.9 |
| | f | % |
| Chert Type | | |
| Onondaga | 11 | 44.0 |
| Kettle Point | 4 | 16.0 |
| Local | 2 | 8.0 |
| Unknown | 8 | 32.0 |
| Total | 25 | 100.0 |
| Number of Points | | |
| One | 13 | 52.0 |
| Two | 3 | 12.0 |
| Three | 4 | 16.0 |
| Four | 4 | 16.0 |
| Five | 1 | 4.0 |
| Total | 25 | 100.0 |
| Number of Utilized Edges | | |
| One | 3 | 12.0 |
| Two | 9 | 36.0 |
| Three | 12 | 48.0 |
| Four | 1 | 4.0 |
| Total | 25 | 100.0 |

worker repeats this action using part of the flake edge adjacent to the original working edge, this results in the production of a second concave working edge and a thin point between them. This action may be repeated around the entire perimeter of the flake, creating a tool with multiple working edges and several small points between them. One tool produced in this manner is shown in Figure 7.4, j, along with two gravers excavated from the Calvert site (Figure 7.4, h-i).

This simple experiment suggested that some gravers may simply represent specialized forms of flakes utilized for scraping and shaving circular shafts of various widths and raw materials. The points are not the working edges of these tools, they are simply the by-product of the use of adjacent concave working edges. Obvious uses for these tools are for the production of arrow and spear shafts, as replicated in my experiment. Bone and antler awls, needles, and punches may also be produced by these tools. Additional controlled experimentation is required to

determine other possible uses and whether it is possible to differentiate among uses on the basis of edge wear.

For the Calvert gravers, metric measurements, chert type, number of points, and number of utilized edges were tabulated for each tool. The total graver sample is only 25 tools and no one phase has more than six gravers; therefore, phase by phase comparisons were not attempted. The graver data are summarized in Table 7.8.

The majority (88%) of the gravers have more than one utilized edge. This is expected since it takes two working edges to produce a distinctive graver point as done in the experiment described above. The average number of scraping edges is 2.44 edges per tool. When compared to the UFL average of 1.47 edges per tool, it is possible to view these Glen Meyer gravers simply as very heavily utilized flakes that have developed a distinctive wear pattern.

## Wedges

Nine wedges or *pièces d'esquillées* occur in the Calvert assemblage. Again this sample is too small to permit a comparative analysis. At Calvert these objects appear to represent tools rather than exhausted bipolar cores.

The distinctive attribute of the wedges is the presence of facets from battering or pounding on two opposite edges. Four of the wedges display battering on two edges, while five have been battered on all four sides. They range in length from 17.0 to 31.6 mm (mean = 24.3), in width from 16.4 to 29.0 mm (mean = 21.2), and in thickness from 4.9 to 12.0 mm (mean = 4.9). Three of these tools are shown in Figure 7.1, e-g.

## Drills

Only four drills are present in the Calvert assemblage. Two types are represented. The first (Figure 7.3, c-d) is bifacially flaked and displays a heavily worn tip with a biconvex cross-section. Two drills of this type measure 37.0 x 15.4 x 8.0 mm and 36.2 x 22.5 x 5.6 mm respectively. The other type is considerably smaller, has a unifacially flaked tip and a triangular tip cross-section (Figure 7.3, a-b). Both drills of this type show tip rounding and use polish. The first

Table 7.9. Rough and ground stone artifacts.

| Artifact | House 1 | Early | Middle | Late | Unknown | Total |
|---|---|---|---|---|---|---|
| Celts | - | 1 | 2 | 1 | 6 | 10 |
| Celt Blanks | - | 3 | 2 | 1 | 5 | 11 |
| Hammerstones | - | - | 1 | 2 | 3 | 6 |
| Hammer-Anvil Stones | - | 1 | 2 | 2 | 2 | 7 |
| Anvil Stones | - | - | - | - | 1 | 1 |
| Metates | 1 | 4 | 2 | 1 | 2 | 10 |
| Abraders | - | - | 1 | - | 1 | 2 |
| Netsinkers | - | - | - | - | 1 | 1 |
| Ground Stone Frags | - | 2 | 1 | - | 13 | 16 |
| Slate Knife | - | - | - | - | 1 | 1 |
| Slate Pendant | - | - | - | 1 | - | 1 |
| Mudstone Effigy | - | - | - | - | 1 | 1 |
| Total | 1 | 11 | 11 | 8 | 36 | 67 |

of these measures 24.4 x 20.6 x 7.6 mm, while the second measures 17.0 x 13.0 x 2.7 mm. While the bifacially flaked drill form is common on Iroquoian sites, the unifacial form is very unusual.

### Rough and Ground Stone Tool Analysis

The rough and ground stone industry at Calvert is not highly developed, as only 67 tools and tool fragments may be assigned to this artifact class. Presumably, many of the tasks inferred for ground stone tools, such as scraping, digging, or hoeing, could have been performed using analogous tools of wood or bone that are not preserved in the archaeological assemblage. Table 7.9 provides a phase by phase breakdown of the rough and ground stone tools. Many rough and ground stone tools were found on the surface and the phase by phase frequencies are quite low making comparisons difficult.

An attempt was made to identify the raw materials present in the Calvert collection through reference to a field identification guide (Chesterman 1978). However, these identifications have not been verified by a geologist and should be regarded as tentative.

Celts and celt blanks dominate the assemblage, comprising 31% of the sample (n=21). The preferred raw material for celts was schist, although limestone, slate, and greenstone were used to a limited extent. Schist was probably chosen for ease of manufacture as it is

easily flaked and ground. Discrete concentrations of schist debitage attest to this activity. Based on the distribution of schist debitage, areas of celt manufacture may be identified. One such area occurs near Feature 156 in House 8 (Late Phase). Over 100 pieces of schist debitage were found in association with a schist celt blank in this feature.

Four of the five complete celts in the collection are quite small, ranging in length from 58 to 88 mm. They have all been flaked and then ground to a fairly sharp bit end (Figure 7.6, a). These tools were probably hafted and used for chopping, woodworking, and hideworking. One unusually large specimen, 125 mm in length, has been pecked and ground and has sustained heavy tip damage indicative of axe or hammer use (Figure 7.6, b).

Several celt blanks were apparently discarded or lost after they were initially shaped by flaking. They vary in size and are usually rectanguloid or ovate in shape.

Of the 13 hammerstones in the assemblage, seven were also used as anvils as indicated by pitted depressions on their top or bottom surfaces. Most of the hammerstones are ovate cobbles of gabbro or granite (both relatively hard igneous-plutonic rocks), displaying hammering facets around their circumference (Figure 7.6, d, h). There is one unusual specimen consisting of a fossiliferous chert cobble (Figure 7.6, i). It is inferred that the primary use of the hammer and

Figure 7.6. Rough and ground stone tools: a-b, celts; c, celt preform;
d, h, i, hammerstones; e, pendant; f, abrader; g, slate knife?

sandstone (n=5) and limestone (n=2), although single specimens of gabbro, granite, and gneiss were recovered as well. Traditionally metates are interpreted as grinding stones for processing corn and other foodstuffs. The Calvert specimens support this inferred function as they all exhibit at least one smooth concave grinding surface.

Only two ground stone abraders are present in the collection, although most of the metates, anvils, and several of the miscellaneous ground stone pieces could have been used as abrading surfaces. The two tools identified as abraders are both of slate and exhibit fine striations on one smooth flat surface (Figure 7.6, f). They vary in the size and depth of striations.

One specimen has been classified as a slate knife, although its precise function remains unknown (Figure 7.6, g). It was found in Feature 285, which has been interpreted as a ritual feature on the basis of its unusual contents (von Gernet and Timmins 1987; see also Chapter 9). This artifact measures 105.7 mm in length, 35.5 mm in width, and is 10 mm thick. It is rectanguloid in shape with a concave working edge. Prominent longitudinal striations occur along this edge while transverse striations are superimposed over the longitudinal wear in the central portion of the working edge. The other edges of the tool are not neatly finished but they have been smoothed and exhibit a dull polish, possibly from hand held use.

Similar slate knives with near identical wear patterns have been found on other Glen Meyer and Uren sites (M. Wright 1986). The wear

anvil stones in the collection was the reduction of chert cobbles and the initial flaking of chert tools.

Metates form an important class of ground stone tools that provide some insight into food preparation techniques. Ten metate fragments were recovered at Calvert, including the nearly complete limestone specimen in Figure 7.7. They are usually made of sedimentary rocks, including

Figure 7.7. Limestone metate.

One unusual specimen of banded slate has been interpreted as a slate pendant (Figure 7.6, e). It is an elongated piece of finely ground and polished slate, broken along the mid-section. One lateral edge is straight while the other is concave. It measures 55.7 mm in length (to the break), is 20.6 mm wide at the widest point, and is 8.7 mm thick. A (suspension?) hole has been drilled from both sides through the bottom of the artifact along the straight edge. This edge also exhibits a series of three small notches superimposed over several longitudinal striations which parallel the edge. The concave top surface has been bevelled to a smooth point.

A remarkable effigy figure made of mudstone was recovered from Feature 100 (phase unknown, Figure 7.8). It is a ground and carved mudstone ring or pipe fragment bearing the head of a small creature with reptilian features. The face displays a short snout, a straight unsmiling mouth, and large sunken eyes. It is best described as salamander-like, but, like other forms of Iroquoian effigy art it is somewhat ambiguous in form. The ring portion of the artifact, which may be the body of the animal, is decorated on one side with a series of short parallel lines. The underside of the effigy is heavily eroded, making it difficult to say whether the figure was at one time attached to a pipe. Since effigy pipes are extremely rare on Glen Meyer sites, and finger rings are not documented at all, it is possible that this specimen is simply an amulet or a charm.

## Discussion - Lithic Assemblage Variability

The explanation of lithic assemblage variability has been a vexing problem for archaeologists, as demonstrated by the classic problem of understanding assemblage variability in the Mousterian (Binford and Binford 1966; Bordes 1968). In the event that sites are used for markedly different purposes, the lithic tool assemblage can be expected to reflect the

pattern and the concave working edge are suggestive of a "drawing" or spokeshave use; however the edge is not sharp. It is possible that these tools were used as beamers or fleshers for the removal of flesh from the inner surface of animal hides. This procedure involves scraping the inner surface of the hide with a tool while resting the hide on a large beam. Such a process would be facilitated by a tool with a concave working edge and could create transverse striations as observed on these artifacts.

Sixteen of the rough and ground stone artifacts are classified as miscellaneous ground stone fragments. In most cases these are small pieces of ground stone tools that are too fragmentary to permit tool identification.

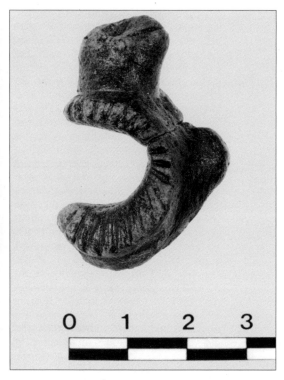

Figure 7.8. Mudstone effigy.

...immediate deposition processes as revealed in debitage are considered along with tool deposition processes which theoretically are not as immediate and are more influenced by curation and transport.

Although Magne's research was conducted on hunter-gatherer sites, the general principles that he developed may be relevant to the explanation of lithic assemblage variability on Early Iroquoian sites that may have served different functions.

Magne has demonstrated that raw material preferences may be evident if certain lithic materials are of higher quality than other available materials. Tools made of the favoured material may be curated and extensively maintained, leading to an abundance of biface thinning and resharpening flakes of that material. Formal tools made of the less favoured material should be more frequently discarded and hence may dominate the archaeological assemblage (Magne 1985:203-220). At the Calvert site, these ideas may be effectively tested by comparing the occurrence and use of the high quality Kettle Point chert with the more abundant but poorer quality Onondaga chert.

Length of occupation may be reflected in the composition of both the tool and debitage samples. On sites occupied for a long time tool assemblages should be large and variable, reflecting a wide variety of tasks. If these tools were maintained there would be a large amount of late stage detritus and maintenance (resharpening) detritus. Conversely, short term occupations with regular tool maintenance, will result in the deposition of fewer tools due to curate behaviour, and the ratio of late stage debitage to tools should be higher (Magne 1985:228, 243).

Finally, settlement strategy or site function may also affect assemblage composition. Tools that are used in related tasks may be expected to co-vary in assemblages. For example, Magne discovered that complete projectile points, spall tools, graver/drills, and unimarginal tools tended to occur together in an assemblage he interpreted as a specialized mammal hunting tool kit. Similarly, bifaces, complete and fragmentary unifaces, utilized flakes, and projectile point

different activities conducted. Unfortunately, the tool categories employed by archaeologists are rarely experimentally verified with respect to their assumed function. Furthermore, several factors other than functional ones may affect assemblage composition. They include occupation span, curate behaviour (removal of artifacts from sites upon abandonment), and raw material preferences or availability (Magne 1985; Schiffer 1987).

Magne (1985) has developed a model of lithic assemblage formation that integrates data on the abundance of tools on sites with the amount and type of lithic debitage recovered from them. This approach is more relevant to questions of site duration and function than other models based simply on the size and complexity of tools, since the by-products of stone tool manufacture are considered. As Magne (1985: 228) states:

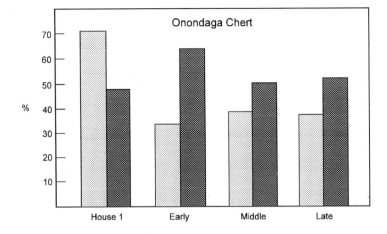

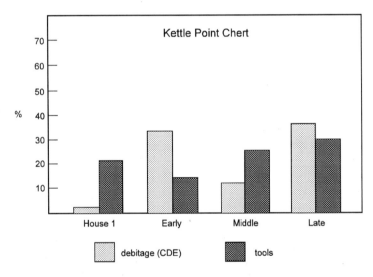

Figure 7.9. Comparative frequency of debitage and tools
of Onondaga and Kettle Point chert.

The differences in the relative frequencies of the chert types among the three phases and House 1 may best be explained by considering chert source locations, inferred procurement patterns, and external relationships. This is particularly useful with respect to Kettle Point chert which is easily recognized and has a known, localized source on the Lake Huron shoreline in the vicinity of Port Franks. James Keron (1986) has conducted an important study of Iroquoian sites in southern Middlesex County in which he examined the frequency of Kettle Point chert in relation to distance from this chert source. Keron's results show that the frequency of Kettle Point chert declines steadily as distance from the source increases, with sites in the Dorchester area generally having 20-25% Kettle Point chert in their lithic assemblages (Keron 1986:204, 205).

The consistency of Keron's results shows that Iroquoian communities in south Middlesex County must have had relatively consistent access to Kettle Point chert, probably through trade networks, since sites within each site cluster exhibit very similar Kettle Point chert frequencies.

Turning to the Calvert data, debitage chert types, which reflect immediate deposition, indicate a dramatic drop in the utilization of Kettle Point chert from the Early to the Middle Phase (32.7% to 12% - Table 7.1). Within House 1 Kettle Point material is barely present, representing less than 2% of the sample. Kettle Point material attains prominence once again in the Late phase when it is almost

fragments were thought to be associated with general purpose/maintenance functions (Magne 1985: 230-233). In the Calvert case, the lengthy occupations may have obscured such patterns, since a wide variety of tasks likely would have been performed with stone tools in every occupational phase. Nonetheless, some differences in assemblage composition may be anticipated in the Late phase sample which would reflect the change to a hunting camp, assuming that the tool categories used have at least some functional significance.

In the following discussion, the variability in the lithic assemblage will be discussed in relation to raw materials, occupation span, curate behaviour, and site function.

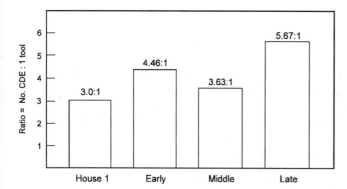

Figure 7.10. Late stage debitage : tool ratios by phase.

that these tools were being exhausted and replaced by Onondaga tools. We have noted that the frequency of utilized flakes made of Kettle Point chert rises significantly in the Middle phase. This increase accounts for much of the overall increase in tool numbers. Utilized flakes are expedient tools that are not generally curated. Thus the increased use of Kettle Point material for UFLs during the Middle phase, at a time when Kettle Point chert was scarce, indicates intentional selection of Kettle Point flakes for utilization.

In the Late phase the percentage of both Kettle Point tools and debitage increases (Figure 7.9), while the frequency of Onondaga tools and debitage changes very little. This suggests that the dynamics between Kettle Point and Onondaga raw materials are approaching a state of equilibrium, in which the occurrence of tools of each chert type corresponds more closely to the frequency of that chert type in the debitage sample.

The apparent fluctuations in the availability of Kettle Point chert and its use and curation may be related to socio-political changes in external relationships to the west during the occupation of the Calvert site. Hostilities with western neighbours who traditionally supplied or permitted access to Kettle Point material could effectively limit the supply. Alternatively, it is possible that the observed fluctuations, especially with respect to the Middle phase and House 1, are the result of different groups of people occupying the site. The changes in lithic raw material frequencies may be related to the origins of these different groups and their traditional access to Kettle Point chert. House 1 and Middle phase peoples may have originated from communities that did not have established access to Kettle Point material.

Regardless of the social and/or political implications of these changes, the evidence from each phase supports the proposition that Kettle Point chert was a favoured raw material that was preferentially selected for utilized flakes and curated as formal tools.

as common as Onondaga in the debitage sample. These figures suggest that access to Kettle Point material may have been restricted during the Middle phase and during the occupation of House 1.

When we consider the cherts used for lithic tools, the evidence suggests more mechanisms in play than simply restricted access. Figure 7.9 plots the percentage of Kettle Point and Onondaga debitage against the corresponding percentage of Kettle Point and Onondaga tools for all phases. House 1 appears anomalous as Kettle Point tools comprise 22% of the sample, even though Kettle Point chert forms only 2% of the debitage. This suggests that the occupants of House 1 did have access to Kettle Point material but were using Onondaga chert for the manufacture of new tools at the time House 1 was occupied. In the Early phase Onondaga and Kettle Point material occur in similar quantities, yet the majority of the tools being deposited are made of Onondaga chert. This may indicate that tools made of Kettle Point chert were being curated or that they were replacing the Onondaga tools, with the Onondaga tools being deposited more frequently. However, given the duration of the Early phase (about 20 years), it is unlikely that curate behaviour would be recognizable.

During the Middle phase, when Kettle Point material is less common in the debitage sample, the frequency of Kettle Point tools increases, while the frequency of Onondaga tools decreases slightly (Figure 7.9). If access to Kettle Point material was indeed restricted at this time, the increase in Kettle Point tools may reflect the fact

With respect to the problem of occupation span and site function, we have noted that the Early phase debitage sample shows a slightly higher occurrence of biface thinning flakes than the other two phases, which tends to support a slightly longer occupation for this phase. These results are supported by the fact that resharpening flakes also achieve their peak during the Early phase (Table 7.2).

Late stage debitage/tool ratios are instructive in understanding the relationship between tool maintenance, deposition, and curation. These ratios were determined by using the percentage of late stage debitage in the analyzed sample to estimate the total amount of late stage debitage in each phase. These numbers were then compared to the tool counts for each phase to determine the ratio. As Figure 7.10 shows, House 1 and the Early and Middle phases have the lowest late stage debitage/tool ratios (3.0:1, 4.46:1 and 3.65:1 respectively). The Late phase ratio is higher at 5.67:1. As a hunting camp, the Late phase probably represents a series of short term occupations. Such occupations may be heavily influenced by curate behaviour as most usable gear would be removed from the site after each visit. This behaviour, in turn, will influence the debitage:tool ratio, contributing to a higher ratio for the Late phase.

While the late stage debitage/tool ratios thus lend some support to the hunting camp interpretation proposed for the Late phase, they do not show the same pattern for House 1, which has also been interpreted as a hunting camp. This is because very little flintknapping occurred in House 1. In fact, of the 364 flakes found in House 1, over 200 were found in the small Feature 280. This suggests that much of the House 1 debitage may relate to a single flintknapping episode.

Other evidence in support of the proposed functional differences between the Early/Middle and Late occupations lies in the tool type frequencies shown in Table 7.4. The Late phase has a significantly lower percentage of utilized flakes and a higher percentage of bifaces. The utilized flake is multi-functional tool that would find more uses in a village where a wide variety of tasks were performed. In contrast, hunting camp activities would involve a few specialized

activities, such as retooling of projectile points, butchering, and processing of the kill. Thus we find a higher occurrence of bifaces and, as noted previously, greater evidence in the form of polish and microflaking that bifaces were used as knives and scrapers. In sum, based on traditional interpretations of tool type functions (not experimentally verified), we may conclude that the changes in the Calvert stone tool assemblage from phase to phase provide additional evidence of a change in site function from village to hunting camp.

## Ceramic Technology

### Background

Throughout the history of Iroquoian archaeology an inordinate amount of time and effort has been expended on the analysis of ceramic artifacts. Since the development of Richard MacNeish's (1952) *in situ* theory of Iroquoian origins, several archaeologists have attempted to trace the evolution of prehistoric Iroquoian groups through the analysis and comparison of their ceramics (Wright 1966; Ramsden 1977; Smith 1983, 1987). Partly as a result of the use of ceramics as temporal and social indicators, the functional analysis of Iroquoian ceramics remains in its infancy.

Ethnohistorical information concerning Iroquoian pot manufacture indicates that women made the pots using what was probably a paddle and anvil technique:

> ...The women ... make them, taking suitable earth which they sift and pulverize very thoroughly, mixing with it a little sandstone. Then when the lump has been shaped like a ball they put a hole in it with their fist, and this they keep enlarging, scraping it inside with a wooden paddle as much and as long as is necessary to complete the work. These pots are made without feet and without handles, quite round like a ball, except for the mouth which projects a little (Sagard 1939:109).

Most studies of Iroquoian pottery assume that potting was learned within the household and

Figure 7.11. Ceramics: a, Vessel 85 (Middle), corded; b, Vessel 27 (Late), corded with two rows of small punctates on upper rim over large punctates on neck; c, Vessel 23 (Early), plain with two rows of small punctates; d, Vessel 20 (Middle), suture stamped; e, Vessel 29 (Early), stamped hatched over incised horizontals over incised opposed; f, Vessel 38 (Unknown), stamped opposed over incised horizontals.

together with evidence of ceramic waste and juvenile ceramics (Pearce 1984). This suggests, not only that Iroquoian potting was learned within the household, but also that distinctive ceramic 'micro-traditions' may have existed at the household level.

Ethnohistorical sources indicate that Iroquoian pots were used for cooking, storing, and gathering food, and for carrying and storing water (Sagard 1939:102,109). Pots occur archaeologically in a wide range of sizes but there have been few detailed arch-aeological studies to determine if functional differences may be related to size. Warrick (1984a:113) examined the rela-tionship between the presence of carbon encrustations on pots (presumably from cooking) and pot diameter at the historic Neutral Fonger village and found that pot size was independent of function. On the other hand, Williamson (1985) demonstrated that mean vessel diameters at special purpose Glen Meyer sites on the Caradoc Sand Plain were smaller than those on village sites, suggesting that smaller, more portable pots were trans-ported to the camps. Given the large size and substantial weight of some large Iroquoian pots, this is hardly surprising.

As mentioned above, most past analyses of Iroquoian ceramics have not been con-cerned with the manner in which pots were made and used, but have focussed instead on developing methods for describing and comparing ceramic designs and techniques in pursuit of classificatory-chronological goals. The first systematic analysis of Glen Meyer ceramics was

taught by a mother and related female kin to female children (Warrick 1984a). The archaeological evidence provides some support for this proposition. For example, a number of prehistoric Neutral cabin sites around the Lawson site have each produced distinctive pottery,

Figure 7.12. Ceramics: a, Vessel 44 (House 1), stamped opposed over stamped platts on neck; b, Vessel 43 (Early), stamped opposed over plain with punctates over incised horizontals over incised opposed.

the typological study conducted by J.V. Wright in *The Ontario Iroquois Tradition* (1966). Wright described the characteristic attributes and temporal trends of a series of Glen Meyer ceramic types from sites across southwestern Ontario. Detailed information on attribute variation within each type was presented, but attribute frequencies for each site were not given, thus limiting the usefulness of the attribute data. Although the ceramic types used by Wright yielded a useful seriation of the Glen Meyer sites

he studied, few have employed this typology in subsequent analyses, largely due to a methodological shift to the use of attribute analysis among Iroquoianists.

Walter Kenyon's attribute analysis of the Pickering Miller site ceramics was not only one of the first Iroquoian pottery studies to examine individual attributes but went beyond single attribute analysis to formulate attribute combinations (W. Kenyon 1968). While Kenyon confined his work to the study of decorative techniques rather than designs, he nonetheless recognized a need to assemble attributes into clusters:

> It was decided ...to analyze the rims in terms of attributes or modes, and through experimentation to see if it were possible to isolate significant attribute clusters or concomitant variations. The resultant clusters would then be types... (W. Kenyon 1968: 36).

To accomplish this goal Kenyon sub-divided the Miller ceramics into categories corresponding to major decorative techniques and then tabulated the frequency of each combination of interior, exterior, and lip decorative technique within each group. Given the lack of comparative data available at the time, Kenyon did not attempt to formalize these attribute combinations into groups corresponding to types (W. Kenyon 1968:45).

A similar concern with decorative techniques rather than motifs was shown by William Noble in his analysis of the Van Besien ceramics (1975a). In this study data were presented on attributes of decorative technique only. This focus on decorative techniques may be related to the wide range of tools and methods used to decorate Early Iroquoian ceramics and the

Figure 7.13. Ceramics: Vessel 77 (Middle), stamped opposed motif over incised horizontals over stamped obliques over incised horizontals (repeated six times on neck).

perception that changes in these techniques could be important chronological indicators.

In Ronald Williamson's (1985) attribute analysis of Glen Meyer ceramics from sites on the Caradoc Sand Plain attribute frequency data were presented for a number of general attributes of rim form, design motif, and design technique.

Following a method used extensively in the seriation of Iroquoian ceramics (Wright 1966; Smith 1983), Williamson calculated coefficients of similarity for each of eight selected attributes and attempted to use the coefficients to seriate the sites for each variable examined (Williamson 1985). This method did not, in his view, yield an acceptable linear order for the sites and suggested only that their ceramics were very similar. He then examined a series of individual attributes that previous studies had demonstrated to be sensitive to chronological change and compared their trends to a chronological sequence derived

from a series of radiocarbon dates. This resulted in the identification of a number of attributes that seemed to correspond with the radiocarbon-derived chronology and these were taken to be attributes that were chronologically sensitive at "micro-temporal" level (ibid: 290). Other attributes were found to be sensitive at a "macro-temporal" level when compared to chronological trends identified in the ceramics from London area Middleport sites which were believed to be descended from the Caradoc Glen Meyer sites (Pearce 1984). Yet, in the end, Williamson was forced to rely heavily on the radiocarbon dates to order his site sequence, because few ceramic attributes showed measurable chronological change.

Smith's recent refinements of seriational methods deal mainly with Late Iroquoian ceramics and have been concerned with the identification of attribute combinations, that may be spatially, chronologically, or culturally significant (Smith 1987). He has developed a method of coding ceramic attributes that begins with the most idiosyncratic attribute states and allows variables to be recoded into more and more inclusive formats, each of which can be tested for variability. Key variables showing the greatest variation are selected and then used to define attribute combinations, which are considered to be higher level analytical entities that contain more information than single attributes. Unfortunately, Smith's methodology cannot be directly applied to Early Iroquoian ceramics because of the variety of techniques and bands of decoration involved. For these reasons modification of his method was considered to be beyond the scope of this study.

Glen Meyer ceramics differ significantly from later Iroquoian ceramics in design complexity, in the number of bands of decoration applied to vessels, and in the variety of impressions present in designs, indicating the use of a wide range of

Figure 7.14. Ceramics: Vessel 82 (Early), linear stamp / incised horizontal / linear stamp / incised horizontal / cord-wrapped stick obliques (4 rows) with punctates / incised horizontals / incised hatched / incised horizontals / incised hatched / incised horizontals.

same site over an estimated period of 50 to 100 years. If these ceramic samples represent an uninterrupted sequence of ceramic development within a single community, it may be possible to identify some chronological trends in the ceramics through seriation. On the other hand, massive social-political change, such as the influx of new people or the occupation of the site by a different community, would be expected to disrupt ceramic traditions and their temporal trends through the introduction of new ceramic types and attributes related to social factors.

In seriating the ceramics we already know the correct chronological sequence of the phases. This information may allow us to determine attributes of chronological significance and distinguish them from socially related attributes. An unknown factor is the 'noise' resulting from possible admixture of ceramics from different phases.

It was also recognized that the Calvert ceramics might show very limited change over the course of the site occupation. As noted above, Williamson's (1985) Caradoc study indicated that Glen Meyer ceramic styles changed very slowly between A.D. 1100 and 1250 in that area. If the Calvert ceramics were produced by a single community evolving over a relatively short period of time, we would expect to find a high degree of ceramic similarity among the different phases.

**Methodology and Results**

The methodology used in the analysis of the Calvert ceramics is described in detail in the

decorating tools and techniques. In my view, none of the approaches described above adequately accounts for the variability observed in Glen Meyer ceramics. Consequently it was necessary to develop a new approach, based in part on previous research, but also addressing the special problems presented by complex Early Iroquoian ceramics.

At Calvert we have four ceramic samples that come from sequential occupations of the

Figure 7.15. Ceramics: a, Vessel 52 (Early), cord-wrapped stick obliques over punctates over incised opposed; b, Vessel 13 (Early), cord-wrapped stick obliques over incised and open triangles and lozenges; c, Vessel 11 (Late), cord-wrapped stick obliques (4 rows) with two superimposed rows of bosses over incised horizontals; d, Vessel 64 (Early), cord-wrapped stick opposed with a row of superimposed bosses over cord-wrapped stick horizontals.

fragmentary rims were sorted into 201 analyzable vessels. To permit the analysis of attribute combinations, variables of technique combination and design motif combination were recorded by combining the sequence of techniques and designs on the interior, lip, upper rim, and neck of each vessel. For example, a vessel with simple oblique bands of cord wrapped stick (CWS) impressions on the interior, lip, rim, and neck would be coded as Simple-Simple-Simple-Simple for the design combination and CWS-CWS-CWS-CWS for the technique combination. All design motifs and techniques are described in Timmins (1992). Examples of the ceramics are shown in Figures 7.11 to 7.15.

Once all vessels were coded the data was entered into a DBASE III+ file and descriptive summary statistics were generated for all attributes of rim form, metrics, design motifs, and design techniques for each occupational phase and for those vessels for which the phase was not known. With the vessel search complete, sample size was reduced to 65 vessels for the Early phase, 33 for the Middle phase, and 41 for the Late phase. Only seven vessels were assigned to House 1, while 55 came from contexts with unknown phase association.

writer's doctoral thesis (Timmins 1992). The methodology and results are only briefly summarized here.

Prior to initiating the ceramic analysis, a detailed vessel search was conducted involving comparison of all rim and neck sherds. In this manner, a total of 447 rim sherds and

Summary data for a number of general ceramic attributes are shown in Table 7.10. The most obvious phase by phase variation apparent in these data occurs in the related metric variables of Diameter at Lip and Lip Width. Specifically, we find that the mean diameter falls from almost 260 mm in the Early phase and 248 mm in the Middle phase, to about

Table 7.10. General ceramic attributes.

| | House 1 | | Early | | Middle | | Late | | Unknown | | Total | |
|---|---|---|---|---|---|---|---|---|---|---|---|---|
| | f | % | f | % | f | % | f | % | f | % | f | % |
| Total Vessels | 7 | 3.5 | 65 | 32.3 | 33 | 16.4 | 41 | 20.4 | 55 | 27.4 | 201 | 100.0 |
| Rim Form | | | | | | | | | | | | |
| Collared | 0 | 0.0 | 7 | 10.8 | 4 | 12.1 | 3 | 7.3 | 8 | 14.5 | 22 | 10.9 |
| Collarless | 7 | 100.0 | 58 | 89.2 | 29 | 87.9 | 38 | 92.7 | 47 | 85.5 | 179 | 89.1 |
| Orientation | | | | | | | | | | | | |
| Outsloping | 5 | 71.4 | 43 | 66.2 | 15 | 45.5 | 25 | 61.0 | 32 | 58.2 | 120 | 59.7 |
| Vertical | 0 | 0.0 | 6 | 9.2 | 6 | 18.2 | 7 | 17.1 | 10 | 18.2 | 29 | 14.4 |
| Insloping | 1 | 14.3 | 7 | 10.8 | 7 | 21.2 | 8 | 19.5 | 7 | 12.7 | 30 | 14.9 |
| Indeterminate | 1 | 14.3 | 9 | 13.8 | 5 | 15.2 | 1 | 2.4 | 6 | 10.9 | 22 | 10.9 |
| Size (mm) | | | | | | | | | | | | |
| Mean Diameter at Lip | 310.0 | | 259.7 | | 247.9 | | 201.9 | | 244.0 | | | |
| Standard Deviation | | | 92.5 | | 81.6 | | 56.2 | | | | | |
| Mean Lip Width | 8.0 | | 7.8 | | 7.0 | | 6.7 | | 7.2 | | | |
| Punctation | | | | | | | | | | | | |
| Interior Punctate | 3 | 42.9 | 28 | 43.1 | 13 | 39.4 | 21 | 51.2 | 21 | 38.2 | 86 | 42.8 |
| Exterior Boss | 2 | 28.6 | 23 | 35.4 | 10 | 30.3 | 16 | 39.0 | 23 | 41.8 | 74 | 36.8 |
| Exterior Punctate | 0 | 0.0 | 6 | 9.7 | 4 | 12.1 | 4 | 9.8 | 3 | 5.5 | 17 | 8.5 |
| Interior Boss | 0 | 0.0 | 6 | 9.7 | 3 | 9.1 | 4 | 9.8 | 2 | 3.6 | 15 | 7.5 |

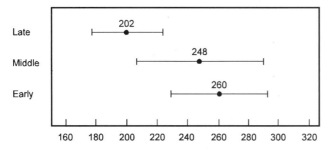

Figure 7.16. Average vessel diameters (mm),
shown with 95% confidence intervals.
(House 1 is excluded due to small sample size.)

200 mm in the Late phase (Figure 7.16). A concurrent trend is a reduction in mean lip width from 7.8 mm in the Early phase to 6.7 mm in the Late phase. These data indicate that Late stage vessels are substantially smaller and thinner than Early and Middle stage ones. The lower standard deviation for Late phase vessel diameters also indicates that they are less variable in size. Bearing in mind Williamson's (1985) demonstration that smaller vessels occur on special purpose sites, these data support our

conclusion that the Late phase at Calvert is a hunting camp.

Tables 7.11 through 7.15 show frequencies and percentages for the variables of interior motif and technique, lip motif and technique, rim motif and technique, and neck motif and technique.

In comparing the percentage occurrence of attribute values for each variable, House 1 appears to be most unusual. As Table 7.13 shows, five (71%) of the seven vessels in House 1 display a suture stamped rim technique. This compares to an occurrence of between 3 and 10% for suture stamped rims in the Early, Middle, and Late phases. Similarly, 43% of the House 1 rims have a suture stamped interior design compared to 10% or less for all other phases (Table 7.11). Despite the small sample size for House 1, this evidence demonstrates that the occupants of House 1 had a distinctive ceramic tradition that was not shared by the occupants of the main village. This strongly suggests that House 1 was occupied by a

Table 7.11. Frequency of interior rim design motifs and techniques

| | House 1 | | Early | | Middle | | Late | | Unknown | | Total | |
|---|---|---|---|---|---|---|---|---|---|---|---|---|
| | f | % | f | % | f | % | f | % | f | % | f | % |
| Motifs | | | | | | | | | | | | |
| Plain | 2 | 28.6 | 10 | 15.6 | 4 | 12.1 | 7 | 17.5 | 10 | 18.2 | 3 | 16.6 |
| Simple | 3 | 42.9 | 46 | 71.9 | 25 | 75.8 | 27 | 67.5 | 40 | 72.7 | 14 | 70.9 |
| Opposed | 0 | 0.0 | 6 | 9.4 | 2 | 6.1 | 3 | 7.5 | 1 | 1.8 | 1 | 6.0 |
| Horizontal | 1 | 14.3 | 0 | 0.0 | 1 | 3.0 | 1 | 2.5 | 1 | 1.8 | | 2.0 |
| Hatched | 1 | 14.3 | 2 | 3.1 | 1 | 3.0 | 2 | 5.0 | 3 | 5.5 | | 4.5 |
| Total | 7 | 100.0 | 64 | 100.0 | 33 | 100.0 | 40 | 100.0 | 55 | 100.0 | 19 | 100.0 |
| Techniques | | | | | | | | | | | | |
| Cord-wrapped Stick | 1 | 14.3 | 35 | 54.7 | 19 | 57.6 | 20 | 50.0 | 31 | 56.4 | 10 | 53.3 |
| Linear Stamp | 0 | 0.0 | 9 | 14.1 | 7 | 21.2 | 7 | 17.5 | 9 | 16.4 | 3 | 16.1 |
| Incised | 1 | 14.3 | 1 | 1.6 | 1 | 3.0 | 1 | 2.5 | 2 | 3.6 | | 3.0 |
| Suture Stamp | 3 | 42.9 | 6 | 9.4 | 1 | 3.0 | 4 | 10.0 | 2 | 3.6 | 1 | 8.0 |
| Stafford Stamp | 0 | 0.0 | 0 | 0.0 | 0 | 0.0 | 0 | 0.0 | 1 | 1.8 | | 0.5 |
| Punctate | 0 | 0.0 | 0 | 0.0 | 1 | 3.0 | 1 | 2.5 | 0 | 0.0 | | 1.0 |
| Corded | 0 | 0.0 | 0 | 0.0 | 0 | 0.0 | 0 | 0.0 | 0 | 0.0 | | 0.0 |
| Plain | 2 | 28.6 | 10 | 15.6 | 4 | 12.1 | 7 | 17.5 | 10 | 18.2 | 3 | 16.6 |
| CWS/Fingernail Imp. | 0 | 0.0 | 2 | 3.1 | 0 | 0.0 | 0 | 0.0 | 0 | 0.0 | | 1.0 |
| CWS/Linear Stamp | 0 | 0.0 | 1 | 1.6 | 0 | 0.0 | 0 | 0.0 | 0 | 0.0 | | 0.5 |
| Total | 7 | 100.0 | 64 | 100.0 | 33 | 100.0 | 40 | 100.0 | 55 | 100.0 | 19 | 100.0 |

different group of people than those who lived in the village.

Seriation was performed to determine if the ceramics from the three village phases formed a time series. House 1 was excluded from further analysis due to its small sample size and the fact that its relative chronological position earlier than the three main construction phases had been established (see Chapter 5). Ceramics of unknown phase were also excluded, since they represent a conglomeration of all periods of occupation.

The seriation was conducted by calculating coefficients of similarity for several ceramic variables and attribute combinations and arranging them into linear orders using the double link method described by Renfrew and Sterud (1969). In the end, only a small number of key attributes and attribute combinations yielded the expected sequence of Early-Middle-Late. For most variables, the coefficients of similarity were very much alike, indicating a high degree of similarity among the ceramics of all phases (Timmins 1992:285). Among the ceramic attributes that appeared to be chronologically sensitive were the presence of simple and horizontal lip design motifs which decreased through time, while plain lips showed a concurrent increase (Table 7.12). In a related trend, cord wrapped stick lip technique decreased through time. The only other attribute that showed a consistent trend was cord wrapped stick neck technique which increased from Early to Late (Table 7.14).

The attribute combination analysis was based on the two attribute combination variables described above, one relating to design motifs and the other involving techniques. Due to the large number of design motifs and techniques recorded, each of these attribute combination variables yielded about 100 initial combinations. Consequently it was necessary to regroup certain motif and technique attributes to reduce the

Table 7.12. Frequency of lip design motifs and techniques.

| | House 1 | | Early | | Middle | | Late | | Unknown | | Total | |
|---|---|---|---|---|---|---|---|---|---|---|---|---|
| | f | % | f | % | f | % | f | % | f | % | f | % |
| Motifs | | | | | | | | | | | | |
| Plain | 4 | 57.1 | 23 | 35.4 | 14 | 42.4 | 19 | 47.5 | 18 | 32.7 | 78 | 39.0 |
| Simple | 0 | 0.0 | 25 | 38.5 | 11 | 33.3 | 13 | 32.5 | 21 | 38.2 | 70 | 35.0 |
| Opposed | 0 | 0.0 | 0 | 0.0 | 0 | 0.0 | 1 | 2.5 | 0 | 0.0 | 1 | 0.5 |
| Horizontal | 3 | 42.9 | 17 | 26.2 | 8 | 24.2 | 7 | 17.5 | 14 | 25.5 | 49 | 24.5 |
| Hatched | 0 | 0.0 | 0 | 0.0 | 0 | 0.0 | 0 | 0.0 | 0 | 0.0 | 0 | 0.0 |
| Horizontal/Simple | 0 | 0.0 | 0 | 0.0 | 0 | 0.0 | 0 | 0.0 | 1 | 1.8 | 1 | 0.5 |
| Notched | 0 | 0.0 | 0 | 0.0 | 0 | 0.0 | 0 | 0.0 | 1 | 1.8 | 1 | 0.5 |
| Total | 7 | 100.0 | 65 | 100.0 | 33 | 100.0 | 40 | 100.0 | 55 | 100.0 | 200 | 100.0 |
| Techniques | | | | | | | | | | | | |
| Cord-wrapped Stick | 1 | 14.3 | 30 | 46.2 | 11 | 33.3 | 12 | 30.0 | 27 | 49.1 | 81 | 40.5 |
| Linear Stamp | 0 | 0.0 | 5 | 7.7 | 6 | 18.2 | 7 | 17.5 | 6 | 10.9 | 24 | 12.0 |
| Incised | 1 | 14.3 | 1 | 1.5 | 0 | 0.0 | 0 | 0.0 | 2 | 3.6 | 4 | 2.0 |
| Suture Stamp | 0 | 0.0 | 3 | 4.6 | 0 | 0.0 | 2 | 5.0 | 2 | 3.6 | 7 | 3.5 |
| Punctate | 1 | 14.3 | 3 | 4.6 | 1 | 3.0 | 1 | 2.5 | 0 | 0.0 | 6 | 3.0 |
| Corded | 0 | 0.0 | 1 | 1.5 | 3 | 9.1 | 1 | 2.5 | 0 | 0.0 | 5 | 2.5 |
| Plain | 4 | 57.1 | 22 | 33.8 | 11 | 33.3 | 17 | 42.5 | 18 | 32.7 | 72 | 36.0 |
| Push-pull | 0 | 0.0 | 0 | 0.0 | 1 | 3.0 | 0 | 0.0 | 0 | 0.0 | 1 | 0.5 |
| Total | 7 | 100.0 | 65 | 100.0 | 33 | 100.0 | 40 | 100.0 | 55 | 100.0 | 200 | 100.0 |

number of combinations represented. The procedure used to regroup the attribute combinations is described in Timmins (1992:288-291) and the frequencies of the various attribute combinations are shown in Table 7.15. At the conclusion of this analysis it was found that 8 of 15 attribute combinations followed consistent trends of increasing or decreasing popularity through time (Table 7.15). In particular, the technique combinations showed a shift from cord wrapped stick decorated vessels to linear stamped vessels through time (Timmins 1992:293), which is a significant general trend in Glen Meyer ceramic development (Williamson 1985; Noble 1975a; Wright 1966). With respect to design motif attributes, there were four combinations that showed steady decrease or increase through time, however, the design motifs were not nearly as temporally sensitive as the techniques (Timmins 1992:293). Overall, compared to our analysis of individual attributes, the attribute combination results showed better agreement with the Calvert sequence (Early,

Middle, Late), lending support to Smith's (1983) assertion that attribute combinations are more sensitive chronological indicators than single attributes.

## Juvenile Ceramics

Most Iroquoian ceramic assemblages include a class of vessels that are interpreted as having been made by children. These are referred to as juvenile ceramics. It is usually assumed that young potters were taught the art of ceramic technology by their mothers. Comparison of the decorative motifs and techniques found on juvenile ceramics with an adult sample may show the degree to which young potters imitated their teachers or, alternatively, experimented with new designs and techniques.

Juvenile ceramics at Calvert are represented by 45 rim fragments, 15 neck-shoulder sherds, and two basal sherds. The rim fragments represent a minimum of 33 vessels.

Table 7.13. Frequency of rim design motifs and techniques.

| | House 1 | | Early | | Middle | | Late | | Unknown | | Total | |
|---|---|---|---|---|---|---|---|---|---|---|---|---|
| | f | % | f | % | f | % | f | % | f | % | f | % |
| Motifs | | | | | | | | | | | | |
| Plain | 1 | 14.3 | 3 | 4.6 | 6 | 18.2 | 0 | 0.0 | 2 | 3.6 | 12 | 6.0 |
| Simple | 4 | 57.1 | 34 | 52.3 | 13 | 39.4 | 20 | 48.8 | 27 | 49.1 | 98 | 48.8 |
| Opposed | 2 | 28.6 | 19 | 29.2 | 11 | 33.3 | 16 | 39.0 | 19 | 34.5 | 67 | 33.3 |
| Horizontal | 0 | 0.0 | 4 | 6.2 | 1 | 3.0 | 2 | 4.9 | 2 | 3.6 | 9 | 4.5 |
| Simple/Horizontal | 0 | 0.0 | 0 | 0.0 | 0 | 0.0 | 1 | 2.4 | 0 | 0.0 | 1 | 0.5 |
| Hatched | 0 | 0.0 | 3 | 4.6 | 2 | 6.1 | 1 | 2.4 | 4 | 7.3 | 10 | 5.0 |
| Simple/Plain | 0 | 0.0 | 1 | 1.5 | 0 | 0.0 | 0 | 0.0 | 0 | 0.0 | 1 | 0.5 |
| Simple/Horiz/Simple | 0 | 0.0 | 1 | 1.5 | 0 | 0.0 | 0 | 0.0 | 1 | 1.8 | 2 | 1.0 |
| Simple/Opposed | 0 | 0.0 | | 0.0 | 0 | 0.0 | 1 | 2.4 | 0 | 0.0 | 1 | 0.5 |
| Total | 7 | 100.0 | 65 | 100.0 | 33 | 100.0 | 41 | 100.0 | 55 | 100.0 | 201 | 100.0 |
| Techniques | | | | | | | | | | | | |
| Cord-wrapped Stick | 1 | 14.3 | 42 | 64.6 | 17 | 51.5 | 23 | 56.1 | 36 | 65.5 | 119 | 59.2 |
| Linear Stamp | 0 | 0.0 | 11 | 16.9 | 7 | 21.2 | 8 | 19.5 | 11 | 20.0 | 37 | 18.4 |
| Incised | 0 | 0.0 | 1 | 1.5 | 1 | 3.0 | 3 | 7.3 | 3 | 5.5 | 8 | 4.0 |
| Suture Stamp | 5 | 71.4 | 6 | 9.2 | 1 | 3.0 | 4 | 9.8 | 2 | 3.6 | 18 | 9.0 |
| Stafford Stamp | 0 | 0.0 | 1 | 1.5 | 0 | 0.0 | 1 | 2.4 | 1 | 1.8 | 3 | 1.5 |
| Punctate | 0 | 0.0 | 0 | 0.0 | 0 | 0.0 | 1 | 2.4 | 0 | 0.0 | 1 | 0.5 |
| Corded | 1 | 14.3 | 3 | 4.6 | 5 | 15.2 | 0 | 0.0 | 1 | 1.8 | 10 | 5.0 |
| Plain | 0 | 0.0 | 0 | 0.0 | 1 | 3.0 | 0 | 0.0 | 1 | 1.8 | 2 | 1.0 |
| Fingernail Impressed | 0 | 0.0 | 0 | 0.0 | 1 | 3.0 | 0 | 0.0 | 0 | 0.0 | 1 | 0.5 |
| Linear Stamp/Incised/CWS | 0 | 0.0 | 1 | 1.5 | 0 | 0.0 | 0 | 0.0 | 0 | 0.0 | 1 | 0.5 |
| CWS/Punctate | 0 | 0.0 | 0 | 0.0 | 0 | 0.0 | 1 | 2.4 | 0 | 0.0 | 1 | 0.5 |
| Total | 7 | 100.0 | 65 | 100.0 | 33 | 100.0 | 41 | 100.0 | 55 | 100.0 | 201 | 100.0 |

The juvenile vessels are small and are generally crudely constructed. They appear to have been made by pinching and molding the clay and many sherds display small finger impressions and fingernail marks.

Functionally, most of the juvenile pots were probably used as toys, although some may have been used for drinking or collecting berries or other small items. They are too small to have been very useful for cooking or storage.

The vessel sample was analyzed to evaluate the degree of correspondence between the juvenile ceramics and those of adult manufacture in the areas of ceramic design and technique. The sample was initially broken down into sub-samples corresponding to different phases, but this reduced sample sizes so much that comparisons were meaningless. It should be noted, however, that juvenile vessels occur in all village phases except House 1. Within the village they show no spatial clustering with respect to distribution within houses.

The frequencies of design and technique attributes displayed by the juvenile ceramics are presented in Table 7.16. As this table shows, almost half of the vessel exteriors are plain, lacking any attempt at decoration. The adult ceramic sample has a much lower frequency of plain rims, ranging from 0 to 18% among the four

Table 7.14. Frequency of neck design motifs and techniques.

| | House 1 | | Early | | Middle | | Late | | Unknown | | Total | |
|---|---|---|---|---|---|---|---|---|---|---|---|---|
| | f | % | f | % | f | % | f | % | f | % | f | % |
| Motifs | | | | | | | | | | | | |
| Plain | 1 | 16.7 | 6 | 13.6 | 6 | 28.6 | 3 | 9.7 | 6 | 17.1 | 22 | 16.1 |
| Simple | 1 | 16.7 | 4 | 9.1 | 2 | 9.5 | 4 | 12.9 | 8 | 22.9 | 19 | 13.9 |
| Opposed | 0 | 0.0 | 6 | 13.6 | 2 | 9.5 | 6 | 19.4 | 2 | 5.7 | 16 | 11.7 |
| Horizontal | 1 | 16.7 | 6 | 13.6 | 4 | 19.0 | 8 | 25.8 | 8 | 22.9 | 27 | 19.7 |
| Simple/Horizontal | 0 | 0.0 | 2 | 4.5 | 0 | 0.0 | 0 | 0.0 | 2 | 5.7 | 4 | 2.9 |
| Hatched/Horizontal | 0 | 0.0 | 1 | 2.3 | 0 | 0.0 | 0 | 0.0 | 0 | 0.0 | 1 | 0.7 |
| Hatched/Opposed | 0 | 0.0 | 1 | 2.3 | 0 | 0.0 | 0 | 0.0 | 0 | 0.0 | 1 | 0.7 |
| Plats | 2 | 33.3 | 7 | 15.9 | 3 | 14.3 | 6 | 19.4 | 2 | 5.7 | 20 | 14.6 |
| Opposed/Plats | 0 | 0.0 | 0 | 0.0 | 0 | 0.0 | 0 | 0.0 | 1 | 2.9 | 1 | 0.7 |
| Horizontal/Simple | 0 | 0.0 | 2 | 4.5 | 1 | 4.8 | 1 | 3.2 | 1 | 2.9 | 5 | 3.6 |
| Simple/Plats | 0 | 0.0 | 1 | 2.3 | 0 | 0.0 | 0 | 0.0 | 1 | 2.9 | 2 | 1.5 |
| Simple/Plain | 0 | 0.0 | 3 | 6.8 | 1 | 4.8 | 1 | 3.2 | 0 | 0.0 | 5 | 3.6 |
| Horizontal/Opposed | 0 | 0.0 | 3 | 6.8 | 2 | 9.5 | 1 | 3.2 | 2 | 5.7 | 8 | 5.8 |
| Simple/Horiz/Simple | 0 | 0.0 | 1 | 2.3 | 0 | 0.0 | 0 | 0.0 | 0 | 0.0 | 1 | 0.7 |
| Simple/Opposed | 0 | 0.0 | 1 | 2.3 | 0 | 0.0 | 0 | 0.0 | 0 | 0.0 | 1 | 0.7 |
| Plain/Plats | 1 | 16.7 | 0 | 0.0 | 0 | 0.0 | 0 | 0.0 | 0 | 0.0 | 1 | 0.7 |
| Indeterminate | 0 | 0.0 | 0 | 0.0 | 0 | 0.0 | 1 | 3.2 | 2 | 5.7 | 3 | 2.2 |
| Total | 6 | 100.0 | 44 | 100.0 | 21 | 100.0 | 31 | 100.0 | 35 | 100.0 | 137 | 100.0 |
| Techniques | | | | | | | | | | | | |
| Cord-wrapped Stick | 1 | 16.7 | 11 | 25.0 | 8 | 38.1 | 13 | 41.9 | 17 | 48.6 | 50 | 36.5 |
| Linear Stamp | 0 | 0.0 | 2 | 4.5 | 0 | 0.0 | 4 | 12.9 | 5 | 14.3 | 11 | 8.0 |
| Incised | 1 | 16.7 | 11 | 25.0 | 4 | 19.0 | 8 | 25.8 | 5 | 14.3 | 29 | 21.2 |
| Suture Stamp | 2 | 33.3 | 6 | 13.6 | 1 | 4.8 | 2 | 6.5 | 0 | 0.0 | 11 | 8.0 |
| Stafford Stamp | 0 | 0.0 | 1 | 2.3 | 0 | 0.0 | 0 | 0.0 | 0 | 0.0 | 1 | 0.7 |
| Corded | 1 | 16.7 | 5 | 11.4 | 4 | 19.0 | 1 | 3.2 | 2 | 5.7 | 13 | 9.5 |
| Plain | 0 | 0.0 | 1 | 2.3 | 2 | 9.5 | 2 | 6.5 | 4 | 11.4 | 9 | 6.6 |
| CWS/Linear Stamp | 0 | 0.0 | 0 | 0.0 | 0 | 0.0 | 0 | 0.0 | 1 | 2.9 | 1 | 0.7 |
| Fingernail Impressed | 0 | 0.0 | 0 | 0.0 | 0 | 0.0 | 1 | 3.2 | 0 | 0.0 | 1 | 0.7 |
| Incised/CWS | 0 | 0.0 | 0 | 0.0 | 0 | 0.0 | 0 | 0.0 | 1 | 2.9 | 1 | 0.7 |
| CWS/Incised | 0 | 0.0 | 3 | 6.8 | 0 | 0.0 | 0 | 0.0 | 0 | 0.0 | 3 | 2.2 |
| CWS/Plain | 0 | 0.0 | 3 | 6.8 | 0 | 0.0 | 0 | 0.0 | 0 | 0.0 | 3 | 2.2 |
| Incised/Linear Stamped | 0 | 0.0 | 1 | 2.3 | 2 | 9.5 | 0 | 0.0 | 0 | 0.0 | 3 | 2.2 |
| Corded/Suture Stamped | 1 | 16.7 | 0 | 0.0 | 0 | 0.0 | 0 | 0.0 | 0 | 0.0 | 1 | 0.7 |
| Total | 6 | 100.0 | 44 | 100.0 | 21 | 100.0 | 31 | 100.0 | 35 | 100.0 | 137 | 100.0 |

Table 7.15. Attribute combination frequencies of interior, lip, and rim motifs and techniques.

| | House 1 | | Early | | Middle | | Late | | Unknown | | Total | |
|---|---|---|---|---|---|---|---|---|---|---|---|---|
| | f | % | f | % | f | % | f | % | f | % | f | % |
| Motif Combinations | | | | | | | | | | | | |
| 1 HO HO | 1 | 14.3 | 2 | 3.3 | 1 | 3.0 | 1 | 2.6 | 1 | 1.9 | 6 | 3.1 |
| 2 SI HO OP | 0 | 0.0 | 2 | 3.3 | 3 | 9.1 | 1 | 2.6 | 5 | 9.4 | 11 | 5.7 |
| 3 SI SI | 0 | 0.0 | 3 | 4.9 | 2 | 6.1 | 3 | 7.7 | 0 | 0.0 | 8 | 4.1 |
| 4 OP OP | 0 | 0.0 | 4 | 6.6 | 1 | 3.0 | 3 | 7.7 | 1 | 1.9 | 9 | 4.7 |
| 5 SI HO SI | 1 | 14.3 | 6 | 9.8 | 3 | 9.1 | 4 | 10.3 | 7 | 13.2 | 21 | 10.9 |
| 6 SI PL OP | 3 | 42.9 | 9 | 14.8 | 7 | 21.2 | 6 | 15.4 | 2 | 3.8 | 27 | 14.0 |
| 7 SI PL SI | 0 | 0.0 | 9 | 14.8 | 4 | 12.1 | 9 | 23.1 | 9 | 17.0 | 31 | 16.1 |
| 8 SI SI OP | 0 | 0.0 | 6 | 9.8 | 4 | 12.1 | 5 | 12.8 | 5 | 9.4 | 20 | 10.4 |
| 9 SI SI SI | 0 | 0.0 | 15 | 24.6 | 4 | 12.1 | 4 | 10.3 | 10 | 18.9 | 33 | 17.1 |
| 10 Residual | 2 | 28.6 | 5 | 8.2 | 4 | 12.1 | 3 | 7.7 | 13 | 24.5 | 27 | 14.0 |
| Total | 7 | 100.0 | 61 | 100.0 | 33 | 100.0 | 39 | 100.0 | 53 | 100.0 | 193 | 100.0 |
| Technique Combinations | | | | | | | | | | | | |
| 1 CW CW CW | 1 | 14.3 | 26 | 42.6 | 10 | 30.3 | 10 | 25.6 | 21 | 39.6 | 68 | 35.2 |
| 2 CW CW | 0 | 0.0 | 14 | 23.0 | 8 | 24.2 | 11 | 28.2 | 12 | 22.6 | 45 | 23.3 |
| 3 LS LS LS | 0 | 0.0 | 4 | 6.6 | 3 | 9.1 | 4 | 10.3 | 2 | 3.8 | 13 | 6.7 |
| 4 LS LS | 0 | 0.0 | 2 | 3.3 | 4 | 12.1 | 3 | 7.7 | 7 | 13.2 | 16 | 8.3 |
| 5 PL PL | 1 | 14.3 | 5 | 8.2 | 4 | 12.1 | 5 | 12.8 | 5 | 9.4 | 20 | 10.4 |
| 6 SU SU | 3 | 42.9 | 6 | 9.8 | 1 | 3.0 | 4 | 10.3 | 2 | 3.8 | 16 | 8.3 |
| 7 Residual | 2 | 28.6 | 4 | 6.6 | 3 | 9.1 | 2 | 5.1 | 4 | 7.5 | 15 | 7.8 |
| Total | 7 | 100.0 | 61 | 100.0 | 33 | 100.0 | 39 | 100.0 | 53 | 100.0 | 193 | 100.0 |

Abbreviations: HO, horizontal; SI, simple; OP, opposed; PL, plain; CW, cord-wrapped stick; LS, linear stamp; SU, suture stamp. Note: Attribute combinations denote the dominant motif or technique. For example, CW CW CW means that Interior, Lip and Rim are all cord-wrapped stick impressed, while LS LS means that two out of the three techniques on the Interior, Lip and Rim are linear stamped.

phases. The high occurrence of undecorated juvenile rims may represent a learning sequence in which shaping and molding of the vessel was taught first, with decoration taught later.

The decorated juvenile vessels display a total of eight different exterior rim designs. The exterior rims are dominated by horizontal motifs (24.2%) (Table 7.16, Figure 7.17, d-f). The relatively high occurrence of horizontal decoration on the exterior rims is not paralleled in the adult sample, where horizontal motifs range between 0 and 6.2%. The most common exterior rim motifs in the adult sample are simple and opposed designs, which comprise 28% to 57% of

the collection. In the juvenile sample these motifs make up only 6.1% of the sample (n=2 in each case). Thus, in the case of exterior rim designs, there are major differences between the adult and juvenile ceramics.

Lip designs on the juvenile vessels are more similar to those in the adult sample. The most common lip designs consist of simple oblique or vertical lines and the juvenile percentage of 27.3% is reasonably close to the range of 32% to 38% observed in the adult samples.

The majority (72.7%) of the juvenile ceramics do not have interior decoration, while in

Table 7.16. Juvenile ceramics, design motif
and technique attribute frequencies.

| | Exterior | | Lip | | Interior | |
|---|---|---|---|---|---|---|
| | f | % | f | % | f | % |
| Design Motifs | | | | | | |
| Plain | 16 | 48.5 | 19 | 57.6 | 24 | 72.7 |
| Horizontal | 8 | 24.2 | 2 | 6.1 | 0 | 0.0 |
| Simple | 2 | 6.1 | 9 | 27.3 | 6 | 18.2 |
| Opposed | 2 | 6.1 | 0 | 0.0 | 0 | 0.0 |
| Hatched | 1 | 3.0 | 1 | 3.0 | 0 | 0.0 |
| Punctate | 1 | 3.0 | 2 | 6.1 | 2 | 6.1 |
| Opposed/Filled Lozenge | 1 | 3.0 | 0 | 0.0 | 0 | 0.0 |
| Simple/Punctate | 0 | 0.0 | 0 | 0.0 | 1 | 3.0 |
| Simple/Blank Lozenge | 1 | 3.0 | 0 | 0.0 | 0 | 0.0 |
| Plain/Inverted U-Shape | 1 | 3.0 | 0 | 0.0 | 0 | 0.0 |
| Total | 33 | 100.0 | 33 | 100.0 | 33 | 100.0 |
| Techniques | | | | | | |
| Plain | 11 | 34.4 | 17 | 54.8 | 22 | 71.0 |
| Corded | 3 | 9.4 | 3 | 9.7 | 0 | 0.0 |
| Punctate | 1 | 3.1 | 1 | 3.2 | 3 | 9.7 |
| Cord-wrapped Stick | 3 | 9.4 | 2 | 6.5 | 2 | 6.5 |
| Incised | 11 | 34.4 | 1 | 3.2 | 2 | 6.5 |
| Linear Stamp | 3 | 9.4 | 7 | 22.6 | 2 | 6.5 |
| Total | 32 | 100.0 | 31 | 100.0 | 31 | 100.0 |

the adult sample at least 70% to 88% display some form of interior rim design. Where interior decoration does occur on the juvenile vessels, it is usually simple, as is the case with the adult sample (Table 7.11).

Turning to the decorative techniques used on the juvenile ceramics, we find that incising is the most common exterior rim technique (34.4%), linear stamping the most common lip technique (22.6%), while punctates, cord-wrapped stick, incising, and linear stamping are about equally represented as interior design techniques (Table 7.16). These figures again differ dramatically from those derived from the adult sample, where incising ranges from 0 to 17.5% on vessel lips. The high frequency of incising on the juvenile ceramics may reflect the simplicity of this decorative technique and the fact that it can be done with any pointed object. Conversely, cord wrapped stick decoration requires a complex tool that may not have been available to child potters.

The use of proper vessel form seems to have been more important to junior potters at Calvert than the replication of adult designs. This is evident in several basal vessel fragments that replicate the globular body shape of adult manufactured pottery. The well made, nearly complete vessel depicted in Figure 7.17, a, is a good example of a juvenile imitation of the adult form.

In summary, the decorative motifs and techniques displayed in the juvenile ceramics show a surprising lack of correspondence with the adult sample. While they seem to share the same pool of techniques and motifs, preferences for certain techniques and motifs in the adult sample are generally not reflected in the juvenile sample. In fact, some of the juvenile vessels show substantial innovation in decorative motifs. One vessel displays a band of incised lozenges filled with incised verticals on the neck, augmented by short rows of linear punctates (Figure 7.17, b). A second pot has an unusual motif of inverted, nested U-shapes incised on the neck (Figure 7.17, c). These data suggest that there was little systematic teaching of ceramic designs to child potters at the stage when they were producing recognizable juvenile vessels. As in other aspects of Iroquoian domestic life, children were apparently permitted much freedom in learning potting skills.

In this regard, it is interesting to note that the favoured motifs (horizontal) and techniques (incising) of the child potters at Calvert are precisely those that become popular in the Middle Ontario Iroquoian stage, which begins shortly after the Calvert occupation. In the past, the widespread occurrence of hori-zontal motifs on Middle Iroquoian

## Smoking Pipes

As on most Glen Meyer sites, the pipe assemblage from Calvert is poorly developed. There are only 18 pipe fragments in the collections, including four stem fragments and 14 bowl fragments.

Two of the stem fragments display D-shaped profiles that are characteristic of many Glen Meyer pipes (Figure 7.18, g-h) (Noble 1975a). Both have a smooth finish, although one displays small horizontal incisions along the bottom edges of the stem. Of the other two stems, one has a rectanguloid cross-section with a smooth finish and the other displays an ovate cross-section and a corded surface treatment similar to that found on many of the ceramic vessels (Figure 7.18, i). The latter specimen is unusual, as cord malleation was rarely used on pipes.

Of the 14 pipe bowls and fragments, 11 are ceramic and the remaining three are stone. Most of the ceramic bowls are too fragmentary to permit identification of the bowl form; however, the single complete bowl is cylindrical with a right angle elbow (Figure 7.18, f). Six of the bowl fragments are plain, one displays vertical incised lines (Figure 7.18, e), one displays at least one horizontal incised line, and three are heavily punctated, sometimes combined with incised horizontals (Figure 7.18, d).

The three stone pipe bowl fragments include a nearly complete barrel shaped specimen made of fine-grained, grey limestone (Figure 7.18, a), a conical bowl fragment made of black slate (Figure 7.18, c), and a cylindrical bowl fragment made of an unidentified dark reddish-brown material (pipestone?) (Figure 7.18, b). All of these pipe bowls were probably fitted with wooden pipe stems, similar to the stone pipe bowls documented among the historic Iroquoians. Certainly, no stone pipe stems were found.

Figure 7.17. Juvenile ceramics: a, complete vessel with stamped rim and incised triangle and open neck motif; b, stamped opposed over incised filled lozenges on neck; c, plain upper rim with incised, nested, inverted U-shaped motif on neck; d-f, rims with incised horizontal motifs.

ceramics has been attributed to a Pickering "conquest" of Glen Meyer peoples, as proposed by J.V. Wright (1966). The Calvert data suggest, on the contrary, that widespread generational changes in ceramic design may have had more to do with this phenomenon. The work of the juvenile potters at Calvert may herald the wave of the future in Iroquoian ceramic design.

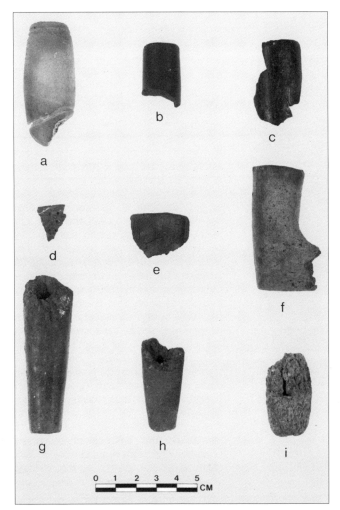

Figure 7.18. Smoking pipes: a, limestone pipe bowl found in association with Carolina parakeet bones in Feature 285; b-c, stone pipe bowls; d-f, ceramic pipe bowls; g-i, ceramic pipe stems.

The limestone pipe bowl was found in Feature 285 in association with the bones of the head, wing, and tail of the now extinct Carolina parakeet and two other artifacts. It has been suggested that the parakeet bones represent the remains of a bird skin (Prevec 1984b). We have proposed that the direct association of a parakeet skin with a stone pipe bowl is more than fortuitous and have argued, on the basis of widely ranging ethnographic analogies, that this pipe was equipped with a wooden pipe stem and decorated with the skin of a Carolina parakeet (von Gernet and Timmins 1987). The possible symbolic significance of this pipe is discussed in Chapter 9.

## Fired Clay Mass

One unusual, sub-rectanguloid lump of clay was found in Feature 92, located within Early phase House 14 (Figure 7.19). This mass of clay measures 146 mm in length, about 65 mm in thickness and is of undetermined width due to breakage. The fired exterior surface shows a series of highly irregular cord-like impressions on the top and two ends. The underside is rough, exfoliated in appearance, and displays at least six circular impressions of various widths and depths created by pressing cylindrical objects into the wet clay (Figure 7.19, b). The clay paste itself is grit tempered. The function of this artifact is not known. To our knowledge, no similar examples have been found in the Northeast.

The prehistoric Iroquoians must have exploited specific localities to obtain clay for ceramic vessels, and it would have been necessary to transport the clay back to the village in some manner. This artifact may be a lump of clay that was shaped, molded, and tempered at a clay source and transported to the village in a net-type bag, resulting in the cord-marked exterior impressions. The circular impressions on one surface may be the result of testing the clay for consistency prior to use. At some point this clay mass became fired; whether this occurred accidently or intentionally is not known.

## Conclusions

In summary, our analysis of the Calvert ceramics has given us insight into the ceramic technology of the Calvert people in the areas of raw material acquisition; manufacture of vessels, pipes, and children's pots; and changing stamped technique is also present on sites of the Younge Phase of the Western Basin Tradition (Lennox 1982:38), although the occurrence of the trait is not well documented. In any case, the high percentage of suture stamped ceramics in House 1 (71%) is viewed as evidence of a distinct ceramic tradition or micro-tradition within that household and suggests that the occupants of House 1 were not ancestral to the later Calvert villagers.

In terms of vessel function, the only attributes showing some correspondence with function are rim diameter and lip width, which are closely correlated with vessel size. The largest Iroquoian vessels were used for storage and are most commonly found in villages, where they were seldom moved. Smaller pots were likely used for collecting, drawing water, and transporting food. Thus smaller vessels are found at special purpose sites. At Calvert the Late phase vessels have a significantly smaller mean vessel diameter, which supports the inter- pretation of the Late phase as a special purpose camp.

While the analysis of individual ceramic attributes yielded few chronologically sensitive traits, the use of attribute combinations was much more successful and generally confirmed the occupational sequence presented in Chapter 5. In brief, it was found that several technique attribute combinations showed regular uni-directional change through time, with cord wrapped stick impressed techniques decreasing and linear stamp techniques increasing in popularity. Almost 80% of the ceramic vessels were found to share technique attribute combinations that followed these temporal trends. Design motifs, on the other hand, were not nearly so sensitive to chronological change and showed little change through time. The design motifs were extremely similar from phase to phase, which has been interpreted as indicating strong continuity in group identity.

Figure 7.19. Fired clay mass: a, top view; b, underside showing circular impressions.

decorative techniques and motifs. In particular, the analysis of the techniques and motifs seen on the adult vessel sample has enabled us to address questions of group identity and relative chronology with respect to the different construction phases.

In comparison to the three main village phases, the House 1 ceramics appear anomalous, with a very high occurrence of the suture stamped technique. In other regions (i.e., the Norfolk Sand Plain) this technique is commonest early in the Glen Meyer sequence, but it always occurs in very low percentages, usually less than 3% (Noble 1975a; Williamson 1985). The suture

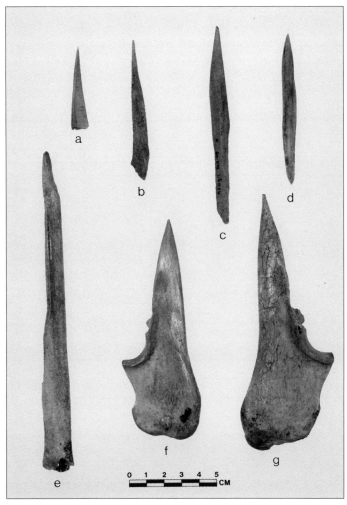

Figure 7.20. Bone awls: a-d, Type 1 awls; e, Type 2 awl; f-g, Type 3 awls (deer ulna punches).

## Bone, Antler, and Shell Technology

A total of 91 bone, antler, and shell artifacts were recovered in the Calvert excavations. While this is a relatively large sample for a Glen Meyer site, these artifacts constitute only .28 of one percent of the total artifact inventory. Since bone preservation in general was excellent at Calvert, the small number of bone tools found provides further support for the observation that the Glen Meyer bone and antler industry was poorly developed (Fox 1982a; Noble 1975a).

The bone tools from Calvert have been described by Rosemary Prevec (1984a), who classified them into 16 descriptive categories and provided faunal identifications where possible. For the present analysis, all of the bone tools were re-examined for specific attributes thought to be related to tool use.

Table 7.17 provides a breakdown of artifact types. It shows that antler artifacts (47.3%) and bone artifacts (50.5%) are almost equally common at Calvert. Shell artifacts are very poorly represented (2.2%).

The bone and antler artifacts were classified within descriptive categories that are related to inferred tool function. No experimental studies were conducted to verify such functions, although some extant bone tool experiments were used to aid interpretations (Callahan 1981).

Although the bone artifacts are broken down by phase in Table 7.17, sample sizes are small and there were too few bone tools to permit meaningful phase by phase comparisons. However, it is noted that bone artifacts were absent from House 1.

On the basis of this ceramic analysis, we conclude that there is no evidence of a drastic, wholesale change in the population occupying the Calvert site during the Early, Middle, and Late phases. The similarities observed in the ceramics indicate that a single community is represented. In contrast, however, the ceramics from House 1 are sufficiently different to suggest not only that House 1 was occupied prior to the Early phase, but also that it may have been occupied by a group unrelated to the later village community.

Table 7.17. Bone, antler, and shell artifacts.

| Artifact Class | Early | Middle | Late | Unknown | Total | % |
|---|---|---|---|---|---|---|
| Bone | | | | | | |
| Bone Awls | 5 | 6 | 4 | 11 | 26 | 28.6 |
| Miscellaneous Modified Bone | 1 | 1 | 2 | 1 | 5 | 5.5 |
| Bone Bead Wastage | 2 | - | 1 | - | 3 | 3.3 |
| Modified Turtle Shell | - | - | - | 7 | 7 | 7.7 |
| Modified Teeth | 2 | 1 | - | 2 | 5 | 5.5 |
| Subtotal | 10 | 8 | 7 | 21 | 46 | 50.5 |
| Antler | | | | | | |
| Antler Awls | 5 | 2 | 4 | 10 | 21 | 23.1 |
| Antler Handles | 2 | 1 | - | 4 | 7 | 7.7 |
| Antler Wastage | 2 | - | 2 | 4 | 8 | 8.8 |
| Antler Projectile Points | - | 1 | - | 3 | 4 | 4.4 |
| Antler Flaker | - | 1 | - | 1 | 2 | 2.2 |
| Antler Ornament | 1 | - | - | - | 1 | 1.1 |
| Subtotal | 10 | 5 | 6 | 22 | 43 | 47.3 |
| Shell | | | | | | |
| Clam Shell Scraper | - | - | - | 1 | 1 | 1.1 |
| Conch Shell Bead | 1 | - | - | - | 1 | 1.1 |
| Subtotal | 1 | 0 | 0 | 1 | 2 | 2.2 |
| Total | 21 | 13 | 13 | 44 | 91 | 100.0 |

## Bone Awls

Twenty-six pointed bone tools were classified as bone awls. Three distinct awl types were recognized on the basis of tip morphology, including tip cross-section and degree of taper. Attribute data are provided in Table 7.18.

Type 1 awls (n=13) are characterized by round tip cross-sections and a gradual taper towards the tip. They are all made of portions of mammal long bone shafts. The points are normally sharp but may in some cases be blunt. Longitudinal striations and some degree of polish are present on all specimens. Working tip widths range from 5.7 to 10.5 mm with a mean width of 9.1 mm. Examples of Type 1 awls are shown in Figure 7.20, a-d.

Type 2 awls (n=7) have tips with flat cross-sections and an acute taper at the point. Of the seven Type 2 awls recovered, four have sharp tips and three display blunt points. The four complete specimens are all quite long with an average length of 147.3 mm and a mean working tip width of 12.9 mm. One example is shown in Figure 7.20, e.

Type 3 awls (n=6) are deer ulna punches, beautiful tools with acutely tapered tips, very sharp points, and flat tip cross-sections (Figure 7.20, f-g). They are fashioned to take advantage of the natural shape of the proximal end of the deer ulna and fit very nicely into the hand. They have an average length of 125.4 mm, and an average width of 19.9 mm. All have longitudinal striations on the tip.

Experimental studies have shown that awls likely performed a wide variety of tasks. Callahan (1981) employed different types of bone and antler awls in his experiments involving the construction of Pamunkey houses using traditional technology. He noted that "several varieties of awls had extensive and critical use as multipurpose tools for such tasks as separating, tucking, piercing, prying, splitting,

Table 7.18. Bone awl attribute data.

| Catalogue Number | Length | Width | Species, Element | Taper Form | Point Form | Cross-section | Striae Direction | Polished Length |
|---|---|---|---|---|---|---|---|---|
| | | | | | | | | |

Type 1 Awls

| Catalogue Number | Length | Width | Species, Element | Taper Form | Point Form | Cross-section | Striae Direction | Polished Length |
|---|---|---|---|---|---|---|---|---|
| 108-71 | (112) | 10 | deer metapodial | gradual | sharp | round | long | 61 |
| 207-197 | - | - | mammal | gradual | blunt | round | long | present |
| 316-46 | - | - | mammal | gradual | blunt | round | long | present |
| 190-2-11 | (84) | 10 | deer metapodial | gradual | sharp | round | long | (84) |
| 9-2-32 | 106 | 13 | bear left tibia | gradual | sharp | round | l/t | 49 |
| 147-5-96 | (71) | 7 | mammal | gradual | sharp | round | l/t | 33 |
| 207-2-8 | (84) | 8 | mammal | gradual | sharp | round | l/t | 39 |
| 161-84 | - | 11 | mammal | gradual | sharp | round | long | (49) |
| 308-1-15 | - | - | mammal | gradual | sharp | round | long | (41) |
| 159-70-147 | - | 6 | mammal | gradual | sharp | round | long | 18 |
| 130-85-319 | - | - | ? | gradual | sharp | flat | long | (43) |
| 311-150 | 87 | 8 | mammal | gradual | sharp | flat | long | 87 |
| 311S-224 | - | - | mammal | gradual | ? | round | long | ?-calcined |

Type 2 Awls

| Catalogue Number | Length | Width | Species, Element | Taper Form | Point Form | Cross-section | Striae Direction | Polished Length |
|---|---|---|---|---|---|---|---|---|
| 316-3-2 | 136 | 14 | deer tibia | acute | sharp | flat | long | none |
| 9-1-2 | 126 | 12 | deer metapodial | acute | blunt | flat | long | 65 |
| 117-5 | 150 | 11 | deer metatarsal | acute | sharp | flat | none | 87 |
| 130-82-319 | 177 | 18 | deer metatarsal | acute | blunt | flat | long | 141 |
| 258-116 | - | 9 | mammal | gradual | sharp | flat | long | 33 |
| 318-1-1 | - | - | deer | acute | sharp | flat | long | none |
| 249-13 | - | - | mammal | acute | blunt | flat | long | present |

Type 3 Awls

| Catalogue Number | Length | Width | Species, Element | Taper Form | Point Form | Cross-section | Striae Direction | Polished Length |
|---|---|---|---|---|---|---|---|---|
| 159-69-146 | - | - | deer ulna | acute | sharp | flat | long | present |
| 161-136-6 | 121 | 21 | deer ulna | acute | sharp | flat | long | present |
| 306-3-15 | 128 | 22 | deer ulna | acute | sharp | flat | long | 50 |
| 321W-2 | (113) | 16 | deer ulna | acute | sharp | flat | l/t | 28 |
| 121-2-1 | 141 | 21 | deer ulna | acute | sharp | flat | long | 62 |
| 148-2-194 | - | - | deer ulna | acute | ? | flat | long | ?-calcined |

Note: ( ) indicates incomplete measurement; long, longitudinal; l/t, longitudinal/transverse

punching, and/or flattening a variety of plant and animal resources needed for house construction" (1981:213). Awls were probably also employed in pottery decoration, clothing manufacture, and food preparation.

## Miscellaneous Modified Bone

Five bone fragments display human modification that is suggestive of tool use, or a stage in bone tool manufacture. These artifacts, and their modifications, are described in Table 7.19.

Table 7.19. Miscellaneous modified bone tools.

| Catalogue Number | Modification |
|---|---|
| 318-2-2 | Deer metatarsal, lateral half; sides worked smooth with transverse striae; gradual taper, tip missing |
| 284-5-1 | Deer, left radius, proximal dorsal portion; hole worked in shaft with polished edge; scored; flesher? |
| 190-7 | Mammal long bone shaft fragment covered with transverse striations on all sides; overall polish; tip missing |
| 156-1-32 | Mammal? bone shaft fragment with one smoothed and polished lateral edge |
| 72-20 | Mammal bone shaft fragment; longitudinal striations, gradual taper, highly polished; probable awl mid-section |

## Bone Bead Wastage

Although no bone beads were recovered at Calvert, three scored and snapped turkey leg bone fragments were found (Prevec 1984a:39). They are interpreted as wastage from bead production.

## Modified Teeth

Three lower beaver incisors and two upper bear canines display worked occlusal surfaces (Prevec 1984a:39) (Figure 7.21, j-k). In all cases the occlusal surface is bevelled to produce a chisel-like working edge.

## Worked Turtle Shell

Seven turtle shell fragments have been modified, probably for use as bowls. One fragment displays a smoothed edge and several others have interior striations (Figure 7.21, c). Both Painted turtle and Blanding's turtle are represented (Prevec 1984a:39).

## Antler Awls

A total of 21 worked antler fragments have been interpreted as antler prong tools, although their precise function remains unknown. They probably served many of the functions attributed to bone awls

above. They are separated into two classes: those that retain tips (n=9) and those that do not (n=12). Table 7.20 presents attribute data for the antler prong tools. All specimens except one display longitudinal striations and eight are polished. The striations may be a result of either use or manufacture, as discussed below.

All antler prong tips are round in cross-section and they may be either sharp (n=5) or blunt (n=3). It is possible that two differing functions are represented by these different tip forms; the sharp pointed tools being used for perforation, the blunt tips used for something else. The majority of the antler prong tools are fragmentary, such that metric measurements are not useful.

## Antler Handles

Seven antler tools exhibiting hollowed ends are interpreted as handles into which other tools were inserted and hafted, creating composite tools (Figure 7.21, h-i). Most of these handles have been detached from the antler by scoring or notching and snapping. Five of the handles also show longitudinal striations. These marks are probably the result of a manufacture technique involving shaving antler prongs with chert flakes to work them to a sharper point. Such a technique would, incidently, contribute to the production of the utilized flakes that are so ubiquitous in the Calvert lithic collection.

## Antler Projectile Points

Four antler tips have been fashioned into projectile points (Figure 7.21, d-f). They all exhibit round tip cross-sections, sharp points, longitudinal striae, and polish. They range in length from 39.7 mm to 75 mm, but three of them cluster at about 40 mm in length, suggesting that this length was considered optimal. They have all been detached by scoring/carving and snapping. Two specimens have a hollow end to facilitate hafting.

## Antler Flakers

Two blunt tipped antler tools are interpreted as flakers used in the pressure flaking of stone tools (Figure 7.21, g). They display a series of small facets on the tip, relating to their use, and longitudinal striations on the tool body, probably from manufacture.

### Antler Ornament

One unusual piece of worked antler is interpreted as a decorative item (Figure 7.21, b). It is a polished antler prong section with five circular grooves around the shaft.

### Marine Shell Bead

One tubular bead worked from conch shell was recovered (Figure 7.21, a). It measures 13 mm long and is 8.3 mm in diameter. Since either the bead or the conch from which it was made probably originated on the Atlantic coast, its presence at Calvert can be taken as evidence of long distance trade.

### Clam Shell Scraper

One fragile piece of a large clam shell shows a continuous series of short striations along one edge that were probably produced by use of the shell in a scraping action.

### Summary

The bone, antler and shell tool collection from Calvert is relatively large for a Glen Meyer site and provides useful data on the nature of Glen Meyer tool assemblages. Bone, antler, and shell tools (n = 91) are less common than lithic tools (n = 689) or ceramic vessels (n = 201) and it is likely that many tools analogous to bone ones were made of wood. Nonetheless, experimental studies indicate that bone tools could have been used to perform a wide variety of domestic activities, suggesting that their importance in Early Iroquoian technology has been underestimated in the past.

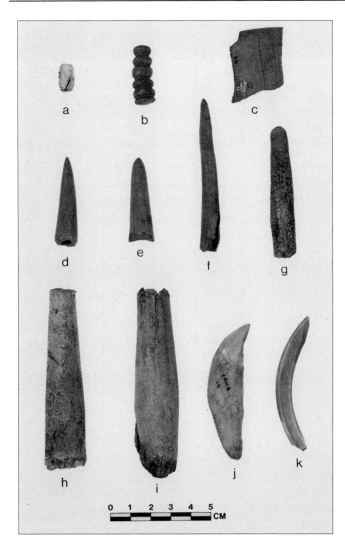

Figure 7.21. Bone, antler and shell tools: a, tubular conch shell bead; b, carved antler ornament; c, worked turtle shell (pottery marker?); d, f, hollow antler projectile points; e, solid antler projectile point; g, antler flaker; h-i, antler handles; j, worked bear canine; k, worked beaver incisor.

### Antler Wastage

Eight pieces of modified antler are classified as antler wastage resulting from the production of antler tools. All display scored and snapped or crushed ends resulting from antler prong removal.

## Feature Function and Formation

Archaeological features on Iroquoian sites not only are the source of much of the artifactual material recovered, but also form an important aspect of the site structure and settlement pattern. In

Table 7.20. Antler awl attribute data.

| Catalogue Number | Portion | Taper Form | Point Form | Cross-Section | Striae | Polish |
|---|---|---|---|---|---|---|
| 284-1 | tip | acute | blunt | round | long | present |
| 161-2-6 | tip | acute | sharp | round | long | present |
| 206-92-123 | tip | acute | sharp | round | long | present |
| 321-1-90 | tip | acute | blunt | round | long | none |
| 282-40 | tip | gradual | blunt | round | long | none |
| 161-82 | tip | acute | blunt | round | long | calcined |
| 20-1-32 | tip | gradual | sharp | round | long | present |
| 104-4-8-9 | partial tip | acute | missing | round | long | present |
| 156-65-521 | tip | acute | sharp | round | long | present |
| 321-177 | tip | gradual | sharp | round | long | none |
| 108-3-41 | distal | n/a | n/a | round | long | none |
| 201-17 | mid | n/a | n/a | round | long | present |
| 284-1-25 | hollow mid | n/a | n/a | round | long | none |
| 92-5 | mid | n/a | n/a | round | long | none |
| 291-31 | hollow mid | n/a | n/a | round | long | none |
| 321-2-41 | mid | n/a | n/a | round | long | none |
| 321E-174 | mid | n/a | n/a | round | long | present |
| 156-136 | distal | n/a | n/a | round | long | present |
| 210-3 | mid | n/a | n/a | round | long | none |
| 159-50 | mid | n/a | n/a | round | long | none |
| 149-2 | partial tip | n/a | n/a | round | none | none |

Abbreviations: long, longitudinal; mid, mid-section

systemic context archaeological features acted as facilities that were used by native people in day to day domestic activities. In this sense, the Calvert site features are artifacts in themselves, and their form, content, and spatial patterning constitute an important part of the record of the domestic activities that were carried out at the site.

The feature analysis presented here is organized as follows. Previous analyses of features are reviewed. The ethnohistorical data, relating to Iroquoian features is then discussed, followed by a description of pit formation experiments conducted by the writer. With this interpretive data in hand, the Calvert features are then analyzed in terms of form, contents, context, and function.

**Previous Feature Analyses**

Past analyses of Iroquoian features have generally provided rather cursory descriptive data relating to feature form and content, from which feature function has been inferred. Feature size (length, width, and depth) is usually considered, as is profile shape or basal configuration. Consideration of feature contents is usually limited to observations concerning the nature of the fill and the presence or absence of certain artifact classes (Williamson 1985: 181-182). In most cases, features are considered as part of the overall site settlement pattern, but feature function within the systemic context has rarely been explored in detail (Noble 1975a; Finlayson 1985). The manner in which features were formed, the type of material found in them, and the role they played as facilities have received little analysis.

An instructive analysis of Early Iroquoian features was undertaken by William Fox (1976: 180-184) in his study of the Dewaele site. In considering the features from Structure 3, Fox recorded feature size, profile shape, and the presence or absence of stratification. He found that the features clustered quite clearly into two distinct groups. Type 1 features were all large in size, (length > 60 cm), flat bottomed, and stratified. Type 2 features were smaller, with variable profile types, and were rarely stratified (Fox 1976:182).

With respect to function, it was proposed that the large Type 1 pits were lined with bark and acted as storage pits for vegetable matter, and that they were gradually backfilled as they were reused over a long period of time. Type 2 pits were seen as having a relatively short use-life, and it was suggested that they were used for disposal of floor debris. The Type 1 pits were found to cluster along the walls and in the corners of the structure, with the smaller Type 2 pits located in the centre. Given the large number of Type 1 pits in House 3 at Dewaele, Fox interpreted this structure as a food storage house, proposing that it could have held enough food to feed a village of 150 people for 60 days (Fox 1976:184).

At the Roeland site, Williamson (1985) excavated over 80 features which were analyzed in terms of size, fill type, and contents. In his analysis, Williamson provided interval data on feature lengths, widths, and depths, and noted the nature of mottling in the feature fill, and the presence or absence of contents. Based on these criteria Williamson stated that the features at Roeland also fell into two groups similar to Fox's types. He noted that the larger pits were usually filled with layers of ceramic and faunal refuse and were distributed under longhouse bunklines and around the perimeter of the village. These pits were interpreted as abandoned storage features. The smaller features showed more mottling with ash and fired soil and were usually aligned down the centre of longhouses in association with hearth features (Williamson 1985: 180).

The Glen Meyer feature types defined by Fox (1976) and Williamson (1985) are empirically quantifiable in terms of size, profile shape, and

stratigraphy. Yet the contents, formation processes, and functions of these feature types have not been considered in relation to ethnohistorical or experimental data. These data are discussed below.

## Ethnohistoric Data

Missionaries and early travellers among the Huron described the interiors of longhouses and in so doing provided important ethnographic data on hearths and storage pits, two of the most common subsurface features found on Iroquoian sites. Sagard (1939:94) and Lalement (Thwaites 1896-1901:17:177) each described large, interior hearths that were aligned down the central corridor of the longhouse (Heidenreich 1971:116-118). These features are usually recognized archaeologically by distinctive orange soil resulting from oxidized iron compounds on the hearth floor (Limbrey 1975:325).

Underground food storage facilities were also described by Sagard (1939:95). These storage pits were lined with bark and grass and were about one metre wide and 1.2 m deep (Heidenreich 1971:119). The early sources do not mention where the pits were located. Pits of similar dimensions are commonly found on some Iroquoian sites and have long been interpreted as storage pits. Within longhouses they are normally distributed beneath bunk lines along interior house walls. In some villages, especially Early Iroquoian ones, these large pits are often found outside houses as well, where they are usually located around the perimeter of the village.

Unfortunately, most of the features archaeologists interpret as storage pits were filled with refuse during a later phase of their use life. Consequently, there are few valid archaeological indicators that can be used to verify storage pit use. It is extremely rare to find food remains preserved in quantity within these pits, although this did happen in at least one feature at Calvert.

Although many archaeological pits were apparently used for refuse disposal, the existence of specific refuse pits is not mentioned in the ethnohistorical record. In fact, the early writers were silent on the topic of refuse disposal. Consequently, we have little ethnohistorical data concerning Iroquoian attitudes towards garbage and how it was dealt with on a daily basis.

Table 7.21. Experimental pit 1: stratum - deposit correlation.

| Excavated Data (from profile) | | | | Deposit Data (litres) | | | | | | |
|---|---|---|---|---|---|---|---|---|---|---|
| Level | Description | Volume | Event | Date | Bone | Veg | Soil | Ash/Char | Other | Total |
| 4 | Black with | 67.92 | 1 | 26/6/86 | 3.0 | - | - | - | 0.2 | 3.2 |
|  | charcoal chunks | | 2 | 30/6/86 | 2.0 | 2.5 | - | 12.0 | - | 16.5 |
|  | | | 3 | 2/7/86 | 2.0 | 8.0 | - | 12.0 | 0.5 | 22.5 |
|  | | | 4 | 4/7/86 | 1.0 | 10.0 | - | 20.0 | - | 31.0 |
|  | | | | Totals | 8.0 | 20.5 | 0.0 | 44.0 | 0.7 | 73.2 |
| 3 | Dark grey | 42.45 | 5 | 7/7/86 | 1.0 | 1.0 | 8.0 | 10.0 | 0.1 | 20.1 |
|  | with char/ash | | 6 | 9/7/86 | 0.5 | 1.0 | 30.0 | 10.0 | - | 41.5 |
|  | mottles | | | Totals | 1.5 | 2.0 | 38.0 | 20.0 | 0.1 | 61.6 |
| 2 | Brown with | 233.50 | 7 | 11/7/86 | 1.0 | 0.5 | 20.0 | 8.0 | - | 29.5 |
|  | yellow subsoil | | 8 | 15/7/86 | - | 10.0 | 40.0 | - | - | 50.0 |
|  | and charcoal | | 9 | 21/7/86 | 1.0 | 10.0 | - | - | - | 11.0 |
|  | mottles | | 10 | 23/7/86 | 1.0 | 12.3 | 50.0 | 5.0 | 0.1 | 68.4 |
|  | (includes light | | 11 | 28/7/86 | - | 13.0 | 30.0 | - | - | 43.0 |
|  | brown lens) | | 12 | 5/8/86 | 1.0 | 4.0 | - | 10.0 | - | 15.0 |
|  | | | 13 | 13/8/86 | 0.5 | 16.5 | 30.0 | - | 0.1 | 47.1 |
|  | | | | Totals | 4.5 | 66.3 | 170.0 | 23.0 | 0.2 | 264.0 |
|  | Level 2-4 Total | 343.88 | | | 14.0 | 88.8 | 208.0 | 87.0 | 1.0 | 398.8 |
| 1 | Dark brown/black humic | 84.9 | | Natural post-depositional infilling | | | | | | |
|  | Total Volume | 428.78 | | | | | | | | |

## Experimental Data

There has been little experimentation conducted dealing with the formation of archaeological pits. Limbrey (1975) has briefly discussed the natural processes involved in the in-filling of pits; however, most of her research concerns the in-filling of trenches associated with experimental earthworks. For both types of features she reports similar processes: the weathering back of the upper pit walls and the formation of basal strata consisting of soil from the upper level. Unfortunately, empty pits and trenches are not a good analogue for Early Iroquoian pits which, we believe, were initially used for storage and later transformed into refuse pits.

Dickens (1985) recognized this problem in a recent study of archaeological pits from the American Southeast. He proposed that prehistoric storage pits underwent the transformation to refuse pits once they became nonfunctional for storage, either because they had become "water-filled, soured, or vermin infested" (Dickens 1985:43). Since the storage pits he examined were used primarily in the fall for nut storage, he reasoned that those pits that were abandoned would probably show evidence of in-filling during the fall as well. Through paleoethnobotanical analysis he was able to demonstrate that this was in fact the case (ibid:56).

The Calvert site storage pits were probably lined with bark or grass as the ethnohistorical record suggests, otherwise they would not have been suitable for the storage of corn, which was the major storable commodity in the village. Following Dickens' line of thought, they would have been

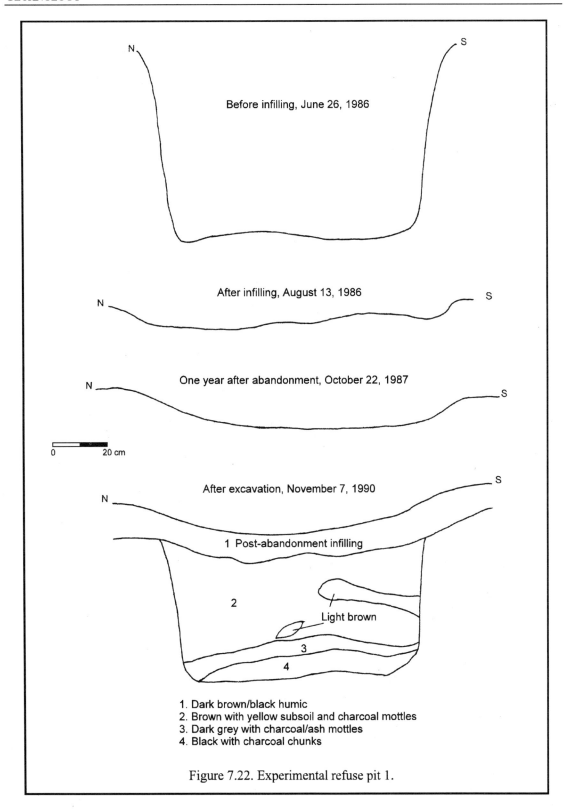

Figure 7.22. Experimental refuse pit 1.

abandoned as storage features for any of the reasons he cites **or** once the liner had begun to rot. Yet unlike the storage pits in the Southeast, the large Calvert pits appear to have been infilled over the long term, as suggested by their stratification and the large quantity and wide variety of debris found in them.

In an effort to understand better the formation of these large pits, a long-term experiment in pit formation was undertaken by the writer beginning in 1986. Although this experiment is ongoing, the objectives, methodology, and preliminary results are summarized here.

## Objectives

The objectives of the pit formation experiment were to address a series of specific problems concerning pit formation that emerged during examination of the Calvert feature profiles. Since it is not possible to recreate the cultural environment in which prehistoric refuse pits were formed, most of the problems involved the study of the natural processes related to pit formation and deformation. Specifically these problems included:

1. the relationship between major depositional events and stratum formation;
2. identification of potential natural disturbance processes and their effects;
3. the effect of short term abandonment of a pit; and
4. the relationship between decomposition of organic material and stratum formation.

These experiments were undertaken with the realization that several complex natural and cultural processes were involved in pit formation. The objective of the project was not to identify or quantify all such processes but, rather, to gain insight into some of the natural processes operative in pit formation as an aid to understanding of the Calvert site features.

## Methodology

Six experimental pits were excavated and in-filled between June 25, 1986 and October 29, 1987, in an effort to model certain aspects of refuse pit formation. In the fall of 1990, Pit 1 and Pit 3 were excavated and profiled using standard archaeological techniques. The remaining four pits were left for later excavation.

Pit 1 was filled over a period of 49 days between June 25 and August 13, 1986. It was excavated and profiled on November 7, 1990, approximately four years and three months after abandonment. Pit 3 was filled over 17 days between July 28 and August 13, 1986. It was excavated on December 12, 1990, four years and four months after abandonment.

The material used for fill ranged from modern domestic debris (mostly organic food wastage) to soil and ash. A log noting the volume and type of deposits was kept for each feature. During the in-filling period observations were made on natural disturbances and processes affecting the pit fill. These observations were entered in the log prior to each deposit. Scale stratigraphic profiles of each pit were drawn at four points in the procedure: 1. when they were initially dug; 2. when they were abandoned (a surface profile); 3. one year after abandonment (a surface profile); and 4. after excavation of half of the pit. A photographic record consisting of colour prints and slides was kept.

Since I was primarily interested in studying the pit profiles, it was only necessary to excavate one half of each pit. Pit profiles were then interpreted and stratigraphic profile drawings were prepared. This was done without reference to the log of deposits that had been made four years previously.

Once the feature profiles were prepared, the control data from the deposit log were assembled in chart form. This chart provided the actual use-life of each feature including the sequence, timing, and nature of deposits. It was then possible to compare the pit profile with the use-life of the pit in terms of the sequence of refuse deposits.

Five of the six pits were dug at the southern end of the Lawson site (off the site but within the fenced area), located at the London Museum of Archaeology in London, Ontario. The sixth pit was dug on the Lawson site in an area excavated by the Museum in 1979. The first five pits were dug through a clay loam topsoil and a yellow clay subsoil, while the pit in the previously excavated area was dug through rocky yellow clay subsoil overlain by a very small amount of topsoil. The pit location data are on file at the London Museum of Archaeology.

It was not possible to replicate several important aspects of Early Iroquoian pit formation during the experiment. One non-replicated condition was soil type, since a sandy soil matrix was not readily available. Further, the pits were not lined with bark due to lack of availability. These factors would be expected to affect the rate of wall collapse since sandy soils are less stable than loams and clays, while a bark lining would retard wall collapse. However, if the hypothesized transition from storage to refuse pit is correct, it is likely that the bark lining in such pits would have deteriorated and perhaps collapsed prior to use as a refuse pit. The experiment attempted to model refuse pit formation rather than storage pit use.

It was also impossible to recreate the environment in which Iroquoian pits were used in systemic context. While the experimental pits were located on the periphery of a partially reconstructed Iroquoian village that is open to the public, they were purposely placed in a remote area and were not affected by much foot traffic; nor were they affected by the many domestic activities that occurred in Iroquoian villages.

Finally, it was difficult to attempt to replicate Iroquoian refuse, both organic and inorganic, due to the obvious differences between modern Canadian material culture and subsistence patterns and prehistoric Iroquoian ones.

Despite these difficulties, valuable information regarding the natural processes involved in refuse pit formation was obtained.

## Results

### 1. Depositional Events and Stratum Formation

To evaluate the process of stratum formation in relation to depositional events, the refuse deposit data were compared to the stratigraphic profile obtained for each pit. Tables 7.21 and 7.22 summarize the refuse deposit data and provide one possible interpretation of the depositional events in relation to the observed pit stratigraphy after excavation. The experimental pit profiles are shown at various stages in Figures 7.22 and 7.23.

Generally, it was not possible to relate single depositional events to specific strata, unless the contents deposited in each event were very distinctive and/or large quantities of similar material had been deposited at once. In this regard, the most recognizable deposit in Pit 3 was Event #1, involving 25 litres of fish bone and fish entrails from a successful fishing trip. This was followed by 90 litres of soil (Event #2) designed to hide the rather unpleasant smell of rotting fish. Both deposits resulted in distinguishable strata. Level 5 in Pit 3 had a distinctive dark brown, greasy soil and yielded many fish bones in contrast to the light brown soil of Level 4. None of the fish bone was burnt, however, and one wonders if the stratigraphic distinction between Levels 4 and 5 would have been lost over several hundred years if this bone had decomposed.

In most cases several deposits seem to have contributed to the formation of individual strata. With the exception of the dark humic layer at the top of each pit (Level 1), most strata were poorly defined. This may be partly attributed to the disturbance and mixture of deposits caused by scavenging animals. Evidence of such disturbance was common and contributed to a homogenization of individual deposits.

Although few individual depositional events could be positively identified, it was possible to observe general changes in the pit strata and relate them to groups of depositional events. For example, in Pit 1, Events #1-6 all involved substantial amounts of ash and charcoal, contributing to the formation of dark grey or black fill in Levels 4 and 3. Subsequent deposits involved less ash and charcoal and more yellow soil, a change that is reflected in Level 2.

### 2. Natural Disturbance Processes

During the in-filling process substantial animal disturbance was documented, especially in Pits 1 and 3, which received the greatest quantity of organic refuse. The main scavengers in these experimental pits were probably raccoons, skunks, and dogs, although none of these animals was actually observed. Once animals were aware of the pits - which happened almost as soon as the experiment was started - the disturbance caused by scavengers was extensive. Covering bones and vegetable refuse with as much as three inches of soil did little to prevent this disturbance. Material that

Table 7.22. Experimental pit 3: stratum - deposit correlation.

| Excavated Data (from profile) | | | Deposit Data (litres) | | | | | | | |
|---|---|---|---|---|---|---|---|---|---|---|
| Level | Description | Volume | Event | Date | Bone | Veg | Soil | Ash/Char | Other | Total |
| 5 | Brown with fish bone | 23.00 | 1 | 28/7/86 | 25.0 | - | - | - | - | 25.0 |
|  |  |  |  | Totals | 25.0 | 0.0 | 0.0 | 0.0 | 0.0 | 25.0 |
| 4 | Light brown with | 85.40 | 2 | 28/7/86 | - | 5.0 | 90.0 | - | - | 95.0 |
|  | subsoil mottles |  |  | Totals | 0.0 | 5.0 | 90.0 | 0.0 | 0.0 | 95.0 |
| 3 | Brown with yellow | 40.20 | 3 | 5/8/86 | 2.0 | 9.5 | - | 10.0 | - | 21.5 |
|  | subsoil mottles |  | 4 | 12/8/86 | 3.0 | 23.0 | - | 14.0 | 0.5 | 40.5 |
|  |  |  |  | Totals | 5.0 | 32.5 | 0.0 | 24.0 | 0.5 | 62.0 |
| 2 | Black with charcoal | 38.5 | 5 | 13/8/86 | 1.5 | 12.5 | 60.0 | 15.0 | - | 89.0 |
|  | mottles |  |  | Totals | 1.5 | 12.5 | 60.0 | 15.0 | 0.0 | 89.0 |
|  | Level 2-5 Total | 187.10 |  |  | 31.5 | 50.0 | 150.0 | 39.0 | 0.5 | 271.0 |
| 1 | Dark brown/black humic | 50.9 | Natural post-depositional infilling | | | | | | | |
|  | Total Volume | 238.00 |  |  |  |  |  |  |  |  |

was completely covered the day it was deposited would be found on the surface the next day. The effect of this mode of disturbance was that some refuse, especially faunal material, tended to migrate upward within the pit as it was filled in, while other bones were simply carried off. For example, one labelled deer bone deposited in the bottom of Pit 3 was later found on the surface - after the pit had been completely filled.

Another natural disturbance process involves wall collapse, partly from weathering and partly from animals climbing in and out. As mentioned earlier, wall collapse in the experimental pits was expected to be minimal since they were dug into clay loam rather than sand. Nonetheless, some wall collapse was observed in most of the pits during in-filling The amount of wall collapse was not sufficient to be observed in the pit profiles. In pits dug into a sandy matrix, however, substantial wall collapse would be expected to form discontinuous lenses extending in from the sides of the pit. Such wall collapse deposits should be observable in pit profiles as artifact free deposits of the same soil type as the surrounding soils into which the pit was dug.

### 3 and 4 . Short Term Abandonment and Decomposition of Organics

The results of the experiment indicated the manner in which decomposition and subsequent settling of organic matter leads to stratigraphic slumping as material becomes consolidated. Since the pit contents were not packed in any way, the debris was loosely arranged and there were several air pockets in the fill. This results in a settling of the pit deposits, creating a depression on the pit surface.

Figures 7.22 and 7.23 document the sinking and compression of Pits 1 and 3 at intervals of approximately one year and four years after they were filled with refuse. In the span of one year each pit had sunk approximately 10 cm. In fact, the compression would have been more than that shown, since there was a concurrent process of in-filling with leaves and other forest debris beginning to accumulate in the depression after abandonment. The effect of such accumulation is the formation of a distinct, sterile, black humic layer in the upper level of both excavated pit profiles.

Observation of the related processes of pit sinking and the formation of a humic layer is relevant to archaeological interpretations for two reasons. First, these processes begin as soon as material is deposited and occur quite rapidly, thus it should be possible to recognize any seasonal or short-term abandonment of a pit by the presence of a thin sterile black organic layer. However, it may take longer for such a layer to form if the pit is located in a cleared area, such as an abandoned village, rather than a forest.

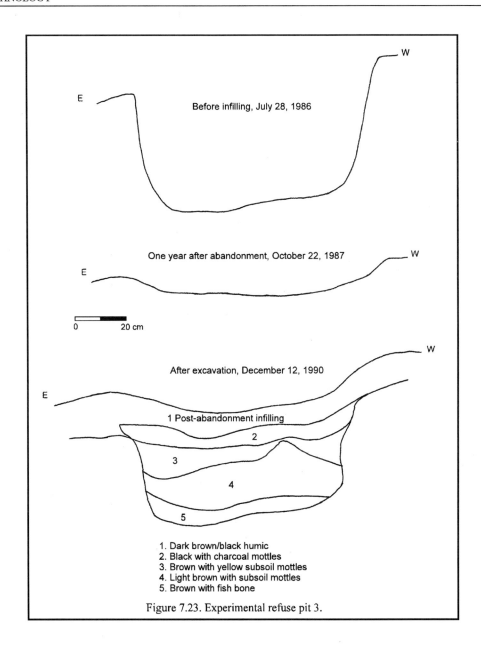

W

E Before infilling, July 28, 1986

One year after abandonment, October 22, 1987 W

E

0    20 cm

W

E After excavation, December 12, 1990

1 Post-abandonment infilling

2

3

4

5

1. Dark brown/black humic
2. Black with charcoal mottles
3. Brown with yellow subsoil mottles
4. Light brown with subsoil mottles
5. Brown with fish bone

Figure 7.23. Experimental refuse pit 3.

The second observation is that virtually all refuse pits that were infilled with perishable material should show the development of a sterile upper layer - unless they were re-used. This observation aids in the interpretation of archaeological pit stratigraphy. Specifically, understanding of these processes indicates that a sterile top layer in a feature does not necessarily mean that the pit was abandoned before it was completely filled as has been suggested in the past (Fox 1982a). Rather it may simply indicate post-abandonment slumping followed by in-filling with leaves and other organic debris as the site returned to forest.

Another case where decomposition of organic material may play an important role in stratum formation involves the decomposition of the bark liner in storage pits. Although such a liner was not employed in the experiments, we have noted that they are documented in the ethnohistoric literature and they would be necessary to keep food, especially seed corn, dry. Experience with reconstructed Iroquoian villages, such as the Lawson site, indicates that elm bark lasts only three to five years on the outside of a longhouse. Elm bark pit liners might deteriorate even faster in the moist conditions of an underground pit, unless conditions were anaerobic in which case decomposition would be slower. In any case, the liner in a storage pit probably had a use-life of only a few years. As mentioned above, it is possible that storage pits were converted to refuse pits once the liner had rotted and the pit had lost its ability to keep corn dry. When this happened the collapse of the bark liner would contribute to the first stratum in the fill of the refuse pit.

## Conclusions

In summary, at least eight significant observations or conclusions relating to the formation processes involved in these experimental pits may be drawn from the initial stages of this experiment. These are summarized below:

1. Most strata appear to involve several depositional events.

2. Distinct strata relating to single depositional events are rare. The creation of such a stratum required a major depositional event involving distinctive material, followed by a subsequent deposit of contrasting material.

3. Refuse pits that were unattended and uncovered were subject to extensive animal disturbance to both their faunal and vegetal contents.

4. Animal disturbance resulted in homogenization of pit deposits.

5. Animal disturbance also resulted in the upward movement of bone in refuse pits. Therefore, the *in situ* archaeological position of faunal remains in pits may not precisely reflect their depositional location.

6. Refuse pits were subject to in-filling from wall collapse. This process may or may not be observable in stratigraphic profiles depending upon soil type and extent of wall collapse.

7. Refuse pits were subject to stratigraphic slumping and compression over the short term after abandonment.

8. Formation of a sterile humic layer in pit depressions began immediately after abandonment. Therefore, the upper layers of pits will often be sterile, while sterile humic layers with overlying layers of refuse may indicate short term abandonment.

Of course, these observations pertain only to the experimental pits created in this study. The use of these data to interpret archaeological refuse pits is based on analogy, and the strength of the analogy depends upon similarities in form and context between experimental and archaeological pits. We have attempted to replicate several aspects of form, but, as discussed above, replication of the systemic context of Iroquoian pit formation is not possible. For this reason, these results are chiefly useful in the interpretation of the natural rather than the cultural processes in pit formation.

## Feature Analysis

### Analytical Method

A total of 19 observations were initially recorded for each excavated feature, with the data entered into a DBASE III+ file. Of the 19 observations recorded, five relate to feature provenience, three document feature size, four describe feature form, and seven document feature content. These data were imported into a Lotus 123 file and additional data were derived using spreadsheet functions. These data included feature volume, depth/length ratio, artifact density per litre, and the density per litre of chipping detritus, fire cracked rock, faunal material, and ceramics. Feature volume was calculated using the formula for the volume of a cylinder or one half the volume of a sphere, depending upon the shape of the feature profile.

Once compiled, the data were grouped to determine whether the feature types defined by Fox

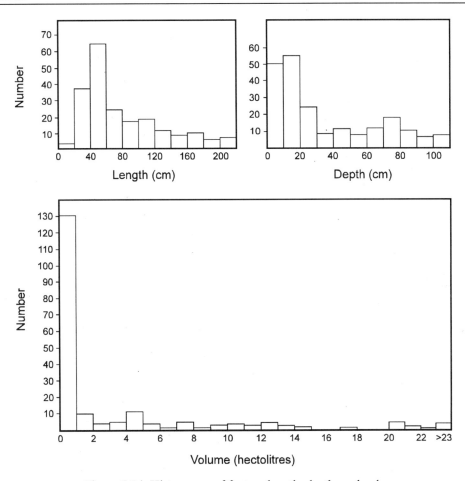

Figure 7.24. Histograms of feature length, depth, and volume.

(1976) were represented in the Calvert sample and whether additional feature types could be defined. Once feature types were defined on the basis of size and form, their contents were examined, their distributions analyzed, and interpretations of feature function and formation were made.

### Feature Form

The definition of feature types was initially attempted using the key attributes of feature size and profile shape employed by Fox (1976). Figure 7.24 shows the distribution of feature lengths and depths for the Calvert features. The distribution of feature lengths is unimodal while the distribution of feature depths is slightly bimodal. Both histograms show that more than half of the Calvert features are

less than 60 cm long and less than 30 cm deep. Most of these features have an average volume of less than 85 litres and a depth/length ratio of less than 0.5. They are essentially similar to the Type 2 features defined by Fox.

The key attribute distinguishing the Type 1 and 2 features defined by Fox is size. Since feature volume is the most accurate measure of feature size, this variable was examined in more detail, with the data converted to interval format in 100 litre (one hectolitre) increments. As Figure 7.24 shows, over half of the features again cluster with volumes less than one hectolitre, while remainder of the sample is more or less evenly distributed with volumes between one and 24 hectolitres. Using 1 hectolitre as a **natural** cutoff point suggested by the

Table 7.23. Feature volume by profile shape.

| Volume | | Cylindrical | Dish | Bowl | Bathtub | Irregular | Cone | Total |
|---|---|---|---|---|---|---|---|---|
| Less than 1 | f | 36 | 35 | 37 | 5 | 14 | 1 | 128 |
| hectolitre | % | 28.1 | 27.3 | 28.9 | 3.9 | 10.9 | 0.8 | 100.0 |
| Greater than 1 | f | 59 | 2 | 5 | 9 | 1 | 0 | 76 |
| hectolitre | % | 77.6 | 2.6 | 6.6 | 11.8 | 1.3 | 0.0 | 100.0 |

histogram of feature volumes (Figure 7.24), we then examined the distribution of profile shapes for features with volumes greater than and less than 1 hectolitre (Table 7.23). The results indicate that the majority (77%) of features with volumes greater than 1 hectolitre have cylindrical feature profiles. In contrast, features with volumes of less than 1 hectolitre display much greater variability in feature shape, with approximately equal numbers of cylindrical, dish shaped, and bowl shaped profiles represented.

Since cylindrical (flat-bottomed) feature profiles are a key attribute in the definition of the larger (Type 1) feature group, we explored the possibility that this profile shape could be a key attribute among the smaller features with volumes of less than 1 hectolitre. The result was the definition of a third group of features characterized by a cylindrical or bathtub shaped profile and a volume of less than 1 hectolitre.

The following criteria of feature volume and profile shape were thus selected to define three feature types. Type 1 features were defined as those features with volumes greater than 1 hectolitre and cylindrical or bathtub-shaped profiles (Figure 7.25). Type 2 features were defined as having volumes of less than 1 hectolitre and dish-shaped, bowl-shaped, or irregular profiles (Figure 7.25). Finally, Type 3 features included those features with volumes of less than 1 hectolitre and cylindrical or bathtub-shaped profiles (Figure 7.25). When these criteria were applied to the complete data base, 94.5% of the Calvert features were subsumed within these three feature types. A small number of large features with irregular profiles were assigned to a residual Type 4 category.

It should be noted that hearth features form a distinct feature type that is generally not included in this analysis. Hearth features are easily recognized by the presence of fired soil and they normally have shallow profiles and yield few artifacts. Since they are both easily recognized and non-productive, very few of the hearth features at Calvert were excavated and few are included in this feature analysis. On the basis of form, most of the Calvert hearths would be classed as Type 2 features.

Table 7.24 provides summary metric data on the three main feature types defined in this analysis. Standard deviations are high for each metric attribute, indicating that considerable variation in size exists within each feature type.

As Table 7.24 shows, the 68 Type 1 features have an average volume of 961 litres, and an average depth of about 70 cm. They are normally stratified: the average number of strata for Type 1 features is 3.5. The total volume of all excavated Type 1 features is 62,478 litres, or about 62 kilolitres.

The Type 2 features are much smaller, with a mean volume of only 21.1 litres and a mean depth of 12 cm. They are rarely stratified and display an average of 1.3 strata per feature. The total volume of all 81 Type 2 features is only 1,752 litres, or about 1.7 kilolitres.

Type 3 features, as defined in this analysis, are intermediate between the Type 1 and 2 features in terms of size, shape, and form. They are slightly larger than Type 2 features, with an average volume of 23 litres and an average depth of 19.6 cm. They are occasionally stratified and have an average of 1.5 strata per feature. The 41 Type 3 features excavated have a total volume of 1,517.7 litres or about 1.5 kilolitres.

Feature Contents

The contents of the Calvert features were analyzed in detail to determine if patterns could be

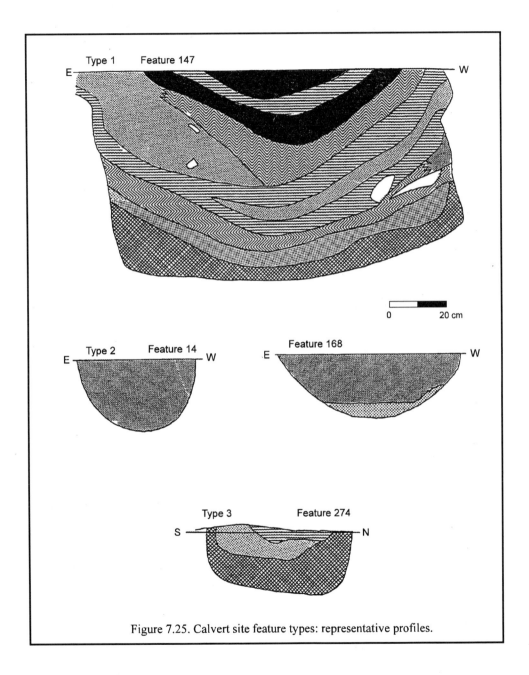

Figure 7.25. Calvert site feature types: representative profiles.

Table 7.24. Feature metric data by feature type.

| Feature Type | Statistic | Length mm | Width mm | Depth mm | Depth/ Length | Volume litres | Strata |
|---|---|---|---|---|---|---|---|
| Type 1 | Average | 127.0 | 112.6 | 69.7 | 0.6 | 961.2 | 3.5 |
| n=68 | Range-Max | 259.0 | 210.0 | 119.0 | 1.3 | 3887.0 | 7.0 |
|  | Range-Min | 54.0 | 51.0 | 26.0 | 0.3 | 110.9 | 1.0 |
|  | Total |  |  |  |  | 62477.9 |  |
| Type 2 | Average | 49.6 | 39.0 | 12.1 | 0.3 | 21.1 | 1.3 |
| n=81 | Range-Max | 104.0 | 68.0 | 29.0 | 0.9 | 98.5 | 3.0 |
|  | Range-Min | 20.0 | 15.0 | 4.0 | 0.1 | 2.4 | 1.0 |
|  | Total |  |  |  |  | 1751.9 |  |
| Type 3 | Average | 51.4 | 42.4 | 19.6 | 0.4 | 23.5 | 1.5 |
| n=41 | Range-Max | 76.0 | 68.0 | 39.0 | 1.0 | 34.8 | 4.0 |
|  | Range-Min | 16.0 | 19.0 | 5.0 | 0.1 | 9.3 | 1.0 |
|  | Total |  |  |  |  | 1517.7 |  |

Table 7.25. Feature content summary data.

| Statistic | Artifacts | CDE | FCR | Faunal | Ceramics | Artifact Density | CDE % | FCR % | Faunal % | Ceramic % |
|---|---|---|---|---|---|---|---|---|---|---|
| Type 1 (n=68) | | | | | | | | | | |
| Mean | 852.1 | 124.8 | 19.7 | 445.8 | 191.3 | 1.7 | 14.7 | 2.3 | 52.3 | 22.4 |
| Maximum | 2420.0 | 807.0 | 105.0 | 1948.0 | 1251.3 | 18.2 | 80.3 | 28.6 | 91.1 | 92.7 |
| Minimum | 14.0 | 3.0 | 0.0 | 1.0 | 1.0 | 0.0 | 0.7 | 0.0 | 1.5 | 2.9 |
| Std Dev | 712.2 | 143.0 | 21.4 | 492.0 | 217.3 | 2.7 | | | | |
| Total | 55385.0 | 8112.0 | 1282.0 | 28975.0 | 12436.0 | | | | | |
| Type 2 (n=81) | | | | | | | | | | |
| Mean | 77.0 | 16.0 | 2.1 | 41.6 | 16.5 | 4.2 | 20.8 | 2.7 | 54.0 | 21.4 |
| Maximum | 950.0 | 260.0 | 50.0 | 699.0 | 583.0 | 40.1 | 100.0 | 100.0 | 100.0 | 100.0 |
| Minimum | 1.0 | 0.0 | 0.0 | 0.0 | 0.0 | 0.0 | 0.0 | 0.0 | 0.0 | 0.0 |
| Std Dev | 156.0 | 40.9 | 6.5 | 106.1 | 73.1 | 7.0 | | | | |
| Total | 6238.0 | 1299.0 | 166.0 | 3370.0 | 1336.0 | | | | | |
| Type 3 (n=41) | | | | | | | | | | |
| Mean | 225.0 | 36.1 | 3.7 | 110.2 | 60.7 | 6.4 | 16.0 | 1.7 | 49.0 | 27.0 |
| Maximum | 1469.0 | 430.0 | 30.0 | 950.0 | 540.0 | 31.1 | 85.7 | 18.2 | 100.0 | 99.5 |
| Minimum | 3.0 | 0.0 | 0.0 | 0.0 | 0.0 | 0.1 | 0.0 | 0.0 | 0.0 | 0.0 |
| Std Dev | 323.0 | 75.6 | 6.3 | 203.7 | 106.9 | 7.4 | | | | |
| Total | 9224.0 | 1479.0 | 153.0 | 4520.0 | 2487.0 | | | | | |

CDE, chipping detritus; FCR, fire cracked rock

Table 7.26. Specialized features.

| Feature Type | Faunal (No Pcs > 1000 or % >80) | Ceramic (No Pcs > 400 or % >80) | Lithic (No Pcs > 250 or % >80) | Near Sterile (Artifact density <0.1) |
|---|---|---|---|---|
| Type 1 | Feat 20, Feat 79 | Feat 9 | Feat 3 | Feat 8 |
|  | Feat 100, Feat 148 | Feat 71 | Feat 24 | Feat 200 |
|  | Feat 151, Feat 156 | Feat 108 | Feat 43 | Feat 243 |
|  | Feat 134,Feat 207 | Feat 134 | Feat 134 | Feat 247 |
|  | Feat 209, Feat 208 | Feat 147 | Feat 156 | Feat 260 |
|  | Feat 258, Feat 308 | Feat 216 | Feat 190 | Feat 278 |
|  | Feat 311, Feat 321 | Feat 261 | Feat 207 |  |
|  |  | Feat 273 | Feat 258 |  |
|  |  | Feat 312 | Feat 270 |  |
| Sub-total | 14 | 9 | 9 | 6 |
| Type 2 | Feat 11, Feat 101 | Feat 10 | Feat 113 |  |
|  | Feat 122, Feat 135 | Feat 44 | Feat 114 |  |
|  | Feat 142, Feat 158 | Feat 58 | Feat 171 |  |
|  | Feat 289, Feat 294 | Feat 114 | Feat 188 |  |
|  | Feat 300, Feat 309 | Feat 251 | Feat 201 |  |
|  | Feat 217, Feat 184 |  | Feat 280 |  |
|  | Feat 219, Feat 221 |  |  |  |
|  | Feat 223, Feat 271 |  |  |  |
|  | Feat 264, Feat 301 |  |  |  |
|  | Feat 304, Feat 315 |  |  |  |
| Sub-total | 20 | 5 | 6 |  |
| Type 3 | Feat 115, Feat 274 | Feat 16 | Feat 205 |  |
|  | Feat 136, Feat 222 | Feat 242 | Feat 112 |  |
|  | Feat 133, Feat 235 | Feat 269 |  |  |
|  | Feat 245, Feat 291 |  |  |  |
|  | Feat 307 |  |  |  |
| Sub-total | 9 | 3 | 2 |  |
| Total | 43 | 17 | 17 | 6 |

identified that were related to the three feature types defined on the basis of form.

Table 7.25 provides summary data on feature content for all three feature types. It shows that approximately 78% of the artifacts from the Calvert site come from Type 1 features. This is not surprising when we consider the these features

comprise about 95% of the excavated feature fill. Much smaller quantities of material, 9% and 13% respectively, were found in the Type 2 and 3 features.

Type 1 features display very low artifact densities (mean = 1.7 artifacts/litre), despite the fact that most of the artifacts are found in them. This is

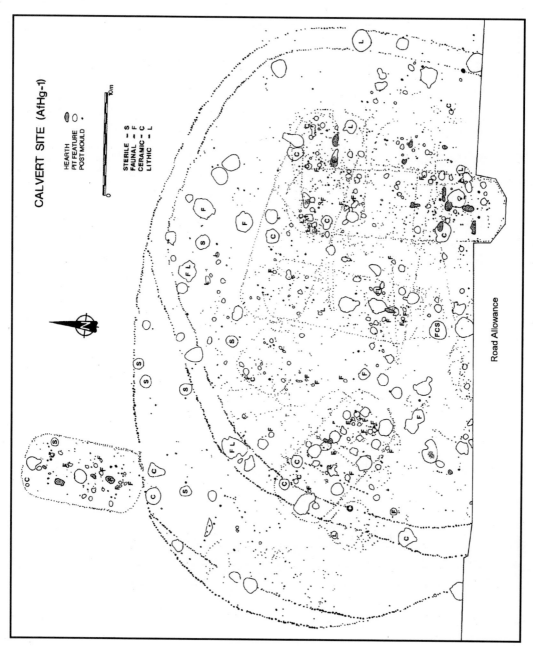

Figure 7.26. Distribution of features with specialized contents.

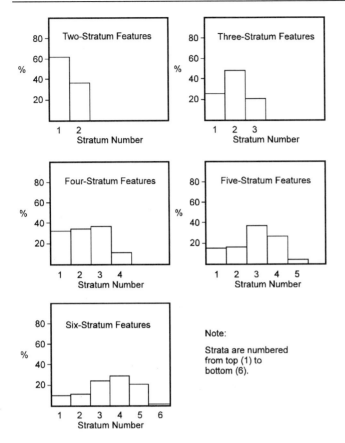

Note:

Strata are numbered
from top (1) to
bottom (6).

Figure 7.27. Artifact percentages by stratum in Type 1 features.

(CDE) shows a clear but weak trend towards higher percentages in Type 2 features (20.8%) and a lower occurrence in Type 1 (14.7%).

Unfortunately, the measures of central tendency provided in Table 7.25 mask a great deal of variability within each feature type. They do not illuminate features that may have had specialized functions. In an attempt to recognize such features, an analysis of artifact contents was conducted to flag those features that were dominated by specific artifact classes. Dominance was established both on the basis of raw numbers of artifacts and their percentages by class within each feature. Thus a feature was considered to be dominant in one artifact class if it contained an established minimum of artifacts of that class or if that class of artifacts dominated the feature assemblage on a percentage basis. The criteria used to establish specialized features are given in Table 7.26.

This analysis resulted in the definition of 38 specialized Type 1 features, 31 specialized Type 2 features, and 14 specialized Type 3 features. These features are listed in Table 7.26, where they are broken down by dominant artifact class and feature type. The distribution of specialized features is shown in Figure 7.26. Their significance is discussed in relation to specialized refuse streams in the section to follow on refuse disposal technology.

The final analysis involving the contents of the Calvert features was documenting the quantity of material within each stratum of the large Type 1 features. This avenue was explored in the hope that it would provide information relevant to the interpretation of the use-lives of these features.

Since it is difficult to compare directly features with different numbers of strata, the sample of Type 1 features was grouped by number of strata (i.e., Two Strata, Three Strata, ...) and summary statistics were generated for each group. Figure 7.27 presents a series of histograms comparing the percentages of artifacts by stratum for each group. These data

due to their large volume and reflects the fact that these features contain many sterile or nearly sterile layers. It is also possible that most of the perishable organic refuse was deposited in Type 1 features, which would tend to fill them without contributing to higher artifact densities. The summary data tend to mask the fact that debris does occur in high density within certain layers of Type 1 pits. The fact that Type 2 and 3 features display significantly higher artifact densities than Type 1 features suggests that the latter were not used for the disposal of large quantities of organic waste.

When we compare the percentage occurrence of the four artifact classes within each feature type, we find a remarkable consistency among feature types. The occurrence of faunal material falls between 49.0% and 54.0%, ceramics between 21.4% and 27.0%, and fire cracked rock (FCR) between 1.7% and 2.7%. Only chipping detritus

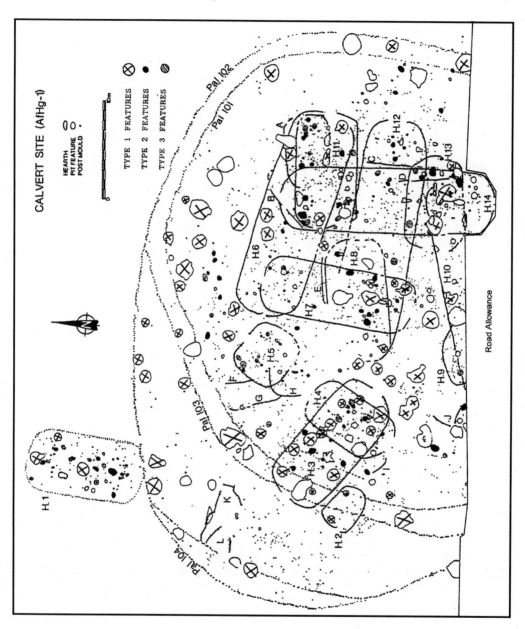

Figure 7.28. Distribution of Type 1, 2, and 3 features.

Table 7.27. Provenience of feature types.

| Type | | Interior | Exterior | Unknown | Total |
|---|---|---|---|---|---|
| 1 | f | 28 | 39 | 1 | 68 |
| | % | 41.2 | 57.4 | 1.5 | 100.0 |
| 2 | f | 68 | 12 | 1 | 81 |
| | % | 84.0 | 14.8 | 1.2 | 100.0 |
| 3 | f | 33 | 6 | 2 | 41 |
| | % | 80.5 | 14.6 | 4.9 | 100.0 |

show that there is a clear pattern in the frequency of debris by strata within Type 1 pits. Specifically, the lowest strata of Type 1 features tend to have the fewest artifacts; the middle strata have the most artifacts; and the top stratum usually has fewer artifacts than the middle strata but more than the lowest ones. This pattern is consistent in all five groups of Type 1 pits I examined and is most certainly related to some standardized behaviour or process in the formation of these features. Interpretations of this pattern are offered below.

Feature Context, Function, and Formation

Figure 7.28 shows the distribution of all Type 1, Type 2, and Type 3 features and Table 7.27 summarizes the provenience of these three feature types.

Type 1 Features

As Table 7.27 shows, the majority of Type 1 features are located outside of houses (57%) and many of these occur around the periphery of the village adjacent to the palisade walls. One exception to this general rule is found at the south end of House 3 where a series of six Type 1 pits cluster between Houses 3 and 12. Within houses, Type 1 features are most often found along interior walls, but they may also be tucked in the corners of longhouses or, occasionally, within the central corridor. These findings are in general agreement with past research on Glen Meyer features conducted by Fox (1976, 1986a) and Williamson (1985).

Type 1 features have traditionally been interpreted as storage/refuse pits. The storage function of these pits has been inferred on the basis of analogy with ethnohistorically described storage pits and the refuse function is attributed on the basis of the feature contents, which normally consist of

large amounts of debris. It has been assumed that most of these large pits were used initially for food storage. Archaeologically we find only pits filled with refuse, and there is usually no reliable archaeological evidence that they were ever used for storing food. One of the objectives of the present analysis was to try determine whether it is possible to distinguish between storage and refuse pits, as well as when the transition from a storage to a refuse function actually took place.

Our analysis of artifact frequencies within Type 1 pits on a stratum by stratum basis yielded some important trends with respect to feature formation. Specifically, we found that the deepest (bottom) stratum in these large pits had, on average, the fewest artifacts (Figure 7.27). There are, however, a small number of Type 1 pits in which the lowest strata have substantial amounts of debris. Some examples include Features 206, 306, 261, 79, 316, and 6. These features were obviously subjected to different formation processes.

It is reasonable to conclude that the pits with minimal artifacts in their basal strata are those that initially served a storage function. A reconstructed use-life of one of these pits would involve initial excavation and lining with bark to make it suitable for food storage. It would be used through the fall and winter, primarily for corn storage, but by the spring most of the corn would have been used up and the pit would fall into disuse. With the pit abandoned over the summer months, it is likely that a small amount of refuse would fall into it as the result of foot traffic and children's play in the vicinity. This material might be incorporated into the basal layer or could be cleaned out prior to fall reuse for food storage. While the storage use-lives of these pits are not known, the bark liner would deteriorate quite quickly, probably within two or three years. It could, of course, be replaced. At some point, however, it was decided that the pit was no longer suitable for food storage - probably because the liner was rotten and collapsing inward. As discussed in the experimental results, the decomposition of this liner would contribute to the formation of the basal stratum. When this process was combined with the small amount of debris incorporated into the basal stratum during the summer months, the end result would have been the formation of a basal stratum with a very low artifact content. Thus the pattern of increasing artifact productivity from the bottom to the middle strata is

Table 7.28. Presence of burnt bone by feature type.

| Type | | Mostly Burnt | Half Burnt | Not Burnt | Total |
|------|---|------|------|------|------|
| 1 | f | 16 | 8 | 44 | 68 |
|   | % | 23.5 | 11.8 | 64.7 | 100.0 |
| 2 | f | 39 | 8 | 34 | 81 |
|   | % | 48.1 | 9.9 | 42.0 | 100.0 |
| 3 | f | 24 | 4 | 13 | 41 |
|   | % | 58.5 | 9.8 | 31.7 | 100.0 |

an important characteristic of the Type 1 storage/refuse pit.

It follows that pits with many artifacts in their basal layers may never have functioned as storage pits; they may have been used as refuse pits only. Further, we may conclude that Type 1 pits lacking significant amounts of refuse in any stratum were either employed primarily as storage facilities or were used for the disposal of perishable organic debris only.

The distribution of sterile or near sterile Type 1 pits shown in Figure 7.26 (Table 7.26) supports the storage pit interpretation. Four of the six sterile pits are located in the outer western area of the site between Palisades 103 and 104. The sterile nature of these pits is the result of their abandonment when the village contracted, before they had reached the refuse disposal stage of their use life.

Our experimental study suggested a relationship between short-term abandonment and the development of sterile strata in Type 1 pits. With this in mind the Type 1 pits were examined for evidence of sterile strata with overlying refuse deposits. Only three Type 1 features displayed such strata (F.1, 209, and 211). Interestingly, all three were associated with the Early phase and outer Palisade 104/102.

A larger number of Type 1 pits (n = 5) displayed sterile upper strata, while nine others had less than 10 artifacts in their upper strata. This trend contributes to the overall decrease in upper strata contents noted in Figure 7.27, and it may be evidence for the process of sterile upper stratum formation noted experimentally. Yet many Type 1 pits clearly contained numerous artifacts in their upper strata - a finding which goes against our

experimental data which indicate that most pits should show an upper humic layer. The Calvert pits were very likely truncated by ploughing and their tops removed when the topsoil was stripped away using power equipment. Thus the upper layer may, in fact, be missing from most of the Calvert pits.

## Type 2 Features

As Figure 7.28 and Table 7.27 show, 84% of Type 2 features are found within houses. Most Type 2 features are hearth related and tend to cluster in the central corridor of the longhouse near the hearths. A small number of Type 2 features are found outside of houses, primarily in two clusters. These clusters are located at the east end of House 12 and the northwest end of House 6. In both cases they are near, and may be associated with, one or two Type 1 pits.

All Type 2 features are small - by definition they have volumes of less than 1 hectolitre - and they also contain few artifacts. Functionally, most Type 2 pits can be classified as casual refuse pits or small refuse filled depressions in living floors that were filled with longhouse floor or hearth debris.

It is significant that Type 2 features contain the highest percentage of chipping detritus in relation to other artifact classes within each feature type (Table 7.25). This may reflect a tendency for small flakes to be incorporated into house floor refuse deposits near the spot where they were created (i.e., around hearths). Ceramics, on the other hand, have their lowest occurrence in Type 2 pits (21%, Table 7.25). As larger pieces of debris, they were more likely to be thrown aside, into Type 1 or Type 3 refuse pits. These processes are in accordance with general principles of site formation relating to artifact size (Schiffer 1987; Stevenson 1986, 1991).

Type 2 pits also contain the highest percentage occurrence of faunal remains (54%, Table 7.25). As Table 7.26 shows, twenty Type 2 pits are dominated by faunal remains; however, most of these are calcined fragments from hearths (Table 7.28). Table 7.28 summarizes the occurrence of burnt bone in features of all types and clearly shows the tendency for fresh bone to occur in exterior Type 1 pits related to butchering, while burnt bone is more common in Type 2 pits related to hearths and cooking activities.

## Type 3 Features

Type 3 pits are found within houses 80% of the time (Table 7.27, Figure 7.28). They are usually located along side walls or in corners, but they may also be found among Type 2 pits in the hearth centred clusters. The primary function of Type 3 pits was probably in-house refuse disposal, judging by their very high artifact density and the nature of their contents. Like the other feature types, the refuse found in these features is usually generalized. However, on a percentage basis they contain the least amount of faunal material, and the highest amount of ceramic debris (Table 7.25).

The high percentage of ceramic debris in Type 3 pits is related to a small number of features with large quantities of ceramic material. Four of these features yielded substantial portions of ceramic vessels. While some of these features may have been used for ceramic refuse dumps, at least one (Feature 242 in House 1) appears to have been used as a vessel support pit. It contains most of Vessel 276 and has a bowl shaped profile.

## Summary

To reiterate, our analysis of the Calvert features has resulted in the definition of three main feature types: large Type 1 features used for storage and refuse disposal; small Type 2 features that are usually clustered around interior hearths and contain living floor debris; and medium Type 3 features that are usually found within houses and have high artifact densities. Within these feature groups it is sometimes possible to identify specialized features containing a dominance of one or two debris types (Table 7.26, Figure 7.26). These features are evidence of specialized refuse streams (Schiffer 1987) and may be related to specific activity areas.

Although most Type 1 features initially served storage functions, at some point the majority of them were filled with refuse, as were most of the Type 2 and 3 features. There is no widespread evidence for short-term abandonment of Type 1 features, although several pits in the western part of the site appear to have been abandoned and not used for refuse disposal after the Early phase palisade was contracted. The role of all three feature types in the refuse disposal process is discussed further in the following section.

# Refuse Disposal Technology

While most of the artifacts we recover from Iroquoian sites are analyzed as tools, at the time that they were deposited most of them were probably considered to be garbage. It follows that a thorough understanding of the formation of any Iroquoian site must seek to understand the modes of refuse disposal that were practised there. Refuse disposal practises are often reflected in site structure and settlement patterns, and they may provide important information on activity areas, site function, and the duration of occupation (Schiffer 1987; Timmins 1989).

In recent years, recognition of the importance of refuse disposal in archaeological formation processes has led to the development of a body of literature concerned with understanding different types of refuse and modes of disposal. Most of this research has been ethnoarchaeological in nature and taken together it constitutes a pool of interpretive theory that can be used in the explanation of refuse disposal patterns at the Calvert site.

## Refuse Disposal Theory

Most archaeological refuse may be defined as either primary refuse, which is deposited where it is produced, or secondary refuse, which is removed and discarded elsewhere. Schiffer (1987) points out that archaeologists rarely find intact primary refuse, simply because refuse in work areas is generally cleaned up on a regular basis so that it does not interfere with ongoing activities. In a cross-cultural study of refuse disposal behaviour, Murray (1980) found that living areas were regularly maintained (cleaned), even in the most mobile societies. At permanent or semi-permanent settlements efficient methods of refuse disposal develop quickly and secondary refuse becomes concentrated in specified areas. Iroquoian villages fall into this category and may display evidence of relatively complex refuse disposal systems.

Given the rarity of primary refuse deposits, Schiffer (1987:58) notes that it may be useful to broaden the definition of primary refuse to include artifacts and debris discarded in "activity related locations". This would include refuse that is swept or kicked into pits, corners, or along walls, but remains close to the activity area in which it was produced.

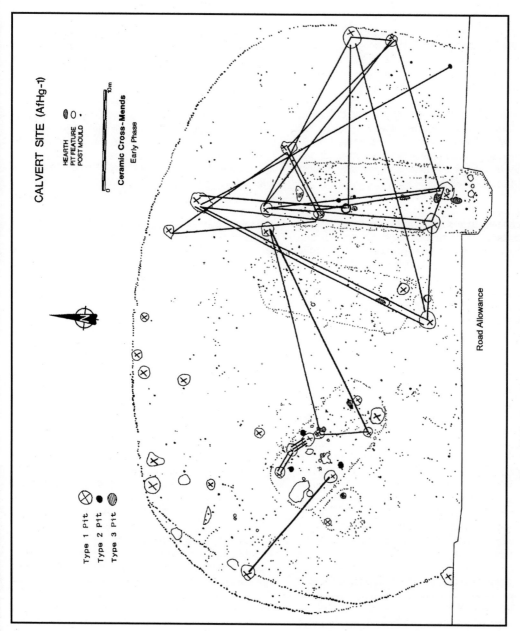

Figure 7.29. Ceramic cross-mends and feature types – Early Phase.

The locations of secondary refuse deposits within settlements are usually quite predictable. They tend to occur around site perimeters and in areas located just outside house doors. The pattern of household refuse accumulation near the house occurs cross-culturally, on some historic Euro-Canadian house sites (South 1977) and on Amazonian Shipibo-Conibo sites (DeBoer and Lathrap 1979), for example. Similarly, on prehistoric Iroquoian sites middens often develop near the ends of longhouses where they are shared by several households. They also tend to cluster around the perimeter of the village adjacent to the palisade or on a hillside (Finlayson 1985).

The phenomenon of refuse attracting refuse has been described as the "Arlo Guthrie refuse-magnet effect" (Schiffer 1987:62). As explained by Guthrie, it simply makes more sense to add to one big pile of garbage, instead of creating several small piles.

Common locations for the disposal of secondary refuse include natural depressions, abandoned structures, and, as we have seen at the Calvert site, abandoned pit features (Dickens 1985; Schiffer 1987:61).

Certain categories of refuse may receive special disposal treatment. Ethnoarchaeological studies have shown that lithic debris is almost never left lying on living floors and is sometimes deposited in specially dug pits (Schiffer 1987). Removal of razor sharp chipping debris is a practical safety precaution, leading to the conclusion that most debitage deposits will be secondary refuse (ibid.). Offensive wastes, such as butchering remains, may also be given special treatment involving immediate disposal and possible burial.

Schiffer (1987) has introduced the concept of waste streams to the archaeological study of refuse disposal. Waste streams are the varied paths that different types of refuse may follow before they are ultimately deposited as secondary refuse. To use a modern example, stages in a domestic waste stream may include initial discard in a kitchen garbage can, removal to exterior garbage cans, and final pick up and deposit in a municipal landfill, where the waste will be deposited along with other trash from industrial and commercial waste streams. Intervening processes may include scavenging at any stage, children's play, and, depending upon the environmental awareness of the community,

recycling of usable materials. Waste streams may vary depending on the type of refuse, the regularity of cleaning, whether activity areas are used regularly or sporadically, and so on. Modelling waste streams is a complex process and, although a number of ethnoarchaeological studies have addressed these problems, there have been few case studies of waste stream modelling based on archaeological data.

Other processes that may affect refuse disposal in the archaeological record include ritual discard and site abandonment behaviour (Schiffer 1987). Abandonment behaviour may lead to a relaxation of standards of cleanliness and fundamental changes in the methods and locations of refuse disposal. Ritual caches usually involve the intentional burial of complete, sometimes unused, artifacts and may be conducted for a variety of ceremonial reasons, including building dedications and offerings. One such feature has been identified at the Calvert site (von Gernet and Timmins 1987). Of course, caching may also be conducted for purely utilitarian reasons.

Some ethnoarchaeological and historical archaeological studies have stressed the role of ideational and symbolic factors as important influences on refuse disposal practises that form the archaeological record (Hodder 1982b:61-65; Deetz 1977). In these cases a correlation is usually shown between an aspect of an ethnographically known belief system or world view and the patterning of material remains. Yet, detractors from this approach point out that the same patterning can often be explained in utilitarian terms and maintain that ideational causality has not been demonstrated (Schiffer 1987:74; Gould 1990:35). In attempting symbolic interpretations of the prehistoric record, it is rarely possible to verify interpretations.

## Refuse Disposal at the Calvert Site

Analysis of the Calvert site features has demonstrated that the majority of them were used for refuse disposal at some time in their use-life. On the basis of feature form, contents, and formation processes, three feature types were defined. We now must determine what waste streams may have been used at the Calvert site and how these features functioned in relation to the different waste streams.

The Type 1 refuse and storage/refuse features found at Calvert are about evenly split between interior and exterior features. As our analysis

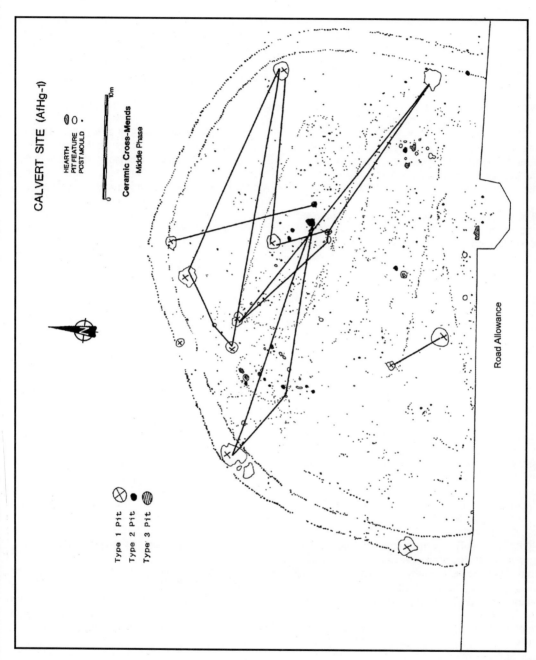

Figure 7.30. Ceramic cross-mends and feature types - Middle Phase.

demonstrated, these features contain the bulk of the refuse at Calvert (78%). They occur both within houses, where they are usually found along side walls or in corners, and outside of houses, generally near house ends or distributed around the palisade. Most Type 1 pits were intentionally filled with refuse over an extended period of time. This refuse must be regarded as secondary refuse, since it does not reflect the precise location of the activities that produced it.

The much smaller Type 2 pits contain very few artifacts and are found inside houses over 80% of the time. They tend to cluster in the central corridor around hearths and contain high frequencies of burnt faunal material and the highest percentage occurrence of chipping detritus. We have suggested that Type 2 pits represent casual refuse pits or refuse filled depressions in living floors that were filled with longhouse floor or hearth debris. As such, the artifacts found in the features are closely associated with hearth activities and may be considered as primary refuse, following Schiffer's broadened definition of the term (1987:58).

The medium sized Type 3 pits are also found in houses 80% of the time, usually in locations similar to the interior Type 1 features. They were used extensively for refuse and have the highest artifact density of any of the three feature types (6.4 pieces/litre, Table 7.25). A large proportion (58%) of these pits contain faunal debris that is mostly burnt (Table 7.28), suggesting that they may be related to hearth activities. However, since they are generally located outside the central corridor, it is probably accurate to consider the material in these pits as secondary refuse.

### Ceramic Cross-Mends and Waste Streams

The goal of waste stream analysis, as defined by Schiffer (1987:67) is to determine how "activity areas contributed, through time, to various secondary deposits." The ceramic cross-mend data, initially discussed in Chapter 5, provide information concerning the movement of debris in systemic context within the village. These data are crucial to understanding the waste streams in operation at the Calvert site. The ceramic cross-mends for each phase are shown in Figures 7.29, 7.30, and 7.31, which also differentiate between the three feature types.

The waste streams that contributed to the distribution of cross-mended ceramics at Calvert are potentially very complex. Among the possible contributing activities are house floor sweeping, removal of refuse from interior refuse pits to exterior ones, scavenging of partially broken vessels from refuse pits for reuse, provisional discard and curation of broken pots to be used again, foot traffic both in houses and around the village, children playing in or around pits; and even sharing or exchange of used, partially broken pots (von Gernet 1982).

The final distribution of debris in pits around the village is the end result of the operation of several waste streams. Ceramic cross-mend patterns provide us with a preserved record of the direction and distance of refuse movement. While it is impossible to infer accurately the precise processes responsible for the lateral transfer of material, it is suggested that most of the movement is related to refuse disposal behaviour. The rationale for this conclusion is outlined below.

If the Calvert people followed refuse disposal practises common to other Iroquoian groups, we would expect refuse to be moved out of longhouses and dumped in middens or pits located either at the ends of houses or around the perimeter of the village. Given the differences in the orientation of houses from phase to phase such patterned refuse disposal behaviour should produce recognizable cross-mend patterns oriented north-south in the Early phase, east-west in the Middle phase, and east-west again in the Late phase.

On the other hand, we can expect to find a certain amount of "noise" in the data, since we know that some later pits are intrusive on earlier ones and some large pits were used over the long term.

To quantify spatial trends in the movement of ceramic debris, the frequency of four different types of cross-mends was calculated. These cross-mend types are:

1. east-west oriented cross-mends involving movement of material out of houses;

2. north-south oriented cross-mends showing movement of material out of houses;

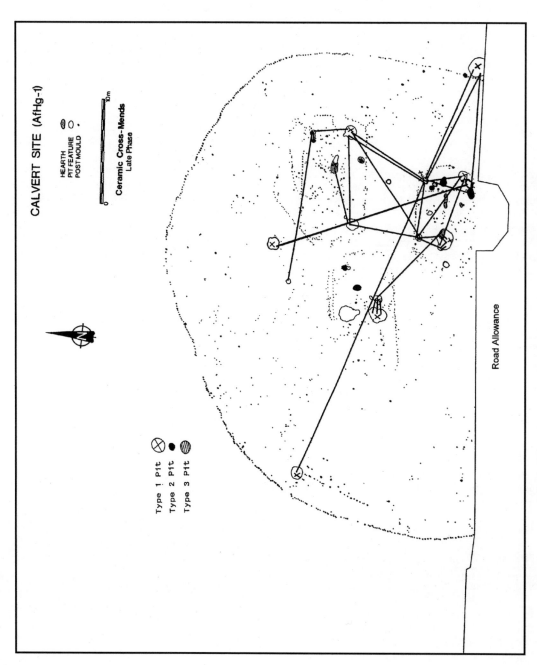

Figure 7.31. Ceramic cross-mends and feature types - Late Phase.

Table 7.29. Percentage occurrence of ceramic cross-mend types.

| | Cross-mend type | | | | | | | | | |
|---|---|---|---|---|---|---|---|---|---|---|
| | North-South | | East-west | | In-House | | House-House | | Totals | |
| Phase | f | % | f | % | f | % | f | % | f | % |
| Early | 12 | 38.7 | 9 | 29.0 | 10 | 32.3 | 0 | 0.0 | 31 | 100.0 |
| Middle | 1 | 7.1 | 10 | 71.4 | 2 | 14.3 | 1 | 7.1 | 14 | 100.0 |
| Late | 2 | 6.7 | 4 | 13.3 | 18 | 60.0 | 6 | 20.0 | 30 | 100.0 |

3. in-house cross-mends reflecting refuse disposal or movement of debris within the structure; and finally,

4. house-to-house cross-mends, which are probably less related to refuse disposal but may indicate interaction between households.

The results of this analysis are presented in Table 7.29. In the Early phase, with the north-south oriented houses, we expect a high occurrence of north-south as opposed to east-west cross-mends. The percentages lend some support to this prediction, as 38.7% of the mends are oriented north-south compared to 29% indicating east-west movement. While 38.7% is not a large plurality, we must remember that this figure primarily involves mends to features at the north end of the village. We do not have evidence of mends to the south end of the village, since this portion of the site was not excavated. Therefore, the 38.7% figure for north-south cross-mends would likely be considerably higher if the south end of the site had been excavated. It should also be noted that a high proportion of the Early phase mends occur within houses (32.3%), primarily within House 3.

No house-to-house mends were noted in the Early phase, although there are cross-mends indicating a transfer of material among House 3 pits and exterior pits associated with Houses 7 and 14 (Figure 7.29).

The predicted pattern of refuse movement emerges more clearly in the Middle phase, when a total of 71.4% of the mends indicate east-west movement. There are only two in-house mends and only one house-to-house mend.

In the final phase a very different pattern emerges. Here, only 13.3% of the cross-mends run east-west indicating refuse transfer out of houses, and 6.6% indicate north-south transfer of material out of houses. However, **in-house** cross-mends comprise 60% of the sample, while house-to-house mends make up 20%. In comparison to the low percentages derived for in-house and house-to-house cross-mends in the two earlier phases, these Late phase patterns indicate that something radically different is happening with respect to the movement of artifacts and debris.

Combining our knowledge of feature types and cross-mend patterns, it is now possible to postulate the existence of several generalized refuse streams that model the disposal of refuse at Calvert. These refuse streams are listed below and are schematically presented in Figure 7.32.

1. Interior Activity Area to Interior Type 2 Feature. This involves the movement of primary debris from interior activity areas (usually around hearths) into adjacent Type 2 pits within the central corridors of houses. This debris may be regarded as a primary deposit, insofar as its location reflects the general area of the activity that produced it (Schiffer 1987).

2. Interior Activity Area to Interior Type 3 Feature. This stream involves the movement of primary debris from hearth activity areas into Type 3 pits located inside house walls. This debris is considered to be secondary refuse.

3. Interior Activity Area to Interior Type 1 Feature. This involves the movement of primary debris from interior activity areas to interior Type 1 pits, where the debris becomes a secondary deposit.

4. Interior Type 1 Feature to Exterior Type 1 Feature/Midden. Secondary refuse deposits within the house are removed to exterior dumping areas. Since most cross-mends involve Type 1 features, the majority of the cross-mends indicate this type of activity.

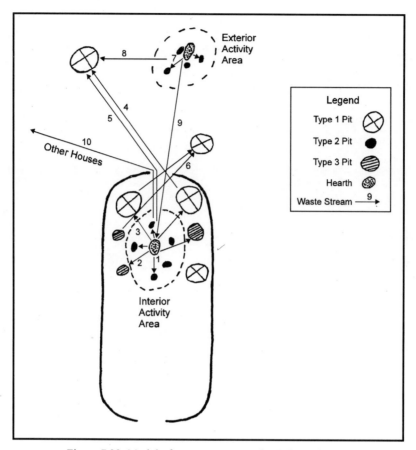

Figure 7.32. Model of waste streams at the Calvert site.

5. Interior Type 2 Feature to Exterior Type 1 Feature/Midden. Only two ceramic cross-mends indicate this refuse stream, involving the movement of material from interior activity related primary deposits to exterior refuse pits.

6. Interior Type 3 Feature to Exterior Type 1 Feature/Midden. This stream involves movement of secondary debris from interior Type 3 refuse pits to exterior Type 1 pits or middens, similar to Stream 4 above.

7. Exterior Activity Area to Exterior Type 2 Feature. This stream involves the deposit of primary refuse in Type 2 pits within or adjacent to exterior activity areas where the activity that produced the debris was carried out. These exterior activity areas

may appear as clusters of Type 2 features (Figure 7.25).

8. Exterior Activity Area to Exterior Type 1 Feature/Midden. Primary debris from exterior activity areas is moved from the area it was produced and deposited in exterior refuse pits.

9. Exterior Activity Area to Interior Activity Area. This waste stream documents the movement of material from outside activity areas into houses. This could occur in the case of butchered animals that may be dispersed around the village from a central exterior butchering location.

10. House to House. This stream involves the movement of debris from activity areas or secondary deposits within one house to a secondary

deposit (Type 1 or 3 pit) in another house. This refuse stream is common in the final phase of the site occupation and may be a product of inter-household interaction and/or cold weather occupation.

## Summary and Discussion

The identification of refuse streams is crucial to understanding the occupational history of any complex archaeological site, since refuse streams may change over the course of the occupation, thus altering the spatial organization of the archaeological deposit (Schiffer 1987:67). At the Calvert site refuse streams appear to have shifted in response to major changes in the community pattern between the Early and Middle phases. As the north-south oriented houses were dismantled and rebuilt with an east-west orientation, the patterns of refuse disposal shifted from north-south to east-west. While some refuse was being deposited within houses, there was systematic removal of refuse from interior refuse pits to exterior pits. These disposal patterns were similar to those documented on other Iroquoian sites, insofar as refuse pits were located at the ends of houses or adjacent to an exterior palisade.

In the Early phase, much of the refuse from Houses 7 and 14 was deposited in a cluster of pits at the north end of the structures (Figure 7.29). Similar refuse pits may have existed south of these houses in the area that was not excavated within the road allowance. The paucity of exterior refuse pits associated with House 3 cannot be explained at this time; although the high occurrence of cross-mends may indicate much refuse disposal within the house as the many storage pits fell into disuse.

In the Middle phase, most of the refuse was deposited in a cluster of pits located northwest of House 6 (Figure 7.30). It is likely that some of the Type 1 pits located west of House 12 were also in use at this time; however, they have not been linked to this phase through ceramic cross-mends or by other means.

With the construction of a series of smaller east-west oriented houses in the Late phase, refuse disposal patterns underwent a dramatic change. In-house refuse disposal became dominant, and house-to-house cross-mends increased substantially (Figure 7.31). There was little concern with removing waste to exterior refuse pits. The increase in house-to-house mends may indicate more interaction between houses, especially Houses 11 and 13. In general, there is evidence for more intensive activity within houses, as suggested by the high percentage of in-house mends and the lack of exterior features assigned to this phase.

The changes in refuse disposal behaviour in the Late phase may be related to several combined factors, including possible changes in the function of the site, the composition of the site population, the season of occupation, and the length of the occupation. Yet the dominant impression is one of relaxing standards of cleanliness and systematic cleaning, as manifested by the use of interior refuse pits and a lack of concern for moving garbage out of houses. This is evidence of classic abandonment behaviour, whereby the rules governing refuse disposal are suspended in light of imminent departure. Nonetheless, if the Late phase had lasted for a lengthy period, we would still expect to see evidence of a more normal pattern of refuse disposal during the early part of the occupation. That this evidence does not appear to be present supports the interpretation that the Late phase involved several relatively brief occupations. The evidence for interior activity further suggests that most of these occupations occurred during the cold season.

Before leaving the topic of refuse disposal, mention must be made of the evidence of specialized refuse streams at the Calvert site. These include special treatment of lithic and faunal debris and at least one case of ritual discard.

During the Early and Middle phases, all Type 1 pits containing large amounts of faunal material were located outside of houses, at the ends of houses, or around the perimeter of the village (Table 7.26, Figures 7.26, 7.29, 7.30). Most of this bone is fresh (unburnt). This pattern demonstrates a concern with faunal refuse disposal outside houses and may also indicate that much butchering activity was conducted outside as well. In contrast, in the final phase, the faunal dominated features (20, 79, 156) were all located inside (Figures 7.26 and 7.31), and most of the bone in these features is burnt. As discussed in the faunal analysis, these results indicate that much skinning and butchering of animals was occurring indoors and the bones were being burned. Such a pattern might best be

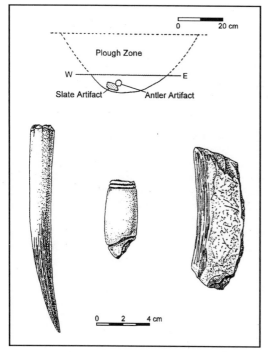

Figure 7.33. Feature 285 and associated artifacts.

explained by the constraints of a cold weather occupation.

In the Early and Middle phases lithic dominated features occurred both inside and outside houses, while in the Late phase they were confined to house interiors (Figures 7.26, 7.29, 7.30, 7.31). Feature 280 in House 1 contains 201 flakes, three utilized flakes, and nothing else. It is a prime example of a specialized lithic waste stream.

Finally, the single case of ritual discard occurs in House 4 and involves Feature 285. This feature, discussed briefly during the faunal analysis, contained bones from the head, wing, and tail of the rare Carolina parakeet (interpreted as the remains of a bird skin), a complete and well made stone pipe bowl, a slate scraping tool, and a antler prong tool (Figure 7.33). All of the artifacts were in excellent condition and none was broken or worn out prior to burial. Through the use of a wide range of ethnographic analogues, the pipe bowl and bird bones in this pit have been interpreted as the remains of a calumet style pipe with a (decomposed) wooden pipe stem upon which the

skin of the Carolina parakeet was impaled (von Gernet and Timmins 1987). A full description of our interpretation of this feature is provided in Chapter 9.

## Building Technology - Settlement Pattern Analysis

Settlement pattern data on Iroquoian sites provide valuable information concerning the location, size, and construction methods of structures and activity areas within villages. Through the use of ethnohistorical analogues, it is also possible to interpret the labour involved in village construction, the functions of structures and activity areas, and the size of the population for individual houses. In this section we present basic data and interpretations of the Calvert settlement patterns. Further explanation of these data and of the changes observed in the settlement pattern from phase to phase is reserved for the following chapter.

### Ethnohistorical, Archaeological, and Experimental Data

Sixteenth and seventeenth century accounts of Iroquoian villages and longhouses provide limited information concerning their construction. Dodd (1984) offers an in-depth review of both ethnohistorical and ethnographic data relating to Iroquoian longhouses.

Longhouses reminded early European explorers and missionaries of European garden arbours or bowers with vaulted (arched) roofs (Sagard 1939:93). Cartier describes the houses in Hochelaga as "built completely of wood and covered in and bordered up with large pieces of the bark and rind of trees..." (Biggar 1924:156-158). Brebeuf notes that cedar, elm, ash, fir, and spruce bark were all used on Huron houses although cedar was preferred (Thwaites 1896-1901:8:105 -107). Estimates of longhouse length vary widely, but they are consistently described as being as high as they are wide. Most accounts describe either one or two platforms or benches running the length of the houses along the inside walls (Heidenreich 1971:118). These were apparently used for seating during meetings and feasts and for sleeping in the summer. We know that the superstructure of the longhouse involved large beams from which corn and fish were hung to dry (Thwaites 1896-1901: 38:247).

Many architectural details of Huron house construction have been gleaned from analyses of Huron vocabulary (Steckley 1987). This source of information has provided valuable information about the superstructure of Huron houses that cannot be obtained archaeologically. For example, Huron vocabulary suggests that vertical wall poles had extension poles that would have allowed longhouses to achieve greater height (ibid:27). Such poles would have been necessary if these houses were as high as they were wide. Steckley's work has also illuminated the nature of longhouse roofs, which had curved rafters forming a vaulted roof structure, and sticks on the outside to hold down the bark sheathing.

The linguistic evidence suggests the use of vertical support poles that were used to suspend corn and other possessions. The presence or absence of such large interior support posts can usually be confirmed archaeologically, and researchers have suggested that these large posts were also used to support side platforms. The ethnolinguistic data suggest that these platforms served primarily as places to put things (ibid:25), rather than as seating or sleeping structures, but multiple uses are possible.

The precise method of wall construction is not detailed in ethnohistorical sources. Archaeologically, at least two wall types are found — staggered or double wall post lines and single wall post lines (Warrick 1988). On some sites, houses with double or staggered post lines seem consistently to display inner post depths that are about twice as deep as the posts on the outer row (Fitzgerald 1990:7; Timmins 1990:14). This pattern suggests that the inner posts acted as the main structural support, while the outer posts were used to hold the bark sheathing in place. The construction method of the single row walls is less clear. It is possible that the outer post rows were shallow and not preserved. Alternatively, it may be that the single row walls were interwoven with bark. This would create a less substantial structure that would provide little winter insulation. Many Early Iroquoian structures have single row walls.

Heidenreich studied longhouse construction using ethnohistorical and archaeological data and estimated the materials and labour involved in the construction of an average village (1971:152-153). Although his calculations were not experimentally verified, he effectively demonstrated that village construction was an expensive proposition in terms of both labour and material requirements. Heidenreich's calculations suggest that the construction of a 2.4 ha village with 36 longhouses would take a work force of 200 men about three months (ibid.).

Experimental work on aboriginal house construction has been conducted by Callahan (1981). His research provides detailed records of the labour, materials, tools, and techniques required in the construction of three Pamunkey houses in the southeastern United States. These houses were much smaller than Iroquoian ones and some of the construction materials differed as well. Nonetheless, construction techniques were sufficiently similar to indicate that Heidenreich's calculations probably underestimate the time required for house construction by a factor of two or three. In particular, the time needed to clear the site, install poles, prepare cordage, and strip and attach the outer bark sheathing were underestimated or omitted in Heidenreich's calculations.

The ethnohistorical literature provides little information on functional differences among longhouses. The majority of structures were undoubtedly multi-family dwellings, and chief's houses, which were used for feasts and meetings, were said to be larger than other houses.

Archaeologically, several Early Iroquoian villages have yielded evidence for small, circular, or oblong houses that have been interpreted as single family dwellings (Williamson 1985; Pearce 1984) or granaries (Tuck 1971). If the former interpretation is correct, these houses should have interior features such as central hearths, refuse pits, and storage pits similar to those found in regular longhouses. If they functioned solely as granaries, one might expect several large storage features but little occupational debris. In some cases, these small structures appear to be associated with larger longhouses.

Ethnohistorical sources are consistent in stating that two families shared a single hearth and that the number of hearths in each house varied between one and 12 (Wrong 1939:94; Steckley 1987). This information has been extensively employed by

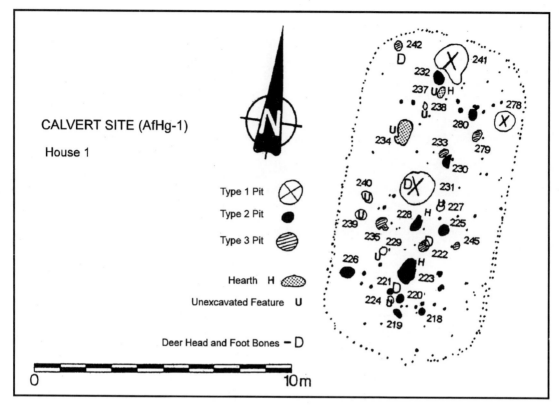

Figure 7.34. House 1 and associated features.

archaeologists to derive population estimates for Iroquoian households on the basis of actual or estimated numbers of hearths. Wright (1974) employed this method at the Middle Iroquoian Nodwell site, using an estimate of 8 people per family, while Warrick (1984a) and Finlayson (1985) adopted a more conservative family of six in their respective estimates of the Fonger and Draper populations. The latter two researchers both found it necessary to round out their data by estimating numbers of hearths in unexcavated areas or where the hearths had been obliterated by plough action.

While many of the Calvert hearths appear to have been well preserved, once the data were separated phase by phase, it became apparent that a significant number of hearths were missing. For this reason it was necessary to derive a technique for estimating hearth number.

Data provided by Dodd (1984:272-4) indicate that the average number of hearths in an Early

Iroquoian longhouse is three and the average house length is 16.3 metres. This yields a figure of one hearth for every 5.4 metres. The validity of this ratio is corroborated by the three Calvert houses that appear to have retained most of their hearth floors: Houses 14, 13, and 1. On average, these houses have a central hearth every 4.8 metres. For the present analysis, a figure of one hearth for every 5 metres of house length will be adopted.

Both Champlain and Sagard mention three-rowed village palisades, "interlaced" to each other, and reinforced with bark (Heidenreich 1971: 139-140). Galleries or watchtowers are mentioned in both accounts. It should be noted that Sagard's description of longhouses and palisades is probably an open plagiarism of Champlain's account of the same features.

Archaeologically, palisade posts are usually staggered and placed 15-40 cm apart, indicating that they must have been interwoven with saplings or

Table 7.30. House 1 feature data.

| Feature Number | Volume (litres) | Artifact Total | CDE | FCR | Faunal | Ceramics | Artifacts per litre | Feature Type |
|---|---|---|---|---|---|---|---|---|
| 218 | 7.93 | 15 | 0 | 1 | 4 | 10 | 1.89 | 2 |
| 219 | 7.26 | 61 | 4 | 0 | 57 | 0 | 8.40 | 2 |
| 220 | 8.77 | 9 | 2 | 0 | 2 | 5 | 1.03 | 2 |
| 221 | 5.54 | 10 | 0 | 0 | 8 | 1 | 1.81 | 2 |
| 222 | 21.77 | 393 | 12 | 0 | 362 | 18 | 18.05 | 3 |
| 223 | 37.87 | 4 | 0 | 0 | 4 | 0 | 0.11 | 2 |
| 225 | 14.52 | 4 | 0 | 1 | 3 | 0 | 0.28 | 2 |
| 226 | 13.74 | 3 | 1 | 2 | 0 | 0 | 0.22 | 2 |
| 228 | 21.38 | 4 | 1 | 0 | 1 | 2 | 0.19 | 2 |
| 231 | 1141.50 | 350 | 58 | 5 | 167 | 114 | 0.31 | 1 |
| 232 | 16.35 | 1 | 0 | 1 | 0 | 0 | 0.06 | 2 |
| 233 | 5.63 | 15 | 2 | 0 | 13 | 0 | 2.66 | 3 |
| 235 | 10.82 | 3 | 0 | 0 | 3 | 0 | 0.28 | 3 |
| 241 | 1480.75 | 754 | 92 | 14 | 266 | 377 | 0.51 | 1 |
| 242 | 12.73 | 115 | 12 | 1 | 3 | 99 | 9.03 | 3 |
| 245 | 10.31 | 8 | 0 | 0 | 8 | 0 | 0.78 | 3 |
| 278 | 302.80 | 14 | 6 | 4 | 3 | 1 | 0.05 | 1 |
| 279 | 21.55 | 3 | 2 | 0 | 1 | 0 | 0.14 | 3 |
| 280 | 7.54 | 203 | 202 | 0 | 0 | 0 | 26.92 | 2 |
| Total | 3148.76 | 1969 | 394 | 29 | 905 | 627 | | |
| % | | 100.00 | 20.01 | 1.47 | 45.96 | 31.84 | | |
| Mean | 165.72 | 103.63 | 20.74 | 1.53 | 47.63 | 33.00 | 3.83 | |

CDE, chipping detritus; FCR, fire cracked rock

bark. On Early Iroquoian sites usually only one or two palisade rows are present, although multiple row palisades with up to nine rows have been found on Late Iroquoian villages (Finlayson 1985; Pearce 1984). The construction and interweaving of a palisade is a time consuming process. At the reconstructed Crawford Lake site, a 600 m palisade consisting of 1500 poles placed 45 cm apart required 6500 man hours to accomplish the weaving alone (Hutton 1990).

Village entrances or gates are poorly known from the ethnohistorical literature. Sagard describes frontier villages as being most heavily fortified with "...gates and entrances, which are closed with bars and through which one is forced to pass turning sideways and not striding straight in..."(Wrong 1939:92). A "baffle-type" entrance like this occurred at the historic Huron Le Caron site

(Johnston and Jackson 1980:194). The prehistoric Neutral Lawson site also had an entrance maze (Pearce 1984:324).

## Settlement Pattern Data

In the following analysis of the Calvert settlement data, each house is described and interpreted in terms of its size, location, construction, interior features, and function.

### House 1

Size and Location: House 1 is located outside the palisade at the northwest corner of the village (Figure 7.34). It is oriented roughly north-south and measures 12.5 m in length by 6.25 m in width, giving it a total floor area of 79 square m. As discussed in Chapter 5, the southern end of House 1

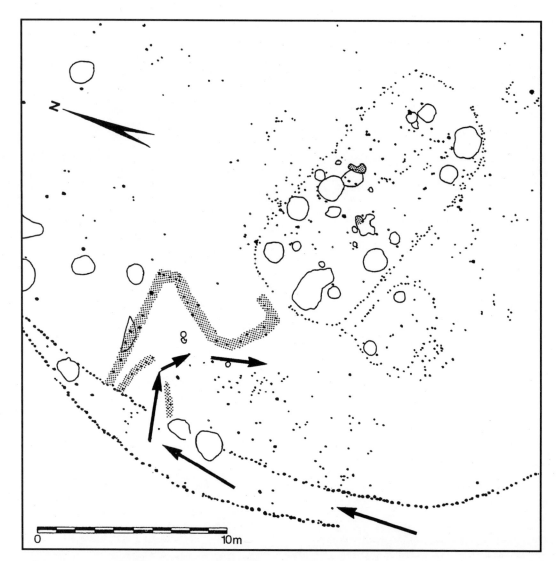

Figure 7.35. Reconstruction of the Early Phase village entrance.

intersects the outer village palisade (Palisade 104), passing inside the palisade wall. This arrangement indicates that these two structures were not contemporaneous.

Construction: The original wall post density of House 1 was estimated at 3.7 posts/m (Chapter 5). It underwent extensive repair involving post replacement along its east wall, resulting in a final post density of 5.91 posts/m. Several interior isolated posts are present, including two irregular rows of large posts located two metres inside both house ends. These may represent interior partitions for storage cubicles. Between 10 and 15 interior support posts occur in groups of two or three, approximately 1.5 - 2.0 m inside the house walls. The house ends are rounded and both have gaps for entrances. It is estimated that the original construction of House 1 required at least 140 wall posts.

Interior Features: Due to its location outside the palisade, House 1 is the only Calvert house that is not overlapped or intersected by another house. As such we can be quite certain that the features within the structure are associated with it. Detailed feature data are provided in Table 7.30. The interior of House 1 includes three centrally located hearths, two in the south half of the structure and one in the north half. A fourth hearth floor is located in the north half, on the west side of the central corridor. These hearths are surrounded by nine Type 2 features and five Type 3 features that cluster in the central corridor. Many of these features contain small quantities of calcined bone. A sixth Type 3 feature (F.242), containing an almost complete ceramic vessel, was located in the northwest corner of the house and is interpreted as a vessel support pit. As mentioned in the previous section, one of the Type 2 features, Feature 280, in the northeast corner of the house, was exclusively filled with Onondaga lithic debris and a few utilized flakes. It appears to be the refuse from a single chert-knapping event. Eight of the small interior features were not excavated.

House 1 contains three Type 1 features, two located in the central corridor and one located along the eastern wall. The latter was almost sterile and is interpreted as a storage pit, while the other two are storage-refuse pits with generalized fill consisting of ceramic, lithic, and faunal debris (Table 7.30). The location of the Type 1 pits within the central corridor is unusual in comparison to most of the houses inside the palisade.

Five House 1 features (F.219, 221, 222, 231, 241) contain deer head and foot bones or foot bones only, as discussed in Chapter 6. Their presence suggests that initial butchering activities were carried out within House 1.

Function: House 1 is interpreted as a multi-family dwelling that housed up to six families (36 people), as suggested by the presence of three central hearths. Its isolated location, combined with radiocarbon and ceramic data, suggests that it pre-dates the three main phases of the Calvert occupation. Post mould densities indicate that House 1 was extensively repaired, which may indicate that it was occupied intermittently over a long time. The ceramics are unusual, compared to the village sample, and suggest that the occupants of House 1 were not related to the later Calvert village. Faunal remains indicate a focus on mammal hunting, with deer butchering taking place within the house. Accordingly, House 1 is interpreted as an isolated house that was used as a hunting camp by a single extended family or hunting group.

## The Early Phase

### Palisade

The Early phase palisade is primarily a single row structure comprised of Palisade Segments 102 and 104, which form a continuous wall (Figure 5.1). This wall splits into two rows at the western end of the site, where there appears to have been a rather elaborate entrance way between the double walls (Figure 7.35). On average, palisade posts are spaced 24 cm apart, and the post density is 4.48 posts/m for Segment 102 and 4.28 posts/m for Segment 104. The similarity in post density between the two segments is difficult to interpret. Our analysis of palisade post densities in Chapter 5 suggests that they are not highly sensitive indicators of length of use-life.

The portion of the Early phase palisade that was excavated involves 523 posts. Estimating the number of posts that would be needed to complete the palisade to the south, in the unexcavated area, we expect that the original palisade would have required between 750 and 800 poles, with an average diameter of 14 cm.

At some point during the Early phase occupation, the western entrance was closed off with a series of smaller stakes. This is indicated by an obvious change in post diameter from 14 cm for the main palisade to 7.4 cm for the closed off entrance way. The location of the subsequent entrance is not known.

The original entrance was not unlike the maze-type entrances described for later Iroquoian villages (Johnston and Jackson 1980; Pearce 1984). It involved passage through a two metre wide corridor for a distance of ten metres. At that point a gap in the inner wall allowed access to the village, but only after passing through a second funnel-like structure that directed one to the east, through a 1.5 m wide opening. Immediately north of this entrance,

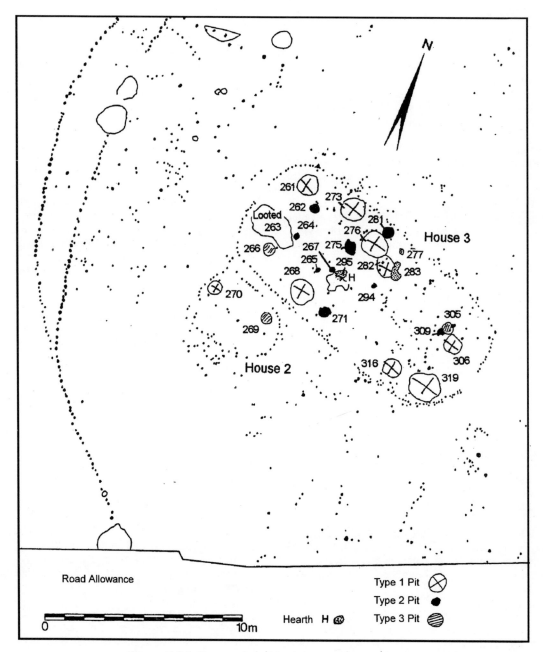

Figure 7.36. Houses 2 and 3 and associated features.

Table 7.31. House 2 feature data.

| Feature Number | Volume (litres) | Artifact Total | CDE | FCR | Faunal | Ceramics | Artifacts per litre | Feature Type |
|---|---|---|---|---|---|---|---|---|
| 269 | 60.77 | 543 | 1 | 0 | 2 | 540 | 8.94 | 3 |
| 270 | 206.41 | 137 | 110 | 0 | 2 | 24 | 0.66 | 1 |
| Total | 267.18 | 680 | 111 | 0 | 4 | 564 | | |
| % | | 100.00 | 16.32 | 0.00 | 0.59 | 82.94 | | |
| Mean | 133.59 | 340.00 | 55.50 | 0.00 | 2.00 | 282.00 | 4.80 | |

CDE, chipping detritus; FCR, fire cracked rock

a line of large post moulds extending east from the palisade wall suggests the former presence of a substantial wall that would have effectively prevented direct passage into the northern part of the village from that point. This wall curves to the south, eventually stopping near the northerly entrance to House 3.

A reconstruction of this interpretation of the original entrance way is shown in Figure 7.35. This arrangement would have routed people coming into the village to the south, where they may have had to pass around Houses 2 and 3 before gaining access to the main part of the village.

## House 2

Size and Location: House 2 is the smallest of the Calvert structures, measuring 4.65 m in length by 3.3 m in width. It is oriented northwest-southeast and is located on the west side of the village adjacent to the northwest corner of House 3 (Figure 7.36). House 2 pre-dates, and is intersected by, Palisade Segments 101 and 103 (Figure 5.1).

Construction: At least 56 exterior wall posts were used in the construction of House 2, giving it a post mould density of 4.15 posts/m. The post lines are straight rather than staggered. An unusual cluster of posts was recorded just outside the south wall of this structure. These posts may represent the remains of a porch, or some type of shelter attached to the house wall. House 2 does not show evidence of large interior support or bench support posts, although there are some smaller posts in the centre that may have served a support function. Some of these posts may be related to the subsequent palisade. Given its narrow width, House 2 was probably constructed by bending wall posts over and tying them in the centre.

Interior Features: House 2 contains only two features, a Type 1 pit located in the northeast corner and a Type 3 pit in the southeast corner (Figure 7.36). These features show an interesting divergence in terms of their contents. Feature 269, the Type 3 pit has a very high artifact density (8.94 pcs/litre) and is dominated by ceramic debris (540 pcs, 99.4%), while the Type 1 pit, Feature 270, has a density of only .66 pieces/metre and is dominated by lithic debris (Table 7.31). There is very little faunal debris in either feature. House 2 does not contain a hearth, nor does it contain any of the small Type 2 features normally located in hearth activity areas.

Function: Given its small size, House 2 cannot be considered a longhouse, and it is hardly large enough to be considered a cabin. The lack of a central hearth in this structure further suggests that it did not function as a dwelling. Spatially, it is associated with House 3, and was probably functionally related to that house. The presence of lithic and ceramic debris within the house indicates that domestic activities were carried out there, including chert-knapping. The separation of this debris between the two interior features is highly interesting, and may relate to the spatial organization of activities carried out within the structure. In light of these data, House 2 is interpreted as a storage/work hut associated with House 3.

## House 3

Size and Location: House 3 is 13.95 m long and 6.4 m wide. It is located on the east side of the village adjacent to and parallel with House 2, and is oriented in an identical northwest-southeast fashion (Figure 7.36). The total floor area within the house is 89.29 square m. The north end of House 3 is

Table 7.32. House 3 feature data.

| Feature Number | Volume (litres) | Artifact Total | CDE | FCR | Faunal | Ceramics | Artifacts per litre | Feature Type |
|---|---|---|---|---|---|---|---|---|
| 261 | 653.03 | 871 | 33 | 45 | 363 | 427 | 1.33 | 1 |
| 262 | 32.57 | 66 | 7 | 2 | 21 | 48 | 2.03 | 2 |
| 264 | 10.13 | 136 | 4 | 3 | 116 | 0 | 13.43 | 2 |
| 265 | 4.78 | 13 | 3 | 1 | 9 | 0 | 2.72 | 2 |
| 267 | 5.99 | 41 | 2 | 1 | 24 | 14 | 6.84 | 2 |
| 268 | 1123.09 | 654 | 77 | 25 | 130 | 286 | 0.58 | 1 |
| 271 | 58.45 | 35 | 0 | 1 | 31 | 1 | 0.60 | 2 |
| 273 | 789.40 | 1622 | 335 | 17 | 555 | 599 | 2.05 | 1 |
| 275 | 54.65 | 28 | 4 | 1 | 4 | 19 | 0.51 | 2 |
| 276 | 1016.54 | 576 | 96 | 32 | 235 | 200 | 0.57 | 1 |
| 277 | 13.17 | 33 | 6 | 6 | 21 | 5 | 2.51 | 3 |
| 281 | 36.15 | 13 | 0 | 0 | 4 | 8 | 0.36 | 2 |
| 282 | 414.86 | 391 | 36 | 14 | 301 | 36 | 0.94 | 1 |
| 290 | 15.61 | 3 | 1 | 1 | 0 | 0 | 0.19 | 2 |
| 294 | 3.80 | 8 | 0 | 0 | 7 | 0 | 2.11 | 2 |
| 305 | 48.09 | 19 | 5 | 2 | 7 | 4 | 0.40 | 3 |
| 306 | 458.17 | 785 | 66 | 39 | 344 | 319 | 1.71 | 1 |
| 309 | 13.60 | 11 | 0 | 0 | 9 | 2 | 0.81 | 2 |
| 316 | 292.64 | 611 | 83 | 13 | 462 | 41 | 2.09 | 1 |
| 319 | 477.13 | 97 | 18 | 10 | 60 | 6 | 0.20 | 1 |
| Total | 5521.85 | 6013 | 776 | 213 | 2703 | 2015 | | |
| % | | 100.00 | 12.91 | 3.54 | 44.95 | 33.51 | | |
| Mean | 276.09 | 300.65 | 38.80 | 10.65 | 135.15 | 100.75 | 2.10 | |

CDE, chipping detritus; FCR, fire cracked rock

intersected by palisade Segments 101 and 103, and the south end of the house is intersected by House 4. These structures all post-date House 3 and presented some problems in assigning features to specific structures.

Construction: The wall posts in House 3 are straight in some areas and staggered in others. It appears to have undergone some repair on the exterior walls. The original post density was calculated at 4.2 posts/m and the final density, after maintenance and repair, was 5.55 posts/m. An estimated 170 posts were required for the initial construction of this house. Well defined entrances about one metre in width are located at both ends. There are a number of large interior post moulds located between one and two metres inside the side

wall that probably represent bench support posts, although it is difficult to say which posts belong to this structure or to other later ones within the area of structure overlap.

Interior Features: Figure 7.36 shows the locations of the interior features that could be confidently assigned to House 3 and Table 7.32 provides data on these features. They include eight Type 1 pits, primarily located along the sides and in corners, ten Type 2 features, mostly located in the central corridor, and two Type 3 features. More Type 2 features associated with this structure are located in its south end, but they could not be distinguished from those belonging to House 4. House 3 contains only one extant central hearth, but typical hearth spacing and Type 2 feature clusters

Table 7.33. House 7 feature data.

| Feature Number | Volume (litres) | Artifact Total | CDE | FCR | Faunal | Ceramics | Artifacts per litre | Feature Type |
|---|---|---|---|---|---|---|---|---|
| 126 | 788.16 | 1851 | 170 | 14 | 55 | 54 | 2.35 | 1 |
| 136 | 13.26 | 412 | 50 | 1 | 335 | 23 | 31.07 | 3 |
| 171 | 6.80 | 8 | 7 | 0 | 1 | 0 | 1.18 | 2 |
| Total | 808.22 | 2271 | 227 | 15 | 391 | 77 | | |
| % | | 100.00 | 10.00 | 0.66 | 17.22 | 3.39 | | |
| Mean | 269.41 | 757.00 | 75.67 | 5.00 | 130.33 | 25.67 | 11.53 | |

CDE, chipping detritus; FCR, fire cracked rock

suggest that there were at least three central hearths in the house when it was occupied. It should also be noted that House 3 contains two features (263 and 292) that were looted prior to excavation.

House 3 displays the classic arrangement of storage pits along the outer walls and smaller Type 2 features within the central corridor. It is particularly notable for the large number of Type 1 features present, which is higher than in any other house in the village. Five of these are classified as storage/refuse pits, two are classified as refuse only, and one is unclassified. They have a total volume of 5222 litres and contain over 5600 artifacts.

Function: House 3 is interpreted as a residential dwelling with a population of approximately 36 individuals (six families). The unusually high volume of pit storage space within this structure suggests that it may have served a subsidiary function as a storage house. A similar structure at the Glen Meyer Dewaele site contained ten storage pits with a volume estimated at 5150 litres. Fox (1976:184) estimated that these pits could have held enough corn (kernels) to feed a population of 150 people through an entire winter, if the diet was supplemented with game. House 3 at the Calvert site may have served a similar function as a central storage house.

## House 7

Size and Location: House 7 is centrally located within the village and is oriented roughly north-south (Figure 7.37). It is 16 m long, 5.4 m wide, and has an area of 86.4 square m. House 7 is overlapped at the north end by House 6 and at the south end by Houses 8 and 12, all of which post-date it.

Construction: The walls of House 7 include both straight and staggered post segments. The original post density has been estimated at 3.4 posts/m. After some maintenance involving post replacement, especially along the east wall, the final post mould density was calculated at 4.31 posts/m. An estimated 145 wall posts were used in the construction of House 7. Interior bench support posts are present and occur between 1.5 and 2 m inside the walls at intervals ranging from 3 to 5 m. Entrances are evident at both ends. The south end displays a line of posts 2 m in length, extending south from the southwest corner. A second line runs east-west perpendicular to the first, creating a rectangular enclosure that encompasses two features. While it is impossible to be sure that these posts have been correctly assigned to House 7, they are interpreted as the remains of a porch-like structure attached to the south end of the house.

Interior Features: Due to the high degree of structure overlap in House 7, only five features could be confidently assigned to this structure. Three of these were excavated and the resultant data are presented in Table 7.33. The excavated features include one Type 1 pit (Feature 126) in the southeast corner of the house that yielded over 1800 pieces of primarily ceramic and lithic debris. It also contained a level of carbonized corn kernels that is believed to have undergone spontaneous combustion. Feature 136, a small Type 3 feature located in the central corridor in the south end of the house, contained over 300 pieces of calcined bone and is associated with the Feature 157 hearth complex. Feature 157 is the only extant hearth within the structure; however, a small feature cluster at the north end indicates that at least one other hearth was present there.

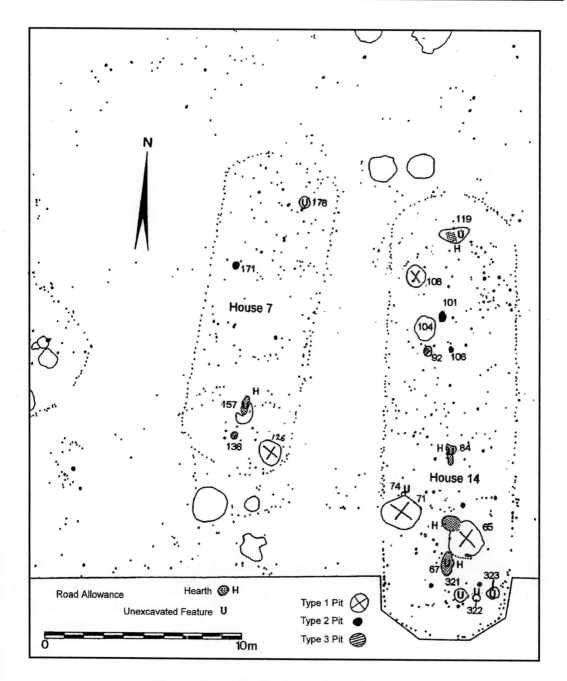

Figure 7.37. Houses 7 and 14 and associated features.

Table 7.34. House 14 feature data.

| Feature Number | Volume (litres) | Artifact Total | CDE | FCR | Faunal | Ceramics | Artifacts per litre | Feature Type |
|---|---|---|---|---|---|---|---|---|
| 065 | 1735.84 | 371 | 21 | 6 | 276 | 65 | 0.21 | 1 |
| 071 | 2045.04 | 1135 | 223 | 41 | 387 | 462 | 0.56 | 1 |
| 092 | 40.06 | 657 | 45 | 9 | 296 | 116 | 16.40 | 3 |
| 101 | 17.49 | 38 | 2 | 0 | 31 | 4 | 2.17 | 2 |
| 106 | 4.01 | 4 | 2 | 2 | 1 | 0 | 1.00 | 2 |
| 108 | 979.37 | 2233 | 44 | 39 | 887 | 496 | 2.28 | 1 |
| Total | 4821.81 | 4438 | 337 | 97 | 1878 | 1143 | | |
| % | | 100.00 | 7.59 | 2.19 | 42.32 | 25.75 | | |
| Mean | 803.64 | 739.67 | 56.17 | 16.17 | 313.00 | 190.50 | 3.77 | |

CDE, chipping detritus; FCR, fire cracked rock. Note: Although Feature 104, Level 4, relates to House 14 this feature was not typed and is excluded here due to its multi-phase use.

Function: House 7 is interpreted as a residential structure with an estimated two hearths, four families, and a population of about 24 people. The lack of interior features within this house is not wholly related to difficulties in assigning features to particular phases. There are, in fact, few features belonging to any phase in the northern and central portions of the structure. This low feature density may indicate that House 7 was not occupied for very long. The low post density of House 7 (4.31 posts/m) compared to House 3 (5.55 posts/m) supports a shorter term occupation. The lack of large storage pits within House 7 reinforces the possibility that House 3 acted as a central storage facility for the entire community.

House 14

Size and Location: House 14 is located on the east side of the village, about 3 m east of House 7, and oriented in the same manner (Figure 7.37). It is 21.5 m in length by 6.3 m in width and covers a total floor area of 135.45 square m. It is overlapped by parts of Houses 6, 11, 12, 13, and 10.

Construction: Wall post lines are straight, with an original post density of 3.6 posts/m and a final density of 4.9 posts/m after repair. A minimum of 200 posts were employed in the walls of House 14. Interior support posts are difficult to assign due to the extensive structure overlapping. There is a line of larger posts located approximately 1.75 m inside both house walls that probably acted as bench supports. A 1 m wide entrance appears at the north

end and a 1.3 m wide entrance is located at the south end.

Interior Features: Fourteen interior features were assigned to House 14 and of these six were excavated. Four of the unexcavated features were central hearths, three of which are located in the south half of the house, while the fourth was located at the extreme north end (Figure 7.37). Two of the hearths at the south end of the house seem too close together to have been used at the same time. A fifth hearth was probably present in the north half, judging by small feature clustering and hearth spacing.

Table 7.34 presents data on the six excavated features. Three of them are large Type 1 pits, two are Type 2 features and one is a Type 3 feature. As usual, the Type 3 pit, Feature 92, has the highest artifact density. It is dominated by burnt faunal material and is probably related to the missing hearth in the north half of the house. The Type 1 pits include storage/refuse pits 108 and 71, located along the west wall, and Feature 65, a storage pit with very low artifact density, located within the central corridor at the south end.

Function: House 14 is the largest structure in the Early phase and is interpreted as a typical multi-family longhouse. If we count the two closely spaced hearths at the south end as one, and add one hearth in the north half of the house, we estimate that it was occupied by eight families comprising about 48 people.

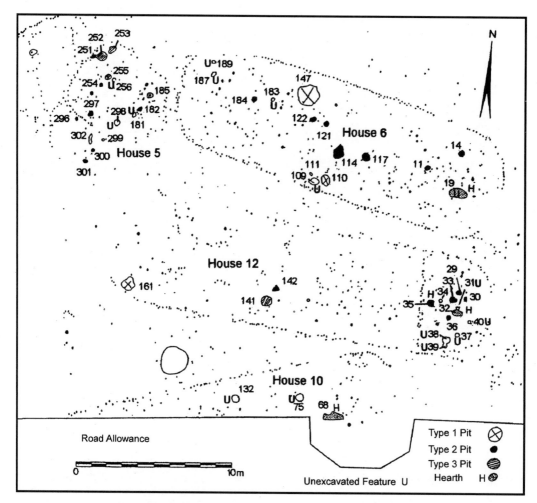

Figure 7.38. Houses 5, 6, 10, and 12, and associated features.

### The Middle Phase

#### Palisade

The Middle phase palisade may include all four palisade segments for at least part of its history. The beginning of the Middle phase was marked by the removal of north-south oriented Houses 2, 3, 7, and 14, and the construction of east-west Houses 6, 12, and 10. At around the same time, the inner village area was contracted on the west by the construction of Palisade Segment 103, which joined the original palisade at the north end of the village and passed 9

m inside the westerly palisade Segment 104 (Figures 5.10 and 7.30). This action effectively reduced the space within the village by 17.6%, from 1.7 ha to 1.4 ha. As discussed in Chapter 5, the outer palisade segment 104 may have remained in use throughout part of the Middle phase or been dismantled with the poles being used to build palisade 103. At some point during the Middle phase a third row (Palisade 101) was added, parallel to combined Segments 102/103 and about 2 m inside.

When the inner palisade Segment 101 was added, a substantial wall seven metres in length was

Table 7.35. House 5 feature data.

| Feature Number | Volume (litres) | Artifact Total | CDE | FCR | Faunal | Ceramics | Artifacts per litre | Feature Type |
|---|---|---|---|---|---|---|---|---|
| 182 | 8.04 | 90 | 12 | 0 | 70 | 8 | 11.19 | 2 |
| 185 | 15.88 | 84 | 12 | 0 | 61 | 7 | 5.29 | 3 |
| 251 | 7.48 | 16 | 2 | 1 | 0 | 13 | 2.14 | 2 |
| 252 | 67.39 | 197 | 16 | 2 | 112 | 67 | 2.92 | 3 |
| 253 | 34.90 | 94 | 25 | 2 | 43 | 23 | 2.69 | 3 |
| 254 | 3.18 | 1 | 0 | 0 | 0 | 0 | 0.00 | 2 |
| 255 | 12.25 | 12 | 1 | 0 | 7 | 4 | 0.98 | 3 |
| 296 | 5.94 | 43 | 1 | 3 | 26 | 8 | 7.24 | 3 |
| 297 | 16.13 | 30 | 12 | 9 | 5 | 2 | 1.86 | 2 |
| 300 | 3.30 | 1 | 0 | 0 | 1 | 0 | 0.30 | 2 |
| 301 | 6.16 | 1 | 0 | 0 | 1 | 0 | 0.16 | 2 |
| Total | 180.65 | 569 | 81 | 17 | 326 | 132 | | |
| % | | 100.00 | 14.24 | 2.99 | 57.29 | 23.20 | | |
| Mean | 16.42 | 51.73 | 7.36 | 1.55 | 29.64 | 12.00 | 3.16 | |

CDE, chipping detritus; FCR, fire cracked rock.

built 2.5 m inside it on the west side of the village where House 3 had been located. This structure may have been part of an entrance arrangement used during the Middle phase, perhaps after the original entrance had been permanently closed. There are a number of other gaps in the Middle phase palisade that may have functioned as entrances, but none of them shows special modifications. It is also possible that additional entrances were located along the unexcavated southern part of the village.

Final post densities for palisade segments 103 and 101 are very similar, at 4.45 and 4.59 posts/m respectively. Contraction of the palisade through construction of Segment 103 involved at least 200 additional palisade posts, although they all may have come from Palisade 104. The addition of the inner palisade Segment 101 required 367 posts in the excavated section and an estimated 270 posts to round out the unexcavated section to the south. Thus at least 837 posts with an average diameter of 14 cm were required to complete the palisade modifications of the Middle phase.

House 5

Size and Location: House 5 is located in the northwest area of the village between the west end

of House 6 and the inner palisade Segment 101. It is a small, squarish structure measuring 5.82 m in length by 5.25 m in width and encompassing an area of 30.56 square m. House 5 appears to have been rebuilt or extended to the south, as indicated by an incomplete curved line of posts extending south from the southwest corner of the structure (Figure 7.38). Most of the post moulds from this proposed rebuilding are missing due to excavation difficulties; however, a series of five small Type 2 and 3 features in the area support the former existence of a structure there. Dimensions of the rebuilt House 5 cannot be ascertained due to its fragmentary nature.

Construction: The House 5 wall sections that are intact display rather haphazard post mould patterns. Some small sections show straight post lines with regular spacing, while in other areas the wall is two to three posts thick. There appears to be extensive maintenance and rebuilding of parts of this structure. A possible entrance appears in the north wall. At least 80 posts were used in the walls of House 5 and the average post density is 5.04 posts/m. Two large interior support posts appear in the opposite southwest and northeast corners.

House 5 abuts the west end of House 6 and may, in fact, have been structurally attached to the end of that house. In any case, the distance between

Table 7.36. House 6 feature data.

| Feature Number | Volume (litres) | Artifact Total | CDE | FCR | Faunal | Ceramics | Artifacts per litre | Feature Type |
|---|---|---|---|---|---|---|---|---|
| 11 | 21.90 | 69 | 1 | 0 | 64 | 4 | 3.15 | 2 |
| 14 | 19.40 | 8 | 3 | 0 | 3 | 2 | 0.41 | 2 |
| 110 | 486.96 | 210 | 29 | 6 | 105 | 66 | 0.43 | 1 |
| 114 | 98.49 | 950 | 260 | 3 | 94 | 583 | 9.65 | 2 |
| 117 | 50.74 | 110 | 54 | 0 | 18 | 36 | 2.17 | 2 |
| 121 | 13.26 | 41 | 28 | 0 | 6 | 6 | 3.09 | 2 |
| 122 | 6.63 | 111 | 7 | 5 | 99 | 99 | 16.74 | 2 |
| 147* | 132.67 | 104 | 1 | 3 | 70 | 29 | 1.28 | 1 |
| 184 | 32.89 | 391 | 8 | 0 | 352 | 29 | 11.89 | 2 |
| Total | 862.94 | 1994 | 391 | 17 | 811 | 854 | | |
| % | | 105.50 | 20.69 | 0.90 | 42.91 | 45.19 | | |
| Mean | 95.88 | 221.56 | 43.44 | 1.89 | 90.11 | 94.89 | 5.42 | |

CDE, chipping detritus; FCR, fire cracked rock; *, Level 4 only.

the two structures is less than 50 cm. House 5 is also attached to the inner village palisade by means of a short house-to-palisade wall running from the middle of the west wall north to the palisade. A similar wall runs between palisade Segment 101 and the rebuilt version of House 5.

Interior Features: Twelve small features occur within House 5 and an additional five features are located in the extended or rebuilt area to the south. Eleven of these features have been excavated and, of those, six were classified as Type 2 and five as Type 3. No Type 1 features were present and there is no central hearth, although the presence of the cluster of Type 2 and 3 features suggests that there may have been a hearth in the structure at one time. This is supported by the fact that many of the features contain calcined bone and five contain fire broken rock. Data on the contents of the features are provided in Table 7.35, which show that faunal material dominates the assemblage at 57.29%. According to Prevec (1984a Appendix A), six of these features are dominated by deer antler, foot, head, and leg bones. Most of the bone is calcined mammal bone, not identifiable to species. This suggests that deer butchering was an important activity conducted inside this structure and that bones may have been burned there.

Function: The features within House 5 indicate that a variety of activities were carried on within the structure, including chert knapping, butchering, and

possibly cooking or intentional burning of bone refuse. The faunal evidence for butchering suggests that this small structure may have been a specialized animal processing area.

House 5 also appears to play an additional role in the spatial organization of the village, insofar as it is strategically situated between House 6 and the inner palisade with a connecting wall running between the house and palisade. As such it effectively prohibited passage through the village from north to south in this area.

House 6

Size and Location: House 6 is located in the north-central part of the village immediately north of House 12 (Figure 7.38). It is oriented roughly east-west. House 6 measures 20.57 m long by 7.0 m in width, making it the widest house in the village. Its total floor area is 145 square m. The east ends of Houses 6 and 12 are only one m apart, while the west ends diverge to about four metres. House 6 overlaps Early phase Houses 14 and 7 and, in turn, is overlapped by Late phase House 11.

Construction: The original wall post density for House 6 was calculated at 4.2 posts/m, indicating that at least 232 posts were required in the initial construction of this structure. At the time of abandonment post density had increased to 5.24 posts/m. Large interior support posts occur between

Table 7.37. House 12 feature data.

| Feature Number | Volume (litres) | Artifact Total | CDE | FCR | Faunal | Ceramics | Artifacts per litre | Feature Type |
|---|---|---|---|---|---|---|---|---|
| 29 | 7.70 | 2 | 0 | 0 | 0 | 1 | 0.26 | 2 |
| 30 | 3.32 | 27 | 4 | 3 | 8 | 12 | 8.13 | 2 |
| 33 | 24.66 | 3 | 2 | 0 | 0 | 1 | 0.12 | 2 |
| 35 | 9.50 | 3 | 1 | 0 | 2 | 0 | 0.32 | 2 |
| 36 | 24.06 | 152 | 60 | 3 | 86 | 2 | 6.32 | 2 |
| 141 | 91.49 | 26 | 7 | 0 | 1 | 15 | 0.28 | 3 |
| 142 | 14.70 | 308 | 0 | 0 | 308 | 0 | 20.95 | 2 |
| 161 | 293.83 | 1008 | 141 | 39 | 656 | 157 | 3.43 | 1 |
| Total | 469.26 | 1529 | 215 | 45 | 1061 | 188 | | |
| % | | 100.00 | 14.06 | 2.94 | 69.39 | 12.30 | | |
| Mean | 58.66 | 191.13 | 26.88 | 5.63 | 132.63 | 23.50 | 4.98 | |

CDE, chipping detritus; FCR, fire cracked rock.

1.75 and 2.0 m inside the walls and are spaced 3 to 5 m apart. The entrance at the east end has been partially obliterated by a Late phase pit, while the west entrance, was only 50 cm wide.

Interior Features: Fourteen features could be assigned to House 6 and of these, eight were excavated. As Figure 7.38 shows, the interior feature arrangement includes several small Type 2 features located within the central corridor. Only two Type 1 pits occur in the house: Feature 147 on the north side and Feature 110, just inside the south wall. The profile of Feature 147 is shown in Figure 7.25. It is a good example of long-term feature use, as levels 5 and 6 relate to the Early phase while level 4 relates to the Middle phase. Although there are only two extant hearths in House 6, it is estimated that at least four hearths were in use when the house was occupied. The feature data are summarized in Table 7.36.

Function: House 6 is interpreted as a multi-family dwelling. With an estimated four hearths and two families of approximately six per hearth, it would have had a population of 48 people.

House 12

Size and Location: House 12 is centrally located within the village, immediately south of House 6 (Figure 7.38). It is also oriented east-west but diverges slightly to the south in relation to House 6. With an estimated length of 24.5 m and a width of 6.5 m, it is the largest house in the village and offers the greatest living space (158.93 square m). House 12 was built over parts of former Houses 7 and 14 and it, in turn, is partially overlapped by Late phase Houses 8, 11, and 13.

Construction: As Figure 7.38 shows, the preservation of posts in House 12 was poor, especially along the northern wall and the western end. The original post density was calculated at 3.83 posts/m, but this figure may be low due to missing posts. Only 128 wall posts were assigned to House 12, but the initial construction would have required at least 237 posts for the exterior frame alone. The post pattern appears to be staggered.

Interior support posts again occur about 1.75 m inside the side walls, although they are poorly represented on the north side of the house. A well defined partition wall was built 4 m inside the east end of the house. It extends from the north wall across to the south wall, where there is a gap, interpreted as a small entrance way, located just inside the wall. If this interior wall is correctly interpreted and the entrance through it was near the south wall, there could not have been a bench or platform in this area.

The east end of the structure has a well defined entrance that is 1.8 m wide.

Interior Features: A total of 16 interior features could be assigned to House 12. Twelve of these

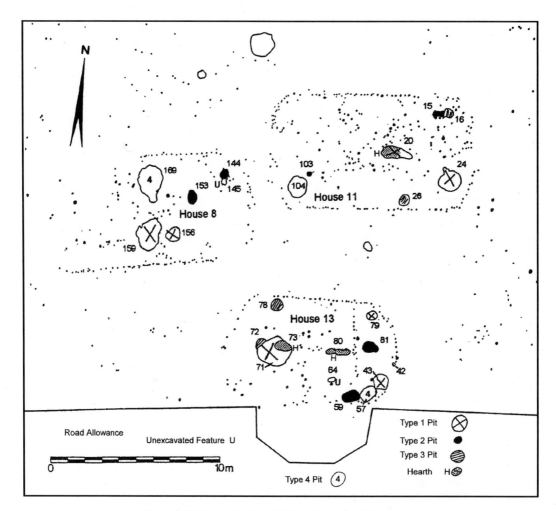

Figure 7.39. Houses 8, 11, and 13, and associated features.

occur in a cluster within the partitioned section at the east end of the house. It is likely that several more features were in use when the house was occupied but they could not all be assigned to House 12 due to structure overlaps.

Table 7.37 presents the data from the eight House 12 features that were excavated. This house is notable for its scarcity of Type 1 features. The single Type 1 pit, Feature 161, is located in the southwest corner and is dominated by faunal material. Type 2 features are most common, with the majority occurring in the partitioned area at the east end of the house in association with two

hearths. It is estimated that three additional hearths existed in the remaining portion of the house.

Function: House 12 is interpreted as a residential multi-family dwelling. Its most unusual feature is the partition wall at the east end. Although ethnohistorical accounts describe storage cubicles in the ends of houses, this area was obviously used as living space, as indicated by the presence of two hearths and several Type 2 features containing occupational debris. Despite the presence of two hearths in this area, it is unlikely that more than two families occupied this rather small space. If we count the two hearths in the east cubicle as one and

Table 7.38. House 8 feature data.

| Feature Number | Volume (litres) | Artifact Total | CDE | FCR | Faunal | Ceramics | Artifacts per litre | Feature Type |
|---|---|---|---|---|---|---|---|---|
| 144 | 8.82 | 17 | 3 | 0 | 10 | 4 | 1.93 | 2 |
| 153 | 35.94 | 81 | 14 | 4 | 62 | 1 | 2.25 | 2 |
| 156 | 449.08 | 2144 | 448 | 32 | 1476 | 171 | 4.77 | 1 |
| 159 | 1335.50 | 952 | 194 | 7 | 554 | 189 | 0.71 | 1 |
| 169 | 1269.41 | 2208 | 28 | 2 | 1936 | 241 | 1.74 | 4 |
| Total | 3098.75 | 5402 | 687 | 45 | 4038 | 606 | | |
| % | | 100.00 | 12.72 | 0.83 | 74.75 | 11.22 | | |
| Mean | 619.75 | 1080.40 | 137.40 | 9.00 | 807.60 | 121.20 | 2.28 | |

CDE, chipping detritus; FCR, fire cracked rock.

estimate that there were three additional hearths, we conclude that House 12 may have housed 8 families comprising 48 people.

## House 10

Size and Location: Only the north wall and part of the east end of House 10 were exposed in the excavations. It is located at the south end of the excavated area, immediately south of House 12. The gap between the east end of House 10 and the wall of House 12 is only 50 cm; however, House 10 is oriented south of west so that the two structures diverge widely at the west end. The dimensions of House 10 are estimated at 21 m in length and 6.75 m in width, giving it a total floor area of 141.75 square m.

Construction: The north wall of House 10 has an original post density of 3.7 posts/m, indicating that initial construction would have required at least 205 posts. The wall lines appear to be staggered but many postmoulds are missing. Only one support post, located 2 m inside the wall, was mapped.

Interior Features: Only three features were assigned to House 10 and none of them was excavated. They include one hearth at the east end and two small features along the north side of the house. Based on hearth spacing, it is possible that House 10 had as many as four central hearths.

Function: While our information on House 10 is extremely limited, it was likely a typical longhouse. An estimate of four hearths and eight families suggests a population of up to 48 individuals for this structure.

The small gap between the east ends of Houses 10 and 12 suggests that these structures may have been strategically placed to limit access to the east and west sides of the village and channel traffic flow in the case of enemy attack (Finlayson 1985).

## The Late Phase

### Palisade

The existence of a palisade in the Late phase has not been demonstrated; nor has it been disproved. A single row palisade (Segment 101) is shown in Figure 7.31; however, its presence during the Late phase is based merely on the fact that this was the final palisade segment built and therefore would be expected to last the longest. It has been described in the previous section as part of the Middle phase.

### House 8

Size and Location: House 8 is located in the centre of the settlement, where it overlaps parts of Houses 7 and 12 (Figure 7.39). It is oriented east-west and measures an estimated 12.8 m in length by 5.8 m in width. Parts of the north side, east end, and all of the west end were not recovered in the field due to poor soil conditions, but enough of the house is intact to permit its recognition.

Construction: Post density for the intact sections of House 8 was originally 3.4 posts/m, increasing to 5.03 posts/m by the time of abandonment. Initial construction required a minimum of 126 posts. The post rows vary from straight to slightly staggered. Interior support posts

Table 7.39. House 11 feature data.

| Feature Number | Volume (litres) | Artifact Total | CDE | FCR | Faunal | Ceramics | Artifacts per litre | Feature Type |
|---|---|---|---|---|---|---|---|---|
| 15 | 7.07 | 11 | 5 | 0 | 1 | 5 | 1.56 | 2 |
| 16 | 63.33 | 233 | 9 | 14 | 0 | 210 | 3.68 | 3 |
| 20 | 574.95 | 1546 | 111 | 22 | 1317 | 70 | 2.69 | 1 |
| 24 | 842.06 | 1295 | 807 | 71 | 114 | 142 | 1.54 | 1 |
| 26 | 35.65 | 5 | 3 | 0 | 2 | 0 | 0.14 | 3 |
| 103 | 2.38 | 26 | 5 | 0 | 19 | 2 | 10.92 | 2 |
| Total | 1525.44 | 3116 | 940 | 107 | 1453 | 429 | | |
| % | | 100.00 | 30.17 | 3.43 | 46.63 | 13.77 | | |
| Mean | 254.24 | 519.33 | 156.67 | 17.83 | 242.17 | 71.50 | 3.42 | |

CDE, chipping detritus; FCR, fire cracked rock.

are present in the west end of the structure but are lacking in the east end. This may be a result of poor post resolution in this area. The interior supports are 1.5 m inside the walls.

Interior Features: As Figure 7.39 shows, six interior features could be assigned to House 8. Five of these features were excavated; selected data on their contents are shown in Table 7.38. Two of the features are Type 1 pits and a third, Feature 169, is a large pit that would have been classed as a Type 1 feature except for its irregular profile. These three features have a total volume of more than 3000 litres and yielded more than 5000 pieces of debris, including almost 4000 pieces of bone. Feature 169 was a highly specialized feature with nearly 2000 faunal fragments, while Feature 156 yielded large quantities of both faunal and lithic debris. These large features are located on opposite sides of the central corridor of the house with only a .75 m passageway between them.

The two remaining features are of the Type 2 variety and are located in the northeast quarter of the structure. Additional Type 2 features were found within House 8 but could not be definitely assigned to it due to structure overlapping. No hearths were found in the house; based on its size it probably had two.

Function: If we apply our standard method of estimating population based on the probable number of hearths, we conclude that House 8 may have had a population of about 24 people. However, the Late phase as a whole is interpreted as a hunting camp, suggesting that this method of estimating population

may not be valid. The social composition of the household may have been determined by the function of the site, with more males present if hunting were the main purpose of the occupation. If so, the ethnohistorical analogue of two families per hearth may not be reliable.

The spatial organization of features within House 8 differs from most of the other houses in that the Type 1 storage/refuse features were located near the centre of the structure and two of the three smaller features were located in a corner, reversing the normal pattern.

House 11

Size and Location: House 11 measures 11.6 m by 6.2 m with a floor area of 71.92 square m. It is located in the northeast quarter of the village and shares an east-west orientation with the other Late phase structures (Figure 7.39). Unfortunately, it overlies Houses 6 and 14 as well as two problematic structures discussed in Chapter 5, making feature-house assignments difficult.

Construction: Wall post lines are generally straight and have an initial post density of 4.0 posts/m. A minimum of 142 posts would have been used in the construction of the house walls. Possible interior support posts lie within the house but it is difficult to assign particular posts to the structure. Well defined entrances 1.5 and 1.3 m in width appear at the west and east ends, respectively.

Interior Features: Seven interior features were assigned to House 11 and all were excavated. Data

Table 7.40. House 13 feature data.

| Feature Number | Volume (litres) | Artifact Total | CDE | FCR | Faunal | Ceramics | Artifacts per litre | Feature Type |
|---|---|---|---|---|---|---|---|---|
| 42 | 2.69 | 2 | 0 | 0 | 1 | 1 | 0.74 | 2 |
| 43 | 438.32 | 1258 | 549 | 19 | 303 | 373 | 2.87 | 1 |
| 57 | 136.73 | 107 | 48 | 5 | 37 | 17 | 0.78 | 4 |
| 59 | 83.13 | 130 | 58 | 15 | 34 | 23 | 1.56 | 2 |
| 72 | 74.99 | 1469 | 171 | 0 | 795 | 371 | 19.59 | 3 |
| 73 | 57.43 | 556 | 91 | 1 | 409 | 52 | 9.68 | 2 |
| 78 | 71.05 | 336 | 33 | 6 | 90 | 121 | 4.73 | 3 |
| 79 | 125.04 | 2281 | 191 | 22 | 1629 | 317 | 18.24 | 1 |
| 81 | 71.68 | 113 | 36 | 50 | 23 | 4 | 1.58 | 2 |
| Total | 1061.06 | 6252 | 1177 | 118 | 3321 | 1279 | | |
| % | | 100.00 | 18.83 | 1.89 | 53.12 | 20.46 | | |
| Mean | 117.90 | 694.67 | 130.78 | 13.11 | 369.00 | 142.11 | 6.64 | |

CDE, chipping detritus; FCR, fire cracked rock.

from these features are summarized in Table 7.39. Feature 104, in the southwest corner of the house, is excluded because the data for this feature are incomplete. Of the remaining features, two are Type 1, two are Type 2, and two are Type 3. The Type 1 features include Feature 24, which is heavily dominated by lithic debris. The presence of over 800 pieces of chipping detritus in an interior pit strongly suggests that a chert-knapping activity area was located in the vicinity. The other Type 1 pit, Feature 20, is a complex hearth/pit containing over 1300 pieces of calcined bone. This Type 1 feature is centrally located, while the Type 2 and 3 features are located around the perimeter of the house which, again, is the opposite of the normal feature distribution pattern.

House 11 contains one hearth in the Feature 20 hearth/pit complex, but it is large enough to have had at least two hearths when it was in use.

Function: The function of House 11 was probably identical to that of House 8. It might have housed as many as 24 people if used by an extended family, but could have housed a hunting party of similar or different size. Type 1 pit refuse suggests that both chert knapping and animal processing were important activities, and were spatially separated.

House 13

Size and Location: House 13, also oriented east-west, is the smallest of the Late phase houses, measuring 9.6 m in length by 5.6 m in width with a floor area of 53.76 square m. It is located near the southern edge of excavation and overlaps parts of Houses 10, 12, and 14 (Figure 7.39).

Construction: Neither the south side nor the west end of House 13 is well defined; yet there are enough extant post moulds to define the structure and its form. The wall posts form a straight line and post density along the intact north wall is 3.3 posts/m, indicating that at least 100 poles were needed for initial construction. Possible interior support posts occur within the structure. They lie between 1.75 and 2 m inside the north wall and between 1 and 1.5 m inside the south wall. Due to the extensive structure overlapping, it is impossible to determine precisely which support posts belong to House 13.

A wall running across the house perpendicular to the long axis is located 2.5 m inside the east end. This is interpreted as a partition wall similar to the one found in House 12. Access through this wall may have been along the south side of the house, where there is a gap in the interior partition. If so,

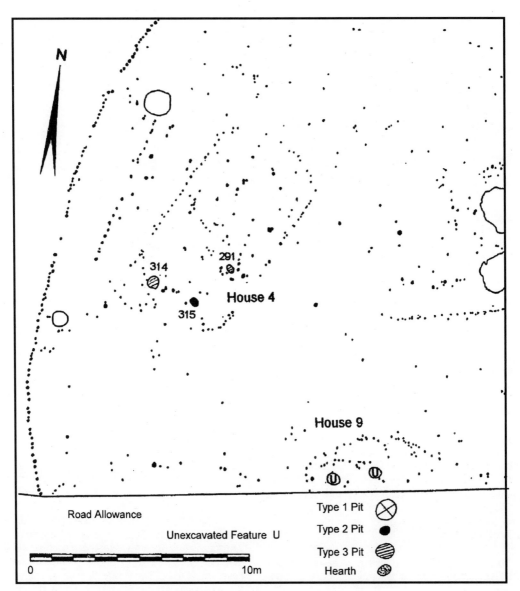

Figure 7.40. Houses 4 and 9 and associated features.

there probably was not a bench on the south side of the house in this area.

Interior Features: A total of 12 interior features were assigned to House 13. Of these, ten were excavated and the data for nine of them are summarized in Table 7.40. Data from Feature 71 are not included in the table, since only Level 1 of this feature is assigned to the Late phase. As Table 7.40 shows, House 13 contains two Type 1 pits, Features 79 and 43. Feature 79 is located in the northeast corner of the house and is dominated by

Table 7.41. House 4 feature data.

| Feature Number | Volume (litres) | Artifact Total | CDE | FCR | Faunal | Ceramics | Artifacts per litre | Feature Type |
|---|---|---|---|---|---|---|---|---|
| 291 | 28.25 | 167 | 8 | 2 | 149 | 7 | 5.91 | 3 |
| 314 | 56.94 | 168 | 23 | 11 | 121 | 7 | 2.95 | 3 |
| 315 | 17.59 | 705 | 4 | 0 | 699 | 0 | 40.08 | 2 |
| Total | 102.78 | 1040 | 35 | 13 | 969 | 14 | | |
| % | | 100.00 | 3.37 | 1.25 | 93.17 | 1.35 | | |
| Mean | 34.26 | 346.67 | 11.67 | 4.33 | 323.00 | 4.67 | 16.31 | |

CDE, chipping detritus; FCR, fire cracked rock.

faunal debris representing an interesting range of animals discussed in Chapter 6. Feature 43, in the southeast corner, is dominated by lithic debris with over 500 pieces present. Both of these specialized features occur within the partitioned area.

The Type 3 features include Feature 72, located in the centre corridor at the west end of the house. This small pit had an artifact density of 19.59 pieces/litre, and included almost 800 pieces of faunal debris. The majority of the bone in Features 72 and 79 was not burnt, which is unusual for an interior refuse pit.

House 13 also contains two hearths, as expected for a structure of this size.

Function: When compared to the other two Late phase houses, House 13 shows a more normal distribution of interior feature types, with the larger Type 1 features tucked into the corners. Although the centrally located Feature 71 is a Type 1 feature, only its top layer has been assigned to the Late phase. Again there is evidence for the spatial organization of chert knapping and animal processing activities. Lithic dominated Feature 43 occurs in the southeast corner, while the faunal dominated features (79 and 72) occur in the central corridor and the northeast corner.

If we apply the usual indices to estimate population for House 13, we arrive at a figure of 24 individuals, as we did for Houses 8 and 11. Since House 13 was used as part of the Late phase hunting camp, it may have been occupied by a hunting group rather than an extended family.

## Unknown Phase

### House 4

Size and Location: House 4 is a small structure located in the west half of the village where it overlaps (and post-dates) the south end of House 3 (Figure 7.40). It is oriented northeast-southwest and measures 9.25 m in length by 4.9 m in width, giving it a floor area of 45.33 square m.

Construction: Wall post lines are straight with a post density of 3.5 posts/m. Construction of the walls of House 4 would have required at least 99 posts. Interior support posts are difficult to identify due to the overlap with House 3. The ends and sides include several gaps that may represent entrances; however, most of these are likely due to poor post resolution in areas of wall/feature overlap.

Interior Features: Only three excavated features (Features 291, 314, and 315) could be confidently assigned to House 4. Feature 315 is a Type 2 pit containing 699 pieces of mostly unburnt faunal material (Table 7.41). Although it was not possible to assign any hearths to House 4, based on its size it probably had two.

Function: As a multi-family dwelling, House 4 could have housed four families or about 24 people. While we know that it is not contemporaneous with the Early phase, we cannot assign it to the Middle or Late phases on the present evidence. If it was part of the Late phase, the possibility exists that it was occupied by a hunting group.

Table 7.42. Calvert site house dimensions.

| House | Length (metres) | Width (metres) | Area (m²) |
|-------|-----------------|----------------|-----------|
| 1 | 12.50 | 6.35 | 79.38 |
| 2 | 4.65 | 3.30 | 15.35 |
| 3 | 13.95 | 6.40 | 89.28 |
| 4 | 9.25 | 4.90 | 45.33 |
| 5 | 5.82 | 5.25 | 30.56 |
| 6 | 20.57 | 7.00 | 143.99 |
| 7 | 16.00 | 5.40 | 86.40 |
| 8 | 12.80* | 5.80 | 74.24 |
| 9 | - | - | - |
| 10 | 21.00 | 6.75* | 141.75* |
| 11 | 11.60 | 6.20 | 71.92 |
| 12 | 24.45* | 6.50 | 158.93* |
| 13 | 9.60 | 5.60 | 53.76 |
| 14 | 21.50 | 6.30 | 135.45 |

*, estimated measurement; -, estimate not possible.

## House 9

House 9 is located along the southern edge of the excavation and is only represented by a corner (Figure 7.40). It appears to be oriented northwest-southeast. Given the fragmentary nature of our data regarding this structure, we cannot estimate its size or comment on its construction, interior arrangements, or function. It intersects House 10; therefore, we know that it was not contemporaneous with the Middle phase. The existence of House 9 creates interpretive problems as it is an unknown addition to one period of occupation. It could therefore skew our interpretations of population and change throughout the occupation of the site.

## Summary and Discussion

### Structure Function and Variability

The preceding analysis of the Calvert settlement pattern has resulted in the identification of at least four different structure types within the village. The variability seen in the Calvert structures is believed to be primarily related to structure function. Table 7.42 summarizes the dimensions of all structures.

The first structure type is the standard Early Iroquoian longhouse occupied by an extended family. It is represented at Calvert by Houses 7, 14, 6, 12, and 10.

The second structure type is a combination residential/storage house characterized by numerous interior storage pits and also occupied by an extended family. The single example of this house type at Calvert is House 3.

The third type is a non-residential structure, represented by Houses 2 and 5. They have been interpreted as work/storage structures in which a variety of domestic activities may have been performed. Structures of this type are small and lack the internal organization of features seen in residential structures (i.e., central hearths and associated features). House 5 may have had a specialized animal processing function, and the separation of lithic and ceramic debris within House 2 suggests that activities were spatially organized within that structure.

The fourth structure type is the special purpose cabin/longhouse used by families or hunting parties for short-term occupation while on hunting and gathering excursions. These structures are usually smaller than regular longhouses and often display a different internal organization of features. The occupants of these structures frequently show little concern with refuse disposal, garbage normally being dumped in pits within houses. Large refuse pits may be located within the central corridor rather than around the house perimeter. Examples of this house type at Calvert include Houses 1, 8, 11, 13, and possibly House 4.

While these types of structures appear to represent the total variability in house types and functions at the Calvert site, no claim is made that the same structure types will be found on other Early Iroquoian sites. The settlement data from each individual site must be analyzed in detail to determine the range in structure types within each community.

### Population

Using ethnohistoric analogues, household population estimates have been calculated for all structures interpreted as residential dwellings at the Calvert site (Table 7.43). It is acknowledged that

Table 7.43. Population estimates based on hearth numbers.

| Phase | House | Length (metres) | Estimated number of hearths | Estimated Population |
|-------|-------|-----------------|------------------------------|----------------------|
| House 1 | 1 | 12.50 | 3 | 36 |
| Early Phase | 3 | 13.95 | 3 | 36 |
| | 7 | 16.00 | 2 | 24 |
| | 14 | 21.50 | 4 | 48 |
| Population Total | | | | 108 |
| Middle Phase | 6 | 20.57 | 4 | 48 |
| | 12 | 24.25 | 4 | 48 |
| | 10 | 21.00 | 4 | 48 |
| Population Total | | | | 144 |
| Late Phase | 8 | 12.80 | 2 | 24 |
| | 11 | 11.60 | 2 | 24 |
| | 13 | 9.60 | 2 | 24 |
| Population Total | | | | 72 |
| Unknown Phase | 4 | 9.25 | 2 | 24 |

these estimates make two important assumptions. The first is that the use of the historic analogue is accurate, and the second is that the Calvert houses were fully occupied. Neither assumption can be wholly justified, but they are necessary to allow interpretations. In any case, the resulting population estimates for each phase show some significant differences.

The population of the Early phase is estimated at about 108 individuals. In the Middle phase an increase in overall house size leads to an increased population estimate of 144 individuals. The Late phase sees a change in site function to a hunting camp and a concurrent reduction in house size. The population estimate is 72 people for Houses 8, 11, and 13, increasing to 96 if House 4 is included. It would be even higher if House 9 belonged to the Late phase. Since there is some evidence for short term occupations in all seasons, it is possible that the Late phase houses were not all occupied contemporaneously. Small hunting parties may have only occupied one or two houses on any given hunting trip.

## Village Organization

The major changes in the organization of space within the village were summarized in Chapter 5. My purpose here is to examine the relationship between village space, population, and living area. The following discussion concerns only the excavated area of the village.

During the Early phase the total area within the excavated palisade was 1700 square metres and the total floor area of the three residential houses was 311.13 square m, or 18.3% of the total site area (Table 7.44). In the Middle phase, with the contraction of the palisade, the inner village area was reduced to 1400 square m, yet the total house floor area increased to 476.23 square m or 34% of the inner village space. At the same time, the population appears to have increased by almost 40% from about 108 people to approximately 150. In short, the structural changes to the village in the Middle phase indicate that there were more people living in less space at that time.

While there was less space within the village in the Middle phase, the organization of that space also underwent deliberate change. The inner palisade, Segment 101, was built, apparently reflecting a greater concern for defense. The house pattern changed from a rather sprawling radial pattern to a tightly clustered radial one in which the east ends of Houses 6, 12, and 10 were less than 1 m apart. At the same time, House 5 was built between House 6 and the inner palisade, and a house-to-palisade wall was constructed between them. All of these modifications had the effect of inhibiting traffic flow within the village. They made it extremely difficult to pass from the east to the west side of the village without walking through the houses or squeezing between them.

The changes in the village between the Early and Middle phases were costly modifications in terms of material and labour and would not have been undertaken lightly. Table 7.45 summarizes the minimum numbers of posts required for construction of the Middle phase houses and palisade. The total of 1591 includes only house wall posts and palisade poles. No attempt was made to calculate requirements for interior supports, wall extension poles, rafters, longitudinal poles, benches, or partitions, so this estimate can likely be doubled. If

Table 7.44. Total house area by phase.

| Phase | Estimated Area (m²) |
|-------|---------------------|
| House 1 | 79.34 |
| Early | 311.13 |
| Middle | 476.23 |
| Late | 306.25 |

Table 7.45. Minimum number of poles required for Calvert structures.

| Structure | Number of Poles |
|-----------|-----------------|
| House 1 | 140 |
| Early Phase | |
| House 2 | 56 |
| House 3 | 170 |
| House 7 | 145 |
| House 14 | 200 |
| Palisade | 800 |
| Subtotal | 1371 |
| Middle Phase | |
| House 5 | 80 |
| House 6 | 232 |
| House 12 | 237 |
| House 10 | 205 |
| Palisade | 837 |
| Subtotal | 1591 |
| Late Phase | |
| House 8 | 126 |
| House 11 | 142 |
| House 13 | 100 |
| Subtotal | 368 |
| Unknown Phase | |
| House 4 | 99 |
| Total | 3569 |

we add the cost of procuring and installing bark sheathing, and the manufacturing of bark, root, or hide cordage, which according to experimental studies was very labour intensive (Callahan 1981), the magnitude of the task becomes more apparent. I have estimated, using data derived from Callahan (1981) and Heidenreich (1971), that the construction of the Middle phase structures would have taken a team of 30 men between one and two months of steady labour. These modifications were

not made without good reason. The rationale for the reorganization of the Calvert village is explored in the following chapter.

## Conclusions

Our analysis of the artifact assemblage and settlement data from Calvert has revealed the technology of the Calvert people and allowed us to address questions of group identity, population changes, seasonality, and site formation. Our conclusions are summarized below.

Inferences with respect to group identity are largely based on artifact analysis, in particular, the comparison of ceramics from the different phases. The pottery of the Early, Middle, and Late phases was found to be quite similar in terms of decorative motifs, suggesting that it is the product of a single community evolving through time. Through seriation of ceramic attributes and attribute combinations, we identified a number of attributes and attribute combinations that show chronological sensitivity, increasing or decreasing in frequency through time. Several attribute combinations involving decorative technique proved to be sensitive to chronological change and supported the occupational history derived in Chapter 5.

House 1, on the other hand, yielded a highly distinctive ceramic assemblage characterized by a high percentage of suture stamped vessels. The House 1 lithic assemblage was also distinctive, containing a very high percentage of Onondaga chert and very little Kettle Point material. Several lines of evidence also indicate that the occupation of House 1 occurred prior to the construction of the main village. I conclude, therefore, that House 1 represents a distinctive group, unrelated to the people of the main village occupation.

Artifactual and settlement pattern data have helped to resolve the questions of seasonality and site function, examined in Chapter 6. For the Late phase, aspects of the lithic assemblage, the smaller size of ceramic vessels, the smaller houses, and the different internal organization of houses further support the hypothesized change to a hunting camp function. Finally, refuse disposal behaviour is radically different in the final phase, reflecting abandonment behaviour associated with a short-term and probably mainly cold weather occupation. These results confirm our conclusion that the Late phase represents a short-term hunting camp that was occupied on a sporadic basis, primarily during the cold season, but during warmer months as well.

Understanding the reasons behind the changes observed at the Calvert site is a more difficult problem. Use of the site as a hunting camp in the House 1 and Late phases poses no problem, as there is a clear economic justification for these occupations. However, the substantial changes in village organization that took place between the Early and Middle phases are less easily explained. Our settlement pattern evidence indicates that, while population was increasing within the village, decisions were made to build additional palisade walls and contract the village area. Houses were rearranged in a tight radial fashion and house-to-palisade walls were constructed that would have inhibited traffic flow within the village. Such modifications were costly in terms of both labour and materials. Moreover, constricting living space would likely not have contributed to improved living conditions. This suggests that the modifications seen in the Middle phase are a response to some type of internal or external stress that may best be explained at the socio-political level of analysis. The social and political organization of the Calvert community is examined in the following chapter.

# Chapter 8

# Social and Political Organization within and beyond the Calvert Community

## Introduction

In this chapter we examine the implications of the Calvert site data for understanding the social and political organization of the Calvert community. Our aim is to explore Early Iroquoian socio-political organization from both a synchronic and a diachronic perspective at the community and regional levels. This involves construction of an interpretive model of Early Iroquoian socio-political development that explains the Calvert data in the context of the general process of Iroquoian development in southwestern Ontario. To address adequately the problem of socio-political organization at the regional level, it is necessary to draw upon data from Glen Meyer sites in other regions of southwestern Ontario.

It is generally held that settlement pattern data are most amenable to the interpretation of the social and political structure of prehistoric societies (Chang 1958, 1968; Trigger 1967, 1968). This is particularly true in Iroquoian archaeology where community patterns and house patterns are often interpreted as reflecting ethnographically defined social units, such as matrilineages or clan segments (Warrick 1984a; Trigger 1981; Finlayson 1985). Ceramic analysis has also been used to study problems of socio-political organization (Whallon 1968; Engelbrecht 1974; Warrick 1984a). This chapter will employ both settlement and ceramic data to develop an interpretive model of Early Iroquoian socio-political organization.

Before proceeding to a discussion of these data it is necessary to review some of the ethnohistorical and archaeological literature that provides the necessary background for the construction of our interpretive model.

## Ethnohistorical Data on Iroquoian Socio-Political Organization

The tribal organization of Iroquoian society in the historical period was a segmentary system consisting of lineages grouped into clan segments, clan segments grouped into villages, villages grouped into tribes, and tribes grouped into confederacies. These entities represent nested levels of socio-political integration. According to Sahlins (1968:15), tribal organization is always built of such compounded segments. It follows that a study of the development of Iroquoian socio-political organization should consider the evolution of the constituent elements of this segmentary system. Historical Iroquoian groups should, therefore, constitute a relevant analogue for prehistoric groups, if their constituent socio-political units are recognizable in prehistory.

The most comprehensive descriptions of Iroquoian social and political organization in the early contact period relate to the Huron and have been gleaned from the accounts of Champlain, Sagard, and the Jesuit Relations. Thorough summaries of the relevant information from these sources can be found in Tooker (1967), Trigger (1976, 1985a, 1990), and Heidenreich (1971). Although the Early Iroquoian Glen Meyer people of southwestern Ontario very likely developed into the historic Neutral, the process of socio-political development from the Early to Late Iroquoian periods was probably generally similar throughout Iroquoia. The following summary of ethnohistorical information is based primarily on the Huron, for whom the best information is available.

At the time of historical contact the Huron were a confederacy of four tribes, living in a relatively small area between the southeastern end of Georgian Bay and Lake Simcoe. Each tribe consisted of a number of villages. Villages and tribes were linked by eight clans that cross-cut village and tribal lines (Trigger 1990:66). The clan was an important socio-political entity serving to integrate communities for social, economic, ritual, and political purposes.

Within the village the clan segment was a fundamental political unit, each clan segment usually having two chiefs or headmen. One of these chiefs dealt with civic affairs, while the other was a war chief. Separate councils were held to discuss civic affairs and matters of war (Tooker 1967:43). Chieftainships usually were the prerogative of a single lineage within the clan segment, so that chiefs were selected from among a deceased chief's relatives (ibid:46). It was sometimes also possible for a man to become a chief solely on the basis of his achievements. Among the peace chiefs or headmen who sat on the village councils was one who acted as spokesman for the entire village.

The rules for clan membership among the Huron are not explicit in the historical sources. Clans appear to have been based on fictive kinship, with all clan members tracing descent from a common female ancestor. Each person belonged to the same clan as his or her mother, and clans were exogamous so that marriages reinforced ties between different clans (Trigger 1990:66).

Large villages consisted of several clan segments and when villages split apart it was usually along clan segment lines (ibid:67). It is likely that the expansion of villages often involved the addition of entire clan segments.

The early sources indicate quite clearly that the Huron observed matrilineal descent, although their residence patterns are more difficult to infer (Tooker 1967:127-128). It is probable that matrilocal residence was preferred, but there are indications in the Jesuit Relations that the observation of rules of residence may have been flexible.

# Archaeological Models of Iroquoian Socio-Political Development

The following discussion of archaeological research relating to Early Iroquoian political organization has been divided into three sections.

The first deals with the relationship between intra-village community patterns and socio-political organization at the village level. The second section deals with the diachronic development of Iroquoian socio-political organization and concerns temporal trends in Iroquoian settlement patterns between the Early and Middle Iroquoian periods. The third section discusses various hypotheses that seek to identify the major causes of socio-political change in Iroquoian prehistory.

## The Determinants of Village Organization

Gary Warrick has examined a broad range of factors that might have influenced the spatial organization of Early Iroquoian villages. These include cosmology, available construction materials, drainage and topography, climate, fire prevention, sanitation, space conservation, defense, and socio-political factors (1984a:22-34). He concluded that, while space conservation and overcrowding (possibly as a result of external hostilities) may have influenced longhouse arrangements in some villages, the major determinants of village organization were probably socio-political in nature.

Working on the assumption that physical and social distance are highly correlated in pre-industrial societies, Warrick argues that closely spaced parallel or radially aligned longhouse clusters represent localized clan segments or "clan-barrios" (ibid: 35). In the Middle and Late Iroquoian periods, large Iroquoian villages were often segmented and contained two or more clan-barrios, each of which functioned as a separate social and political entity. These interpretations accord well with the ethnohistorical data concerning Iroquoian clan segments discussed above.

In contrast to Warrick's model, William Finlayson (1985) offers an alternative explanation of Iroquoian village organization which is equally political but places much greater emphasis on defense as a major determinant of village layout. Finlayson argues that the multiple expansions of the late prehistoric Draper site, as well as several aspects of its internal organization, were motivated by a concern for defense (1985:439). The coalescence of groups into large villages is generally accepted as a defensive response in which people sought strength in numbers. Both Finlayson (ibid.) and Pearce (1984:317) have further argued that radially aligned houses with narrow corridors between them and walls connecting houses and palisades are defensive measures designed to channel attacking warriors within the village. This interpretation of Iroquoian warfare has been challenged by Warrick, who argues that large scale raids and fighting within palisades were not typical of Iroquoian warfare of the early contact period and notes that aboriginal weaponry was largely ineffective against palisaded villages (1984a:32). He believes that Iroquoian warfare was similar to that practised in other stateless societies, involving small scale raids, ritual battles, and ambushes outside villages (ibid:33).

The socio-political model proposed by Warrick and the defense model proposed by Finlayson need not be mutually exclusive. Each model provides parsimonious explanations of settlement pattern data, and there is no reason that some aspects of intra-village settlement patterns could not have served both socio-political and defensive ends. For example, radially aligned longhouse clusters with doorways in close proximity may reflect social cohesion, even clan segments; yet, at the same time, they would serve effectively to channel attacking warriors if they did gain access to the village interior.

Several of the longhouse clusters that were added to the Draper core village involve parallel or radially aligned structures. These longhouses undoubtedly relate to distinct socio-political groups, thus their spatial organization lends support to the interpretation that they constitute clan segments and to the assertion that villages are most likely to cleave or grow through the budding off or addition of clan segments. Yet, at the same time, the causal factors underlying the growth of the Draper village may well have been related to warfare and the external tensions associated with increasing military activity. Thus the models proposed by Warrick and Finlayson may be seen as complementary explanations that address different aspects of Iroquoian village organization.

### Settlement Patterns and Socio-Political Development

The prevailing view of Early Iroquoian socio-political organization was established by William Noble as early as 1969, when he concluded that the apparent disorganization of Early Iroquoian

villages implied a lack of village planning (1969:19). This opinion was reinforced by Noble in his analysis of the Van Besien site (1975a) and was later echoed by Warrick (1984a) in his reconstruction of Iroquoian socio-political development based on the analysis of village settlement patterns. Most recently, Ferris and Spence have re-stated the view that Early Iroquoian village settlement patterns reflect "a lack of formal village organization" (1995:107).

Warrick defined four sequential types of village patterns:
1. an Early Iroquoian pattern characterized by small, often overlapping houses, in small disordered villages;
2. a Middle Iroquoian pattern typified by larger villages, larger longhouses, and parallel house alignments sometimes forming a segmented village pattern;
3. a Late Prehistoric-Protohistoric pattern involving large villages, diverse house sizes, radial clusters of houses, and complex palisades; and
4. a Historical pattern, based on Huron data, involving large palisaded villages with smaller houses arranged in parallel rows (Warrick 1984a:61).

Warrick explained the changes in Iroquoian community patterns in terms of a three phase evolutionary scheme. Phase 1 involved the transition from small, unplanned Early Iroquoian villages to the larger, well planned villages of the Middle Iroquoian period, a change that was thought to have occurred in a time of climatic deterioration combined with increasing warfare, long-distance trade, and the development of pipe complexes and ossuary burial. Political organization was thought to have been dominated by influential lineages, since clans and tribes had not yet developed. Warrick also postulated the existence of village endogamy during this period as a result of "a state of chronic war" (ibid:66).

According to Warrick, clans and tribal alliances did not develop until Phase 2, in the Late Prehistoric period, which saw "unprecedented warfare and socio-political upheaval, followed by a relatively peaceful period" (ibid:59). During this peaceful period, it was postulated that village exogamy developed for the first time.

| Model of Tribal Evolution | Expected Settlement Pattern |
|---|---|
| Bilateral Band | Restricted Wandering: small temporary camps less than a half acre; average population less than 50 |
| Patrilocal Band | Central-based Wandering: seasonal base camps less than one acre; population 50 to 150 |
| Multi-lineage Community | Semi-sedentary or sedentary villages: average more than one acre; population 150 to 400 or 500 |
| Tribe | Semi-sedentary or sedentary villages clustered or within a defined territory; intervillage homogeneity |

Figure 8.1. Niemczycki's model of tribal evolution operationalized in terms of settlement (Niemczycki 1984: 86).

Phase 3 occurred during the protohistoric and historical periods and involved the gradual erosion of Iroquoian socio-political systems as a result of European contact (ibid:58-69). In sum, within Warrick's scheme, the fundamental institutions of Iroquoian socio-political organization did not develop until the fifteenth century, during Late Iroquoian times. A variety of variables, including climatic change, increasing warfare, population pressure, and trade, were viewed as causal factors stimulating change.

Another important model of Iroquoian socio-political development was proposed by Niemczycki to explain the development of the Seneca and Cayuga tribes of New York State (Figure 8.1). Niemczycki drew upon Service's (1971) scheme of cultural evolution to propose four stages of development leading to the formation of the tribe.

The first stage **bilateral band** was characterized by fluid membership, loose territoriality, and a trend towards patrilocality in what were essentially hunting and gathering societies (Niemczycki 1984:81).

The second stage **patrilocal band** was larger and more stable than the bilateral band and was based on a more reliable resource base, which allowed related males to remain together most of the time. It was thus a patrilocal hunting and gathering society composed of a core of male siblings and their families. Because most band members were related, marriage was exogamous. Patrilocal bands rarely exceeded 150 individuals, after which classification of relationships became difficult and bands would either become segmented or fission into smaller, more manageable groups (ibid:82).

The third stage **multi-lineage community** involved the amalgamation of several intermarrying lineages to create a marriage isolate in which endogamy could have been practised. This was considered to have been a higher level of socio-political integration than the band (ibid:83).

Finally, the fourth stage saw the development of the **tribe** as a result of the growth or amalgamation of multi-lineage communities. It often involved territorial consolidation, leading to large aggregates of people in small geographical areas. Such developments were often seen to occur under conditions of competition or warfare, leading to alliance formation between villages (ibid:84).

Niemczycki "operationalized" this model for archaeological application using settlement pattern data to test its applicability to Iroquoian socio-political development. She initially tested the model against Tuck's (1971) settlement pattern data relating to Onondaga development and modified it somewhat to produce a specific model of tribal development that was applicable to the Seneca and Cayuga sequences. This interpretive model begins with the patrilocal band following a pattern of central-based wandering, which is thought to have characterized Early Owasco hunting and gathering communities between A.D. 1000 and 1100 (Niemczycki 1984:91). The Middle Owasco period, between A.D. 1100 and 1250 is seen as a period of fusion and fission during which patrilocal band organization and central-based wandering seems to have continued. However, there is some development of semi-sedentary, multi-lineage communities which appear to have been short-lived attempts at higher levels of community organization. They were unsuccessful and were followed by a return to the patrilocal band. This fusion-fission period continues until we see the emergence of stable multi-lineage communities, which did not appear until after A.D. 1250 in western New York. The coalescence and clustering of these multi-lineage villages eventually led to the formation of tribes sometime between A.D. 1450 and 1600 (Niemczycki 1984).

While the specific model of Iroquoian tribal organization developed by Niemczycki may not apply to southwestern Ontario Iroquoians, the general model that she proposes constitutes a useful framework for the analysis of Early Iroquoian political development. Niemczycki's general model of Iroquoian cultural development is summarized in Figure 8.1, which also shows the expected archaeological correlates of each stage in terms of settlement patterns.

## Forces of Change in Iroquoian Socio-Political Development

Several hypotheses have attempted to identify the causal factors behind the development of Iroquoian socio-political groups. We are primarily concerned here with the dramatic changes that occurred between the Early and Middle Iroquoian periods as this was the political milieu of the Calvert community. Relevant hypotheses are reviewed below.

### 1. Warfare and a "Pickering Conquest Hypothesis"

At the beginning of the Middle Iroquoian period, ca. A.D. 1300, Iroquoian assemblages across southern Ontario began to show a high degree of homogeneity. Incised horizontal ceramic motifs came to dominate ceramic assemblages, vessel motifs became uniformly less complex, and the decorative techniques of linear stamping and cord-wrapped stick impression became rarer (Dodd et al. 1990). The explanation of the apparent homogeneity of Middle Iroquoian assemblages has become one of the most controversial problems in Iroquoian prehistory.

Wright (1966) proposed that this cultural homogeneity arose as the result of a conquest of the Glen Meyer people by easterly Pickering groups. He defined the Uren substage as the product of the Pickering conquest and assimilation of the Glen Meyer. The Uren substage is thus characterized by continuity with Pickering in terms of material culture and by the persistence of some Glen Meyer traits in southwestern Ontario (Wright 1966:58-59). Wright cited the presence of pottery gaming discs and cup-and-pin deer phalanges, which appear in Pickering and Uren assemblages, but not in Glen Meyer ones, as evidence for this migration and conquest.

The Pickering conquest hypothesis has been challenged by several researchers. One of the first to question the hypothesis was William Noble, who challenged the validity of the concept of the Uren substage and "the precise mode of fusion between Glen Meyer and Pickering peoples... " (1975a:52).

Based on his analysis of both old and new data from the Uren site, the type site of the Uren substage, Milton Wright (1986) has argued that the original definition of the Uren substage was flawed as a result of the use of a non-representative ceramic sample from the Uren site itself. He further noted that artifact frequency data may not be particularly useful in addressing problems of prehistoric cultural change, and suggested that settlement pattern data may be more revealing. Finally, he proposed that the entire concept of Glen Meyer and Pickering as distinct cultural entities may not be valid, given the accumulating evidence for regional variation during the Early Iroquoian period (ibid:66).

Along similar lines, Pearce (1984, 1996:257) has argued that continuous local developmental sequences can be traced from Early to Late Iroquoian times in many areas. However, he has recently repudiated this view, citing new data from

Uren substage sites in the London area (Pearce 1996: 371). Pearce now agrees with J.V. Wright that there were "major discontinuities from Glen Meyer to Uren" (ibid.), concluding that "the Middle Ontario Iroquoian Stage was initiated by a Pickering conquest of southwestern Ontario, leading to the Uren substage..." (ibid:374). In support of this argument Pearce compared ceramic data from several recently investigated Uren substage sites with earlier Glen Meyer and later Middleport substage sites, all from the London area. However, rather than showing a discontinuity between Glen Meyer and Uren, the coefficients of similarity presented by Pearce place the Uren sites squarely in an intermediate position between the earlier Glen Meyer and subsequent Middleport substage components (Pearce 1996:372-374). One wonders how such evidence of continuous stylistic change can be interpreted as a major discontinuity in the archaeological record. In this writer's view, the recent research in the London area has helped demonstrate the validity of the Uren substage as an archaeological taxon, and filled a gap between Glen Meyer and Middleport with further evidence of continuous development. It is possible to accept the Uren substage as a valid cultural horizon without invoking the conquest hypothesis to explain its origins.

Gary Warrick (1984b) has argued convincingly that a Pickering conquest of Glen Meyer peoples is inconsistent with our knowledge of Early Iroquoian political organization and Iroquoian warfare in general. Most critics of the conquest hypothesis agree that the "Pickering culture" does not constitute a cohesive socio-political entity such as a tribe or a confederacy (Williamson 1990). This alone makes the conquest hypothesis untenable.

In a recent reassessment of the conquest hypothesis J.V. Wright argued that additional evidence in support of the hypothesis has accumulated over the past 25 years (1992). He cited settlement pattern, artifactual, and burial data in support of this view, however, his analysis was limited to data from a small number of sites that did not encompass the regional variability that is now apparent in Early Iroquoian societies. As data accumulate from regional studies there is an increasing need for a comprehensive inter-regional comparative study to examine the socio-political nature of Early Iroquoian groups, their material culture, burial practices, settlement patterns, and the mechanisms involved in their interaction.

Several other researchers have emphasized the role of warfare in Iroquoian socio-political development. Engelbrecht (1978) has argued that warfare played a major role in the formation of the League of the Iroquois, while Tuck stressed the importance of the Iroquoian complex of warfare, torture, and cannibalism in leading to the formation of large villages in Late Iroquoian times (1978:330). We have already noted the importance accorded to warfare in Finlayson's (1985) explanation of the development of the Draper village.

All of the above explanations point to internal warfare with Iroquoians fighting Iroquoians, as incentives to socio-political change. As an alternative, Warrick (1984b) has suggested that the Early and Middle Iroquoians may have been at war with external enemies, as the Neutral were in the historical period. In southwestern Ontario, the Glen Meyer people would have been in contact with Younge Phase groups of the Western Basin Tradition, who were probably Algonkians (Murphy and Ferris 1990). Younge Phase sites are common within the Thames River drainage just west of the Caradoc Sand Plain (ibid; Fox 1982b), but the nature of interaction between the Younge people and the Glen Meyer people remains a matter of speculation. Younge Phase groups show little evidence for defensive concerns, although single row palisades were found at the Van Bemmel site, and possibly at the Dymock site (Murphy and Ferris 1990). Dymock is the most easterly known Younge Phase site and thus may be considered to be on the Western Basin frontier (Fox 1982b).

## 2. Multi-Factor Hypotheses

It has recently become more common to stress several contributing factors as explanations for socio-political change in the Early to Middle Iroquoian transition. Several researchers have suggested multi-factor hypotheses.

Warrick (1984b) has proposed a "peaceful interaction model" to explain Iroquoian developments from the Early to Middle Iroquoian periods. This explanation involves a combination of population growth and ecological stress resulting from a dry climatic episode beginning ca. A.D. 1300, which would have made it more essential for Iroquoian groups to move off the drought-stricken sand plains onto more fertile soils. Other factors include the possibility of external warfare with

Western Basin Tradition peoples, discussed above, which would have encouraged community alliances in the Middle Iroquoian period. This, in turn, would have facilitated exchange and contributed to the broad cultural homogeneity of the period observed in artifact assemblages.

In his analysis of Iroquoian development in the London area, Robert Pearce suggested that several social and political factors must have been involved in the changes from the Early to Middle Iroquoian periods (1984:379). While he did not explore these factors in detail, he suggested that Early Iroquoian villages were likely exogamous. Thus amalgamating several villages in the Middle Iroquoian period would have offered the social benefit of eliminating the need for long distance travel to acquire spouses.

Finally, Niemczycki's reconstruction of Seneca and Cayuga development placed considerable emphasis on the combination of maize production, competition, and warfare as causal factors in the formation of multi-lineage villages (Niemczycki 1984:93).

### 3. Mississippian Influences

Most recently, some researchers have proposed that several aspects of Iroquoian development in both Ontario and New York State may be related to external pressures caused by the growth and far-reaching influence of Mississippian society after A.D. 1000 (Dincauze and Hasenstab 1989; Hasenstab 1987; Little 1987). Employing a core-periphery model and world systems theory, they have argued that prehistoric Iroquoia was within the range of economically viable travel from the Mississippian heartland in the American Bottom, where Cahokia, the largest prehistoric centre in North America, is located. They argue that the Iroquoian people may have participated in a trade in deer hides and other high value commodities to provision a burgeoning Mississippian population. Dincauze and Hasenstab state that the process of "Iroquoianization" seems to have progressed from west to east, and they view this as further support for their hypothesis of Mississippian influence. I have also noted, based on an analysis of extant radiocarbon dates, that the basic elements of Early Iroquoian culture seem to occur earlier in southwestern Ontario than elsewhere in Iroquoia (Timmins 1985). This lends some support to the

possibility that general "mid-continental" influences were felt first in the western parts of Iroquoia.

Jamieson has elaborated upon this core-periphery model, arguing that a general process of "Mississippification" affected several Late Woodland societies in the Upper and Middle Ohio valley, the Piedmont and Ridge and Valley provinces of the Middle Atlantic Region, and southern Ontario, beginning as early as A.D. 900 (1992:80). Rather than invoking direct links between Early Ontario Iroquoians and major Mississippian centres like Cahokia, Jamieson suggests that southern Ontario groups had extensive interaction with "Mississippified" societies in the Ohio, Richilieu-Hudson and Upper Delaware drainages. Archaeological evidence of this interaction is seen in the adoption of artifact traits such as horizontal ceramic motifs, triangular Levanna projectile points, pebble pendants, and a developed bone tool industry, by Ontario Iroquoian groups (Jamieson 1992:72-74).

Yet there are several problems with a core-periphery model that views Mississippian influence or interaction as an explanation for Iroquoian development in southern Ontario. To begin with, Muller has demonstrated that Mississippian population estimates have been wildly exaggerated and that the Mississippians were probably largely self sufficient (Muller 1986). On the basis of settlement pattern data, Muller suggests that large centres like, Kincaid, may have had only populations of 2-3000 within a 15 km radius. He also demonstrates that such a population could easily be self sufficient practising hoe horticulture and have supplied its own needs for hides (1986:210-216). Similar low population estimates have been offered for Mississippian centres in the American Bottom based on recent salvage research (Bareis and Porter 1984).

It appears unlikely that Early Iroquoians in Ontario took an active part in the Mississippian trade. This proposal is not supported by archaeological evidence on either the Mississippian or the Iroquoian side. Exotic trade goods are extremely rare on Early Iroquoian sites in Ontario and on Owasco sites in New York State (Pearce 1984:335; Ritchie 1969). The few known trade goods include Busycon and Marginella shell beads (Fox 1976:190; Ritchie 1969), both of which must have originated along the eastern seaboard although

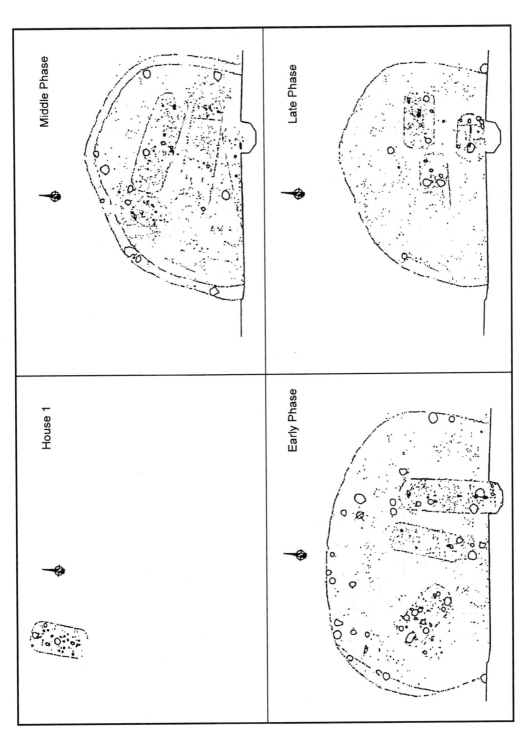

Figure 8.2. The occupational history of the Calvert site.

they may have been traded up the Mississippi River from the Gulf of Mexico. A small amount of Ohio chert occurs on Ontario Glen Meyer sites (Noble 1975a:49; Noble and Kenyon 1972:17) and there is also some steatite that may have been brought in from Pennsylvania (Noble 1975a). Native copper implements occur in very small quantities and undoubtedly originated in the Upper Great Lakes region. Trade items found on the Calvert site include a conch shell bead from the eastern seaboard and the inferred Carolina parakeet skin, which was likely traded up from the south. While some of these items may have originated in Mississippian territory, or in the territories of the "Mississippified" societies discussed by Jamieson (1992), they are simply too few in number to demonstrate an ongoing and extensive trade relationship of the magnitude suggested by Dincauze and Hasenstab.

Williamson and Robertson have proposed an alternative to the core-periphery model that involves interaction between groups at similar levels of socio-political complexity within the Great Lakes region (1994). They also note the lack of exotic materials indicative of Mississippian trade on Early Ontario Iroquoian sites, and they point out that most of the traits that Jamieson derives from "Mississippified" groups to the south can be traced to Early or Middle Woodland times in Ontario (Williamson and Robertson 1994:31).

One might ask why the Western Basin tradition peoples living around the western end of Lake Erie did not respond to Mississippian pressures in like manner and succumb to the process of "Iroquoianization"? There is also the evidence that the essential elements of Early Iroquoian culture, including a palisaded village, proto-longhouses, and maize horticulture were established at the Porteous site by ca. A.D. 900, at which time the Mississippian culture had only reached its Emergent stage and would have exerted little peripheral influence. While it is surely useful to view Iroquoian development in a broader geographical and cultural context, the archaeological evidence suggests that the origins of Iroquoian cultural uniqueness pre-date the beginnings of any Mississippian influence in the region.

## The Social and Political Organization of the Calvert Site

It is now possible to move on to consider the archaeological evidence for the social and political organization of the Calvert community itself.

As we have seen, Iroquoianists have failed to address adequately problems of community organization during the Early Iroquoian period. This is because past researchers have not attempted detailed reconstructions of the occupational histories of complex Early Iroquoian sites. With the successful separation of the Calvert settlement pattern data into a series of three main occupational phases, the Calvert site provides our first clear view of Glen Meyer community organization. Contrary to previous beliefs, the resulting community pattern is anything but chaotic and unplanned. Figure 8.2 summarizes the occupational history of the site. The inferred socio-political organization of each occupational phase is summarized below.

### House 1

As discussed in previous chapters, House 1 is an isolated structure located outside the village palisade (Figure 8.2). On the basis of super-positional data, artifactual evidence, and a single radiocarbon date, it is believed to pre-date the Early phase of the village. In Chapters 6 and 7 House 1 was interpreted as a hunting camp occupied by an extended family or hunting group.

The high percentage of suture stamped ceramics found in this structure differentiates it from all later phases at Calvert and argues strongly for the existence of a household ceramic "micro-tradition" for the occupants. Post mould densities, discussed in Chapter 5, indicate that House 1 shows substantial evidence of repair; thus it may have been occupied on a seasonal basis for several years. The persistence of this household ceramic tradition throughout this period suggests a matrilocal residence pattern. It further suggests that the occupants of House 1 were an extended family, rather than a hunting party composed of unrelated men. Therefore, House 1 may provide evidence for the presence of matrilocal lineage-based households at special purpose camps in the mid to late twelfth century, ca. 1150-1200 A.D..

The dominance of suture stamped ceramics in House 1 also suggests that the occupants of that house were unrelated to the subsequent occupants of the main village. Research to examine the cultural affiliation of the occupants of House 1 and their relationship (if any) to the occupants of the main village is ongoing.

## The Early Phase

The Early phase village is surrounded by a single row palisade which is doubled at the village entrance located in the northwest corner of the site, implying some concern for defense (Figure 8.2). Within the palisade are found three widely spaced longhouses, each of which would have housed an extended family. One of these structures, House 3, appears to have doubled as a food storage house. There is also a very small structure that has been interpreted as a work or storage shed (House 2). The population of the Early phase is estimated as 108 individuals and residential space comprised only 18.3% of the 1700 square metre village area. Houses 7 and 14 shared a parallel to radial alignment and their north entrances were three metres apart. House 3 was rather isolated on the western side of the village. The area between the houses and the palisade was substantial during the Early phase.

It is probable that each of the longhouses in the Early phase housed a group of matrilineally related women with their husbands and families. Thus the Calvert village consisted of three extended families at this time.

Interpretation of House 3 as a food storage structure implies a degree of organization and leadership to coordinate the storage and distribution of a food surplus. More importantly, the massive changes in village organization at the end of the Early phase indicate careful planning and a high degree of community cooperation, which in turn suggests a well integrated community.

## The Middle Phase

The community re-organization in the Middle phase involved the dismantling of Houses 3, 7, and 14 and the construction of larger Houses 6, 10, and 12 in a radially aligned east-west pattern. The small House 5 was constructed at the west end of House 6. At the same time the palisade was contracted with the construction of Segment 103 and later doubled with the addition of Segment 101. The population of the Middle phase (assuming full occupancy) would have increased to about 144 people, living within an area of 1400 square m inside the palisade. Residential space now covered 34% of the village and increases in house length suggest the growth of the three extended families. House 5 has been interpreted as a non-residential work/storage structure.

The decision by the Calvert villagers to contract their village space and create more crowded conditions seems to make little sense from a planning point of view. However, if we examine these changes in light of the determinants of village organization suggested by Warrick (1984a) and Finlayson (1985), meaningful social and political motives become more apparent.

To begin with, large scale rebuilding of the house structures may have been necessary due to reasons of decay and infestation. This is one of the reasons why historically known Huron groups relocated their village every ten to thirty years (Heidenreich 1971). On many Early Iroquoian sites the villages were simply rebuilt in the same location. Our analysis of the post densities in the Early phase houses indicated that they had probably been occupied for about 20 years and had undergone some maintenance prior to their abandonment (Chapter 5). It is likely then, that the Calvert houses had to be replaced due to problems of increasing decay and infestation. Yet this does not explain why the village contracted or the way that the houses were reorganized.

The decision to build larger houses was likely a response to a natural population increase. An increase of 40 people over 20 years indicates a growth rate of about 2 people per year or 0.02% of

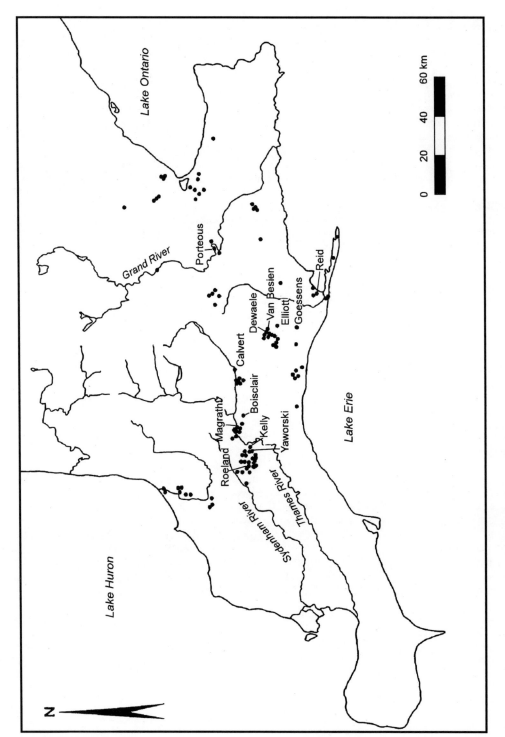

Figure 8.3. Early Iroquoian site locations in southwestern Ontario.

the total population. This is, in fact, quite slow compared to average Neolithic population growth rates, which are estimated at around 0.1% (Hassan 1978:68).

In all probability, the decision to build the three houses in a tight radial pattern with the eastern entrances of all three houses close together had social significance. The close clustering of longhouses observed during the Middle phase may reflect increased social and political cohesion among the Calvert people. The orderly and purposeful re-organization of space within the village at this time is indicative of the operation of effective socio-political institutions rather than of a lack of social control.

The causal factors underlying the development of greater social cohesion in the Calvert village during the Middle phase have yet to be identified. The Middle phase coincides with the construction of a second palisade around the site in an obvious attempt to strengthen the village fortifications. This suggests an increasing concern with defense on the part of the Calvert people. At the same time a house-to-palisade wall was constructed between House 5 and the inner palisade. When combined with the layout of the radially aligned longhouses, these arrangements would have made it difficult to move through the village from west to east without passing either through one of the houses or through a narrow corridor between them. If enemy forces penetrated within the village limits, the internal organization of structures would have aided in its defense through the strategies outlined by Finlayson (1985).

In sum, the organization of longhouses within the village during the Middle phase is interpreted as exemplifying increased social and political integration among the Calvert villagers. It is suggested that the causal factors underlying this development may be related to a political environment involving increased warfare.

### The Late Phase

The Late phase at Calvert sees a dramatic decrease in house size, wider house spacing, and no evidence of an associated palisade. On the basis of observed changes in the faunal assemblage, the artifact assemblage, and modes of refuse disposal, we have argued that this phase represents a hunting

camp. It follows, therefore, that the Late phase community pattern represents a departure from the socio-political institutions of the Middle phase. The Late phase structures differ from House 1 in that they are all smaller and show less evidence of repair. Given their small size they were probably not occupied by matrilineal extended families, although there is evidence that children were sometimes present. As discussed in Chapter 7, these houses were likely occupied by small hunting parties or task groups on a short term basis. It follows that their social composition would have differed from that of the matrilocal longhouse. They were probably occupied by groups of males or by one or two nuclear families. This change in social composition and site function is further reflected in the interior organization of the houses and the refuse disposal practises, which involved little systematic cleaning of houses and little use of exterior refuse pits. Taken together, the houses of the Late phase do not represent a socio-political entity such as the communities of the Early and Middle phases.

The contrast between the settlement patterns of the Middle and Late phases at Calvert provides a strong argument for the existence of matrilineal, matrilocal residence in Early Iroquoian villages and alternate residence patterns on some non-village special purpose sites. Williamson (1985) reached similar conclusions in his Caradoc study which demonstrated that socio-political organization and residence patterns in the Early Iroquoian period were highly flexible.

## External Relationships of the Calvert Community

In this section we explore the social and political relationships between the Calvert community and other Iroquoian communities located within and beyond the middle Thames River drainage during the time of the Calvert occupation in the twelfth and thirteenth centuries. Our goal is to understand the socio-political context of the Calvert people on a broad regional level; to grasp what may have been the political realities of the time. To understand the historical context of the Calvert site it is also necessary to consider subsequent developments in Iroquoian socio-politics, namely those that occurred at the beginning of the Middle Iroquoian period around A.D. 1300. These developments post-date the Calvert occupation by

Figure 8.4. The Dorchester area site cluster.

perhaps 50 to 75 years, but the data from Calvert and other late Early Iroquoian sites are crucial for understanding the changes that initiated the Middle Iroquoian period. To explain socio-political developments during the Early to Middle Iroquoian transition we will build an interpretive model, based partially on previous archaeological models and partly on data from Calvert and the surrounding region.

To begin this discussion it is necessary to examine the relationship of the Calvert site to other Glen Meyer sites in the region. This is accomplished through comparative analysis of ceramics and intra-site settlement patterns.

## Regional Comparisons

### Sites and Site Clusters

At the local and regional level there are several Glen Meyer sites and site clusters that may have been contemporary with Calvert (Figure 8.3). Within the Thames River drainage other sites are found in the Dorchester area in the immediate vicinity of Calvert (Keron 1984, 1986), while distinct site clusters are found on the Caradoc Sand Plain west of London (Williamson 1983, 1985), and in the Byron area on the western edge of the city (Timmins 1983; Poulton 1985). Several Glen Meyer sites have been documented to the southeast on the Norfolk Sand Plain (Fox 1976, 1986a; Noble 1975a), within the Catfish Creek drainage to the southwest (Poulton 1980), on the Ausable drainage to the northwest (Lee 1951, 1952), and in the Horner Creek/Nith River/Grand River drainage to the east (Nixon 1985). The Ausable and Grand River drainage site clusters have not been investigated in detail.

The best known of these site clusters are briefly described here and their relationship to the Calvert site is then assessed through comparisons of ceramic and settlement pattern data. Unfortunately, the quantity and quality of data available for these site clusters are extremely uneven, thus limiting interpretations. Only four sites that lie outside the Thames drainage are considered in the following comparisons. These sites are the Goessens, Elliott, Van Besien, and Porteous sites, all of which are located on the Norfolk Sand Plain and have been the subject of systematic excavations. They do not form a single cluster as they are widely distributed.

They are included in these comparisons primarily to highlight regional variations.

### The Dorchester Cluster

A series of five other Glen Meyer sites are (or were) located on the sand hills bordering the Dorchester Swamp in the immediate vicinity of the Calvert site. These are the Mustos (AfHg-2), Larch Lookout (AfHg-17), Keith (AfHg-19), Andrew (AfHg-18), and Cedar Ravine (AfHg-32) sites, shown on Figure 8.4. These sites are known only through surface collection.

The Mustos site is a small village or a special purpose camp located on a sandy knoll just 300 m southwest of Calvert (Keron 1986:71). Based on a small surface collection, this site may post-date Calvert or be contemporaneous with it.

The Larch Lookout, Keith, and Andrew sites were all located 300 to 400 m northwest of Calvert on the crest of a sandy ridge overlooking the Thames River valley. Unfortunately, all three of these sites have been destroyed in recent years by the same housing subdivision that impacted the Calvert site. Information provided on their Borden forms suggests that they were related to Calvert (Ontario Ministry of Culture and Communications Site Data Files).

The sixth known Glen Meyer site in the Dorchester cluster is the Cedar Ravine site, located about 1.3 km south of Calvert on a small tributary that drains into Dorchester Swamp Creek. It is a small site discovered by Jim Keron, who interpreted it as a hamlet or work station (1984:78).

A final important site in this area is the Dorchester site, a large Middle Ontario Iroquois village located along the Thames River just east of the Village of Dorchester. Keron estimates this site to be between two and three ha in extent and dates it to the late thirteenth century on the basis of the surface assemblage (Keron 1986:76). Although it is not a Glen Meyer component, it is important to the present discussion as evidence of the continuity of the Iroquoian sequence in this area after the abandonment of the Calvert site. Moreover, the large size of the Dorchester site (six times larger than Calvert) indicates that it may have been formed by the coalescence of two or more smaller villages, which seems to have been a common occurrence in

Middle Iroquoian times in this part of southern Ontario (Pearce 1984:269).

The extremely high concentration of Glen Meyer sites near Calvert raises the possibility that some of these poorly known sites could have been contemporaneous with Calvert. It is also possible that more Early Iroquoian sites remain to be discovered in the area, since large areas around the Dorchester Swamp have not been surveyed. If the descendants of Calvert and other communities in the area eventually amalgamated to form the Dorchester site, it is very likely that the Calvert people had strong social and political ties with the other communities prior to this event.

Unfortunately, since none of the sites in the Dorchester cluster other than Calvert has been excavated in detail, it is impossible to draw detailed conclusions concerning their relationship to Calvert. However, given our knowledge of Early Iroquoian site clusters in other localities, especially the Caradoc Sand Plain located west of London (Williamson 1985), we may conclude that most of these sites were related as parts of a complex settlement-subsistence system involving semi-permanent villages, hunting and gathering camps, and other special purpose centres.

The Byron Cluster

In recent years a number of Glen Meyer sites have been discovered on a series of sand hills in the Byron area of west London. Regrettably, many of these sites have been heavily impacted or completely destroyed by construction activities. Although some limited mitigative activity has occurred, our understanding of the Glen Meyer occupation of the area is spotty at best. The best documented Glen Meyer site in the Byron cluster is the Magrath site (AfHh-61), which was completely excavated by the Museum of Indian Archaeology in 1983 (Poulton 1985). The other known sites include the London Ski Club site (AfHi-78), Dunn (AfHi-50), Mariem I (AfHi-51) and Mariem II (AfHi-74), Boisclair (AfHh-28), Praying Mantis (AfHi-178), Off-The-Beaten-Path (AfHi-176), Grasshopper Ridge (AfHi-177), Baby Hawk (AfHi-179) and several small unnamed sites (AfHi-76, AfHi-75, AfHi-60, AfHi-61, AfHi-57) (Timmins 1983; Pearce 1984, 1996).

The Magrath site yielded an artifact assemblage dominated by chipped stone tools and stone debris (Poulton 1985:24). No structural remains and few features were found, prompting Poulton to interpret this small site as a briefly occupied hunting camp used by Glen Meyer people between A.D. 1150 and 1250 (ibid: 11). It is significant to note that Poulton found evidence for the presence of men, women, and children at Magrath, indicating that the site was occupied by a family.

The London Ski Club site was situated on a high point of land overlooking the Thames valley. Unfortunately, this site has been almost completely destroyed by construction activities associated with the ski hill. A small artifact collection from the site was donated to the Museum of Indian Archaeology by the late Mr. George Connoy. The ceramics in this collection have been briefly analyzed by the writer and are described later in this chapter. Judging by its favourable location, it is possible that the Ski Club site was a village (Pearce 1996:322).

The Dunn site is located on the extreme western edge of the City of London within one km of the Thames River. An indeterminate portion of the site has been destroyed by a sand pit. In 1982 the site area was systematically tested by the writer as part of the City of London Archaeological Survey (Timmins 1983). This testing determined that at least 0.2 ha of site remained intact, suggesting that it was probably a small village.

The Boisclair site was discovered when the excavation of a swimming pool in a Byron subdivision unearthed human remains in the early 1980s. Rescue excavations conducted by William Fox of the Ontario Ministry of Culture and Communications recovered human remains and artifacts from a number of exposed pit features. Unfortunately, there is no way of knowing whether or not Boisclair was a village. However, the presence of pit features suggests that it was a substantial site. For the present comparative study the small rim sherd sample from Boisclair was analyzed by the writer.

The Praying Mantis site is a 0.23 ha village located on a sandy ridge beside a tributary of Dingman Creek in south Byron, less than 1 km from the London Ski Club site (Pearce 1996:323). The site was completely salvage excavated by the London Museum of Archaeology in 1993 and 1994.

The village consisted of three east-west oriented longhouses surrounded by a palisade varying from one to two rows, with a gap in the northeast corner (ibid.). The houses ranged in length from 19 to 22 metres, and in width from 6.1 to 7.1 metres (ibid.). While the artifact collection has not been described in detail, Pearce has reported that a range of classic Glen Meyer ceramic types such as Ontario Oblique and Glen Meyer Oblique are present (ibid.).

The Off-The-Beaten-Path, Grasshopper Ridge, and Baby Hawk sites are all small components located near the Praying Mantis site (Pearce 1996:326). Investigations conducted by the London Museum of Archaeology yielded small artifact collections but no subsurface cultural features. All three sites are interpreted as special purpose sites related to the Praying Mantis village (ibid.).

The Byron area is unique in having yielded evidence of Glen Meyer burials on several sites including Dunn, Ski Club, Boisclair, and Praying Mantis. Glen Meyer burials are not normally associated with village sites in other areas, so their presence in the Byron cluster is unusual.

The remaining Byron area sites are probably all special purpose camps judging by their small size. None of them has been excavated and they need not be further described here except to note that their presence indicates that Glen Meyer people made intensive use of the Byron area.

## The Caradoc Cluster

Several years of archaeological survey and excavations of Early Iroquoian sites on the Caradoc Sand Plain, located just west of London, have been conducted by Ronald Williamson (1983, 1985). This research, which is reviewed in Chapter 2, resulted in the documentation of five Glen Meyer villages and 20 special activity sites. One of the village sites, Roeland, was partially excavated, as were five of the hamlet sites: Kelly, Yaworski, Berkmortel, Little, and Crowfield.

The Roeland village is a typical late Glen Meyer settlement with evidence of structure overlapping indicating at least two distinct phases of site occupation. Two rows of palisade suggest at least one major village expansion or contraction. The area circumscribed by the inner palisade is 0.6

ha, while the outer palisade surrounds a much larger area of 1.5 ha. (Williamson 1985:177).

The hamlet sites investigated by Williamson are indicative of a wide range of seasonal resource extraction functions. The Kelly site, which yielded evidence of a single longhouse, is interpreted as a warm weather plant and animal processing site. The Yaworski site had at least four structures including both circular and longhouse forms. This site was interpreted as a fall-winter hunting camp (ibid:207).

Other special purpose functions are suggested by the Little, Berkmortel, and Crowfield sites. Little is a unique site, consisting of a circular pattern of post moulds 16 m in diameter, open at one end, and surrounding a cluster of interior features. One of these features yielded over 10,000 faunal remains, dominated by white-tailed deer, but including raccoon, squirrel, chipmunk, turkey, and grouse as well. Accordingly, this site is interpreted as a deer drive and butchering location - the first of its kind to be documented in eastern North America (ibid:248).

While Williamson argues that the Glen Meyer sites on the Caradoc Sand Plain represent a single community moving through time, it is possible that more than one community is represented on the sand plain. Although only five sites were interpreted as villages, a rather arbitrary distinction was made in designating sites over one hectare in size as villages and sites of less than one hectare as hamlets. We have seen that many small Glen Meyer villages (like Calvert and Elliott) are much less than one hectare; hence, it is possible that other villages exist among the 20 hamlets discovered during the Caradoc survey. When we consider that Glen Meyer villages may have been occupied for up to 75 years, it is possible that there are enough village sites on the sand plain for there to have been more than one community.

## The Norfolk Sand Plain Sites

The Glen Meyer sites on the Norfolk Sand Plain are briefly described as they occur, from west to east.

The Goessens site is located in the drainage of South Otter Creek, near the village of Glen Meyer. It was excavated by Thomas Lee (1951) but never fully reported. A large artifact sample was analyzed by Wright (1966) and used for comparative

Table 8.1. Radiocarbon dates from selected Glen Meyer sites.

| Site | Lab No. | Radiocarbon years B.P. | Calibrated Age(s) A.D. | Calibrated 1-sigma range A.D. |
|------|---------|------------------------|------------------------|-------------------------------|
| Calvert | I-12176 | 900 ± 80 | 1133, 1136, 1156 | 1023 - 1218 |
| Calvert | I-12174 | 860 ± 80 | 1191 | 1036 - 1260 |
| Calvert | I-12173 | 820 ± 80 | 1219 | 1131 - 1277 |
| Calvert | I-12175 | 800 ± 80 | 1230, 1243, 1256 | 1160 - 1279 |
| Calvert | I-12476 | 740 ± 75 | 1277 | 1220 - 1284 |
| Boisclair | I-13094 | 950 ± 80 | 1033, 1143, 1147 | 997 - 1189 |
| Kelly | I-12061 | 850 ± 80 | 1195, 1196, 1208 | 1039 - 1261 |
| Kelly | I-11474 | 790 ± 80 | 1257 | 1162 - 1280 |
| Roeland | I-12773 | 700 ± 80 | 1280 | 1259 - 1287 |
| Roeland | I-12774 | 750 ± 80 | 1264, 1268, 1276 | 1214 - 1284 |
| Yaworski | I-12060 | 830 ± 80 | 1215 | 1068 - 1276 |
| Yaworski | I-12059 | 890 ± 80 | 1158 | 1024 - 1225 |
| Dewaele | I-6411 | 900 ± 90 | 1133, 1136, 1156 | 1020 - 1224 |
| Dewaele | I-6412 | 855 ± 55 | 1193, 1202, 1206 | 1067 - 1256 |
| Elliott | I-13095 | 890 ± 80 | 1158 | 1024 - 1225 |
| Elliott | I-13096 | 820 ± 80 | 1219 | 1131 - 1277 |
| Elliott | I-13097 | 750 ± 80 | 1264, 1268, 1276 | 1214 - 1284 |
| Van Besien | I-6167 | 1005 ± 90 | 1002, 1010, 1018 | 978 - 1154 |
| Van Besien | I-6847 | 1010 ± 90 | 1001, 1012, 1017 | 904 - 1153 |
| Porteous | I-4972 | 1125 ± 100 | 897, 921, 940 | 776 - 1000 |
| Porteous | DIC-126 | 1200 ± 100 | 780, 790, 802 | 680 - 980 |

Calibrations based on Calib version 2.0 (Stuiver and Becker 1986).

purposes by Noble (1975a). Thus ceramic data from the site are available while settlement pattern information is largely lacking. Goessens is reputed to be a large 2.8 ha village.

The Van Besien site, discussed in Chapter 2, is located within a cluster of Glen Meyer sites on Big Otter Creek (Noble 1975a). Noble's work at this village yielded a large artifact sample and important settlement data. The site exhibits evidence of sequential palisade expansion and contraction and appears to have passed through least three phases of occupation.

The Elliott site, is situated on Big Creek, not far from Van Besien. Salvage excavations conducted by Fox (1986a) revealed the presence of three sequential village occupations, only two of which were investigated. Raw settlement data are

available from a published map but the artifacts have not been described.

Finally, the Porteous site is located farther east along the Grand River, near the "oxbow" at Brantford. It lies on a northeasterly extension of the Norfolk Sand Plain. Excavations conducted initially by Noble and I. Kenyon (1972), and later by Stothers (1977), revealed four houses of variable form surrounded by a single row palisade with external middens. Full artifact and settlement pattern analyses are available for this important site.

## Chronology of Compared Sites

Before proceeding to detailed comparisons it is necessary to establish the chronological position of the sites considered. This is essential to determine if differences noted among the sites are related to

Table 8.2. Percentage frequency of interior rim design motifs on seven Glen Meyer sites.

| Site, Sample size | Calvert 192 | Magrath 20 | Ski Club 17 | Boisclair 12 | Roeland 217 | Kelly 87 | Yaworski 163 |
|---|---|---|---|---|---|---|---|
| Plain | 16.1 | 15.0 | 17.7 | 16.7 | 14.3 | 18.4 | 9.8 |
| Simple | 71.9 | 70.0 | 76.5 | 41.7 | 60.4 | 55.2 | 43.3 |
| Opposed | 6.3 | 5.0 | 0.0 | 0.0 | 2.3 | 1.1 | 4.9 |
| Horizontal | 1.6 | 0.0 | 5.9 | 8.3 | 7.8 | 3.4 | 14.0 |
| Horizontal/Simple | 0.0 | 0.0 | 0.0 | 0.0 | 0.0 | 0.0 | 0.6 |
| Simple/Horizontal | 0.0 | 0.0 | 0.0 | 0.0 | 0.9 | 0.0 | 2.4 |
| Hatched | 4.2 | 0.0 | 0.0 | 33.3 | 11.5 | 14.9 | 17.7 |
| Hatched/Simple | 0.0 | 0.0 | 0.0 | 0.0 | 1.8 | 3.4 | 1.2 |
| Hatched/Horizontal | 0.0 | 0.0 | 0.0 | 0.0 | 0.0 | 0.0 | 2.4 |
| Stafford Stamp/Simple | 0.0 | 0.0 | 0.0 | 0.0 | 0.0 | 0.0 | 1.2 |
| Simple/Criss-Cross | 0.0 | 5.0 | 0.0 | 0.0 | 0.0 | 0.0 | 0.0 |
| Linear Punctate | 0.0 | 0.0 | 0.0 | 0.0 | 0.0 | 1.1 | 0.0 |
| Punctate | 0.0 | 0.0 | 0.0 | 0.0 | 0.9 | 2.3 | 2.4 |
| Irregular | 0.0 | 5.0 | 0.0 | 0.0 | 0.0 | 0.0 | 0.0 |
| Total | 100.1 | 100.0 | 100.1 | 100.0 | 99.9 | 99.8 | 99.9 |

spatial variation or temporal change. Fortunately, many of the sites considered have one or more associated radiocarbon dates. These have been analyzed in detail by the writer in a previous study (Timmins 1985). For the present study the radiocarbon dates were calibrated using the University of Washington's Quaternary Isotope Lab program Calib Version 2.0 (Stuiver and Becker 1986). The resulting dates and date ranges are presented in Table 8.1.

A brief examination of Table 8.1 reveals that the Byron and Caradoc clusters are temporally close to the estimated span of the Calvert occupation between A.D. 1150 and 1250, although the Roeland site on the Caradoc falls slightly later and the Boisclair site may be a bit earlier. Thus substantial differences in the ceramics among these three areas can likely be attributed to spatial and social variation, that is, to the development of local ceramic traditions, rather than temporal differences.

On the other hand, two of the dated sites on the Norfolk Sand Plain fall earlier than the more westerly sites, with Van Besien being about 100 years older and Porteous perhaps dating 2-300 years prior to Calvert. Thus some of the observed differences between these sites and Calvert may be related to temporal factors. The Elliott and Dewaele sites have calibrated date ranges similar to those for Calvert.

It should be noted that the chronological data for Glen Meyer sites are consistent with a hypothesis that sees the initial development of Glen Meyer in the Grand River valley, followed by a westerly spread across the Norfolk Sand Plain and ultimately into the Dorchester, Caradoc, and Ausable areas. The fact that none of the sites in the latter areas dates much earlier than A.D. 1100 suggests that this movement took place between A.D. 1000 and 1100.

## Ceramic Comparisons

Ceramic data were compiled from existing reports for five attributes that were more or less consistently observed by previous researchers (Poulton 1985; Williamson 1985; Noble 1975a). The material from the Byron Ski Club and Boisclair sites in the Byron Cluster was analyzed by the writer. The ceramic attributes compared were: Rim Design, Rim Technique, Interior Design, Interior Technique, and Punctation.

Table 8.3. Percentage frequency of interior rim techniques on ten Glen Meyer sites.

| Site, Sample size | Cal-vert 192 | Ma-grath 20 | Ski Club 18 | Bois-clair 12 | Roe-land 215 | Kelly 86 | Yawor-ski 164 | Port-eous 53 | Van Besien 779 | Goes-sens 494 |
|---|---|---|---|---|---|---|---|---|---|---|
| Cord-wrapped Stick | 54.7 | 25.0 | 33.3 | 8.3 | 12.1 | 20.9 | 11.6 | 67.9 | 5.2 | 18.0 |
| Linear Stamp | 16.7 | 45.0 | 38.9 | 33.3 | 47.0 | 41.8 | 43.3 | 9.4 | 12.8 | 24.7 |
| Incised * | 2.6 | 0.0 | 0.0 | 16.7 | 1.4 | 8.1 | 8.5 | 0.0 | 1.7 | 8.3 |
| Suture Stamp | 6.8 | 5.0 | 0.0 | 16.7 | 0.0 | 2.3 | 0.0 | 0.0 | 0.0 | 0.0 |
| Stafford Stamp | 0.5 | 0.0 | 11.1 | 8.3 | 16.7 | 4.7 | 12.8 | 0.0 | 0.0 | 0.0 |
| Punctate | 1.0 | 0.0 | 0.0 | 0.0 | 1.9 | 3.5 | 1.8 | 0.0 | 0.0 | 0.6 |
| Linear Punctate | 0.0 | 0.0 | 0.0 | 0.0 | 0.9 | 1.2 | 0.0 | 0.0 | 0.0 | 0.0 |
| Corded or Sm Over Cord | 0.0 | 0.0 | 0.0 | 0.0 | 0.0 | 0.0 | 0.0 | 1.8 | 1.3 | 0.0 |
| Plain | 16.1 | 15.0 | 16.7 | 16.7 | 14.4 | 16.3 | 11.6 | 20.7 | 78.0 | 40.5 |
| CWS/Fingernail Impressed | 1.0 | 0.0 | 0.0 | 0.0 | 0.0 | 0.0 | 0.0 | 0.0 | 0.0 | 0.0 |
| Crescent Stamp | 0.0 | 5.0 | 0.0 | 0.0 | 0.0 | 0.0 | 0.0 | 0.0 | 0.2 | 4.7 |
| CWS/Linear Stamp | 0.5 | 5.0 | 0.0 | 0.0 | 0.5 | 0.0 | 0.6 | 0.0 | 0.0 | 0.0 |
| Combination | 0.0 | 0.0 | 0.0 | 0.0 | 0.5 | 0.0 | 1.8 | 0.0 | 0.0 | 0.0 |
| Dentate | 0.0 | 0.0 | 0.0 | 0.0 | 3.3 | 1.2 | 1.2 | 0.0 | 0.6 | 0.4 |
| Stafford Stamp/Incised | 0.0 | 0.0 | 0.0 | 0.0 | 0.5 | 0.0 | 0.6 | 0.0 | 0.0 | 0.0 |
| Stafford Stamp/Lin Stamp | 0.0 | 0.0 | 0.0 | 0.0 | 0.0 | 0.0 | 3.0 | 0.0 | 0.0 | 0.0 |
| Fingernail Impressed | 0.0 | 0.0 | 0.0 | 0.0 | 0.0 | 0.0 | 1.8 | 0.0 | 0.0 | 0.0 |
| Chevron Linear Stamp | 0.0 | 0.0 | 0.0 | 0.0 | 0.0 | 0.0 | 0.0 | 0.0 | 0.0 | 1.4 |
| Linear Stamp/Incised | 0.0 | 0.0 | 0.0 | 0.0 | 0.9 | 0.0 | 1.2 | 0.0 | 0.0 | 1.4 |
| Other | 0.0 | 0.0 | 0.0 | 0.0 | 0.0 | 0.0 | 0.0 | 0.0 | 0.0 | 0.0 |
| Total | 99.9 | 100.0 | 100.0 | 100.0 | 100.1 | 100.0 | 99.8 | 99.8 | 99.8 | 100.0 |

* some Incised rims not differentiated from Linear Stamp in Porteous, Van Besien, and Goessens analyses (Noble 1975a)

For these comparisons the House 1 ceramic sample from Calvert was excluded, as it has been demonstrated that the occupation of House 1 was not related to the village occupations. The remaining collection has been treated as a single sample since our analysis indicated that the three village phases represented a single community.

Summary data for each of the ceramic attributes is presented in Tables 8.2 through 8.6. Coefficients of similarity were calculated comparing Calvert to each of the other sites on an attribute by attribute basis. The results are presented in Table 8.7, which ranks the sites most similar to Calvert for each attribute and gives the coefficients of similarity. If the placements of the sites with respect to each ceramic attribute are weighted, assigning 1 point for the most similar and six points for the least similar site, it is possible to derive a summary ranking that indicates the sites that are most similar to Calvert overall. This summary ranking is shown at the bottom of Table 8.7. The sites of the Byron Cluster,

including Magrath and Ski Club were most similar to Calvert, with Magrath judged to be closest. The Byron area sites are also those in closest proximity to the Dorchester cluster.

The attribute of punctation as secondary decoration is particularly interesting as both Williamson (1985:289) and Warrick (1984b:9) have noted that it appears to show significant spatial variability. This is borne out in the present analysis as shown in the triangular coordinate plot in Figure 8.5. The Caradoc sites form a discrete cluster since they lack exterior punctates. On the other hand, Porteous, Boisclair, and Calvert display a relatively high occurrence of exterior punctation.

Surprisingly, the Porteous site, which is the most distant from Calvert temporally and spatially, also had the highest coefficient of similarity for the attributes of interior technique and rim technique. This is due to the shared high frequency of cord-wrapped stick decoration. Cord-wrapped stick

Table 8.4. Percentage frequency of exterior rim design motifs on seven Glen Meyer sites.

| Site, Sample size | Calvert 194 | Magrath 19 | Ski Club 22 | Boisclair 12 | Roeland 210 | Kelly 93 | Yaworski 153 |
|---|---|---|---|---|---|---|---|
| Plain | 5.7 | 10.5 | 9.1 | 8.3 | 9.5 | 5.7 | 5.2 |
| Simple | 48.5 | 63.2 | 81.8 | 41.7 | 52.9 | 40.9 | 39.9 |
| Opposed | 33.5 | 15.8 | 4.6 | 25.0 | 7.6 | 13.6 | 12.4 |
| Horizontal | 4.6 | 0.0 | 4.6 | 16.7 | 9.5 | 5.6 | 12.5 |
| Simple/Horizontal* | 0.5 | 0.0 | 0.0 | 0.0 | 3.4 | 2.2 | 3.3 |
| Hatched | 5.2 | 5.3 | 0.0 | 8.3 | 10.5 | 25.0 | 19.0 |
| Hatched/Simple | 0.0 | 0.0 | 0.0 | 0.0 | 4.3 | 2.3 | 3.3 |
| Hatched/Opposed | 0.0 | 0.0 | 0.0 | 0.0 | 0.0 | 1.1 | 0.0 |
| Hatched/Horizontal | 0.0 | 0.0 | 0.0 | 0.0 | 0.0 | 2.3 | 2.0 |
| Horizontal/Simple | 0.0 | 0.0 | 0.0 | 0.0 | 0.5 | 0.0 | 0.7 |
| Punctate | 0.0 | 0.0 | 0.0 | 0.0 | 0.0 | 1.1 | 0.7 |
| Stafford Stamp/Simple | 0.0 | 0.0 | 0.0 | 0.0 | 1.9 | 0.0 | 1.3 |
| Simple/Plain | 0.5 | 0.0 | 0.0 | 0.0 | 0.0 | 0.0 | 0.0 |
| Simple/Horiz/Simple | 1.0 | 5.3 | 0.0 | 0.0 | 0.0 | 0.0 | 0.0 |
| Simple/Opposed | 0.5 | 0.0 | 0.0 | 0.0 | 0.0 | 0.0 | 0.0 |
| Total | 100.0 | 100.1 | 100.1 | 100.0 | 100.1 | 99.8 | 100.3 |

* includes Simple by Horizontal from Williamson (1985).

decoration on Glen Meyer pottery was thought to be an early decorative technique, partly due to its dominance at Porteous and at earlier Princess Point sites in the Grand River Valley (Noble 1975a; Stothers 1977). The high frequency of both cord-wrapped stick decoration and exterior punctation at Calvert appears aberrant. Yet it is simply further evidence for the development of distinctive local ceramic traditions in the Early Iroquoian period. This example thus reveals the folly of attempting ceramic seriation across regional site clusters that are spatially separated by great distances.

The small Boisclair assemblage displays a mixture of relatively complex design motifs, similar to Calvert, but a minority of the Boisclair ceramics displays traits typical of the Younge Phase of the Western Basin Tradition. These include complex, incised neck designs with open areas, a dominance of tool impression in which the tip of the tool is pressed deeply into the clay, and the use of shallow punctates (Murphy and Ferris 1990). Thus, Boisclair may be one of very few sites in the London area with evidence of interaction between

Glen Meyer and Younge Phase peoples. Our analysis of the Boisclair rim sherds reflects this in the high frequency of complex oblique motifs executed primarily by linear stamping and suture stamping, which would both be classed as "tool impressed" in Younge Phase terminology (Fitting 1970; Lennox 1982).

Despite the strong ceramic similarity demonstrated between Calvert and some of the Byron area sites, it is unlikely that the Dorchester and Byron area sites are the product of a single community. The tendency for Glen Meyer sites to occur in clusters suggests that most Glen Meyer communities confined their activities to fairly small circumscribed areas. The ceramics between the two areas also differ in the use of punctation. Further, it may be noted that the coefficients of similarity among the Early, Middle, and Late Calvert phases are significantly higher than the coefficients between Calvert and the Byron area sites (Timmins 1992:296, 474). This indicates that the Byron sites are not contemporaneous seasonal sites occupied by the Calvert community. The presence of Middle Iroquoian sites in both areas further suggests that

Table 8.5. Percentage frequency of exterior rim techniques on ten Glen Meyer sites.

| Site, Sample size | Cal-vert 194 | Ma-grath 19 | Ski Club 23 | Bois-clair 12 | Roe-land 215 | Kelly 86 | Yawor-ski 164 | Port-eous 53 | Van Besien 779 | Goes-sens 494 |
|---|---|---|---|---|---|---|---|---|---|---|
| Cord-wrapped Stick | 60.8 | 31.6 | 30.4 | 8.3 | 14.8 | 21.8 | 11.1 | 44.7 | 8.0 | 21.7 |
| Linear Stamp | 19.1 | 42.1 | 43.5 | 41.7 | 45.2 | 54.0 | 47.1 | 3.9 | 38.2 | 48.6 |
| Incised * | 4.1 | 0.0 | 4.4 | 8.3 | 1.9 | 1.1 | 7.2 | 9.2 | 22.5 | 3.9 |
| Suture Stamp | 6.7 | 5.3 | 0.0 | 16.7 | 0.0 | 3.4 | 2.0 | 2.6 | 0.2 | 0.0 |
| Stafford Stamp | 1.5 | 0.0 | 8.7 | 8.3 | 15.3 | 6.9 | 15.0 | 0.0 | 0.0 | 0.0 |
| Punctate | 0.5 | 0.0 | 0.0 | 0.0 | 1.9 | 0.0 | 1.3 | 7.9 | 0.1 | 0.0 |
| Linear Punctate | 0.0 | 0.0 | 0.0 | 8.3 | 2.4 | 0.0 | 0.0 | 0.0 | 0.0 | 0.0 |
| Corded or Sm Over Cord | 4.6 | 5.3 | 0.0 | 0.0 | 1.4 | 1.1 | 1.3 | 18.4 | 14.9 | 3.2 |
| Plain | 1.0 | 5.3 | 8.7 | 8.3 | 8.1 | 4.6 | 4.6 | 11.8 | 12.2 | 8.7 |
| CWS/Incised | 0.0 | 0.0 | 0.0 | 0.0 | 0.0 | 0.0 | 0.0 | 1.3 | 1.3 | 0.0 |
| Crescent Stamp | 0.0 | 5.3 | 0.0 | 0.0 | 0.0 | 0.0 | 0.0 | 0.0 | 1.0 | 5.9 |
| CWS/Linear Stamp | 0.0 | 0.0 | 4.4 | 0.0 | 0.9 | 1.1 | 0.0 | 0.0 | 0.0 | 0.0 |
| Combination | 0.0 | 0.0 | 0.0 | 0.0 | 1.4 | 0.0 | 0.7 | 0.0 | 0.0 | 0.0 |
| Dentate | 0.0 | 0.0 | 0.0 | 0.0 | 2.8 | 1.1 | 1.3 | 0.0 | 0.7 | 2.6 |
| Stafford Stamp/Incised | 0.0 | 0.0 | 0.0 | 0.0 | 0.0 | 0.0 | 1.3 | 0.0 | 0.0 | 0.0 |
| Stafford Stamp/Lin Stamp | 0.0 | 0.0 | 0.0 | 0.0 | 1.9 | 0.0 | 2.0 | 0.0 | 0.0 | 0.0 |
| Fingernail Impressed | 0.5 | 0.0 | 0.0 | 0.0 | 0.0 | 0.0 | 0.7 | 0.0 | 0.3 | 0.0 |
| Corded/Incised | 0.0 | 0.0 | 0.0 | 0.0 | 0.0 | 0.0 | 0.0 | 0.0 | 0.2 | 0.0 |
| Linear Stamp/Incised/CWS | 0.5 | 0.0 | 0.0 | 0.0 | 0.0 | 0.0 | 0.0 | 0.0 | 0.0 | 0.0 |
| CWS/Punctate | 0.5 | 0.0 | 0.0 | 0.0 | 0.0 | 0.0 | 0.0 | 0.0 | 0.0 | 0.0 |
| Other | 0.0 | 0.0 | 0.0 | 0.0 | 0.5 | 0.0 | 0.0 | 0.0 | 0.0 | 5.4 |
| Linear Stamp/Incised | 0.0 | 5.3 | 0.0 | 0.0 | 1.4 | 4.6 | 4.6 | 0.0 | 0.0 | 0.0 |
| Total | 99.8 | 100.2 | 100.1 | 99.9 | 99.9 | 99.7 | 100.2 | 99.8 | 99.6 | 100.0 |

* some Incised rims not differentiated from Linear Stamp in Porteous, Van Besien, and Goessens analyses (Noble 1975a)

Table 8.6. Percentage frequency of punctates on nine Glen Meyer sites.

| Site, Sample size | Calvert 194 | Magrath 17 | Boisclair 12 | Roeland 215 | Kelly 86 | Yaworski 164 | Porteous 53 | Van Besien 779 | Goessens 494 |
|---|---|---|---|---|---|---|---|---|---|
| Exterior | 8.8 | 0.0 | 16.7 | 0.0 | 0.0 | 0.0 | 28.9 | 4.7 | 3.2 |
| Interior | 36.6 | 47.1 | 16.7 | 40.0 | 32.0 | 35.9 | 2.6 | 19.5 | 35.2 |
| Absent | 54.6 | 52.9 | 66.7 | 60.0 | 67.0 | 64.1 | 68.4 | 75.7 | 61.5 |
| Total | 100.0 | 100.0 | 100.1 | 100.0 | 99.0 | 100.0 | 99.9 | 99.9 | 99.9 |

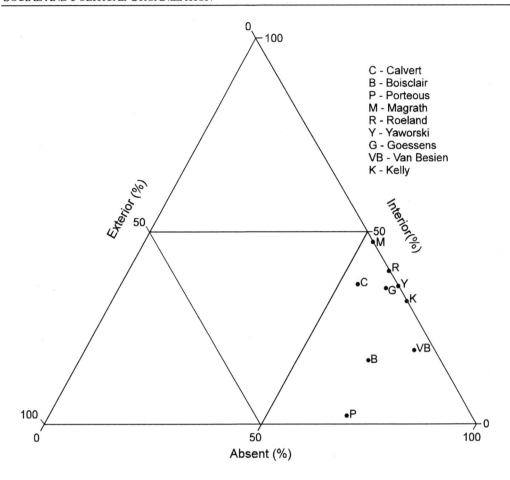

Figure 8.5. Triangular coordinate plot of rim punctate attributes for nine Glen Meyer sites.

community development occurred *in situ* from Early to Middle Iroquoian times in both areas.

## Settlement Pattern Comparisons

The selection of sites for settlement pattern comparisons was largely dictated by the availability of data and the necessity to restrict comparisons to village sites. Comparative data were available for only one site located west of Calvert, that being the slightly later Roeland site. The Van Besien, Elliott, and Porteous sites on the Norfolk Sand Plain have also been included. With the possible exception of part of the Elliott site occupation, none of the sites considered seems to be entirely contemporaneous with Calvert; thus some of the observed variation in settlement patterns may be attributed to temporal

change. For each site, observations were made on village size, house size and form, palisades, the distribution of large and small features, refuse disposal, and village organization. These data are summarized in Table 8.8.

### Village Size

The sites vary from 0.1 to 1.5 ha in size, which is a greater range of variation than that previously documented by Dodd for several Early Iroquoian villages (1984:280). It is notable that the Calvert and Elliott sites are similar in size, between 0.3 and 0.4 ha in extent. Both of these sites were largely rebuilt in the same location rather than expanded. On the other hand, the Van Besien and Roeland sites, which underwent significant expansions or

Table 8.7. Ranked coefficients of similarity
for five ceramic variables.

| Sites | Coefficient of Similarity | Point Rank |
|---|---|---|
| Interior Design Motif | | |
| Calvert and Magrath | 180 | 1 |
| Calvert and Ski Club | 179 | 2 |
| Calvert and Roeland | 166 | 3 |
| Calvert and Kelly | 157 | 4 |
| Calvert and Yaworski | 128 | 5 |
| Calvert and Boisclair | 127 | 6 |
| Interior Technique | | |
| Calvert and Ski Club | 133 | 1 |
| Calvert and Magrath | 124 | 2 |
| Calvert and Kelly | 120 | 3 |
| Calvert and Boisclair | 102 | 4 |
| Calvert and Roeland | 93 | 5 |
| Calvert and Yaworski | 89 | 6 |
| Rim Design Motif | | |
| Calvert and Boisclair | 164 | 1 |
| Calvert and Magrath | 152 | 2 |
| Calvert and Roeland | 144 | 3 |
| Calvert and Kelly | 141 | 4 |
| Calvert and Yaworski | 135 | 5 |
| Calvert and Ski Club | 127 | 6 |
| Rim Technique | | |
| Calvert and Magrath | 123 | 1 |
| Calvert and Ski Club | 112 | 2 |
| Calvert and Kelly | 98 | 3 |
| Calvert and Yaworski | 82 | 4 |
| Calvert and Boisclair | 82 | 5 |
| Calvert and Roeland | 81 | 6 |
| Punctate Attributes | | |
| Calvert and Roeland | 182 | 1 |
| Calvert and Yaworski | 181 | 2 |
| Calvert and Magrath | 179 | 3 |
| Calvert and Kelly | 174 | 4 |
| Calvert and Boisclair | 160 | 5 |

| Summary Ranking of Coefficients of Similarity | | |
|---|---|---|
| Site | Rank | Points |
| Magrath | 1 | 6 |
| Ski Hill | 2 | 11 |
| Kelly | 3 | 14 |
| Boisclair | 4 | 16 |
| Roeland | 5 | 17 |
| Yaworski | 6 | 20 |

contractions, share a size range of 0.5 to 0.6 ha for their inner village limits and 1.2 to 1.5 ha for their outer limits. These sites are significantly larger than Calvert and Elliott but like Calvert suggest a pattern of population growth rather than simple rebuilding, although this has not been demonstrated through extensive excavation on either site.

The villages considered all show evidence of structure rebuilding in the form of either overlapping houses, houses that were rebuilt in almost the same location, or house-palisade overlaps.

## Houses

At all sites houses show significant variability in size and form. This is most pronounced, however, at Calvert, Elliott, and Roeland, where two house sizes are discernible, including small structures in the five to 13 m length range and larger structures in the 13 to 24 m range. The Porteous structures include small proto-longhouses and a single circular structure. These houses are significantly smaller than those at Calvert, but they are also much earlier.

The similarities between the Calvert and Elliott site houses are intriguing, especially in the association of large and small structures. This has been noted at Calvert where the substantial Houses 3 and 6 are associated with the smaller Houses 2 and 5, which are interpreted as work huts. At Elliott, this pattern appears to be repeated at least two times in different stages of the site occupation (Fox 1986a).

## Feature Distribution

Turning to feature distribution, our comparisons differentiated only between the general location of large and small features, rather than dealing with feature types, since not all researchers analyzed features in the same manner. There is a definite pattern in the occurrence of large exterior pit features: they are rarely found on the Norfolk Sand Plain villages, yet become more common as one moves west to the Dorchester and Caradoc areas. This may be related to cultural influence from more westerly Younge Phase people, who commonly used exterior pits for food storage (Lennox 1982; Murphy and Ferris 1990). It may also indicate that the later, more westerly Glen Meyer groups were more reliant upon horticulture

Table 8.8. Glen Meyer village settlement pattern comparisons.

| Site (Source) | Size (ha) | House Data | Palisades | Large Feature Distribution | Small Feature Distribution | Comments |
|---|---|---|---|---|---|---|
| Calvert (this report) | 0.3 | Length, 5.8-24.4 m Large (13-24 m) Small (5-13 m) overlapping | Initially 1 row; later two rows, contracted | Around village edge; along interior house walls | Small exterior activity areas; around interior hearths | Three phase occupation |
| Roeland (Williamson 1985) | 0.6-1.5 | Length, 6-25+ m overlapping | 1 or 2 rows; expanded or contracted | Around village edge; along interior house walls | Around interior hearths | At least two phases of occupation |
| Van Besien (Noble 1975a) | 0.5-1.2 | Length, 14.6-22.5 m Houses overlap palisade | At least 5 rows; two expansions | Around interior hearths; few exterior features | Around interior hearths | Three phase occupation; exterior middens present |
| Elliott (Fox 1986a) | 0.35 | Length, 6-21.5 m overlapping, rebuilding | At least 5 rows; possible expansion, contractions, rebuilding | Along interior walls and in corners | Small exterior activity areas; around interior hearths | Three phase occupation; complete rebuilding |
| Porteous (Stothers 1977) | 0.1 | Length, 6.1-11.4 m Small proto-longhouses; one circular house; overlapping | Two rows; no expansions or contractions | Few present; middens outside palisade | Around interior hearths | At least a two phase occupation |

and were producing a surplus to be stored in such pits.

Within houses large pits are distributed along interior walls and in house corners at Roeland and Elliott, as they are at Calvert. Yet Van Besien does not follow this pattern; large features there seem to cluster around interior hearths. The lack of large storage pit features at Van Besien and Porteous suggests that these communities must have practised an alterative food storage method, if indeed they were producing an agricultural surplus for storage. They are both early horticultural communities in which the importance of cultigens in the diet may have been minimal.

The distribution of small pit features around interior hearths appears to be fairly consistent among the sites compared (Table 8.8). In addition, both Calvert and Elliott display clusters of small exterior pits; these have been interpreted as exterior activity areas at Calvert.

Refuse Disposal

At Calvert and Roeland the re-use of large storage pits for refuse disposal was common. For Calvert, several streams of refuse disposal involving the movement of refuse from interior pits to exterior ones have been documented. A similar pattern can be traced at Roeland through examination of ceramic cross-mends (Williamson 1985: 179). However, the pattern of refuse disposal in large pits does not preclude the use of surface middens as noted previously. A portion of a basal midden was discovered at Roeland and surface middens were noted at Calvert prior to excavation (Fox: personal communication). At the more easterly Van Besien, Elliott, and Porteous sites large storage pits are less common and the pattern of refuse disposal in pits is less pronounced.

## Palisades

It is notable that all of the sites compared are palisaded. While several palisade lines appear on some sites, the maximum number of lines of palisade that can be demonstrated to have been in use at the same time is three (at Van Besien) and most sites had at least two lines of palisade at some point in their occupation. This tends to negate the argument that palisades were meant primarily as snow fences or to keep animals out, since only a single row would be required for that purpose. Thus we may conclude that at least some concern for defense was common at these villages. We have already discussed the evidence for defensive planning within the Calvert village.

## Village Planning

I have argued that the Calvert site displays evidence of purposeful village planning during the Early and Middle phases of the site occupation. The degree of planning at the Roeland and Van Besien villages is difficult to assess, since only small portions of them were excavated and no attempt was made to separate the occupational phases. Yet the fact that these villages both appear to have undergone expansions or contractions is indicative of purposeful change. Some degree of planning must have been involved.

A preliminary separation of the Elliott village data into sequential periods has been published by Fox (1986a). It shows one occupation as a series of well ordered predominantly north-south oriented houses in a fairly close parallel pattern, with smaller structures clustered in the northeast part of the village. In contrast, a later occupation consists of small, widely spaced houses oriented primarily east-west, and is reminiscent of the Late phase at Calvert. These changes in the Elliott community pattern show evidence of planning.

## Summary

In general, there does not appear to be marked regional variation in settlement patterns among these villages. There is a significant increase in the use of exterior pits for food storage as one moves west. This appears to be a cultural trend, probably related to food storage practises. Refuse disposal practises vary in similar fashion, with the more easterly communities using surface middens and the more westerly villages making more use of abandoned storage pits for refuse. It is likely that all villages had surface middens, but the pattern of re-use of storage pits for refuse disposal on more westerly sites is marked.

In terms of house patterns, the similarities between the Calvert site and Elliott site on the Norfolk Sand Plain are quite striking, while those between Calvert and Roeland to the west are less so. This may well be a function of time, as the well-ordered Roeland houses seem to be slightly later than those at Calvert, whereas at least some of the Elliott houses are probably contemporary with Calvert.

The range in village size is also quite striking, although it is not a regional trend. This suggests that Glen Meyer village populations may have been quite variable in size. If the larger villages grew even partly through the incorporation of smaller groups, the pattern of village coalescence may have begun earlier than was previously thought. This has socio-political implications for Glen Meyer society as it pertains to social integration at the community level.

In sum, the overall impression of the settlement patterns of this small sample of villages is that there was considerable similarity in both structure types and village layout, with some significant variations in feature distribution and use. These are the only readily identifiable geographical trends in community patterns.

## Discussion and Conclusions

## A Model of Socio-Political Development in the Early to Middle Iroquoian Transition

In constructing a model of socio-political development for the Early to Middle Iroquoian periods, we must consider the segmentary nature of historic Iroquoian tribal organization, as suggested at the beginning of this chapter. Since historical Iroquoian tribal groups were built of extended families, lineages, clan segments, and villages, our ability to trace the development of Iroquoian political organization rests largely with our success in recognizing these constituent groups in the archaeological record. Niemczycki (1984) has taken an important first step in outlining a general framework for tribal development from the patrilocal band to the multi-lineage village to the tribe. I have employed this general framework and modified it in accordance with the archaeological evidence from southwestern Ontario. The resulting model is built largely on regional settlement patterns and remains to be verified through detailed study of regional site sequences. Such verification is a problem for future research.

Early Iroquoian sites in southwestern Ontario tend to occur in clusters and are usually located inland from major rivers on elevated, sandy soils. In the preceding analysis we examined four of these site clusters, located respectively in the Norfolk Sand Plain, Dorchester, Byron, and Caradoc areas. Figure 8.3 shows the locations of many of these sites.

The majority of Early Iroquoian villages in southwestern Ontario are located in areas that permit easy access to a wide variety of environmental zones. Specifically, most villages are situated on sandy soils in close proximity to swamps and/or mast producing forests, both of which provide excellent deer habitats. In the case of the Calvert village, the location selected was an optimal one that permitted access to no less than six micro-environmental zones, each of which offered a different range of resources (Chapter 4). Other Early Iroquoian villages are located in similarly diverse ecological situations (Williamson 1985).

It is suggested that the selection of site locations with high environmental diversity is related to the continued importance of hunting and gathering in Early Iroquoian subsistence systems. This has been aptly demonstrated by the wide range of floral and faunal material recovered from Calvert, and by Williamson's study, which documented a variety of special purpose sites related to hunting and gathering (1985). Our analysis clearly indicates that deer were the preferred game of the Calvert people, comprising more than 85% of the faunal sample in all phases. A similar focus on deer has been documented on some other Glen Meyer villages (i.e., Van Besien); however, other Glen Meyer sites show an emphasis on fish, birds, and small mammals (i.e., Porteous, Dewaele, Force, Reid) (Prevec 1984a:59). As demonstrated in Chapter 2, regional adaptations and variability in subsistence systems is a hallmark of the Early Iroquoian period.

Sandy soils are usually considered to have serious limitations for horticulture due to their generally low fertility. Thus the location of Glen Meyer villages on sandy soils did not provide optimal conditions for horticulture. The locational characteristics of most Early Iroquoian villages suggest that hunting and gathering were as important as horticulture. The abundant evidence of rebuilding found on most Early Iroquoian sites, as well as the post mould replacement evidence from Calvert, suggests that these villages were occupied for a very long time, perhaps 50 to 75 years. This, in turn, suggests that Early Iroquoian village positions were highly valued, since the occupants would rather rebuild than move a short distance away. It follows that good village locations and, perhaps more importantly, hunting territories, may have been tenaciously protected against incursions from outsiders. Thus territorial disputes may have been a potential source of tension between regional Glen Meyer communities.

The populations of Early Iroquoian communities probably ranged from about 100 to several hundred people, judging by size variability in the villages we compared. As noted, sites tend to occur in clusters; however, insufficient research has been conducted to indicate if two or more villages could have been occupied at the same time within a

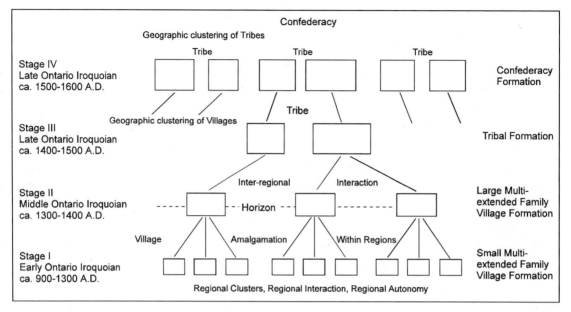

Figure 8.6. A model of Iroquoian socio-political development in southwestern Ontario.

specific cluster, or if the site clusters indicate sequential occupations. The model of group aggregation in the Middle Iroquoian period tends to favour the existence of several contemporary communities within a regional cluster. These communities would have been closely related to each other, and may have shared a common, valued resource base such as a hunting territory. For example, in the Dorchester area it is quite possible that the two or three communities that eventually coalesced to form the Dorchester site shared a common hunting territory that included the Dorchester Swamp. Similarly, the Glen Meyer villages on the Caradoc Sand Plain are clustered in the vicinity of black ash-tamarack swamps and it is conceivable that more than one community shared this resource base.

Such economic cooperation would have fostered other social and political relations, possibly including spousal exchange and alliances in warfare, while at the same time predisposing these people for the eventual decision to amalgamate into large villages and became more dependent upon agriculture.

Although they were occupied for long periods, Early Iroquoian villages were still semi-sedentary and were moved after 50 to 75 years. The settlement pattern evidence indicates that residence rules were flexible, especially at special purpose camps, but within the village residence in longhouses appears to have been the norm. These community patterns indicate that most Early Iroquoian villages consisted of multiple extended families, with the occasional nuclear family or individual possibly living in a small house. There is no evidence that Early Iroquoian villages were segmented.

Villages like Calvert may have practised village exogamy, and, if so, it is likely that spouses were obtained from other communities within the regional cluster. Such local interaction would have promoted the development of regionally distinct ceramic traditions. These regional groups of villages probably cooperated in other matters involving warfare and ceremonies. Thus the regional community may have formed a loosely knit socio-political entity.

Within or near each of the clusters of Early Iroquoian sites are documented Middle Iroquoian sites that were very likely occupied by the descendants of the Early Iroquoian occupants. In all cases, these Middle Iroquoian villages are significantly larger than the preceding Glen Meyer ones; they are also less numerous. Thus it can be reasonably suggested, if not demonstrated at this time, that the formation of many Middle Iroquoian villages involved the amalgamation of two or more Early Iroquoian villages. It is likely that the reasons for this regional integration involved a complex interplay of economic, social, and political factors.

In the Middle Iroquoian period, we definitely see the development of segmented villages, for example, at the Uren site (M. Wright 1986). Such community patterns are precisely what would be expected as a result of the amalgamation of two or more smaller villages. It is possible that Middle Iroquoian villages could have become marriage isolates, as several clans would almost certainly have been present within one village. Yet village exogamy may still have been practised as a way to foster social and political relations with adjacent groups. The formation of larger regional villages in Middle Iroquoian times may have created a void in external relations, since formerly cooperative neighbours were now living together. This void could have been filled through the establishment of ties with adjacent villages, leading to an unprecedented level of inter-regional interaction and integration. This, in turn, may have contributed to the widespread homogeneity of material culture during the Middle Iroquoian period. The development of incised ceramics with horizontal motifs seems to be a generational phenomenon, as child potters were already using these techniques at Calvert late in the Early Iroquoian period.

The degree to which the formation of large Middle Iroquoian villages was a defensive response to external political factors such as a Mississippian threat cannot be adequately assessed on the present evidence. The Middleport substage Edwards site, which may have eventually been occupied by the descendants of the Caradoc Glen Meyer population, has produced no evidence of a palisade (Pearce 1984). Moreover, the Dorchester site is located on the Thames River and thus does not display a withdrawal to inland defensive positions, as suggested by Dincauze and Hasenstab (1989).

On the other hand, the Uren site was heavily palisaded and shows ample evidence of prisoner torture and cannibalism (M. Wright 1986). Thus the evidence for an increase in Iroquoian warfare in the Middle Iroquoian period varies from region to region. As a form of inter-regional interaction, warfare among regional communities may have contributed to the homogenization of material culture through the movement of prisoners of war.

This interpretive model of Early to Middle Iroquoian socio-political development is summarized in Figure 8.6. This model has recently been adopted by Williamson and Robertson in their discussion of Early and Middle Iroquoian interaction (1994:35).

Socio-political developments in southwestern Ontario appear to have been quite different from the sequence Niemczycki has reconstructed for New York. The model suggests that most Glen Meyer villages can be characterized as multi-extended family communities, although they were not segmented. This "stage" of socio-political development appears in southwestern Ontario by ca. A.D. 900 (at Porteous) and was common until the late thirteenth century. In contrast, it does not seem to have become well established in New York until after A.D. 1250 (Niemczycki 1984).

The regional integration of the Early to Middle Iroquoian transition involved the development of segmented villages, such as Uren. This led to a new level of socio-political interaction among regional villages that may have been based upon the extension of clan ties across tribal divisions.

The final stages in Iroquoian socio-political evolution in southwestern Ontario are beyond the scope of this study, although one possible scenario for these later developments is outlined in Figure 8.6. Eventually there may have been a geographic clustering of the regional communities that would have led to the formation of distinct tribes, probably early in the Late Iroquoian period shortly after A.D. 1400. Finally, in the Late Iroquoian period, there was a poorly documented long-distance movement and aggregation of these tribal groups, leading to the formation of the Neutral confederacy. It was this latter development that resulted in the clustering of the several Neutral tribes within a restricted area around the west end of Lake Ontario and on the Niagara peninsula, where they were found at the time of European contact.

# Chapter 9

# Ritual, Belief, and Death at the Calvert Site

## Introduction

As part of the ideational component of Iroquoian society, ritual and belief systems lie at the top of the interpretive pyramid and are the most inaccessible through archaeological inference. This is because many aspects of belief systems, ceremonialism, and ideology leave few traces in the archaeological record that can be unambiguously interpreted. Much cultural and ideational behaviour is specific to particular historical and cultural contexts; thus direct historical or continuous ethnographic analogies are most useful as interpretive data and there is usually little scope for generalization. Yet broad patterns and widespread underlying themes in symbolic and belief systems are often recognized ethnographically and archaeologically, so that useful interpretive analogies can sometimes be drawn cross-culturally. Such analogies achieve relevance either through historical connections or by sharing similar preconditions or mechanisms that give rise to similar cultural phenomena (Wylie 1982:43; von Gernet and Timmins 1987).

What we may infer about the ideational component of the Calvert people must, therefore, be viewed against the culturally specific backdrop of Iroquoian belief systems and the broader background of native American religion. This body of potential source side data is vast and we cannot do more than touch upon it here. In the overall context of this study, the amount of archaeological data from Calvert that is relevant to this problem is quite limited. Thus we will limit our discussion to a brief summary of historically documented Iroquoian belief systems and ritual, followed by an analysis and interpretation of the relevant data from Calvert.

## Ethnohistorical Background

According to Tooker (1985) historically documented Iroquoian ceremonies may be grouped into two major categories: calendrical thanksgiving ceremonies conducted for and by the social groups and curing ceremonies conducted for individuals. To these two types, I would add mortuary ceremonies conducted for the dead. These types of ceremonies are not necessarily mutually exclusive. For example, it is possible to conduct curing rituals for individuals as part of calendrical ceremonies.

Apart from the various types of ceremonies, the Iroquoians also possessed a repertoire of games, dances, and songs that could be conducted as part of various ceremonies. As Tooker noted, "the basic rule seems to be that any rite may be used in a ceremony addressed to any being, though certain rites are more often used than others" (1970:33). This created considerable variability in the content of ceremonies and made them appear quite complex to historical and modern observers (ibid:32).

The calendrical ceremonies were, and still are, held at different times of the year to give thanks to particular beings or spirits that were essential to Iroquoian life. These ceremonies include the Strawberry, Maple, Planting, Green Bean, Green Corn, and Harvest ceremonies which were held in honour of their respective spirits. The calendrical ceremonies are obviously closely related to the horticultural economy of the historic Iroquoians. It is quite possible that many elements of these ceremonies diffused into Iroquoia from the south. Thus they were probably not an important part of Iroquoian belief systems until the horticultural economy became fully established and they may have been of limited significance in Early Iroquoian times. There is, in fact, no convincing evidence that these ceremonies were a part of Huron culture in the first half of the seventeenth century.

Tooker (1985) notes that eighteenth and nineteenth century ethnographers among the Iroquois paid much more attention to calendrical ceremonies than did seventeenth century observers, who took greater notice of medicine societies and curing rituals. This suggests that the calendrical ceremonies may have been a rather late and primarily historic development among the Iroquoians.

In contrast, the curing ceremonies are believed to be of considerable antiquity in the Northeast, inasmuch as they are thought to be related to an ancient shamanic belief system that was derived from Siberia and was common to most cultures of the New World (La Barre 1972). In historic Iroquoian society curing rituals were performed by a variety of medicine societies, each of which possessed its own rituals and myths (Tooker 1970:16). Individuals who were cured by members of a medicine society often became members of that society (ibid.). As Weston La Barre states:

> Cure is much like initiation into a secret ritual one witnesses and learns. Thus, all the members of the Bear Society, for example, share "bear power" taught them by the shaman and ultimately originating in the shaman's supernatural "vision". Shaman and clients form a psychic sodality (La Barre 1972:275).

In this way, the medicine societies became important integrative institutions, crosscutting clan, village, and even tribal lines (Trigger 1990:116).

The role of the shaman or medicine man is always that of an intermediary between the natural and the spirit world. Thus, the basic shamanic role of curing societies involves an appeal to the spirit world to heal a sick individual. Some of the specific shamanic elements of Iroquoian medicine societies include the use of bone tubes to suck or blow medicine or power on the sick person, the use of tobacco as a sacrifice to the spirits or as a stimulant to facilitate the shaman's interaction with the spirit world, and the ability of the shaman or medicine man to achieve a trance-like state during his communication with the spirit world.

The specific details of Iroquoian ceremonies are those that were likely most culturally restricted and the specific content of ceremonies clearly varied among Iroquoian nations. For example, there was obviously considerable variation in burial practises, and presumably in burial ceremonies, between the Huron and the Neutral (Lennox and Fitzgerald 1990:452). During the seventeenth century, Neutral burial practises became much more variable than

Huron ones, as the Neutral began using cemeteries with single and multiple interments. This historic variability in Neutral burial suggests that direct historical analogies with Glen Meyer burial are risky, while analogies with Huron practises would be unwise. We are left to reconstruct Glen Meyer burial ritual largely on the basis of archaeological evidence and a general knowledge of Iroquoian burial treatments, without recourse to detailed and relevant historical documentation.

## Archaeological Evidence of Ritual and Belief at Calvert

### Calendrical Ceremonies and Feasting

There is little archaeological evidence to suggest that any of the historically documented calendrical ceremonies were practised by the Calvert people. As noted above, very few types of archaeological residues can be confidently assigned to ceremonial activities, and it is even more difficult to recognize specific ceremonies in the archaeological record. One of the most common activities carried out at calendrical festivals was feasting - an activity that may appear in the archaeological record as a large concentration of preserved food remains.

The contents of Feature 79 at Calvert may conform to the pattern expected from a feast. This feature contained over 1300 animal bones comprising the almost complete, but butchered, skeletons of a deer, a bear, a bobcat, and a raccoon. Moreover, almost all of this material occurred in a mass of bone within the basal layer of the pit, suggesting that it originated from a one-time deposit. The presence of the skeletons of these animals in one deposit suggests that they were butchered, eaten, and disposed of as part of a single event, such as a feast.

However, the context of Feature 79 does not suggest that it was formed as part of a calendrical ceremony. This feature is unambiguously associated with House 13 and the Late phase, which, of course, is the hunting camp phase. It would be unusual to hold a calendrical festival in a hunting camp; historically such festivals were usually related to horticulture and were normally held within villages. It seems more likely that the remains in Feature 79 are indicative of a different sort of feast -

perhaps one involving a ceremony to celebrate and give thanks for a particularly successful hunt.

## Shamanism and Curing Societies

It is impossible to say whether the medicine societies of the Iroquoians had developed into the integrative institutions that were observed historically by the time of the Calvert occupation. Yet there is strong evidence to indicate that elements of shamanic religion were known to the Calvert people.

Feature 285 yielded an unusual artifact assemblage consisting of bones from the head, wing, and tail of a Carolina parakeet, a stone pipe bowl, an antler prong tool, and a slate knife. These items appear to have been intentionally buried in the pit, which was only 34 cm in diameter and 15 cm deep (below the plough zone level). It was located in the area of overlap of Houses 3 and 4 and, therefore, cannot be definitely assigned to any one phase of the occupation. Feature 285 and the associated artifacts are illustrated in Figure 7.33.

The discovery of the Carolina parakeet in this archaeological context is significant from a zoological point of view since southern Ontario lies north of the known range of this species. Upon identifying the bones, Rosemary Prevec suggested that they represented the remains of a bird skin, since they all came from the extremities of the bird. It was further suggested that the bird skin may have had a ritualistic use (Prevec 1984b). The fact that the bird skin is from a rare southern bird noted for its colourful plumage strongly suggests that it may have been traded north.

In a previous article Alexander von Gernet and the writer explored the meaning of the bird skin/pipe association and argued that the intentional burial of these artifacts together may best be interpreted in the context of shamanic beliefs involving the use of tobacco, bird symbolism, guardian spirits, and soul flight (von Gernet and Timmins 1987). This research will be briefly summarized here.

At the heart of our argument is the suggestion that the bird skin was used to decorate a long wooden pipe stem attached to the stone pipe bowl. The pipe bowl has a large hole for the insertion of a wooden or reed pipe stem. It also displays a circular groove around the bottom of the bowl which may

have been used for the attachment of a safety string to prevent loss of the pipe bowl (Figure 7.18, a).

The use of bird feathers, bird skins, and other bird motifs to decorate pipe bowls and stems is widespread in the New World. The best known bird/pipe association is that involving the calumet, the elaborately decorated pipe used in rituals among eastern tribes in the historic period (ibid:35-37). Of particular interest to the Calvert problem are two pipes found in the Public Museum of Milwaukee, described by Alanson Skinner:

> The first specimen belonged to the Wolf gens of the Iowa, and on its highly ornamented stem "is impaled the skin of a Carolina Paroquet, the head of which is missing but had been pointed toward the bowl" (Skinner 1926 p. 229, Plate 32, Figure 2)....A second example, from the Thunder gens (Iowa), also has bound to the stem "a well preserved skin of the rare Carolina Paroquet, with the head towards the bowl and the bill bent back" (Skinner 1926, p. 233, Plate 32, Figure 4) ...(von Gernet and Timmins 1987:36)

The calumet ceremony itself may have had a prehistoric origin in the western Great Lakes and Mississippi Valley regions, but ethnohistoric evidence suggests that it did not spread to the eastern woodlands until the historical period (Fenton 1953). Thus the occurrence of a calumet-like pipe at the Calvert site appears to pre-date the diffusion of the calumet ceremony into the eastern woodlands by several centuries. Yet bird motifs associated with pipes have considerable antiquity in the Northeast, extending back to at least Adena-Hopewell times. We have suggested that the appearance of the feathered pipe at Calvert indicates a more fundamental and ancient relationship between smoking and bird symbolism that is common in the shamanic belief systems of numerous New World groups (von Gernet and Timmins 1987:37).

Native Americans used a wide variety of hallucinogenic plants to produce altered states of consciousness and enhance the visionary experiences that were essential to the shaman's communication with the spirit world. The potent native tobacco *Nicotiana rustica* is regarded by some researchers as a hallucinogen (Janiger and

Dobkin de Rios 1976). There is no doubt that it was capable of producing "major dissociational states," including the sensation of flight, when consumed in sufficient quantities (von Gernet and Timmins 1987:38). According to La Barre, "...tobacco is the supernatural plant par excellence of the American Indian" (1972:276).

With respect to bird symbolism, it is significant to note the importance of man-animal transformations in both shamanism and Iroquoian ideology (Furst 1976). During visionary experiences it is common for the shaman's soul to be transformed into a bird to facilitate flight to and in the spirit world. In a Mississippian context, Furst has interpreted the "Eagle Dancer" conch shell engraving from Spiro Mound as an expression of the shaman's ecstatic ascent, showing the merging of the shaman and his tutelary spirit, the eagle. Furst feels that the bird motif:

> ...seems to stand for the power of flight that is the shaman's special gift and that is activated by the hallucinogen. It should be noted that birds are often regarded as guardian spirits or even manifestations of specific psychoactive plants, especially tobacco; this observation provides one clue for the meaning of bird-shaped tobacco pipes in North American Indian art. (Furst 1976:154)

In summary, although the specific details of the ritual event will never be known, we feel that the association of the Carolina parakeet skin and the stone pipe at the Calvert site is related to the practise of ancient rituals involving tobacco use, bird symbolism, and soul flight as part of the visionary shamanic experience. Shamanism "is everywhere the religion of hunting peoples" (La Barre 1972:272) and would have dominated the spiritual life of the Iroquoian peoples prior to their adoption of horticulture. Elements of this ancient substratum of beliefs persisted into the historic period, particularly in the shamanistic aspects of Iroquoian curing societies.

## Mortuary Practises

No human burials were discovered at Calvert, nor was any other evidence of mortuary ritual uncovered. Only one fragment of human bone was recovered in a refuse context. However, recent research has improved our understanding of Early Ontario Iroquoian burial practises (Spence 1988, 1994; Mullen and Hoppa 1992) and will be briefly reviewed here.

Human burials have been recovered from 22 Early Ontario Iroquoian sites, including 17 classified as Glen Meyer and five classified as Pickering (Spence 1994:9-14). The following discussion will be confined to the evidence from sites in southwestern Ontario that have been classified as Glen Meyer.

Both primary and secondary burials are known, and some burials consist of only discarded elements of exhumed primary burials (Spence 1994:10). The number of individuals involved in each burial ranges from one to 28 (ibid.). These burials occur within houses, outside houses but within villages, at the edges of villages, and in sites with no known associated settlement (ibid.).

The data suggest that several different burial programmes were followed and that Early Iroquoian groups developed burial practises that fit their own particular situations (Spence 1994:17). For example, the burial programme for Glen Meyer groups on the Norfolk sand plain appears to be closely tied to their settlement-subsistence system. That system involved seasonal movement from inland villages along Big Otter Creek and Big Creek (i.e. the Van Besien and Elliott sites) to lakeshore spring-summer fishing camps or villages (i.e. Bruce Boyd, Reid). These groups may have practised some type of scaffold or exposure burial of the winter dead in or near the inland village followed by sorting of the bones, discard of non-essential or non-articulated elements, and removal of retained elements for secondary burial at the lakeshore camps (Spence 1988).

On the other hand, Glen Meyer groups in the Byron area of London appear to have followed a different programme. Single primary burials have been found in villages, such as the London Ski Club site, and an exhumed primary burial was recovered at the Praying Mantis village (Spence 1994:9). Yet multiple secondary burials also occur within these villages, including a pit containing the disarticulated elements of eight individuals at Praying Mantis and one containing six individuals at the Boisclair site (ibid.). The Boisclair burial may represent the annual exhumation and reburial of the dead of the village. However, the multiple burial from the Praying Mantis site was found within a longhouse and could represent the dead of the household, perhaps accumulated over a longer period (Spence 1994:15). Thus there is considerable variability in burial practises even within the same site cluster.

A third type of mortuary programme is indicated by the Rogers Ossuary located near Brantford. It has been assigned to the Early Iroquoian period on the basis of two radiocarbon dates of $1110 \pm 60$ BP that yield a calibrated range of AD 833-992 (Mullen and Hoppa 1992:37). The excavation of this site occurred in 1935 and its circumstances are poorly understood, however in their recent analysis Mullen and Hoppa determined that a minimum number of 28 individuals were interred in a communal burial (1992:37). These were probably secondary burials repesenting the accumulation of the dead over a considerable length of time (ibid.; Spence 1994:15). A burial like the Rogers ossuary may have occurred upon the re-location of a village or the death of a leader, thus the cycle from primary to secondary burial would have been longer than that inferred for either the Norfolk or Byron group.

In summary, Early Iroquoian mortuary programmes varied from region to region, just as the settlement-subsistence systems of these groups differed on a regional basis. As Michael Spence has pointed out, there is no uniform set of practises that characterize Glen Meyer or Pickering burials, and this raises questions about the "social integrity" of "Glen Meyer" and "Pickering" as archaeological constructs (Spence 1994:17). The only consistent trend appears to be some adherence to the practise of multiple secondary burial. Such burials, and their attendant ritual, undoubtedly served a socially integrative function for participating groups. However, the timing of these events and the breadth of participation varied from place to place (Spence 1994:16). The regional variability observed in burial practises can be taken as further evidence that Early Iroquoian socio-political organization operated largely at the local community level with limited inter-regional integration.

Unfortunately, as there are no data available on the burial practises of the Dorchester group the nature of the Calvert site mortuary programme remains a mystery.

## Conclusions

As is usually the case when drawing archaeological inferences at the top of the interpretive pyramid, we find that our ability to interpret the ideational component of the Calvert community is greatly restricted. While historical data concerning Iroquoian calendrical ceremonies and belief systems appear to have little direct relevance to the Calvert data, there is some evidence to suggest that the Calvert people led active spiritual lives and participated in ancient shamanistic practises characteristic of hunting societies throughout the New World. This is not surprising when we consider that the Early Iroquoians were in essence still hunters with an emerging horticultural economy.

This study develops a general methodology for the interpretation of archaeological data and applies this methodology to the study of an Early Iroquoian community that occupied the Calvert site near London, Ontario, between ca. A.D. 1150 and 1250. The results of this analysis show that, contrary to previous interpretations of Early Iroquoian communities, the Calvert village was not unplanned or disordered; instead the Calvert people planned their village in a systematic manner through four sequential periods of rebuilding and spatial reorganization that involved substantial economic and socio-political change. This demonstrates that at least some Early Iroquoian villages were planned multi-extended family communities approaching a higher level of socio-political organization than was previously thought.

The theoretical perspective of the study is concerned with strengthening archaeological interpretations through the development and application of interpretive theory. Interpretive theory is defined as a body of archaeological principles employing analogical reasoning to relate archaeological residues to the natural processes or cultural behaviours inferred to have produced them. Interpretive theory represents a broadening of the concept of middle range theory to incorporate all social, cultural, and natural processes that condition the archaeological record. As such, it subsumes ethnoarchaeology and experimental archaeology as well as arguments based on ethnographic and ethnohistoric analogy.

Interpretive theory differs from middle range theory in that it may be general or particular; it may utilize culturally specific ethnographic data or it may be concerned with general principles that have widespread cross-cultural applicability. Compared to middle range research, interpretive theory involves an expansion of the source side data base for archaeological inference and recognizes the value of textual sources, especially in relation to the interpretation of culturally specific phenomena. Existing bodies of interpretive theory may include well established archaeological interpretations and these are also accepted as appropriate source side data as long as they can be shown to have a sound basis. Interpretive theory recognizes that similar processes of analogical reasoning underlie a wide range of middle range approaches and traditional culture-historical methods and it seeks to integrate these. The concept of interpretive theory thus draws together the seemingly disparate goals of archaeology as a nomothetic, generalizing science and as idiographic, particularistic culture history.

Integral to this interpretive method is the model of the interpretive pyramid (Figure 1.1), an adaptation of the traditionally recognized ladder of archaeological inference which notes the increasing difficulty of inference as one proceeds from interpretations relating to space and time through interpretations of technology, economy, socio-political organization, religion and ideology (Hawkes 1954). The pyramid is chosen as an appropriate model for the organization of archaeological inference partly because the spatio-temporal inferences at the broad base of the pyramid have the greatest scope for generalization. This scope narrows as one rises within the pyramid. Thus inferences of technology and economy have narrower applicability, interpretations of socio-political organization are even more culturally constrained, and phenomena such as ideology and belief systems may be highly culturally specific. The types of analogy employed in archaeological inference usually change from general comparative to direct historical as one moves up the pyramid. Separate bodies of interpretive theory are recognized at the distinct levels of spatio-temporal, techno-economic, social, and cultural analysis.

The interpretive pyramid may also be used to structure archaeological inquiry. It formed the basic structure for the organization of the substantive portion of this study. We began with a spatio-temporal analysis of the Calvert community, proceeded to a techno-economic analysis, a socio-political analysis, and finally, a cultural analysis.

The task of developing interpretive theory for the problems encountered at each level of analysis is part of the ongoing methodological work of archaeology in general. Bodies of interpretive theory accumulate over years of research through experimental archaeology, ethnoarchaeology, ethnohistory, and applications of the biological, geological, and physical sciences. It was beyond the scope of this study to attempt to develop comprehensive bodies of interpretive theory for all aspects of the Calvert analysis. However, the attempt was made to draw upon relevant source side data whenever possible.

We entered the interpretive pyramid at the spatio-temporal level.

## Spatio-Temporal Analysis

To situate the Calvert site spatially and ecologically, a reconstruction of the environmental setting of the site was presented, based on a consideration of glacial history, physiography, drainage, soils, and climate, combined with modern and historical data regarding resident plant and animal communities. This analysis led to the definition of five distinct micro-environmental zones within a five kilometre radius of the site: (1.) the sandy upland plateau on which the site is situated, (2.) the littoral environment of the Thames River and Dorchester Swamp Creek adjacent to the site, (3.) the Dorchester Swamp, a large wetland located just southeast of the site, (4.) the upland forests that ring the sandy plateau, and (5.) a series of glacial ponds (Foster and Beattie ponds) located to the south. Thus it was demonstrated that the Calvert site was optimally situated to provide ready access to a diversity of environmental zones offering different natural resources.

Still at the spatio-temporal level, a detailed analysis of stratigraphic evidence (feature and post superpositions), spatial data, ceramic cross-mends, post mould densities, and radiocarbon dates was performed to provide interpretations of the occupational history of the Calvert site. This analysis yielded three products:

1. four sets of settlement pattern data corresponding to four occupational episodes;

2. four sub-samples of feature, artifactual, and ecofactual data corresponding to the four phases of occupation; and

3. an estimate of the dating of the site on the calendrical time-scale, together with estimates of the duration of each occupational episode.

The occupation of the Calvert site was initiated with the construction of a single house (House 1) which was probably used as a seasonal hunting camp in the mid-twelfth century (Figure 8.2). This was followed, perhaps with an intervening temporal gap, by the Early village phase, consisting of three longhouses and one small shed surrounded by a single row palisade. It was occupied for about 20 years in the early thirteenth century.

The Early phase was terminated and the Middle phase initiated by a village reorganization that involved dismantling the houses and rebuilding them in an east-west pattern. The palisade was contracted and a second line of palisade was constructed. This phase of occupation is interpreted as being sequential and continuous with the Early phase and is thought to have lasted for about 20 years in the early to mid-thirteenth century (Figure 8.2).

The Late phase was marked by the removal of the Middle Phase houses and the construction of three or four much smaller east-west oriented houses, possibly surrounded by a single palisade. There was no major gap in occupation between the Middle and Late phases. The Late phase may have been occupied, perhaps intermittently, for about 20 years in the mid-thirteenth century (Figure 8.2).

## Techno-Economic Analysis

The analysis of the economy and technology of the Calvert community involved the study of all classes of artifactual and ecofactual remains recovered from the site. The economic analysis incorporated the results of floral and faunal analyses conducted by specialists and involved a comparison of data from the four occupational phases to determine if changes in site function occurred.

The faunal data were divided into sub-samples and compared on a phase by phase basis. This analysis indicated a focus on mammal hunting in House 1, a shift to a broad spectrum hunting and fishing pattern in the Early and Middle phases, and a return to a strategy based on mammal hunting in the Late phase. The evidence for this shift lies in a lack of fish remains associated with House 1 and the Late phase and changes in the percentages of mammal species hunted in the Late phase. Throughout the occupation white-tailed deer were the principal prey of the Calvert people. In the final phase, however, the overall percentage of white-tailed deer decreased, while the percentage of other mammals of economic importance increased. This trend, combined with the evidence for a decline in fishing, suggests that a generalized hunting strategy became important during the Late phase.

The floral remains were analyzed and compared on a phase by phase basis. There were no notable changes in the diversity of floral species among the three main phases, but fewer species were identified from House 1. While it was evident that maize constituted the main plant food of the Calvert people, squash, bean, and sunflower were also cultivated and several fleshy fruits were collected during all phases. Evidence of seasonality from both faunal and floral indices leaves little doubt that the Calvert site was used in all seasons during all phases. However, warm weather indicators are less common in the Late phase and House 1, whereas cold weather indices are more plentiful in these samples. This suggests that the House 1 and Late phase occupations occurred primarily during the cold season, with intermittent use in the warm seasons as well.

To assess the catchment area of the Calvert community, the preferred habitats of the floral and faunal species represented in each phase were compared to the five micro-environmental zones defined previously. It was determined that the most important environmental zones in all phases were the sandy upland plateau surrounding the site and the Dorchester Swamp area to the southeast. Thus the local catchment area of the Calvert community was likely ovate in form, extending from the sand plateau to the Dorchester Swamp and incorporating part of the Thames River/Dorchester Swamp Creek zone as well. It was noted, however, that, with the expansion of mammal hunting in the Late phase, the catchment was probably modified to include more of the upland forest zone.

The analysis conducted at the technological level included all major artifact classes as well as some aspects of Iroquoian technology that have not traditionally been considered in detail. The technological categories considered were lithic technology, ceramic technology, bone, antler, and shell technology, feature function and formation, refuse disposal technology, and building technology and structure function.

The lithic artifacts and debitage were analyzed using traditional tool categories with no attempt made to create source side data through extensive experimentation. Analysis of raw material frequencies for both debitage and tools indicates that high quality Kettle Point chert was being preferentially selected by the Calvert people during the Early and Late phases. A decrease in Kettle Point chert in the House 1 and Middle phase samples suggests that access to the Kettle Point source may have been restricted at those times, possibly as a result of changes in socio-political relationships. Analysis of debitage/tool ratios indicates that the Late phase has a much higher ratio of late stage debitage to tools. This supports the interpretation of the Late phase as a series of short term occupations, since such occupations are more affected by curate behavior which, in turn, should be reflected in the late stage debitage/tool ratio. Moreover, it was found that a significantly higher number of the bifaces from the Late phase showed use polish and microflaking, suggesting that many of them were used in butchering, as would be expected at a hunting camp.

The pottery of the Early, Middle, and Late phases was found to be very similar, suggesting that it was the product of a single community evolving through time. Several technique-attribute combinations demonstrated chronological sensitivity, increasing or decreasing in frequency through time. House 1, on the other hand, yielded a highly distinctive ceramic assemblage, dominated by suture stamped ceramics, which form only a minority of the main village ceramic samples. This suggests that the occupants of House 1 were not related to the group that later lived in the main village.

The analysis of feature formation and function led to the definition of three distinct feature types at Calvert: large Type 1 features used for storage and refuse disposal, small Type 2 features that are usually clustered around interior hearths and contain living floor debris, and medium sized Type 3 features that are most often found within houses and contain very high concentrations of artifact debris. Experiments in refuse pit formation aided in the feature analysis, especially with respect to understanding sources of disturbance, stratum formation, and the effects of short-term abandonment. It was observed that any short-term abandonment of a refuse pit was characterized by rapid organic decomposition of refuse leading to stratum slumping and accumulation of sterile humic fill. This suggested that any significant abandonment of the Calvert site between the Early and Middle phases should have resulted in the formation of a dark layer of sterile fill within pits that were used in both phases. Such a pattern was not observed. Yet documentation of this process helped to interpret several features with dark, sterile upper layers of fill as the product of post-depositional slumping and in-filling. The stratum by stratum analysis of Type 1 features also successfully documented their transition from storage pits to refuse pits on the basis of stratigraphic content.

The analysis of feature function at Calvert is directly related to the study of refuse disposal technology. This analysis was based on refuse disposal theory, a body of interpretive theory that is growing rapidly as a result of numerous experimental and ethnoarchaeological studies (Schiffer 1987). Ceramic cross-mends were analyzed from a behavioral point of view to help identify refuse streams at Calvert. A total of ten different refuse streams was postulated, linking activity areas within and outside houses to specific feature types. In general, these refuse streams involved movement of debris from hearth activity areas to interior features and the subsequent removal of debris to exterior refuse pits. This pattern was observed for both the Early and Middle phases; the direction of the refuse streams changing, as expected, with the reorientation of houses. However, the Late phase revealed a very different pattern, involving mainly in-house refuse disposal streams and a high proportion of house-to-house refuse transfer. This is interpreted as evidence of abandonment behaviour which reflects a lack of concern for moving refuse out of houses, as well as evidence for a high degree of interaction between households. These observations further support the interpretation of the Late phase as a hunting camp occupied mainly in the cold season.

The analysis of building technology and village settlement patterns is grounded in a body of ethnohistorical, archaeological, and experimental data. With these data in mind, each structure at Calvert was described and interpreted in terms of its size, location, construction, associated features, and function. A total of four different structure types were defined. These include the standard Early Iroquoian longhouse occupied by an extended family, the residential/storage house characterized by a very high proportion of interior storage pits, the small non-residential work/storage hut or shed, and the small cabins and longhouses occupied by families or task groups while on hunting expeditions.

Population estimates based on ethnohistorical data indicating that two families shared a hearth, suggest an increase from about 108 people in the Early phase to 144 in the Middle phase. The maximum Late phase population could have been about 90, but it is possible that the Late phase structures were not all occupied at the same time, given the hunting camp interpretation. The inferred population changes raise some important issues when they are considered in conjunction with the evidence for village reorganization. First, a contraction of the palisade during the Middle phase, coupled with the proposed population increase, would have led to more crowded village conditions. Second, it was argued that the Middle phase reorganization involved defensive considerations, including the construction of a second row of palisade, the radial alignment of houses to inhibit movement between them, and the construction of a house-to-palisade wall. Finally, it was demonstrated that the structural modifications of the Middle phase involved a large expenditure of labour and materials and hence were not likely undertaken without good cause. All of these lines of evidence suggest that the Calvert village was reorganized under some form of stress, possibly of a socio-political nature.

## Socio-Political Analysis

This analysis was concerned with reconstructing socio-political organization within the village and the greater region and exploring how the socio-political organization of the Calvert community related to the general process of Iroquoian development in southwestern Ontario. Previous archaeological and anthropological models of Iroquoian socio-political development were reviewed as potential interpretive data, as were ethnohistorical descriptions of Iroquoian social and political systems.

At the community level two competing hypotheses concerning the determinants of village organization were considered. The first is that developed by Warrick (1984a), which suggests that Iroquoian village organization is largely a reflection of the degree of socio-political integration of the community, while the second, advocated by Finlayson (1985), relates many elements of Iroquoian community patterns to defensive planning. The changes in the Calvert community patterns were examined in light of these models, with the conclusion that they need not be mutually exclusive and that elements of both processes were operative at the Calvert site. Thus, while the changes in village organization between the Early and Middle phases appear to have been motivated by defensive concerns, it is also likely that this was a time of increased social and political integration within the community. Certainly, the planning and implementation of such sweeping and purposeful changes imply a high degree of political organization and cooperation.

The shift in community settlement patterns in the Late phase, notably the change to smaller houses, is correlated with the shift in site function to that of a hunting camp and a concomitant alteration in the social composition of the occupying groups. These small houses were probably occupied by small task groups comprised primarily of men or small family units, rather than the extended family units of the Early and Middle phase longhouses. In fact, the contrast between the Early/Middle phase longhouse forms and the shorter Late phase forms, when considered in connection with the strong evidence for a change in site function, supports the argument for the existence of matrilineal, matrilocal residence patterns on Early Iroquoian villages and more flexible residence patterns at special purpose sites (Williamson 1985).

At the regional level, a number of past archaeological explanations that attempt to explain regional Early Iroquoian socio-political change were reviewed. These include models such as Wright's (1966) "Pickering Conquest Hypothesis," which relies heavily on warfare as a "prime mover," Dincauze and Hasenstab's (1989) "Mississippian hypothesis," and a number of multi-factor hypotheses, such as those proposed by Warrick

(1984b) for the Ontario Iroquoians and Niemczycki (1984) for the Seneca and Cayuga. Turning to the archaeological data, settlement patterns and ceramics from Glen Meyer communities in the Dorchester, Byron, Caradoc, and Norfolk Sand Plain areas were compared to evaluate their socio-political relationships. Ceramic styles among these site clusters were shown to be very heterogeneous, with each local group developing distinctive elements of its own ceramic tradition. As expected, adjacent groups were found to have ceramics that were most similar. Intra-village settlement patterns were less variable, but there were still significant differences in village layouts and feature distributions. Overall, the general impression was that the communities represented by these site clusters must have been largely politically autonomous and economically self sufficient.

Finally, a new model of Early to Middle Iroquoian political development in southwestern Ontario was proposed which seeks to account for several aspects of Early and Middle Iroquoian settlement patterns and material culture. It was proposed that each of the clusters of Glen Meyer sites in southwestern Ontario represents two or three village communities, living in a circumscribed area and sharing a diversified resource base which was exploited through a combination of hunting, collecting, and horticulture. The presence of multiple communities within each site cluster is suggested by the large numbers of known Glen Meyer villages in well surveyed areas (i.e., the Caradoc Sand Plain), the long-term occupation of these sites, and the relatively short time span during which they are thought to have existed (i.e., ca. A.D. 1100- 1300 on the Caradoc). Such groups would have been socially and politically autonomous, probably practising village exogamy, although they were likely regionally endogamous.

Economic and socio-political cooperation among these people would have preconditioned them for the eventual amalgamation of several of these small villages to form much larger, often segmented villages at the beginning of the Middle Iroquoian period ca. A.D. 1300. This major development, which occurred across southwestern Ontario, may have been precipitated by several interrelated social, political, and economic factors that remain to be identified. What we do know is that these villages were larger and hence more easily defended, and by the mid-fourteenth century they were located on heavier soils that were much more productive for horticulture. Thus the changes of the Early to Middle Iroquoian periods addressed both economic and socio-political (defensive) needs. The requirement for environmental diversity to accommodate a dominant hunting and gathering economy gave way to the need for fertile soil, as the southwestern Ontario Iroquoians became committed horticulturalists.

At the same time, these local developments led to important changes on the inter-regional level. With former neighbors now living together in large regional villages, new inter-regional ties would have been established for political alliances, defense, trade, and perhaps spouse exchange. This new, and unprecedented level of inter-regional interaction may have led to the rapid spread across southern Ontario of the ceramic motifs and associated artifacts that have been recognized as the Middle Ontario Iroquoian horizon.

## Cultural Analysis

At the cultural level the limited evidence for the belief systems, ritual, and mortuary practises of the Calvert community allow for little discussion. Interpretive data were drawn from ethnohistorical and ethnographic sources concerning Iroquoian calendrical ceremonies, curing societies, and mortuary programmes. No definitive evidence for calendrical ceremonies was detected at Calvert and it may be that these horticulturally related festivals had not yet developed in Early Iroquoian times. Curing societies, however, have a strong shamanistic element and some evidence for shamanic belief systems was discovered at Calvert in the form of the association of a Carolina parakeet skin and a stone pipe bowl with implications of attendant ritualism (von Gernet and Timmins 1987).

The Calvert mortuary program remains a mystery. No human burials were recovered in the excavations, nor were any deposits of discarded human bones recovered that could be interpreted as discard burials. The burial programmes reconstructed for other Early Iroquoian communities in southwestern Ontario are quite variable, but all seem to have involved some type of primary burial followed by multiple secondary burial at a later date (Spence 1994). However, it is not possible to say if the Calvert people followed similar practises.

## Conclusion

One of the principal aims of this study has been to demonstrate the use of a general methodology for the interpretation of archaeological data through the analysis and interpretation of an Early Iroquoian village. The application of interpretive theory, as implemented here, requires that we become explicit about the sources of our archaeological interpretations and recognize their analogical nature in bridging the gap between known processes and archaeological residues. Approached in this manner interpretive theory has the potential for strengthening archaeological inferences at all levels of the interpretive pyramid.

With respect to the substantive culture-historical problems addressed in this study, it has been demonstrated that Early Iroquoian villages may be successfully analyzed once their occupational histories have been reconstructed through the careful study of site formation processes. In the case of the Calvert community, this reconstruction of occupational history has permitted us to trace, in detail, the development of a single community over the course of three generations. The result has been our first clear picture of the economic and socio-political realities of stability and change in Early Iroquoian society. We have shown that, contrary to earlier beliefs, Early Iroquoian groups had developed effective socio-political institutions to cope with village planning and defense. These institutions were of no small importance as they were the early antecedents of the highly developed political institutions of the historic Ontario Iroquoians.

# References Cited

Ascher, R.
    1961. Analogy in Archaeological Interpretation. *Southwestern Journal of Anthropology* 17, pp. 317-325.

Baerreis, D., and R. Bryson.
    1965. Climatic Episodes and the Dating of Mississippian Cultures. *Wisconsin Archaeologist* 46, pp. 203-220.

Baerreis, D., R. Bryson and J. Kutzbach.
    1976. Climate and Culture in the Western Great Lakes Region. *Midcontinental Journal of Archaeology* 1, pp. 39-57.

Bareis, C.J., and J.W. Porter, editors.
    1984. *American Bottom Archaeology*. The University of Illinois Press. Urbana.

Banfield, A.W.F.
    1974. *The Mammals of Canada*. University of Toronto Press. Toronto.

Biggar, H.P., editor.
    1924. *The Voyages of Jacques Cartier*. Publications of the Public Archives of Canada, No. 11. Ottawa.

Binford, L.R.
    1962. Archaeology as Anthropology. *American Antiquity* 28, pp. 217-225.
    1967. Smudge Pits and Hide Smoking: The Use of Analogy in Archaeological Reasoning. *American Antiquity* 32, pp. 1-12.
    1972. *An Archaeological Perspective*. Seminar Press. New York.
    1977. General Introduction. In *For Theory Building in Archaeology*, edited by L.R. Binford, pp. 1-10. Academic Press. New York.
    1978a. Dimensional Analysis of Behaviour and Site Structure: Learning from an Eskimo Hunting Stand. *American Antiquity* 43, pp. 330-361.
    1978b. *Nunamiut Ethnoarchaeology*. Academic Press. New York.
    1980. Willow Smoke and Dog's Tails: Hunter-Gatherer Settlement Systems and Archaeological Site Formation. *American Antiquity* 45, pp. 4-20.
    1981a. *Bones: Ancient Men and Modern Myths*. Academic Press. New York.
    1981b. Behavioral Archaeology and the "Pompeii Premise." *Journal of Anthropological Research* 37, pp. 195-208.
    1983a. *In Pursuit of the Past*. Thames and Hudson. New York.
    1983b. *Working at Archaeology*. Academic Press. New York.
    1984. Butchering, Sharing, and the Archaeological Record. *Journal of Anthropological Archaeology* 3, pp. 235-257.

Binford, L.R., and S. Binford.
    1966. A Preliminary Analysis of Functional Variability in the Mousterian of Levallois Facies. *American Anthropologist* Vol. 68, pp. 238-295.

Bordes, F.H.
    1968. *The Old Stone Age*. McGraw-Hill. New York.

Bowman, I.
    1979. The Draper Site: Historical Accounts of Vegetation in Pickering and Markham Townships with Special Reference to the Significance of a Large, Even-Aged Stand Adjacent to the Site. In *Settlement Patterns of the Draper and White Sites*, edited by B. Hayden, pp. 47-58. Simon Fraser University, Department of Archaeology, Publication 6. Burnaby.

Bowman, S.
    1990. *Radiocarbon Dating*. University of California Press. Berkeley.

Callahan, E.H.
    1981. Pamunkey Housebuilding: An Experimental Study of Late Woodland Construction Technology in the Powhatan Confederacy. Ph.D. Thesis, Catholic University of America, Washington D.C. University Microfilms. Ann Arbor.

Carr, C.
    1984. The Nature of Organization of Intrasite Archaeological Records and Spatial Analytic Approaches to their Investigation. In *Advances in Archaeological Method and Theory*, Vol. 7, edited by M.B. Schiffer, pp. 103-222. Academic Press. Orlando.

Chapman, L.J., and D.F. Putnam.
    1984. *The Physiography of Southern Ontario, Third Edition*. Ontario Geological Survey, Special Volume 2. Toronto.

Chang, K.C.
    1958. Study of the Neolithic Social Grouping: Examples from the New World. *American Anthropologist* 60, pp. 298-334.
    1967. Major Aspects of the Interrelationship of Archaeology and Ethnology. *Current Anthropology* 8, pp. 227-234.

Chang, K.C., editor.
    1968. *Settlement Archaeology*. National Press. Palo
        Alto.

Chaplin, R.E.
    1971. *The Study of Animal Bones from Archaeological
        Sites*. Seminar Press. New York.

Charlton, T.H.
    1981. Archaeology, Ethnohistory, and Ethnology:
        Interpretive Interfaces. In *Advances in
        Archaeological Method and Theory*, Vol. 4, pp.
        129-176. Academic Press. New York.

Chesterman, C.W.
    1978. *The Audobon Society Field Guide to North
        American Rocks and Minerals*. Alfred A. Knopf.
        New York.

Clarke, D.L.
    1979. Archaeology: The Loss of Innocence. In
        *Analytical Archaeologist: Collected Papers of
        David L. Clarke*, pp. 83-103. Academic Press.
        London.

Coles, J.
    1973. *Archaeology by Experiment*. Scribner. New
        York.

Courbin, P.
    1987. *What is Archaeology? An Essay on the Nature
        of Archaeological Research*. The University of
        Chicago Press. Chicago.

Crabtree, D.E.
    1982. *An Introduction to Flintworking*. Occasional
        Papers of the Idaho Museum of Natural History,
        Number 28, Second Edition. Pocalello, Idaho.

Crawford, G.W.
    1982. Late Archaic Plant Remains from West-Central
        Kentucky: A Summary. *Midcontinental Journal of
        Archaeology* 7, pp. 205-224.

Day, G.M.
    1953. The Indian as an Ecological Factor in the
        Northeastern Forest. *Ecology* 34, pp. 329-346.

Deal, M.
    1985. Household Pottery Disposal in the Maya
        Highlands: An Ethnoarchaeological Interpretation.
        *Journal of Anthropological Archaeology* 4, pp.
        243-291.

DeBoer, W.R., and D.W. Lathrap.
    1979. The Making and Breaking of Shipibo-Conibo
        Ceramics. In *Ethnoarchaeology: Implications of
        Ethnography for Archaeology*, edited by C.

Kramer, pp. 102-138. Columbia University Press.
        New York.

Deetz, J.
    1967. *Invitation to Archaeology*. The Natural History
        Press. New York.
    1971. Must Archeologists Dig? In *Man's Imprint From
        the Past: Readings in the Methods of Archaeology*,
        edited by J. Deetz, pp. 2-9. Little, Brown and
        Company. Boston.
    1977. *In Small Things Forgotten*. Anchor Books. New
        York.

Dickens, R.S., Jr.
    1985. The Form, Function, and Formation of
        Garbage-filled Pits on Southeastern Aboriginal
        Sites: An Archaeological Analysis. In *Structure and
        Process in Southeastern Archaeology*, R.S.
        Dickens and H.I. Ward (eds.), pp. 34-59. University
        of Alabama Press. Tuscaloosa.

Dincauze, D.F., and R.J. Hasenstab.
    1989. Explaining the Iroquois: Tribalization on a
        Prehistoric Periphery. In *Centre and Periphery,
        Comparative Studies in Archaeology*, edited by
        T.C. Champion, pp. 67-87. Unwin Hyman. London.

Dodd, C.F.
    1984. *Ontario Iroquois Tradition Longhouses*.
        National Museum of Man, Archaeological Survey
        of Canada, Mercury Series, Paper 124, pp.
        181-437. Ottawa.

Dodd, C.F., D.R. Poulton, P.A. Lennox, D.G. Smith and
        G.A. Warrick.
    1990. The Middle Ontario Iroquoian Stage. In *The
        Archaeology of Southern Ontario to A.D. 1650*,
        C.J. Ellis and N. Ferris (eds.). Occasional
        Publication No. 5, Ontario Archaeological Society,
        London Chapter. London.

Dragoo, D.
    1977. Prehistoric Iroquoian Occupation in the Upper
        Ohio Valley. In *Current Perspectives in
        Northeastern Archaeology*, R.E. Funk and C.F.
        Hayes (eds.), pp. 41-47. New York State
        Archaeological Association. Buffalo.

Dunnell, R.C.
    1984. The Americanist Literature for 1983. *American
        Journal of Archaeology*, 88, pp. 489-513.

Ellis, C.J.
    1979. Analysis of Lithic Debitage From Fluted Point
        Sites in Ontario. Unpublished M.A. thesis,
        Department of Anthropology, McMaster
        University. Hamilton.

Ellis, C.J., and D.B. Deller.
1982. Hi-Lo Materials from Southwestern Ontario. *Ontario Archaeology* 38, pp. 3-22.
1988. Some Distinctive Paleo-Indian Tool Types from the Lower Great Lakes Region. *Midcontinental Journal of Archaeology* 13, pp. 111-158.

Eley, B.E., and P.H. von Bitter.
1989. *Cherts of Southern Ontario*. Royal Ontario Museum. Toronto.

Engelbrecht, W.
1974. The Iroquois: Archaeological Patterning on the Tribal Level. *World Archaeology* 6, pp. 52-65.
1978. Ceramic Patterning Between New York Iroquois Sites. In *The Spatial Organization of Culture*, edited by I. Hodder, pp. 141-152. Duckworth. London.

Fecteau, R.D.
1985. The Introduction and Diffusion of Cultivated Plants in Southern Ontario. Unpublished M.A. thesis. York University. Toronto.
1992. Preliminary Report on the Archaeobotanical Remains from the Calvert Site (AfHg-1), North Dorchester Township, Middlesex County. Report submitted to Peter Timmins. London.

Fenton, W.N.
1953. The Iroquoian Eagle Dance: An Offshoot of the Calumet Dance. *Smithsonian Institution Bureau of American Ethnology*, Bulletin 156, pp. 1-222.

Ferris, N., and M.W. Spence.
1995. The Woodland Traditions in Southern Ontario. *Revista de Arqueologia Americana* 9, pp. 83-138.

Findlay, P.
1978. Late Eighteenth Century-Nineteenth Century Vegetation Patterns, Wildlife and Native Indian Recordings in the County of Middlesex. Manuscript and maps on file, Ontario Ministry of Culture and Communications, London.

Finlayson, W.D.
1985. *The 1975 and 1978 Rescue Excavations at the Draper Site: Introduction and Settlement Patterns*. National Museum of Man, Archaeological Survey of Canada, Mercury Series, Paper No. 130. Ottawa.

Finlayson, W.D., R.J. Pearce, P.A. Timmins and B. Wheeler.
1990. *London, Ontario: The First 11,000 Years*. The Museum of Indian Archaeology. London.

Fitting, J.E.
1970. *The Archaeology of Michigan*. The Natural History Press. Garden City.

Fitzgerald, W.R.
1990. Preliminary Observations on the Ivan Elliot (AiHa-16) Village and the Raymond Reid (AiHa-4) Hamlet, Wellington County, Ontario. *KEWA* 90-6, pp. 2-16.

Flannery, K.V.
1976. The Village and its Catchment Area. In *The Early Mesoamerican Village*, edited by K.V. Flannery, pp. 91-95. Academic Press. New York.
1982. The Golden Marshalltown: A Parable for the Archaeology of the 1980s. *American Anthropologist* 84, pp. 265-278.

Ford, R.I.
1982. Paleoethnobotany in American Archaeology. In *Advances in Archaeological Method and Theory, Selections for Students from Volumes 1 through 4*, edited by M.B. Schiffer, pp. 281-332. Academic Press. New York.

Fox, W.A.
1976. The Central North Erie Shore. In *The Late Prehistory of the Lake Erie Drainage Basin*, edited by D.S. Brose, pp. 162-192. Cleveland Museum of Natural History. Cleveland.
1982a. The Calvert Village: Glen Meyer Community Patterns. *KEWA* 82-7,8, pp. 5-9.
1982b. An Initial Report on the Dymock Villages (AeHj-2). *KEWA* 82-1, pp. 12-17.
1982c. The Princess Point Concept. *Arch Notes* 82-2, pp. 17-26.
1982d. Glen Meyer Points. *KEWA* 82-1.
1982e. Dewaele Points. *KEWA* 82-3.
1986a. The Elliott Villages (AfHc-2) - An Introduction. *KEWA* 86-1, pp. 11-17.
1986b. The Breaks on the Elliott Site. *KEWA* 86-2, pp. 28-29.
1990. The Middle to Late Woodland Transition. In *The Archaeology of Southwestern Ontario to A.D. 1650*, C.J. Ellis and N. Ferris (eds.), pp. 171-188. Occasional Publication No. 5, Ontario Archaeological Society, London Chapter. London.

Furst, P.T.
1976. *Hallucinogens and Culture*. Chandler and Sharp. Novato.

Gellner, E.
1982. What is Structuralisme? In *Theory and Explanation in Archaeology*, C. Renfrew, M.J. Rowlands and B.A. Segraves (eds.), pp. 97-123. Academic Press. New York.

Gould, R.
1980. *Living Archaeology*. Cambridge University Press. Cambridge.
1990. *Recovering the Past*. University of New Mexico

Press. Albuquerque.

Gould, R.A., and P.J. Watson.
1982. A Dialogue on the Meaning and Use of Analogy in Ethnoarchaeological Reasoning. *Journal of Anthropological Archaeology* 1, pp. 355-381.

Grayson, D.K.
1984. *Quantitative Zooarchaeology*. Academic Press. New York.

Griffin, J.
1960. Climate Change: A Contributory Cause of Growth and Decline of Northern Hopewell. *Wisconsin Archaeologist* 41(2), pp. 21-33.

Guthe, A.
1960. The Cultural Background of the Iroquois. In *Essays in the Science of Culture*, G.E. Dole and R.L. Carneiro (eds.), pp. 202-215. Crowell. New York.

Hasenstab, R.J.
1987. Canoes, Caches, and Carrying Places: Territorial Boundaries and Tribilization in Late Woodland Western New York. *The Bulletin Journal of the New York State Archaeological Association* No. 95, pp. 39-49.

Hassan, F.
1978. Demographic Archaeology. In *Advances in Archaeological Method and Theory*, Vol. 1, edited by M.B. Schiffer, pp. 49-103. Academic Press. New York.

Hawkes, C.
1954. Archeological Method and Theory: Some Suggestions From the Old World. *American Anthropologist* 56, pp. 155-168.

Heidenreich, C.
1971. *Huronia. A History and Geography of the Huron Indians, 1600-1650*. Historical Sites Branch, Ontario Ministry of Natural Resources. McClelland and Stewart Ltd. Toronto.

Hilborn, W.H.
1970. Forest and Forestry of the Norfolk Sand Plain. M.A. Thesis, Department of Geography, University of Western Ontario. London.

Hill, J.N.
1968. Broken K Pueblo: Patterns of Form and Function. In *New Perspectives in Archeology*, S.R. Binford and L.R. Binford (eds.), pp. 103-142. Aldine. Chicago.

Hodder, I.
1982a. *Symbols in Action*. Cambridge University Press. Cambridge.
1982b. *The Present Past: An Introduction to Anthropology for Archaeologists*. Pica. New York.
1985. Postprocessual Archaeology. In *Advances in Archaeological Method and Theory*, Vol. 8, edited by M.B. Schiffer, pp. 1-26. Academic Press. New York.
1986. *Reading the Past: Current Approaches to Interpretation in Archaeology*. Cambridge University Press. Cambridge.

Hutton, G.
1990. A Village Rises Again. *The Palisade Post* 10, No. 4, pp. 10-11.

Janiger, O., and M. Dobkin de Rios.
1976. Nicotiana an Hallucinogen? *Economic Botany* 30, pp. 149-51.

Jamieson, S.M.
1986. Late Middleport Catchment Areas and the Slack Caswell Example. *Ontario Archaeology* 45, pp. 27-38.
1992. Regional Interaction and Ontario Iroquois Evolution. *Canadian Journal of Archaeology* 16, pp. 70-88.

Johnson, W.C.
1976. The Late Woodland Period in Northwestern Pennsylvania: A Preliminary Survey and Analysis for the Symposium on the Late Woodland Period in the Lake Erie Drainage Basin. In *The Late Prehistory of the Lake Erie Drainage Basin*, edited by D. Brose, pp. 48-75. The Cleveland Museum of Natural History. Cleveland.

Johnston, R.B., and L.J. Jackson.
1980. Settlement Patterns at the Le Caron Site, a 17th Century Huron Village. *Journal of Field Archaeology* 73, pp. 173-99.

Jury, W.W.
1948. *Crawford Prehistoric Village Site*. The University of Western Ontario, Bulletin of the Museums No. 7. London.

Justice, N.
1987. *Stone Age Spear and Arrow Points of the Midcontinental and Eastern United States*. Indiana University Press. Bloomington.

Kapches, M.
1987. The Auda Site: An Early Pickering Iroquois Component in Southeastern Ontario. *Archaeology of Eastern North America* 15, pp. 155-175.

1990. The Spatial Dynamics of Ontario Iroquoian Longhouses. *American Antiquity* 55, pp. 49-67.

Kenyon, W.A.
1968. *The Miller Site*. Royal Ontario Museum, Art and Archaeology, Occasional Paper, No. 14. Toronto.

Keron, J.
1984. Archaeological Survey of the Township of Westminster and North Dorchester - 1983. Report on License 83-42 submitted to the Ontario Ministry of Culture and Communications. Toronto.
1986. The Iroquoian Occupation of Southeast Middlesex County, Ontario. Unpublished Honours B.A. Essay, Department of Anthropology, University of Waterloo. Waterloo.

Kramer, C., editor.
1979. *Ethnoarchaeology: Implications of Ethnography for Archaeology*. Columbia University Press. New York.

La Barre, W.
1972. Hallucinogens and the Shamanic Origins of Religion. In *Flesh of the Gods: the Ritual Use of Hallucinogens*, edited by P.T. Furst, pp. 261-78. Praeger. New York.

Lee, T.
1951. A Preliminary Report on an Archaeological Survey of Southwestern Ontario in 1949. *National Museum of Canada, Bulletin 123*, pp. 42-48. Ottawa.
1952. A Preliminary Report on an Archaeological Survey of Southwestern Ontario for 1950. *National Museum of Canada, Bulletin 126*, pp. 64-75. Ottawa.

Lenig, D.
1965. *The Oak Hill Horizon and its Relation to the Development of Five Nations Iroquois Culture*. Researches and Transactions of the New York State Archaeological Association, 15(1). Buffalo.

Lennox, P.A.
1982. *The Bruner-Colisanti Site: An Early Late Woodland Component, Essex County, Ontario*. National Museum of Man, Archaeological Survey of Canada, Mercury Series, Paper 110. Ottawa.

Lennox, P.A., and W.R. Fitzgerald.
1990. The Culture History and Archaeology of the Neutral Iroquoians. In *The Archaeology of Southern Ontario to A.D. 1650*, C.J. Ellis and N. Ferris (eds.), pp. 405-456. Occasional Publication No. 5, Ontario Archaeological Society, London Chapter. London.

Limbrey, Susan.
1975. *Soil Science and Archaeology*. Academic Press. London.

Little, E.A.
1987. Inland Waterways in the Northeast. *Midcontinental Journal of Archaeology* 12, pp. 55-76.

MacDonald, J.
1986. New Dates for Old Chronologies: Radiocarbon Dates for the Varden Site. *KEWA* 86-9, pp. 8-22.

MacDonald, R.
1988. Ontario Iroquoian Sweat Lodges. *Ontario Archaeology* 48, pp. 17-26.

MacNeish, R.S.
1952. *Iroquois Pottery Types: A Technique for the Study of Iroquois Prehistory*. National Museum of Canada, Bulletin 124. Ottawa.

Magne, M.
1985. *Lithics and Livelihood: Stone Tool Technologies of Central and Southern Interior British Columbia*. National Museum of Man, Archaeological Survey of Canada, Mercury Series, Paper No. 133. Ottawa.

Maycock, P.F.
1963. The Phytosociology of the Deciduous Forests of Extreme Southern Ontario. *Canadian Journal of Botany* 41, pp. 379-438.

McAndrews, J.H.
1981. Late Quaternary Climate of Ontario: Temperature Trends from Fossil Pollen Data. In *Quaternary Paleoclimate*, edited by W.C. Mahaney, pp. 319-333. Geoabstracts. Norwich.

McKern, W.C.
1939. The Midwestern Taxonomic Method as an Aid to Archaeological Study. *American Antiquity* 4, pp. 301-13.

Miksicek, C.H.
1987. Formation Processes of the Archaeobotanical Record. In *Advances in Archaeological Method and Theory*, Vol.10, edited by M.B. Schiffer, pp. 211-247. Academic Press. New York.

Moore, J.A., and A.S. Keene, editors.
1983. *Archaeological Hammers and Theories*. Academic Press. New York.

Mullen, G.J., and R.D. Hoppa.
1992. Rogers Ossuary (AgHb-131): An Early Ontario Iroquois Burial Feature from Brantford Township.

*Canadian Journal of Archaeology* 16, pp. 32-47.

Muller, J.
1986. *Archaeology of the Lower Ohio River Valley*. Academic Press. New York.

Munson, P.J., P.W. Parmalee and R.A. Yarnell.
1971. Subsistence Ecology of Scovill, a Terminal Middle Woodland Village. *American Antiquity* 36, pp. 410-431.

Murphy, C., and N. Ferris.
1990. The Late Woodland Western Basin Tradition in Southwestern Ontario. In *The Archaeology of Southern Ontario to A.D. 1650*, C.J. Ellis and N. Ferris (eds.), pp. 189-278. Occasional Publication No. 5, Ontario Archaeological Society, London Chapter. London.

Murray, P.
1980. Discard Location: The Ethnographic Data. *American Antiquity* 45, pp. 490-502.

Niemczycki, M.
1984. *The Origin and Development of The Seneca and Cayuga Tribes of New York State*. Rochester Museum and Science Center, Research Records, No. 17. Rochester.
1986. The Genesee Connection: The Origins of Iroquois Culture in West-Central New York. *North American Archaeologist*, Vol. 7, pp. 15-44.

Nixon, C.
1985. Middle Iroquoian Settlement Along the Lower Nith River and Horner Creek Drainages. *KEWA* 85-7, pp. 2-8.

Noble, W.C.
1969. Some Social Implications of the Iroquois "*in situ*" Theory. *Ontario Archaeology* 13, pp. 16-28.
1975a. *The Van Besien Site: A Study in Glen Meyer Cultural Development*. Ontario Archaeology 24.
1975b. Corn and the Development of Village Life in Southern Ontario. *Ontario Archaeology* 25, pp. 37-46.

Noble, W.C., and Ian T. Kenyon.
1972. Porteous (AgHb-1): A Probable Early Glen Meyer Village in Brant County, Ontario. *Ontario Archaeology* 19, pp. 11-18.

Norcliffe, G.B., and C.E. Heidenreich.
1974. The Preferred Orientation of Iroquoian Longhouses in Ontario. *Ontario Archaeology* 23, pp. 3-30.

Ontario Ministry of Culture and Communications Site Data Files.

n.d. Borden forms on file with the Ministry of Culture and Communications, Heritage Branch. London.

Ontario Ministry of Natural Resources.
1982a. *Aggregate Resources Inventory of North Dorchester Township, Middlesex County, Southern Ontario*. Ontario Geological Survey, Aggregate Resources Inventory Paper 74. Ontario Ministry of Natural Resources. Toronto.
1982b. An Analysis of Dorchester Swamp Creek, May - July 1981. Report on file with the Ontario Ministry of Natural Resources. Aylmer.
1986. The Dorchester Swamp Area of Natural and Scientific Interest. Report on file with the Ontario Ministry of Natural Resources. Aylmer.

Ounjian, G.L.
1988. Plant Remains of the Calvert Village Site. Report submitted to Peter Timmins. London.

Parker, A.C.
1916. The Origin of the Iroquois as Suggested by their Archaeology. *American Anthropologist* 18, pp. 479-507.
1922. *The Archaeological History of New York State*. New York State Museum, Bulletins 235-238. Albany.

Pearce, R.J.
1978. Archaeological Investigations of the Pickering Phase in the Rice Lake Area. *Ontario Archaeology* 29, pp. 17-24.
1984. Mapping Middleport: A Case Study in Societal Archaeology. Ph.D. Thesis. Department of Anthropology, McGill University. Montreal.
1996. Mapping Middleport: A Case Study in Societal Archaeology. *London Museum of Archaeology, Research Report* No. 25. London.

Poulton, D.R.
1980. A Preliminary Report on the 1980 Archaeological Survey of the Catfish Creek Drainage, East Elgin County, Ontario. *Museum of Indian Archaeology, Research Report*, No. 11. London.
1985. Salvage Archaeology in the City of London: The 1983-1984 C.O.E.D. Program and the Magrath, Willcock and Pond Mills Sites. Manuscript on file at the Museum of Indian Archaeology. London.

Prevec, R.
1984a. Calvert Site (AfHg-1) Faunal Report. Report submitted to the Ontario Ministry of Citizenship and Culture, Archaeology and Heritage Planning Branch. London.
1984b. The Carolina Parakeet - Its First Appearance in Southern Ontario. *KEWA* 84-7, pp. 4-8.

Raab, M.L., and A.C. Goodyear.
1984. Middle-Range Theory in Archaeology: A Critical Review of Origins and Applications. *American Antiquity* 49, pp. 255-268.

Ramsden, P.
1977. *A Refinement of Some Aspects of Huron Ceramic Analysis*. National Museum of Man, Archaeological Survey of Canada, Mercury Series, Paper No. 63. Ottawa.

Redman, C.L., M. Berman, E. Curtin, W. Langhorne Jr., N. Versaggi and J. Wanser , editors.
1978. *Social Archeology: Beyond Subsistence and Dating*. Academic Press. New York.

Reid, C.S.
1975. *The Boys Site and the Early Ontario Iroquois Tradition*. National Museum of Man, Archaeological Survey of Canada, Mercury Series, Paper No. 42. Ottawa.

Renfrew, C.
1984. Social Archaeology, Societal Change and Generalisation. In *Approaches to Social Archaeology*, edited by C. Renfrew, pp. 3-21. Edinburgh University Press. Edinburgh.

Renfrew, C., and G. Sterud.
1969. Close Proximity Analysis: A Rapid Method for the Ordering of Archaeological Materials. *American Antiquity* 34, pp. 265-277.

Ridley, F.
1958. The Boys and Barrie Sites. *Ontario Archaeology* 4, pp. 18-40.

Ritchie, W.A.
1944. *The Pre-Iroquoian Occupations of New York State*. Rochester Museum of Arts and Sciences, Memoir No. 1.
1949. *An Archaeological Survey along the Trent Waterway in Ontario, Canada*. Researches and Transactions of the New York State Archaeological Association, 12(1). Buffalo.
1961. *A Typology and Nomenclature for New York Projectile Points*. New York State Museum and Science Service Bulletin No. 384.
1969. *The Archaeology of New York State, 2nd Edition*. The Natural History Press. New York.

Ritchie, W.A., and R.S. MacNeish.
1949. The Pre-Iroquoian Pottery of New York State. *American Antiquity* 15, pp. 97-124.

Ritchie, W.A., and R.E. Funk.
1973. *Aboriginal Settlement Patterns in the Northeast*. New York State Museum and Science Service

Memoir, 20. Albany.

Roper, D.C.
1979. The Method and Theory of Site Catchment Analysis: A Review. In *Advances in Archaeological Method and Theory*, Vol. 2, edited by M.B. Schiffer, pp. 120-140. Academic Press. New York.

Rowe, J.S.
1972. *Forest Regions of Canada*. Department of Fisheries and the Environment, Canadian Forestry Service Publication No. 1300. Ottawa.

Rozel, R.
1979. The Gunby Site and Late Pickering Interactions. Unpublished M.A. Thesis, Department of Anthropology, McMaster University. Hamilton.

Sagard, G.
1939. *The Long Journey to the Country of the Hurons*, edited by G. Wrong. The Champlain Society. Toronto.

Sahlins, M.D.
1968. *Tribesmen*. Prentice-Hall. London.

Salmon, M.H.
1982. *Philosophy and Archaeology*. Academic Press. New York.

Schiffer, M.B.
1972. Archaeological Context and Systemic Context. *American Antiquity* 37, pp. 156-165.
1976. *Behavioral Archeology*. Academic Press. New York.
1978. Methodological Issues in Ethnoarchaeology. In *Explorations in Ethnoarchaeology*, edited by R.A. Gould, pp. 229-247. University of New Mexico Press. Albuquerque.
1983. Toward the Identification of Formation Processes. *American Antiquity* 48, pp. 675-706.
1985. Is There a "Pompeii Premise" in Archaeology? *Journal of Anthropological Research* 41, pp. 18-41.
1987. *Formation Processes of the Archaeological Record*. University of New Mexico Press. Albuquerque.
1988. The Structure of Archaeological Theory. *American Antiquity* 53, pp. 461-485.

Scott, W.B., and E.J. Crossman.
1973. *Freshwater Fishes of Canada*. Fisheries Research Board of Canada, Bulletin 184. Ottawa.

Service, E.R.
1971. *Primitive Social Organization: An Evolutionary Perspective*. Second edition. Random House. New

York.

Small, J.P.
  1978. Natural Areas in Middlesex County: A
  Systematic Empirical Evaluation of Selected Sites
  with Special Reference to Overstory Vegetation.
  Unpublished M.A. Thesis, Department of
  Geography, The University of Western Ontario.
  London.

Smith, B.D.
  1978. *Prehistoric Patterns of Human Behaviour*.
  Academic Press. New York.

Smith, D.G.
  1983. An Analytical Approach to the Seriation of
  Iroquoian Pottery. *Museum of Indian Archaeology
  Research Report* 12.
  1987. Archaeological Systematics and the Analysis of
  Iroquoian Ceramics: A Case Study from the
  Crawford Lake Area, Ontario. Unpublished Ph.D.
  Thesis, Department of Anthropology, McGill
  University. Montreal.

Smith, D.G., and G. Crawford.
  1995. The Princess Point Complex and the Origins of
  Iroquoian Societies in Ontario. In *Origins of the
  People of the Longhouse*, A. Bekerman and G.
  Warrick (eds.), pp. 55-70. Ontario Archaeological
  Society. North York.

Snow, D.R.
  1980. *The Archaeology of New England*. Academic
  Press. New York.
  1995. Migration in Prehistory: The Northern Iroquoian
  Case. *American Antiquity* 60, pp. 59-79.

South, S.
  1977. *Method and Theory in Historical Archaeology*.
  Academic Press. New York.

Spence, M.
  1988. The Human Skeletal Material of the Elliott Site.
  *KEWA* 88-4, pp. 10-20.
  1994. Mortuary Programmes of the Early Ontario
  Iroquoians. *Ontario Archaeology* 58, pp. 6-26.

Starna, W.A., and R.E. Funk.
  1994. The Place of the In Situ Hypothesis in Iroquoian
  Archaeology. *Northeast Anthropology* 47, pp. 45-
  54.

Steckley, J.
  1987. An Ethnolinguistic Look at the Huron
  Longhouse. *Ontario Archaeology* 47, pp. 19-32.

Stevenson, M.G.
  1986. *Window on the Past, An Archaeological*

*Assessment of the Peace Point Site, Wood Buffalo
National Park, Alberta*. Parks Canada. Ottawa.
  1991. Beyond the Formation of Hearth-Associated
  Artifact Assemblages. In *The Interpretation of
  Archaeological Spatial Patterning*. E.M. Kroll and
  D. Price (eds.), pp. 269-299. Plenum Press. New
  York.

Stothers, D.
  1977. *The Princess Point Complex*. National Museum
  of Man, Archaeological Survey of Canada,
  Mercury Series, Paper No. 58. Ottawa.

Stuiver, M., and B. Becker.
  1986. High Precision Decadal Calibration of the
  Radiocarbon Time Scale, A.D. 1950-2500 B.C.
  *Radiocarbon* 28, pp. 863-910.

Stuiver, M., and G.W. Pearson.
  1986. High Precision Calibration of the Radiocarbon
  Time Scale, A.D. 1950-500 B.C. *Radiocarbon* 28,
  pp. 805-838.

Taylor, W.W.
  1948. *A Study of Archeology*. American
  Anthropological Association, Memoir 69.
  Washington, D.C.

Thomas, D.H.
  1971. On Distinguishing Natural from Cultural Bone in
  Archaeological Sites. *American Antiquity* 36, pp.
  366-371.
  1976. *Figuring Anthropology: First Principles of
  Probability and Statistics*. Holt, Rinehart and
  Winston. New York.

Thomas, D.H., R.R. Kautz, W.N. Melhorn, R.S.
  Thompson and D.T. Trexler.
  1983. *The Archaeology of Moniter Valley 1:
  Epistemology*. Anthropological Papers 58. Part 1.
  American Museum of Natural History. New York.

Thwaites, R.G., editor.
  1896-1901. *The Jesuit Relations and Allied
  Documents*. 73 Vols. Burrows Brothers. Cleveland.

Timmins, P.A.
  1982. The Education of W. Wilfrid Jury. Manuscript
  on file with the author.
  1983. The Final Report on the City of London
  Archaeological Survey. Report submitted to the
  Ontario Ministry of Culture and Communications.
  Toronto.
  1985. The Analysis and Interpretation of Radiocarbon
  Dates in Iroquoian Archaeology. *Museum of Indian
  Archaeology, Research Report* No. 19. London.
  1989. The Butler's Woods Site and the Middle
  Woodland Occupation of the Middle Thames River

Drainage. *KEWA* 89-9, pp. 2-18.
1990. The Southdale Site: A Multi-Component Historic and Prehistoric Site in London, Ontario. *Museum of Indian Archaeology, Research Report* No. 20. London.
1992. An Interpretive Framework for the Early Iroquoian Village. Ph.D. Thesis. Department of Anthropology, McGill University. Montreal.

Tooker, E.
1967. *An Ethnography of the Huron Indians 1615-1649.* The Huronia Historical Development Council. Midland.
1970. *The Iroquois Ceremonial of Midwinter.* Syracuse University Press. Syracuse.

Tooker, E., editor. .
1979. *Native North American Spirituality of the Eastern Woodlands.* Paulist Press. New York.
1985. *An Iroquois Source Book, Volume 2, Calendric Rituals.* Garland. New York.

Tringham, R.
1978. Experimentation, Ethnoarchaeology, and the Leapfrogs in Archaeological Methodology. In *Explorations in Ethnoarchaeology,* edited by R.A. Gould, pp. 169-199. University of New Mexico Press. Albuquerque.

Trigger, B.G.
1967. Settlement Archaeology - Its Goals and Promise. *American Antiquity,* 32, pp. 149-160.
1968. The Determinants of Settlement Patterns. In *Settlement Archaeology,* edited by K.C. Chang, pp. 53-78. National Press. Palo Alto.
1970. The Strategy of Iroquoian Prehistory. *Ontario Archaeology* 14, pp. 3-48.
1976. *The Children of Aataentsic: A History of the Huron People to 1660.* McGill-Queen's University Press. Montreal.
1978a. Iroquoian Matriliny. *Pennsylvania Archaeologist* 48, pp. 55-65.
1978b. *Time and Traditions.* Columbia University Press. New York.
1980. Archaeology and the Image of the American Indian. *American Antiquity* 45, pp. 662-676.
1981. Prehistoric Social and Political Organization: An Iroquoian Case Study. In *Foundations of Northeast Archaeology,* edited by D.R. Snow, pp. 1-50. Academic Press. New York.
1984. Archaeology at the Crossroads: What's New? *Annual Review of Anthropology* 13, pp. 275-300.
1985a. *Natives and Newcomers.* McGill-Queen's University Press. Montreal.
1985b. Draper: Past and Prologue. In *The 1975 and 1978 Rescue Excavations at the Draper Site: Introduction and Settlement Patterns,* National Museum of Man, Archaeological Survey of

Canada, Mercury Series, Paper No. 130, pp. 5-19. Ottawa.
1989. *A History of Archaeological Thought.* Cambridge University Press. Cambridge.
1990. *The Huron: Farmers of the North.* Second Edition. Holt, Rinehart and Winston, Inc. Toronto.
1995. Expanding middle-range theory. *Antiquity* 69, pp. 449-458.

Tuck, J.
1971. *Onondaga Iroquois Prehistory.* Syracuse University Press. Syracuse.
1978. Northern Iroquoian Prehistory. In *Handbook of North American Indians, Volume 15, Northeast,* edited by B.G. Trigger, pp. 322-333. Smithsonian Institution. Washington.

Upper Thames River Conservation Authority.
1952. *Upper Thames Valley Conservation Report.* Conservation Authorities Branch, Ontario Department of Lands and Forests. Toronto.
1986. Dorchester Mill Pond Management Plan. Report on file with the Upper Thames River Conservation Authority. London.

Vita-Finzi, C., and E.S. Higgs.
1970. Prehistoric Economy in the Mount Carmel Area of Palestine: Site Catchment Analysis. *Proceedings of the Prehistoric Society* 36, pp. 1-37.

von Gernet, A.
1982 . Analysis of Intrasite Artifact Spatial Distributions, The Draper Site Smoking Pipes. M.A. Thesis, Department of Anthropology, McGill University. Montreal.

von Gernet, A.D., and P.A. Timmins.
1987. Pipes and Parakeets: Constructing Meaning in an Early Iroquoian Context. In *Archaeology as Long-Term History,* edited by I. Hodder, pp. 31-42. Cambridge University Press. Cambridge.

Ward, B.
1982. An Analysis of Dorchester Swamp Creek. Report on file with the Ontario Ministry of Natural Resources. Aylmer.

Warrick, G.
1984a. *Reconstructing Ontario Iroquoian Village Organization.* National Museum of Man, Archaeological Survey of Canada, Mercury Series, No. 124, pp. 1-180. Ottawa.
1984b. Pottery from the Cooper Village Site and Ontario Iroquois Development. *KEWA* 84-8, pp. 2-17.
1988. Estimating Ontario Iroquoian Village Duration. *Man in the Northeast* 36, pp. 21-55.

Watson, P., S. Leblanc and C. Redman.
  1984. *Archeological Explanation: The Scientific Method in Archeology*. Columbia University Press. New York.

Whallon, R.
  1968. Investigations of Late Prehistoric Social Organization in New York State. In *New Perspectives in Archeology*, S.R. Binford and L.R. Binford (eds.), pp. 223-44. Aldine. Chicago.

White, M.E.
  1961. *Iroquois Culture History in the Niagara Frontier Area of New York State*. Anthropological Papers, Museum of Anthropology, University of Michigan, No. 16. Ann Arbor.
  1963. Settlement Pattern Change and the Development of Horticulture in the New York-Ontario Area. *Pennsylvania Archaeologist* 33(1-2), pp. 1-12.

White, T.E.
  1953. A Method of Calculating the Dietary Percentage of Various Food Animals Utilized by the Aboriginal Peoples. *American Antiquity* 13, pp. 396-398.

Willey, G., and P. Phillips.
  1958. *Method and Theory in American Archaeology*. The University of Chicago Press. Chicago.

Willey, G., and J.A. Sabloff.
  1980. *A History of American Archaeology, Second Edition*. W.H. Freeman. San Francisco.

Williamson, R.F.
  1983 . The Mill Stream Cluster: The Other Side of the Coin. *KEWA* 83-1, pp. 3-12.
  1985. Glen Meyer: People in Transition. Unpublished Ph.D. Thesis. Department of Anthropology, McGill University. Montreal.
  1990. The Early Iroquoian Period of Southern Ontario. In *The Archaeology of Southern Ontario to A.D. 1650*, C.J. Ellis and N. Ferris (eds.), pp. 291-320, Occasional Publication No. 5, Ontario Archaeological Society, London Chapter. London.

Williamson, R.F., and D.A. Robertson.
  1994. Peer Polities Beyond the Periphery: Early and Middle Iroquoian Regional Interaction. *Ontario Archaeology* 58, pp. 27-48.

Wilmsen, E.
  1968. Functional Analysis of Flaked Stone Tools. *American Antiquity* 33, pp. 156-161.

Wintemberg, W.J.
  1928. *Uren Prehistoric Village Site, Oxford County, Ontario*. National Museum of Canada, Bulletin, No. 51. Ottawa.

  1931. Distinguishing Characteristics of Algonkian and Iroquoian Cultures. *National Museum of Canada, Bulletin*, No. 67, pp. 65-126. Ottawa.

Wright, J.V.
  1966. *The Ontario Iroquois Tradition*. National Museum of Canada, Bulletin, 210, Anthropological Series No. 75. Ottawa.
  1974. *The Nodwell Site*. National Museum of Man, Archaeological Survey of Canada, Mercury Series, No. 22. Ottawa.
  1992. The Conquest Theory of the Ontario Iroquois Tradition: A Reassessment. *Ontario Archaeology* 54, pp. 3-15.

Wright, J.V., and J.E. Anderson.
  1969. *The Bennett Site*. National Museum of Canada, Bulletin, 229. Ottawa.

Wright, M.
  1986. *The Uren Site AfHd-3 An Analysis and Reappraisal of the Uren Substage Type Site*. Monographs in Ontario Archaeology 2. Toronto.

Wrong, G.M., editor.
  1939. *The Long Journey to the Country of the Hurons*. The Champlain Society. Toronto.

Wylie, A.
  1982. Epistemological Issues Raised by a Structuralist Archaeology. In *Symbolic and Structural Archaeology*, edited by I. Hodder, pp. 39-46. Cambridge University Press. Cambridge.
  1985. The Reaction Against Analogy. In *Advances in Archaeological Method and Theory*, Vol. 8, edited by M.B. Schiffer, pp. 63-111. Academic Press. Orlando.
  1989. Matters of Fact and Matters of Interest. In *Archaeological Approaches to Cultural Identity*, edited by S.J. Shennan, pp. 94-109. Unwin Hyman. London.

Yarnell, R.A.
  1982. Problems of Interpretation of Archaeological Plant Remains of the Eastern Woodlands. *Southeastern Archaeology* 1, pp. 1-7.

Yellen, J.E.
  1977. *Archaeological Approaches to the Present: Models for Reconstructing the Past*. Academic Press. New York.